Interfirm Networks

'This will almost surely become a standard reference on business analysis.'

Nicholai Foss, *Copenhagen Business School*

A wide range of economists and policy-makers are now aware that there is a distinct correlation between the economic success of a country or region and that unit's capacity to develop networks of relatively high-trust relationships among firms. This has drawn deserved attention to this organizational form. *Interfirm Networks* examines the nature of such networks and their role in promoting industrial competitiveness.

Where previous work in this area has tended to be purely descriptive rather than analytical, the distinguished contributors to this volume present a balanced, theoretical and empirical approach to interfirm networking drawing on a variety of international case studies. Issues covered in *Interfirm Networks: Organization and Industrial Competitiveness* include:

- the role of networks in regulating conflict and producing cooperation
- the role of networks in developing knowledge and competences
- network governance and conflict intensive networks

Students and researchers working on industrial and managerial economics, as well as those in business in general will find this an indispensible resource on the role of contemporary interfirm networks.

Anna Grandori is Professor of Organization and Management, University of Modena and Bocconi University, Milan.

Routledge Studies in Business Organizations and Networks

Interfirm Networks

Organization and Industrial Competitiveness

edited by Anna Grandori

London and New York

First published 1999 by Routledge
11 Fetter Lane, London EC4P 4EE

Simultaneously published in the USA and Canada
by Routledge
29 West 35th Street, New York, NY 10001

Typeset in Baskerville by Exe Valley Dataset, Exeter, Devon, England
Printed and bound in Great Britain by MPG Books Ltd, Bodmin

British Library Cataloguing in Publication Data
A catalogue record for this book is available from the British Library

Library of Congress Cataloging in Publication Data
Interfirm networks: organization and industrial competitiveness /
    edited by Anna Grandori.
        p.   cm. — (Routledge studies in business organization and
    networks; 15)
    Includes bibliographical references and index.
    1. Business networks.   I. Grandori, Anna.   II. Series.
HD69.S8158   1999
658.4´095–dc21   98-33131
                                                          CIP
                ISBN 0–415–20404–6

Contents

PART 3
The externalities of networks

Tables and Figures

Contributors

Anna Grandori is Professor of Organization and Human Resource Management and Head of the Business Administration Department at the Economics Faculty, University of Modena; and Professor of Methods of Organization and Management Research at Bocconi University, Milan.

Massimo Neri is Research Fellow at the University of Modena, Department of Business Administration. His research has focused on organizational justice as applied to a variety of organization analysis and design problems.

Erhard Friedberg is Senior Researcher at the Centre National de la Recherche Scientifique (CNRS), Paris, Director of the Centre de Sociologie des Organisations (CSO), and Director of the Doctoral Program in Sociology at the Paris Institute of Political Science (IEP).

Jean-Philippe Neuville is Assistant Professor of Sociology at the National Institute for Applied Sciences (Lyon) and Research Associate at the Center for the Sociology of Organisations (Paris).

Bart Nooteboom is Professor of Industrial Organization at the School of Management and Organization at Groningen University, the Netherlands. His research interests have been entrepreneurship, innovation and diffusion, technology policy, transaction cost theory, interorganizational relations and learning.

Andrea Lipparini PhD teaches at the University of Bologna and at the Catholic University in Milan. His research interests lie in the areas of interorganizational relationships and organizational competencies.

Alessandro Lomi is a member of the Strategy and Organization Group at the School of Economics of the University of Bologna. His main research interests include social network analysis, ecological models of organizations and simulation models of social processes.

Chris Hendry is Centenary Professor in Organisational Behaviour at City University Business School, London.

James Brown is Research Associate at City University Business School, London.

Robert J. DeFillippi is Associate Professor at Suffolk University School of Management, Boston, Massachusetts, USA.

Dr Robert Hassink is a Research Fellow at the University of Dortmund, Germany.

Keith G. Provan is a Professor in the College of Business and Public Administration at the University of Arizona, Tucson, Arizona, USA. He holds joint appointments with the School of Public Administration and Policy and the Department of Management and Policy.

Sherrie E. Human is an Assistant Professor in the Department of Management and Entrepreneurship at Xavier University, Cincinnati, Ohio, USA. Her research interests include interorganizational relationships such as strategic networks and franchises.

Paul B. de Laat is Assistant Professor of Science Studies at the University of Groningen, the Netherlands. His current research interests focus on R&D management, both within organizations (matrix management) and between organizations (strategic alliances), and on intellectual property rights in software.

Peter Smith Ring is a Professor of Strategic Management at Loyola Marymount University in Los Angeles, CA. His current research interests focus on the structure and processes of networks and strategic alliances and on the role of trust in economic exchange.

Andrew Godley is a Lecturer in Economics at the University of Reading. He has published widely in business and economic history, especially on the development of the fashion industries, and his book on Jewish entrepreneurship in Britain and America will be published in 1999.

Giuseppe Soda, PhD, is Assistant Professor of Organization Theory at Università L. Bocconi, Milan.

Alessandro Usai is a PhD student at Università degli Studi di Bologna and Research Assistant at Università L. Bocconi, Milan.

Mark J. Scher is Economic Affairs Officer, International Economic Relations Branch, United Nations General Secretariat, where he is responsible for monitoring and analysing economic and financial developments in Japan.

Introduction

Interfirm networks: Organizational mechanisms and economic outcomes

Anna Grandori

Why do networks and interfirm coordination need further analysis? The growth in the economic relevance and in the variety of forms of interfirm cooperation has been accompanied by a possibly even more marked growth in the literature devoted to it in many areas of economic and social studies (Sydow 1997; Oliver 1990). These studies have analysed in both theory- and practice-oriented terms the features and properties of a wide variety of interfirm coordination modes that differ from price- and exit-based exchange and competition, ranging from social networks of interfirm joint decision-making, to contract-based bureaucratic networks as franchising or consortia, to proprietary networks as joint ventures and other forms of equity alliance. In spite of this richness, the proliferation of analyses and approaches has been the outcome of a phase of disclosure and exploration in a field that is far from being consolidated and which is actually largely unchartered. In particular, recent reviews of the field of 'network research' have detected a variety of blind spots and under-researched themes that deserve attention.

- Among disciplinary approaches, 'macro' economic and sociological perspectives are prevailing (Oliver and Ebers, 1998), while more micro-analytic organizational analyses are underdeveloped, especially as applied to interfirm coordination (Grandori and Soda 1995).
- Static analyses of network structures are more developed than process studies of network formation and evolution (Ebers and Grandori 1997).
- Comparative studies are more concerned about the properties of networks as an overall third type of governance structure, an alternative to firms and markets, than about the relative superiority of different forms of networks with respect to each other (Grandori 1997).
- Research on antecedents and contingencies of networks—such as industry structure and technology or country and culture—is much more clearly articulated than research on outcomes (Oliver and Ebers, 1998).

- Some categories of outcomes are much more considered than others: in economic studies, cost efficiency and innovation prevail, while in sociological studies power is the most frequently considered variable, both as an outcome and as a predictor of network forms (Oliver and Ebers, 1998).
- Among the costs and benefits of networks, the latter have received much more attention than the former (Ebers and Grandori 1997) and the intent of explaining and justifying this form of economic organization has ended up in a widespread pro-network bias.

This book makes a contribution by enhancing our knowledge on all the above issues. Before discussing the specific ways in which the various essays, and their combined effect, do so, let me explain the reasons why they do so. This collection of papers is primarily, albeit not exclusively, drawn from the final conference on interfirm networks held within the 'EMOT Programme'.[1] One of the thematic groups into which the programme was divided was devoted to reviewing, comparing and integrating interfirm network research which progressed from the analysis of network formation, to the description and classification of network structures and processes, to the understanding of their contingencies, and to the explanation and prediction of their outcomes.[2] The fourth and final EMOT conference on networks was called as a synthetizing event which focused on network consequences and outcomes as linked to network forms and antecedents. Therefore, on the one hand, the papers contribute to our understanding of what the consequences of interfirm networking are, broadening the effectiveness and efficiency notions which are usually considered. In particular, they explore the properties of interfirm networks in making a virtue of the very differentiation of firms' interests and competences. On the other hand, the papers link these outcomes to the structures and processes through which they are achieved, broadening the set of coordination mechanisms usually considered as typical of networks, whereby they are conceived as an 'alternative' to markets and firms. The various papers, as a whole, illustrate how these mechanisms encompass rules and conventions, brokers and intermediaries, interfirm authorities, joint decision-making and negotiation, and incentive schemes (from prices to pledges and hostages). Therefore, *in this book an interfirm network will be conceived and defined as a set of firms, generally characterized by different preferences and resources, coordinated through a mix of mechanisms not limited to price, exit and background regulation.* The overall contribution made by the selected papers also contributes in some theoretical debates that, deriving especially from network research, are investing and unsettling some of the conceptual divides and oppositions most used in organization and management theorizing, such as those between trust and opportunism, between formal and informal organization and between governance 'alternatives' themselves. These considerations are outlined below.

Network outcomes

The most widely analysed consequences of networks are the economies in transaction and production costs that these structures may allow, and the opportunities for value creation that the pooling of complementary resources may yield. The former type of assessment of interfirm networks has been the central concern of transaction cost economics, while the latter has been a distinctive feature of the resource-based view of the firm. Many important economic consequences of networks have been typically neglected in these research traditions, even when considered as a whole, but they lie at the centre of interest of this book. Naturally these cost and benefit criteria are, in general, present in economic and organizational research but have not yet been applied systematically in network research.

In the first place, interfirm networks, whatever their form, have consequences not only for the participating firms but also for outsiders. Economists have been concerned with externalities, but the dominant view has been that the relevant categories of external consequences are either negative externalities generated by reduced competition—to be opposed by public regulation—or positive externalities represented by the 'public good'—to be sustained and protected by public intervention.

The *private and negotiated allocation of externalities* has been quite neglected, as has the properties of interfirm networks in achieving a sensible order. The papers in Part 3 are explicitly focused on how and when what types of networks can generate improvements in general welfare and at what cost. Andrew Godley illustrates through a business history study how the highly risky investments in the growing London and New York fashion industries, which would not have been financed by the traditional capital market institutions, were successfully financed, with almost no failure in repayment, by the soft loan system created by the the Jewish community, using the ethnic-based social network as a monitoring system. This paper offers a capital market failure explanation of the formation of network-based alternative financial intermediaries and an examination of the improvement in general welfare and allocative efficiency of these institutions. On the other hand, he highlights the possible negative consequences of that system in terms of opportunity costs and the maintenance of underperforming firms at the expense of others not belonging to the network. Therefore, the system has both positive and negative externalities that should be traded-off if a proper assessment is to be reached, and the matter is not simply an issue of 'striking the right balance' between cooperation and competition (Jorde and Teece 1989). The qualitative nature of the coordination mechanism employed, in this case social and cultural norms and group control, matters a lot, and the advantages and disadvantages of that specific mechanism should be evaluated—not only the extent of competition or of cooperation.

The papers by Giuseppe Soda and Alessandro Usai, and by Mark Scher

unveil the dark side of networking, especially of the high 'socially embedded' variety, in institutional and cultural contexts that are often
celebrated for the easiness of interfirm networking, that is, in Italy and
Japan. In the Italian study, the positive and negative consequences, in
terms of efficiency (economies of scale and coordination costs) and of
externalities (opportunity costs, right of access by outsiders, quality and
costs for final users), of networking among construction firms are explored,
under different governance structures (consortia and H-form integration)
and under different levels of competitive pressure. Important aspects of the
myth of Japanese high-culture, high-trust management, as far as interfirm
collaboration is concerned, are criticized in Scher's study, through a first-
hand analysis of restrictive norms of access and hidden authority and
domination relations, and of their likely negative consequences for both
some of the player firms and outsiders. Therefore, these studies add new
evidence and arguments that enrich the thesis that there are 'costs of
embeddedness'. They do not consist only of a *deficit of innovation* due to
'cognitive', 'political' and 'functional' lock-in, as Gernot Grabher (1993) has
nicely illustrated in the case of some German industrial districts. In
addition, these studies highlight the possible 'costs of embeddedness' in
terms of a *deficit of fairness*: domination and highly asymmetric distribution
of resources among insiders and discrimination against outsiders.

Peter Smith Ring widens the treatment to a variety of other costs of
interfirm networking. He offers an analysis and classification of these costs
that goes beyond production and transaction costs in their usual operationalization. Not only costs for external stakeholders are considered, but
also the dynamic costs of learning and change, or 'transition' costs. He
considers those interfirm networks that are based on 'relational contracting'
and configured as fully connected webs of long-lasting relationships among
players with complementary competences and resources. Then he argues
that, if so configured, they should provide advantages with respect to both
firms and markets, as well as to other forms of networks, with regard to
learning (for example, networks coordinated primarily by hierarchy,
programming and standardization, rules and routines). More specifically, his
argument about learning costs can be read as an application to networks of
the knowledge-based evaluation of governance forms (Demsetz 1993):
networks maintain the advantage of not having to acquire the same
knowledge of an exchange partner but do allow some knowledge exchange.
In addition, he highlights that, whatever the advantages provided by the
form of coordination adopted by a given set of firms, opportunity costs
should also be considered. This is a particularly fruitful suggestion on how
to renew and enlarge the current ways of approaching network analysis, and
actually inspires a criticism of the logic of transaction cost economizing on
its own grounds, by having neglected some important economic variables
rather than for being 'too economic'. Fitting nicely with the papers on
network negotiation and network learning outcomes, the core idea is that

the search for value-creating matches with other firms and the time and resources spent in negotiation should be seen as an investment rather than a cost to be minimized; these are the very processes that can lead to the discovery of superior encounters and reduce opportunity costs.

In a positive framework, *fairness* and *learning outcomes* are the core concerns of Parts 1 and 2 respectively. In spite of the division between the two parts, the results are tightly linked. For example, Grandori and Neri's case studies on the negotiation of the governance structures of complex multiple-firm industrial projects show how the investments in search for partners and for suitable agreements, although increasing process costs, are the only means for finding superior matches and superior ways for regulating matches, both in terms of total value created (the Pareto-efficiency of a network arrangement) and in terms of how resources are divided among parties (the fairness of a network arrangement). Where network arrangements are not designed through problem-solving but through less creative processes—such as non-cooperative bargaining or routinized contracting—the process may be more efficient but there are losses in the quality of solutions. In addition, in their in-depth field observation of the appearently hazardous and asymmetric relation between car manufactures and their suppliers of components, Friedberg and Neuville demonstrate how a reasonably fair distribution of resources among firms can be achieved, at least in relational contracting forms of networking, also in the ongoing contract implementation processes. There, even though some parties enjoy less negotiation power and are more substitutable *ex ante*, it is shown that they have the chance to condition cooperation to the reciprocation of concessions *ex-post*, in terms of information disclosure, tolerance of defects and technical help, so as to win back some of the benefits that were unattainable *ex ante*.

On the other hand, the analyses focused on the learning properties of networks also provide insights on how organizational arrangements should be shaped in a way that simultaneously solves the cognitive problem of allowing knowledge exchange and the interesting problem of providing adequate incentives and protection. This double constraint on effective network structures is particularly clear in Provan and Human's comparative analysis of trade association structures seen as 'brokers' of interfirm relations, and in Paul De Laat analysis of joint ventures as systems of hostages and pledges exchange under a quasi-third-party guarantee. In fact, taken together, these contributions show that, on one hand, the realization of learning advantages, especially when the exchanged knowledge is tacit and the sought outcome is innovative, requires all-to-all, face-to-face problem-solving-oriented communication channels; while on the other hand, when know-how is the basis of a firm's competitive strength, additional guarantees against expropriation and in support of reciprocal information exchange are needed.

This hypothesis is consistent with Bart Nooteboom's dynamic theory of network efficiency, arguing that 'disintegration and differentiation are required for radical innovation by means of novel combinations in tacit knowledge'. The mode of coordination that can integrate this differentiation and transform it into reciprocal learning and innovative problem-solving seems to be necessarily based on joint problem solving, or at least on intense and diffused knowledge exchanges. A more incremental type of learning would be likely in conditions of lower differentiation and lower integration. This principle is well known when applied to internal organization (Lawrence and Lorsch 1967; Lawrence and Dyer 1983) and Nooteboom's analysis shows that it applies equally well—at higher levels of differentiation—to external organization. In fact, Nooteboom also downplays the differences between internal and external organization, suggesting that firms can emulate network structures to reach high levels of innovation. In addition, as shown in Hendry and associates' case studies on the development of the highly innovative sector of opto-electronics in six regions in the UK, US and Germany, the effective patterns of integration may differ according to further contingencies, such as: what processes they regulate—for example, commercial versus knowledge transfer and generation; what type of interdependence they regulate—for example, vertical transactions or horizontal relations; and on what supporting institutions private integration efforts can rely upon. In fact, the study shows that, in a vertically interdependent industry with international rather than local markets, the networks most relevant for innovation are extraregional and centrally coordinated by 'hub firms' in commercial processes; while they are more local but not always 'dense' and 'intimate' even in technical knowledge-exchange processes.

Some further general implications of the reported arguments and results are as follows. In the first place, as far as learning outcomes are concerned, a differentiated and integrated network-like organization form seems more important than the allocation of activities within or across firms' boundaries.[3] In the second place, the effect of uncertainty and information complexity on governance structures seems to be much more complicated than it is usually assumed in relevant models, most notably in organizational economics: for both scale economies and competence differentiation reasons, very high levels of information complexity seem to favour networked and integrated but external organization rather than proprietary integration into one firm (Grandori 1995). In the third place, a methodological implication of these analyses of network outcomes is that with respect to both learning and fairness (as with any outcome, actually), *the properties of networks cannot be assessed in general, but different types of learning and fairness outcomes are generated by networks employing different types of coordination mechanisms*. It is to these mechanisms that we now turn.

Network coordination mechanisms

It has been said that interfirm networks are different from markets because they employ a wider set of coordination mechanisms, and are different from firms because they keep (at least some) property rights separated (Langlois and Robertson 1995). While this is a useful general characterization, the management and organization of interfirm relations needs a more fine-grained analysis of what the coordination mechanisms applicable and applied to interfirm-relations governance are (Grandori and Soda 1995). Taken together, the papers gathered here cover a wide range of salient organizational mechanisms and their relations to economic outcomes.

Appropriate *rules of the game*, combined with repeated interactions sustaining cooperative gaming strategies, are revealed to substantiate 'trustful' exchanges in the case of industrial districts, in the analysis by Sebastiano Brusco. He maps out a set of rules of the game that regulate successful cooperation; these can be broadly classified as: a rule of 'cautiousness' (it is legitimate and expected to protect oneself from extreme dependence on partners and related risks), a rule of 'truthfulness' (it is not legitimate to obtain gains through guile) and a rule of 'soberness' (it is not legitimate to waste resources that could be of high value to other parties). In the quite value-laden and apologetic literature on 'trust' that has been diffused in recent years, this approach indicates a useful alternative. It is supported by other data and conceptualizations such as the recent comparative and extensive field study on Italian industrial districts by Ivana Paniccia (1998), describing how the relative incidence of *ex ante* reliance on trust on the basis of rule acceptance, with respect to *ex post* judgement that a specific partner is trustworthy on the basis of repeated experience, varies greatly across different districts, even in the same region; and that the *content* of rules and norms matters a lot—in that, for example, they may prescribe diffidence and individualism rather than openness and co-operativeness. Grandori and Neri also report results on the importance of rules and routines—industry-specific and site-specific as well as partner-specific—providing tested contractual schemes in the definition of sub-contracting agreements in industrial districts. Both Grandori and Neri's and Friedberg and Neuville's papers also highlight the importance of *gaming and negotiation* as network coordination mechanisms, and the conditions sustaining the adoption of cooperative behaviours and the realization of fair dealing. Economic actors do 'refrain' from exploiting all the available negotiation power and squeezing their counterparts into a corner of perceived unequity. The apparent negotiation rationale behind this behaviour is that when economic action involves repeated interaction in time—as in the car manufacturers/components suppliers relationship—and repeated similar contracts with many partners—as in franchising chains—a clearly unfair division of resources is self-defeating and not sustainable, because it decreases the attractiveness for other high-quality partners, and because it discourages the provision of help and adaptation beyond formal contractual provision in the ongoing common activity. Even in the absence of significant direct negotiation, such as in franchising agreements, for example, larger shares of quasi-rents are distributed to franchisees with respect to those that would be secured by their best alternative deals (Grandori and Neri).[4] Or even when *ex ante* contracts do not grant reasonable profit shares to subcontractors, they are able to win back resources in the implementation and working process (Friedberg and Neuville) and to transform the governance system from a hierarchical and control-based sub-contracting form into a 'co-makership' relational contracting form. In large one-shot endeavours, as in complex construction projects, significant investments in *ex ante* search for partners and negotiation over governance structures are worthwhile for improving outputs while reducing technical and behavioural risks and allocating risk efficiently among partners (Grandori and Neri).

When the number of actors is large and networked firms are in a potential or actual competitive relation—as in horizontal relations among competitors or in vertical buyer–seller relations on a value chain—coordination can be usefully supported by *intermediating third parties as brokers, liaison roles, common staff and quasi-authorities*. The range of these mechanisms is wide. They include trade association staff (Provan and Hemer); enterpreneurs (Lipparini and Lomi); 'hub' firms (either small or large, depending on their centrality and criticality in the value system), universities and knowledge-generating nodes, as well as public agencies and common goods-provider nodes (Hendry *et al.*; Lipparini and Lomi).

As already noted in connection with learning outcomes, *group-like, knowledge-sharing*, problem-solving-oriented mechanisms are described as the core mechanisms capable of supporting radical innovation, especially when complex and tacit know-how is involved (Nooteboom; De Laat). A possible objection to the use of teams and groups to foster knowledge exchange at an interfirm level is, however, that more knowledge than desired may be exchanged and that dangerous spillovers of people and competence may occur. In spite of the fact that internal organization and hierarchy are supposed to be a defence against competence spillovers, these studies may be read as leading to the following two-fold suggestion: on one side, there are feasible interfirm arrangements for making 'dangerous knowledge-exchange liaisons' sustainable; on the other side, that analogous problems may exist within firms as well, in the absence of appropriate mechanisms for encouraging and supporting knowledge sharing. On the first issue, Paul De Laat develops the idea of using hostages to support exchange in an explanation of joint venture as a form of 'third party' deposit and guarantee. Some relevant properties of JV with respect to other forms of *hostages, pledges and sureties* are noticed, such as being able to solve the problem posed by the fact that once transferred, information cannot be returned. Acknowledging that the need for information and knowledge exchange and sharing should be responded to by taking simultaneously into account the need for protecting know-how from the risk of early expropriation and exploitation, De Laat proposes a double-sided organization structure: a fully integrated organization within the joint venture, and a delayed full disclosure of information toward the mother firms. On the second issue, Nooteboom suggests that firms can emulate networks in constructing a sufficiently differentiated and integrated internal network structure so that problem-solving and creative learning can take place. This contention fits with other recent studies on the management of learning and diversity in large firms, maintaining that a coordination network based on hierarchy, procedures and standards for routinized and non-core activities is overlaid on and juxtaposed to a group-like and fully connected network-coordinating core and innovation oriented activities in multinational corporations (Amin and Cohendet 1997). On the other hand, these exchanges of knowledge may encounter difficulties and impasses in internal organization as well, especially when tacit knowledge is involved. In fact, property rights are ill-defined on this type of know-how and people rather than firms 'possess' the relevant knowledge as a matter of fact rather than as a matter of right. Therefore the problem of retaining these human resources and of providing them with adequate incentives to share their knowledge with other actors and units without fear of creating internal competitors is important in internal organization as well. Firms could emulate interfirm networks even in this respect, constructing internal joint ventures and 'knowledge owner' units, holding rights to the utilization of the created know-how and/or to some shared rewards deriving from its utilization.

Network explanation and design: beyond conceptual divides

Markets and hierarchies

A further and more general implication of these studies and arguments seems to be that the traditional and coarse-grained divides between governance structures such as 'firms', 'networks' and 'markets' not only obscure a comparative assessment of coordination properties, which differ substantially according to what types of internal and interfirm organization are considered, but that they have also apparently undergone a substantial convergence through the hybridization in the type of coordination mechanisms used. Firms can use pricing and other 'market' mechanisms within their boundaries, emulate network mechanisms, and may combine a 'hierarchical' or 'capitalistic' organization of some property rights (e.g. on basic equipments) with islands of 'collective' property of know-how and/or with 'enterpreneurial' inside contracting. On the other hand, interfirm networks may intensively use hierarchy, programmes and groups as coordination devices (Part 2); and market exchanges can be extensively defined by rules, codes and standards, are often completed and made more fair by negotiation, and can be made more efficient by social control on performance (Parts 1 and 3).

Trust and opportunism

Another opposition that does not fit well with the evidence and arguments presented in this book is that between trust and opportunism. The development of neo-institutional economics, and of transaction cost economics in particular, has contributed in reinforcing this divide by introducing opportunism as a 'behavioural assumption'. This is not to deny that interesting results have been reached using opportunism as an analytic device—such as demostrating how many cooperative behaviours we can predict starting with an assumption of possibly opportunistic agents. On the other hand, a universalistic interpretation has prevailed, dividing those who believe that 'human nature' is basically opportunistic, from those who believe that that it is basically cooperative or at least honest and trustworthy. Leaving aside heavy methodological discussions on whether these types of assumptions on human nature are a good basis for developing scientific models of economic behaviour, I wish only to highlight how the researches reported here would be better interpreted in a framework in which these 'assumptions' are 'endogenized' and the emergence of opportunistic or trustworthy behaviours is seen as a dependent variable, as something to be explained—and as a strategic dilemma to be solved in practice by economic actors.

To start with, behavioural research has shown that supposed individual attributes and predispositions used in economic modelling—such as a propensity toward risk, opportunism or fairness—are actually quite context dependent and vary within the same individuals. Research on interfirm networks, sharing an interest in understanding the cognitive foundations of economic behaviour, has shown that the formation of trust relationships depends, for example, on the amount of possible losses involved (Nooteboom 1996), on the amount of possible joint gains envisaged (Grandori and Neri), and on the awareness that, in continued relations and negotiations, it pays to refrain from being too calculating (Friedberg and Neuville) whilst not forgoing the ability to make cautionary moves (such as never becoming unilaterally dependent on a single partner) (Brusco).

The hypothesis that economic agents are generally lacking the relevant information for judging the trustworthiness of business partners (justifying the suspicion of opportunism in transaction cost economics) seems to be falsified by empirical evidence; as it seems false that trust is generally conceded to any partner in high trust contexts or cultures (Scher; Paniccia 1998). The identity and evaluation of single partners is dramatically important in practice and relevant information about the past performance of actors is often available from key informants, intermediaries, previous partners and other sources, and it is in fact used in many industries for partner evaluation and selection (Ebers 1997). And even when the web of relationships external to a particular business transaction does not provide enough information, the very creation of the partner specific knowledge and competence that tends to 'lock in' actors in bilateral monopolies, at the same time gives the information for judging whether or not the partner is trustworthy (Ring and Van de Ven 1994; Grandori and Neri). In addition, by definition, asset specificity creates surplus and quasi-rents, and parties are not and should not be willing to lose a bigger portion by bargaining too hard for their share of the pie. Even more, they do and should 'invest' in search and negotiation activities (i.e. increase transaction cost) for conquering partners and types of agreements that increase the total value that can be shared with respect to possible alternative agreements and partners (i.e. increase the specificity and co-specialization of assets) (Ring).

Therefore, it is too easy to treat trust and opportunism as assumptions: they are behaviours to be explained. In practice, economic actors find it important to understand when they should defend themselves as fully as possible against misbehaviour through formal and guaranteed contractual structures, authorities, hostages, third parties and the like; and when all these costs can and should be avoided (Powell 1997). In addition, informal agreements can be self-enforcing not in spite but usually thanks to relation-specific investments and the possibility of joint gains (Grandori 1997). Assets specificity can also be governed strategically by economic actors in most situations and should also be endogenized if our models should capture the variety of games that economic actors play and the variety of structures governing them. Game and negotiation structures (the variety of moves and alternatives open to the various parties, the amount of jointly created value, the number of possible players) rather than specificty or small numbers per se, and feasible decision logics (from value maximizing calculations to automatic rule-guided behaviour) rather than uncertainty per se, look to be promising variables for predicting whether trust or opportunism will prevail.

Finally, trust and opportunism not only can be both present in a relationship, but can even reinforce each other, as Friedberg and Neuville have illustrated in the case of supply relationships. If a party has gained a reputation of trustworthiness, its incentives to behave opportunistically usually increases because it expects less control efforts.

Formal and informal organization

The opposition between formal and informal organization is a long-lasting one in organization theory and has sharply and unfortunately re-emerged in the field of 'interorganizational' research, after having been overcome in the analysis of internal organization. However, the lessons learned about the inadequateness of this divide for understanding and designing internal organization should not be forgotten and would appear to be valid also for the analysis and design of external organization. Informal organization is not more 'natural' and not necessarily better, in any sense, than formal organization, as the studies by Scher, Soda and Usai, and Friedberg and

Neuville illustrate. These studies also reinforce the view that formal and informal governance mechanisms—no matter of what type—are likely to complement each other, reinforce each other, and be embedded in each other, rather than the view that they are governance alternatives or that 'social embeddedness' has a sort of primacy with respect to 'rational-legal embeddedness'. For example, informal negotiations in the car assembly process are as they are because of the type of contracts that have been signed and the types of quality control procedures that have been adopted; in turn, the nature of the negotiation process has a substantial impact on what types of rules will be in fact implemented. Also the deep restructuring of both social and contractual relationships in the Italian construction industry after the change in the juridical climate, as illustrated by Soda and Usai, support this view. In addition, the mere formalization of rules may not change their basic regulatory properties (Grandori *et al.* forthcoming): for example, if the firms clustered in an industrial district were to formalize in a 'constitutional chart' their unwritten constitution about fair-dealing and acceptable codes of conduct—as it has in fact occured in various industries such as telecommunication—this would probably imply only a reinforcement and an explicitation of an already existing system of regulation.

On the other hand, other studies gathered here actually illustrate that the formalization of interfirm coordination mechanisms into documents and contracts may be of help in achieving the types of outcomes especially considered here—learning and fairness—under certain conditions. For example, transparency is likely to reinforce procedural justice (Greenberg 1990) in interfirm relationships as well as in other relationships, especially if the number of involved actors is high; explicitation and awareness is likely to reduce the degree of inertia of institutions (North 1990), especially at their deeper level of principles and values; and formalization as an effort to formulate knowledge (technical as well as behavioural) in a more abstract and generalizable way, rather than in a highly context specific and concrete way, should facilitate its diffusion and flexible application to new contexts (Heylighen 1992).

Concluding remarks

After the transversal reading of the papers offered in the above paragraphs, let me conclude by summarizing some of the substantive implications that may be offered by each section.

- Interfirm networks in general, and different forms of network in particular, have distinctive properties in the resolution of conflicts, because they allow interfirm direct communication, negotiation and agreement over the allocation of resources. Therefore, they can con-tribute to increase the distributive and procedural justice of an economy, by regulating those types of resource allocation problems that are difficult to solve by either unilateral competitive decision-making or by central planning, arbitration and 'fiat' (Part 1).

- Interfirm networks in general, and specific forms of networks in particular, have distinctive properties in the development and exchange of knowledge and competences, thanks to the double feature of the separation of some property rights and the sharing of communication and decision rights (Part 2).
- Interfirm networks in general, and different forms of network in particular, achieve the above results at a cost. While the costs of market and firm coordination have been widely analysed, the enthusiasm for networks have led to neglect the internal and external costs that they entail, which are widely analysed in the last section of the book (Part 3).

Notes

1 European Management and Organization in Transition (EMOT), a research programme of the European Science Foundation, directed by myself and Richard Whytley, existed for five years (1993–1997) as an ongoing forum for European researchers to debate research questions about the comparative and evolutionary analysis of organization and management solutions in and across European firms and countries. It was divided into five interest groups, one of which was the interfirm network group, coordinated by Mark Ebers. I had been particularly involved in the substantive debate of this group from the beginning of its life and acted as the convenor of its final conference, held at the Faculty of Economics, Modena University, in September 1996.
2 This framework was laid down as a series of connected research questions in the planning workshops for the EMOT Programme and then kept alive and refined thanks to the contributions of a group of people who acted as convenors of workshops or as key and committed participants. Their role has been invaluable for achieving learning across five years and four conferences. My warmest acknowledgments go, in addition to Mark Ebers, coordinator of the network group, to George Blanc, Carlos Jarrillo, Bart Nooteboom and Peter Smith Ring.
3 Other leading participants in the EMOT programme, anchoring their observations to the research on large differentiated firms as MNC, have drawn a similar conclusion (Cantwell and Colombo 1997).
4 References to the chapters of this volume are reported in the text without a date and are not listed in the Bibliography.

Bibliography

Amin, A. and Cohendet, P. (1997) 'Learning and adaptation in decentralized business networks', ESF-EMOT Final Conference, Stresa.
Cantwell, J. and Colombo, M. (1997) 'Technological and output complementaries, and interfirm cooperation in information technology ventures', ESF-EMOT Final Conference, Stresa.

Demsetz, H. (1993) 'The theory of the firm revisited', in O. Williamson and S. Winter (eds) *The Nature of the Firm: Origins, Evolution and Development*. Oxford: Oxford University Press.

Ebers, M. (ed.) (1997) *The Formation of Inter-organizational Networks*. Oxford: Oxford University Press.

Ebers, M. and Grandori, A. (1997) 'The forms, costs and development dynamics of inter-organizational networking' in *The Formation of Inter-organizational Networks*. Oxford: Oxford University Press.

Grabher, G. (1993) 'The weakness of strong ties', in G. Grabher (ed.), *The Socially Embedded Firm*. 255–77. London: Routledge.

Grandori, A. (1995) *L'organizzazione delle attività economiche*, Bologna: Il Mulino (new english edition *Organization and Economic Behavior*, London: Routledge, forthcoming).

Grandori A. (1997) 'An organizational assessment of interfirm coordination modes', *Organization Studies* 18(6): 897–925.

Grandori, A. and Soda, G. (1995) 'Inter-firm networks: antecedents, mechanisms and forms', *Organization Studies* 16(2): 183–214.

Grandori, A., Delmestri, G., Soda, G. and Usai, A. (forthcoming) 'Rules as a mode of governance', in L. Engwall and G. Morgan (eds) *Regulation and Organization*, London: Routledge.

Greenberg, J. (1990) 'Organizational justice: yesterday, today and tomorrow'. *Journal of Management* 2(6): 399–432.

Helylighen, F. (1992) 'Making thoughts explicit: advantages and drawbacks of formal expression', paper submitted to the *Journal of Applied Philosophy*.

Jorde, T. M. and Teece, D. J. (1989) 'Competition and cooperation: Striking the right balance', *California Management Review* Spring: 25–37.

Langlois, R. N. and Robertson, P. L. (1995) *Firms, Markets and Economic Change*, London: Routledge.

Lawrence, P. and Dyer, D. (1983) *Renewing American Industry*, New York: The Free Press.

Lawrence, P. and Lorsch, J. (1967) *Organization and Environment*, Boston: Harvard Business School.

North, D. C. (1990) *Institutions, Institutional Change, and Economic Performance*, Cambridge: Cambridge University Press.

Oliver, A. and Ebers, M. (1998) 'Networking network studies', *Organization Studies Special Issue 'The organizational texture of interfirm relations'*, August.

Oliver, C. (1990) 'Determinants of interorganizational relationships: integration and future directions'. *Academy of Management Review* 15: 41-265.

Paniccia, I. (1998) 'One, a hundred, thousands industrial districts. Organizational variety of local networks of SMEs', *Organization Studies, Special Issue: 'The organizational texture of interfirm relations'*, August.

Powell W. (1997) 'Disentagling inter-organizational cooperation', ESF-EMOT Final Conference, Stresa.

Ring, P. Smith and Van de Ven, A. (1994) 'Developmental processes of cooperative interorganizational relationships', *Academy of Management Review*, 19(1): 90–118.

Sydow, J. (1997) 'Inter-organizational relations', in *The Handbook of Organizational Behaviour, International Encyclopedia of Business and Management*, A. Sorge and M. Warner (eds), 211–225, London: Routledge.

Part 1

Differentiated interests, coordination mechanisms and fairness outcomes

1 The rules of the game in industrial districts

Sebastiano Brusco

Statistics from the industrial censuses show that from 1971 to 1991 industrial districts have been a resounding success. In twenty years their share of the total manufacturing employment in Italy has risen from 32 to 42 per cent. This success is attributable to the specific ability of the districts to harmoniously resolve conflict and cooperation both among firms, and within the firm (Brusco 1992; Brusco and Fiorani 1995). The aim of this essay is to study the way in which these dilemmas are dealt with in order to create an efficient system. The basic idea is that specific rules that allow parties to express themselves generate behavioural patterns that, instead of producing destructive effects, make the system more competitive.

Relationships among firms, competition and collaboration

Besides the ability to create innovations, discussed elsewhere (Brusco 1995), the second competitive factor to be considered in the ideal district is the relationships among firms; such relationships simultaneously create competition and cooperation.

The characteristics and rules of competition

It is not difficult to argue that there is competition among the firms within a district. The presence of nearby sellers allows buyers to choose a preferred product in terms of quality, price, delivery terms, customization, and customer service. Each of these elements represents an opportunity to build competitive advantage, and in each of these areas firms compete in a lively way. Each firm identifies its strong points and can draw on the experience of the others to strengthen its market standing. The spread of information makes it possible to know what the various firms' strategies are and enables each one to measure the level of efficiency of all firms and, if need be, to take advantage of this by imitating one or more of them. In this

---

Rules are indented and italicised; citations from personal interviews are indented only.

respect, at least, an industrial district is very transparent. Strategies are indeed clear, understandable and replicable.

Information on product innovations circulates freely and it is very difficult to keep them secret. Fairs, fashion shows and even shop windows are an opportunity to watch what others are doing. When manufacturers in Carpi use felt for the first time, or some Prato manufacturers use synthetic fur, or canning machinery manufacturers in Bologna use relays, or Montebelluna ski-boot manufacturers use plastic, or machinery manufacturers introduce more complex planning, or construction firms utilize new motors in their cement-making machines, specifications of all these innovations become public and it is possible for anyone to retrace the processes that created them and apply them for a better and more efficient product, one which would be better received on the market. It is the incremental nature of innovations that favours imitations, and therefore competition.

As was said some time ago about Japanese entrepreneurs (and it would be easy to quote anecdotes showing how similar the conditions are), the district can count on a specific type of professionalism in taking either machinery or products apart in order to copy them and make small changes to improve the product without running into charges of patent infringement. This is true for imitations of innovations realized outside the district, by large Italian or foreign firms, as well as for incremental innovations carried out within the district. In either case, the small size of the firms is already a defence against intellectual property holders, since the number of lawsuits necessary to enforce the patent would be too expensive. There are several examples of farm machinery that have been copied in terms of quality, efficiency and price; similarly rapid is the spread of innovations introduced by firms within the district.

The frequent use of innovations, creative as it may be, has led to the claim that the district structurally entails a situation of dependence and parasitism that will cause it to fail. On the other hand, one could argue that the easy reproduction of innovations produced inside the district, together with the lack of institutional protection of the results, might discourage any research and development investments. In any case, both remain open problems. However, it could also be that the ability to innovate by imitation is based on a high professionalism, and that improving others' products should be interpreted with the same attitude shown towards the copying of Xerox machines by Minolta or Canon. This discussion is, anyway, irrelevant. The point is that within districts competition is very high and expresses itself in product or process innovation. It should also be mentioned that—as Russo (1985) has demonstrated through significant empirical evidence—there is widespread awareness that it is easy to get a hold of ideas belonging to others, to the extent that firms in Modena and Bologna forgo patenting their innovations for fear that the registration of their new designs at the patent office will be a source of information too easily accessible to their competitors.

Along the same lines, market innovation does not represent an obstacle to competition. A success story with a product in a specific market immediately involves the advent of new competitors. (A small example of this type of market is the gold-leaf faucet market which was a resounding success a few years ago in the Arab world.)

This wild competition in product and market innovations is simplified even further: the presence of a new market or the introduction of a new product are usually simple processes in terms of the necessary capital and the resources needed. A production system entirely based on sub-contracting and the availability within the district of complex and expensive machinery that can be utilized only for a fraction of their saturation time, lowers entry barriers. The low level of vertical integration and, paradoxically, the small dimensions highlight the competitive advantage of the adversaries. The comparative advantage of someone who produces a new product or explores a new market is always only temporary and is based on pure know-how as well as on a network of relationships. The latter is always the only 'protection' for the innovator while the efficiency of the firms in the district is always dynamic.

All conditions regarding competition are therefore exceptional: an extraordinary market transparency, a significant diffusion of information, and the easy access of new firms or existing ones to the market. This lively competition and the very rapid circulation of information, given the large number of highly enterprising firms, on the one hand eliminate rents but, on the other, are crucial factors in ensuring that firms inside the district attain a competitive advantage as against those remaining outside.

The large number of firms and their common attempts to distinguish themselves and grow, render them particularly open to large and small innovations in order to equip themselves with new products and markets. Many of these innovation attempts fail; however, they create precedents and have lessons to teach. At times, there is a feeling of certainty that a specific plan of action is completely wrong; in other circumstances, feedback is gained for future efforts if changes are made to the original strategy. In yet other cases, new experiences are positive and successful to the extent that they are acquired by others and copied. The advantage that innovators enjoy is only temporary since the district's flexibility, its mobility and its ability to react are very high.

In sum, the district is constantly engaged in a trial and error process. Work is usually not carried out on projects that require large investments, given that the actors involved are small in terms of gross sales and capital. However, as has already been mentioned, if the project is a worthwhile one, the strategy, modified here and there as discussed earlier, can bring the effort to fruition. In addition, the strategy focuses on various directions and the commitment is quite significant, given that the rewards are rich and no firm is willing to share them with any other, at least for a while. Simultaneously, groups of firms carefully monitor the situation of thousands of other single firms pursuing old and new strategies and are able rapidly to process the feedback received, whether positive or negative. It is this ability to observe and copy success stories with care and creativity that explains how, even without a strategy and a means of coordination, the district can read and interpret occurrences within technology and markets, so as to compete efficiently with more aggressive actors.

This imitation and replication practice, combined with the ability to value and learn from others' experiences, obviously creates problems—at times serious ones—as far as commercial ethics are concerned. However, the districts' behavioural codes precisely regulate the conditions by which private knowledge can become public knowledge, defining in detail what is just, as opposed to what is unfair, competition. The rule established by the community reads as follows (keep in mind that the reference is to an ideal district even though the empirical evidence obviously refers to the study of actual districts):

> *Final market firms should be competitors and can exploite all final market firms by exploiting all legitimate opportunities to gain success from others as in the case of fairs, fashion shows, exhibits, shop windows. Supplier firms are also competitors, along the same lines. Supplier firms can, if they deem it appropriate, play the game by gambling their future on final markets. However, it is considered unfair and shameful competition to corrupt a supplier or employee in order to acquire information on a competing firm's strategy.*

Towards a typology of cooperation rules

Despite the lively competition we have just discussed, cooperation does exist; it assumes various shapes and plays quite a relevant role. The idea that among district firms there is only collusion is an off-the-cuff remark that at times is expressed by economists who tend to think that collusion is the only alternative to competition. What is the social and cultural structure that enables competition and cooperation to coexist? What is the institutional framework in which cooperation is made possible and developed?

It does not seem reasonable to trust explanations that assign a relevant role to goodwill, a willingness to cooperate or, in the end, to character features of the actors and people involved. It is most certainly naive to think that this cooperation is based upon the fact that people from the Emilia-Romagna or Veneto regions have a particular inclination to be fair and good-hearted. Rather, this collaboration is underpinned by a complex body of rules that can be studied as carefully as law. In particular, norms regulating cooperation among firms can be categorized in three groups: rules of caution, interaction rules, and sanctions. The distinctions among them are quite precise. The first are norms that are unilaterally applied to single agents, as necessary conditions to create a new cooperation agreement. Interaction rules, on the other hand, define the behaviour that the agents will have to follow once the relationship is established. Lastly, sanctions identify who is in charge of ascertaining violation of the norm, determining the fine applicable and issuing the sentence.

Cautions

As already pointed out by Lorenz (1988) in the case of the Lyon steel workers, the practice of apportioning contracts among various suppliers and soliciting orders from various clients is also widespread within Italian districts. This is done in order to prevent damage to the firm's viability in the event of a betrayal or a defection, thus leaving the contractor without his habitual tried and tested subcontractors who could be quickly assigned the work that was previously assigned to the offending party, or alternatively leaving a subcontractor without a reliable client. 'Never put all your eggs in one basket' is the oft-quoted saying. It must be noted that this turns out to be an expensive rule to observe. In fact, building trust among various suppliers and contractors requires more time and effort than dealing with only one or two opposite parties. The additional costs inevitably involved with this method represent a kind of insurance against possible defections or betrayals. To confirm this attitude towards cautions, we can argue that only rarely do subcontractors in districts purchase specific machinery, as discussed by organizational economists. The models used for the printing of steel plates, for example (or for moulding in the steel industry), almost always belong to the contracting company and are lent to the chosen supplier as the occasion demands. When this does not happen, it means that the machinery is of low value, and its cost is charged entirely on the first supply batch.

Both attitudes are made possible by a general rule without which no form of collaboration would be possible.

> *It is a good thing to trust those who deserve it, even though prudent attitudes are legitimate and allowed. These attitudes are not necessarily evidence of a lack of trust in and esteem for the opposite party; rather, they merely represent cautions, typical of any careful entrepreneur.*

The true significance of the rule can be appreciated only by contrast, i.e. by reflecting on how often this norm is not applied and when prudent behaviour is not deemed desirable and legitimate. For example, this procedure is felt to be normal and fair in Emilia-Romagna and Tuscany, but is interpreted as a sign of blinkeredness in Veneto, where it is normal for an entrepreneur to ask his subcontractor to work exclusively with him/her. At the same time, in Southern Italy only those who trust others unconditionally, through total commitment, have the right to ask for special treatment and support in times of need. These two different behaviours, unusual as they may seem, are actually quite similar. Indeed, in both cases the relationship is based on very strong dichotomies: 'either we are friends or we are enemies'. If we are friends, we are expected to give and get back; any refusal will be interpreted as a betrayal. If we are enemies, any unfair behaviour is possible and all interactions will be characterized by fear and suspicion of cheating.

Interaction rules

The type of collaboration that best reflects the daily life of the district is the one between final-market firms and subcontractor firms. This collaboration relies, above all, on the readiness to invest significant resources in order to 'learn how to work together'. The investment is made by both contractor and supplier. The point is to understand and harmonize two different work-styles as well as two ways of organizing the production process. In this setting, transfers of knowledge (even technological) often occur in both directions. The requirements are a common language and a set of mutually agreed-upon precedents that facilitate communications. Through a series of subsequent orders, costs can be agreed upon and a price can be established. Then, multiple visits to each others' plants enable a better acquaintance with and understanding of the respective technologies. The ongoing relationship then leads to a sample contract that can be later defined on the phone before being put into writing, if a written form is necessary. In almost every case, when firms in the textile or steel industries with less than fifty employees are involved, the only written agreements defining delivery contracts are the order vouchers that are frequently not even signed by the supplier. These contracts, informal as they may seem, even detail the procedures for handling possible communication mis-understandings. A typical case requiring a standard procedure to share damages equally is a situation when, in good faith, the supplier delivers a product that is different from what the contractor requested (e.g. sewing buttonholes that are too big or producing metal pieces with too high or too low endurance).

The basic rule governing these cases of collaboration is quite simple:

> *Two agents who work together on a continuous basis will never fully take advantage of the market power that is available to them, owing to their reciprocal interdependence, or some other phenomenon. Each of them will take into consideration the survival needs and the success opportunities of the other; both are tied to profit margins, and to the ability to keep their respective technological standards high and to retain the best and most skilled workforce.*

It is precisely for this reason that, among firms that regularly collaborate with each other, prices for subcontractor transactions change less frequently than on the open market where non-collaborative firms usually operate. During a crisis, it is the subcontractor who has the most advantage; in a period of strong demand, the contractor is the winner. In any case, both have a larger profit, both can afford better profit and investment planning, and both feel less uncertainty for the future. And if in a longer time frame each partner ends up balancing advantages and disadvantages, both will enjoy a better profit stability and less uncertainty. The same result holds for the widespread custom where the contractor ensures that a regular supplier reaches a certain volume of gross sales even in times of crisis, and the supplier ensures that his best clients receive their orders in a timely fashion despite peak demands.

In a relationship between final-market firms and subcontractor firms, some particular procedures for the fixing of the price may play a role, notwithstanding the general rule described above. In the Veneto region, for example, the contractor is acknowledged to have the right to fix the price; on the other hand, the subcontractor is accorded the option of requesting a price change if the workmanship should be more complex than expected. In yet other cases, contractor and supplier can agree that the price be determined *ex post*, i.e. after production is completed, and when reasonably certain that the proposed schedule is respected. In both cases, the parties enjoy a substantial saving both in terms of cost estimates and negotiations.

However, the interaction between contractor and supplier can develop into more complex situations than those described above: 'The contractor goes to the supplier not with a plan but with a problem' and asks him/her for help in resolving it (Brusco and Sabel 1981). In this case, it is not only a matter of working together through the production process where procedures and results are known; the two firms need to learn to work together creatively, with the common aim of creating a new product or a new production process. In this way, the creativity of the one who perceives a new need within the market goes hand in hand with the familiarity that the other party has with all the details of the production method. It often happens that a firm having an idea presents it to various suppliers, with the aim of finding the best technical solution. The advantages of this collaboration for the end firm are obvious. In turn, the subcontractor carefully selects the firms with which to work, knowing that the 'consultancy' will eventually translate into fair compensation later on when dealing with some other clients. This support and assistance in the planning process is reflected in the firm's budget, both in terms of gross sales realized and in the promotional value that it inevitably assumes.

Russo (1996a) also describes an activity similar to the one just analysed for which definite procedures have been codified, and which focuses on the ceramic production sector. Russo cites several cases in which a metal worker, thinking he has a good idea for solving bottlenecks in the manufacturing process, asks for help from a tile factory owner and for extended periods spends time there experimenting on his prototype. His presence causes problems and eventually increases costs until at length he manages to improve the product. In this instance, the value added for the worker trying to produce a new machine entails having available both a testing site and a machine on which to test his prototype. On the other hand, the advantage for the tile factory owner is that once the worker's new machine is completed, he will be the first to take advantage of it.

Among the various forms of technological cooperation, it is worth citing the indirect cooperation that takes place among similar firms through the personal relationships between technicians: 'We could not seem to get this machine to work properly. Our technician called his friend at firm B to find out how they resolved the problem.' Hence, firm A and firm B, although competitors for final products, can cooperate to improve a new piece of machinery. The issue did not concern a machine particularly critical for product quality; rather, it was a question of handling the problem in the best possible way.

As we have attempted to explain, each of the forms of cooperation described (within end firms, within subcontractor firms and within both) improves, at one and the same time, the efficiency of the system and the financial situation of the firm. However, all this is possible only because there is a basic rule that supports and promotes this collaboration.

> *It is wrong and shameful for a client, a consultant, a subcontractor or an employee to use information, knowledge or a network of relationships for personal gains to the detriment of the firm that has involved them in specific initiatives with good faith.*

Thus, if Joe calls Bill to invite him to work together on a large order of clamps or hinges, Bill should stay in the shadows so as not to try to develop a working relationship with Joe's client in order to promote himself as an alternative supplier for possible future orders. All this is even more evident in the case of a taxi driver who dispatches a colleague to help him with a large number of customers: it would be very unfair if the driver called upon tried to steal customers from his colleague. Along the same lines, a sub-contractor who receives a plan cannot use it to manufacture a product in direct competition with that of his client; the same is true for a supplier who should not use an idea that was shared with him and exploit it for his own interest. Lastly, these examples also describe the possible relationship between designers such as Trussardi or Cardin and the artisan who shares with them an item that he himself has designed and could produce (and that they would later sell under their own trademark). If the offer is refused, the artisan is sure to be able to share his product with other potential buyers, feeling reasonably certain that the idea will not be taken away from him.

All this would seem obvious and to be taken for granted. However, it is useful to remember that very often the absence of this rule creates serious obstacles in cooperation among firms and prevents the system from reaching its potential. Without such rules, the subcontractor—and, above all, a similar firm to whom a part of the work is contracted out—is often perceived as a tough competitor, someone to be avoided at all costs, given that avoidance is the only guarantee against the subcontractor's using plans or projects for his own ends or even attempting to seduce a contractor by offering lower prices. This is what some managers relate about furniture companies in Cyprus (personal interviews):

> How is it possible [an entrepreneur from Cyprus asks himself in commenting on the situation in Emilia-Romagna] for someone to share a plan with a supplier? If it were me, in order to obtain that plan, I would have to look for a trustworthy Italian architect; I would have to explain to him the rules of the market, and I would have to pay him a generous compensation. He would sustain no expenses . . . If he copied my plan, he could sell a piece of furniture identical to mine at a 30 per cent discount and force me out of the market.

The same, most probably, happens in Southern Italy where even medical doctors are afraid of being replaced while on vacation.

Sanctions

Lastly, cooperation is also based on sanctions that are applied to those who betray anyone trusting them; these sanctions seldom involve law suits or arbitration. Sanctions can be categorized in various ways. In some cases, when there is reasonable doubt that the missed commitment may be owing to *force majeure* or non-fraudulent causes, the sanction can merely involve a reduction in orders.

> He delivered late and the work was not perfect. However, we have been working together for a long time and I realized that if I reduced the contract, he would understand that he must take more care.

In other cases, however, the sanction takes the form of a cancellation of orders or refusal to accept them; this, in turn, involves a loss of the initial investment in the form of the sunk costs necessary to establish the cooperation.

The interested party is not necessarily the one responsible for the sanction. In a small community, information travels fast: if relationships between two firms are discontinued, everybody finds out since the contractors' staff is no longer seen around town. People talk about the news in bars, at meetings, at social events. There is the need to know what happened and the why and wherefore of the break-up. At the end of this process, all those firms that have witnessed the violation of a rule know, or they think they know, what happened and act accordingly. This is why, generally speaking, the loss of reputation usually connected with loss of trust has repercussions on the relationships among all the firms within the district.

The firm's internal relationships, conflict and participation

The other characteristic typical of a civil society that is linked with the economic system and the territory—enabling the firm to maintain a position on the international market—is the quality of the relationships between workers and firms. Even in this case, the district witnesses a tension between opposing forces regulated in such a way as to produce a positive effect. This phenomenon can be labelled 'balance between conflict and participation' and concerns relationships between workers and entrepreneurs within the same firm.

Within the argument we attempt to develop here, there is a focal point: the relationship of competition/cooperation discussed in the previous section specifically refers to a sample of small-sized firms. It requires that in the firm there be an atmosphere of collaboration and trust between entrepreneur and workers. For relationships among firms do not merely involve relationships among the owners of those firms. There are highly productive relationships among production managers, project leaders and foremen who, through collaboration, are often able to resolve complex and different balances among various loyalties. Only a strong participation in the well-being of one's own firm together with the traditional custom of fairness can lead to fruitful relationships.

The role and nature of participation

All arguments about post-Fordism lead to the same conclusions (we shall not recall them here). The fragmentation and volatility of the demand, together with the need for rapid production of what the market requests (and could reject tomorrow) and the need to ensure that the product meets the expected quality standards, require that the workers be committed in a different way compared to those employed in Ford's time.

In order to be efficient and competitive, the firm needs the active collaboration of the workers both in the design and planning stages and the production stage; in addition, collaboration is essential in the delicate and critical testing phase until the product is finally completed. In sum, competitiveness and efficiency call for, 'additional doses of intelligence, commitment, and diligence' on the part of the workers who are no longer asked merely to provide work at 'standard' levels (Gallino 1978).

The precise meaning of 'standard', and hence also the true sense of 'additional doses of commitment', can be defined by referring to analytical and cultural contexts quite different from each other. One could refer to an *ordinary* workforce, identifying it with the one described by Marx in his *Manifesto*: 'The extensive use of machinery and the division of labour have led the proletariat to lose independence and therefore the workers do not feel any appeal for their jobs. The worker becomes a mere accessory to the machine, an accessory asked to perform very simple, repetitive and easy-to-learn tasks.' In this specific case, additional commitment presumes a different organization of labour, at least one in which the worker can assume more complex tasks as well as more important responsibilities.

Alternatively, one can use as a comparison the situation, theorized in the classics of Taylorism and Fordism, by which the conception and execution of work are strictly separated and the additional doses of commitment are necessary, at least partially, to connect the two types of activity. Alternatively, standardization can stem from the nature of the work contract and the control exercised by the firm over subordinate labour. The point, in this case, is that the work contract imposes a precise and efficient performance but cannot, for obvious reasons, demand creativity. Along the same lines, hierarchical control is by nature insufficient and unable to force a subordinate to perform to extraordinary standards. In this context, additional doses of commitment are what no contract could ever require or guarantee; what the worker adds or takes away from the production process is at his own discretion and this remains outside the sphere of control, since the controller cannot really control it.

All in all, additional doses of commitment are, in fact, evidence of a true involvement by the worker in the production process; they are evidence that the worker takes part in the process with heart as well as hands and thinks of the work as useful and important—from his/her own point of view as well as that of the firm. It is obvious that when such situations occur and workers' participation in the production process and the future of the firm reaches very high levels, firms are more able to be competitive both in terms of quality and price.

All this should be properly labelled: it could be useful to use the terms 'participation' and 'involvement' to describe firm situations where workers take part in the production process in the generous and committed way we have sought to define above.

Rules of participation

Based on what premises, with what content and in what form are negotiations carried out in the district, which will lead to participation and involvement of the workers in the firm's activities? As in the previous case, it is worthwhile to distinguish between rules of *caution*, *interaction rules* and *sanctions*.

Cautions

Participation is not easy to control. It can be granted and taken away at will, i.e. without notice and without any verbal intervention alerting that the behaviour is about to change or has changed. As a matter of fact, except for formal work rules, a certain amount of time may be necessary for the entrepreneur to understand that the situation has changed and that there is less willingness to offer 'additional doses of commitment'. In this perspective, participation is seen as a daily decision, one that must be reiterated and confirmed all the time. One measures a cautious behaviour, above all, by the fact that it is a game that is played only when, in specific situations, it is felt to be worth playing. However, there are also other strategies that are more complex, are played on the basis of more important decisions and refer to a wider time frame with consequently higher costs for those who make them.

Moratorium is the first of these strategies. Solinas (1996) has highlighted and demonstrated that a worker at the beginning of his career changes jobs two, three, even four times before finding the most suitable position. This search includes learning about the firm's work rules, and the process of getting used to a strict and severe discipline is somewhat hidden in the search. There is also a search for a pleasant work environment and co-workers easy to get on with. Every young person beginning a working career is looking for the place and environment deemed most appropriate to their tastes. The 'best' place could be the one where a flexible schedule would allow one to take half a day off to go fishing, or where the pay is generous enough to make it possible to buy a house.

Among all these alternatives, there are also people who look for work environments that involve professional growth, where it is possible to continue learning, and where a personal commitment to the job is recognized through incentives, higher income and more responsibilities. Only in this case is it worth playing the entire game: it is in this way that one pursues challenging objectives in terms of respect, learning opportunities and salary. Therefore, in the *moratorium* the search for the place and the environment in which to give one's best is apparent. And this search obviously implies the establishment of conditions set in such a unilateral and preliminary way as to reveal that a caution is being observed not to overcommit oneself before ascertaining that the commitment will be rewarded. The search for mobility between one position and another is not so different. In this case, too, motivations may vary, but just as often mobility means searching for opportunities where one's extra commitment is most acknowledged.

The last case worth quoting on this issue is the easiest to interpret. It is the case of the worker who, asked to develop a new line of products, in turn asks the entrepreneur to become a partner in the newly created company that will market the new product. The worker in this case prudently asks that the entrepreneur make a firm commitment about sharing the profits with him/her, abandoning the usual tendency to 'trust' the partner in favour of defining clear responsibilities regulated by law.

> We really needed to work hard to realize the new line of products we designed. Knowing that I would have to put a lot of energy into the job, I wanted to make sure that at least part of the profits came my way. That is why I asked to become a partner in the company producing a new plough.

On this basis, it is possible to formulate a rule governing these behaviours and resembling the one already cited for the relationships among firms:

> *Besides being a good thing, it is also fair to contribute to the best of one's abilities to the success of the firm for which one works. However, prudent behaviour is also allowed and is legitimate. The fact that the worker demands adequate recognition for the commitment demonstrated is not a sign of low esteem or lack of trust towards the entrepreneur; it is simply evidence of admirable wariness and caution.*

The meaning of the rule, in this case, is very clear, just like in the case previously discussed. High commitment is subject to negotiation and conditions. The two parties enjoy equal dignity and can negotiate freely. Being a subordinate does not imply a feeling of inferiority, thus one refuses to submit to the employer's orders without negotiating the conditions.

Interaction rules

Workers have a significant role in defining new products, identifying the techniques and obtaining the best results from the production process.

> Nowadays the firm can no longer decide alone what are the best products to manufacture; it needs to pay attention to the market and, given that we are all consumers, even workers can participate in the production process in order to improve results which will eventually benefit them too.

> I shared all my plans with our workers and I took into consideration their feedback; I do think that those who work with every aspect of the production can really offer good advice on both the process and internal management.

> We rely heavily on daily exchanges with the workers; the worker can express judgement on what he is doing, and on what is about to take shape; a strong relationship with him/her is very stimulating.

Such a participative attitude has benefits for both the worker and the entrepreneur. The former distances him/herself from a complex and authoritarian hierarchical system and sees that his skills and craftsmanship are being recognized. The latter improves his product as well as the efficiency of the production process of which he is in charge.

However, the price that both parties have to pay is high. If it is true that workers are asked to express consensus and offer strong commitment in order to meet the firm's objectives, the commitments of the entrepreneur are no less significant. He needs to shift from an authority-based hierarchy to a competence-based one, the latter being more complex and difficult to implement. The entrepreneur finds him/herself having to submit his own ideas to other people, he needs to commit a significant amount of his time to fostering relationships with his employees in order to hear their opinions and proposals. It is obviously not a case of simply reading what has been put in the suggestion box.

There is an important implication here that influences the organization of labour. To leave room for the 'additional doses of commitment' discussed above, it is necessary for the hierarchical system to lose explicitness and detail to the point where it becomes informal and poorly defined. In other words, the firm needs to abandon the Fordist hypothesis and admit that it cannot know in detail the alternatives of action available and cannot keep all the variables involved in the production process under control. Analysed in this way, informality requires precise behavioural rules which allow the workers to be very independent. Informality therefore becomes an organizational mode whereby unpredictable circumstances can be faced by mutual adaptation, thus blurring the Taylorian distinction between spheres of decision and spheres of action.

> What hierarchies? Each worker is responsible for all kinds of machines and we do not just produce one model, rather several ones. The foreman decides on the division of work even when the owners are not around; each worker has then to set up his own machine accordingly.

> We have a very open mentality with our workers; they are always involved if there is a concern related to the shop floor; they are usually not if it is an external matter.

> Although I am in charge of overseeing operations, each worker is responsible for his own accomplishments; it is the worker him/herself who feels he has to carry out the work with a professional attitude.

> If there is a problem, the workers usually get involved in trying to solve it: they feel it is their problem also; if a shipment is late they do their best to ensure that it gets out quickly; they are familiar with our customers' needs for quality products without being reminded of them all the time.

It is possible to regulate informality in various ways. Sometimes all rules are implicit and are legitimized in the custom and the work style of the firm. In other cases, however, the rules regulating discretionality can be negotiated explicitly, on an individual or collective basis. In this case the rules are not the result of spontaneity or community spirit, but rather of a social framework that can be modified along the way and later adapted to various and changing needs.

However, cases reflecting the first example are quite rare. An informal organization of labour is almost always a difficult structure to create. It is a target that needs to be pursued with tenacity and persistence against reluctant entrepreneurs who are often ready to ask for collaboration but not to pay the price. Even when objectives are met, the success is always ephemeral since it needs to be consolidated during the daily life of the firm, and thus over a long period of time. In this sense, then, conflict paradoxically ends by being the guarantee for participation and efficiency. Without the potential for the sanctions inherent in a conflict, participation is nothing but goodwill and kindness of heart or, alternatively, an unbalanced exchange and an unconditional surrender. Supposing that the fall of Fordism can naturally bring this about leads one to assume that the technical aspects of production are sufficient to determine consciousness: in other words, one is here supposing that technical conditions precisely determine the style of social relationship within and outside the firm.

Regardless of their origin in struggling workers or enlightened owners, the practice of workers' participation in the production process and the division of labour (as well as their discretion in carrying out tasks) have an important implication that is indissolubly tied to the informal organization. This is a clear admission that the only differences between entrepreneur and workers are those of role and authority and that there are no differences of respectability, intellectual status or rank. In sum, it is the mutual recognition of equal dignity.

In the organizational context described above, the workers' autonomy and discretion do not depend on the entrepreneur's good-hearted attitude, but rather on the realization that the achievement of quality and efficiency depends on the active involvement of the workers. Workers therefore are no longer passive followers: they become leading actors despite their role differences. These are, in turn, accepted because they are based on competence. Along the same lines, the entrepreneur is free to choose to remain competitive. As premiss and result of this situation, it is necessary for both workers and entrepreneurs to see each other as people having equal dignity, and that as equals they are committed to the exchange of ideas and the building of personal relationships not only in the workplace but also through a wide range of interests, values and settings within community, political and social life.

> He who thinks merely about work in life is a closed-minded person and cannot produce. He who has other interests has a wider perspective and finds the energies to strive.
>
> We are fortunate to employ workers who do not just see work, and for whom work is not their only reason for being. One has to work hard, but at the same time have other interests.
>
> It is not true that firms prefer workaholics; rather workaholics are seen as stiff and tormenting. The person who finds a balance and has a spontaneous attitude yields better results.
>
> We need conscientious people who can carry out the work, at times, if necessary, even against the boss's opinion.

This assumption is enough to eliminate any hypothesis of paternalism, given that paternalism always presumes the recognition of deep differences that have an impact not only on the life of the firm but also on the relationships outside the firm.

The awareness that conflicts are always possible is at the basis not only of one's work situation and income but also of the esteem that one feels for oneself at work or outside the workplace; when, with friends, one goes out for amusement or socializing.

All this can be translated into a rule that has an important significance:

> *The premiss for participation is the awareness, on everybody's part, that the roles exercised within the firm—both of an entrepreneur or a worker—do not imply any hierarchy in terms of subordination, culture or politics; they also do not label workers with a judgement of professional inferiority. The firm needs a hierarchical structure but in their own job everyone should have room for discretion and initiative; each individual should also assume their responsibilities and should be willing to pay for their own mistakes.*

However, the entrepreneur does not only have to face a change in relationships if he/she wants to enjoy the advantages of participation. There are also significant problems connected with the distribution of surplus. What is interesting is that these issues are arrived at indirectly, and through logical itineraries and firm behavioural rules: one could say they are not tackled up-front. Specifically, there are two guarantees that entrepreneurs are asked to produce. They need to be committed to furnishing clear and precise information concerning the affairs of the firm; and they must also be committed to a particularly sober lifestyle. Let us take a look at what exactly this commitment to 'truth' and 'sobriety' means.

Truth in divulging firm information means, above all, establishing transparency within relationships.

> We do not keep secrets. We do not withhold information in order to use it only at opportune times.

I need to provide the workers with all kinds of information, so as to make them feel comfortable in their work.

For the entrepreneur, providing information on the successes and the hardships of the firm means setting the premises for the acceptance of a relationship between productivity and wages, or introducing some form of profit participation. What happens then is that when the firm is going through a crisis, the entrepreneur can call for help from his employees, e.g. can request that wage increases be limited to a minimum based on national guidelines. However, in order to obtain this help, the entrepreneur must be willing to grant substantial wage increases when the firm is profitable. In these circumstances, it would not be possible to tell the workers that wage increases are out of the question; basically, the worker pays a price when conditions are unfavourable and receives a prize when they are favourable. The following is a statement from a worker from Parma: 'If the company is not doing well we do not even talk about it; if things look up, we demand the money.'

Similar considerations can be made regarding the 'sobriety' of the entre-preneur. What emerges from the examination of attitudes and behaviours, of statements and recriminations, is that in this context it is natural that the entrepreneur will have a higher income than the worker (a bigger house, a house in the mountains and perhaps also one at the seaside, and a Mercedes instead of a Fiat); but what is not permitted is conspicuous consumption or the wasting of resources. An entrepreneur who gambles his profits in Monte Carlo is not deemed to deserve and should not count on 'additional doses of commitment' and participation. The point here is that the entrepreneur is only able to ask his workers to do all they possibly can to save the company if he, too, 'had done his share'. This obviously means that when the firm is profitable it must invest and that workers are entitled to work using the best machines and technology that the market allows. The sobriety in question is not equality in income received and in resources spent but, rather, the commitment to investment in order to keep the company on the frontier of efficiency. Without this commitment the request for participation is seen as cheating and the owner is labelled as unreliable: 'I work like a dog, but he has to provide me with the best possible machine.'

The two conditions described above—transparency and truth in the sharing of information and sobriety in the work- and lifestyles of the entre-preneur—are nothing less than a commitment to participation in the profit-sharing and ploughing back of such profits into the firm.

The rule describing the above can be expressed as follows:

The entrepreneur must be committed to truth (whence a wage condition is directly connected with merit and the success of the firm) and to sobriety (whence comes a high rate of investment of the profits to guarantee use of the best possible technology.

Sanctions

There are two possible sanctions that can be applied to the entrepreneur who does not follow these rules. The first one is set by the workers who can use their 'voice' to complain or who can leave the firm, thus removing all the know-how learned over the years that the entrepreneur will inevitably have to replace. Entrepreneurs are very aware of this danger.

> My main resource is my workforce—people in whom I have been investing for a long time. The women you see working here need to be taken care of, even during a crisis, because it is they who make the company function and grow.

The second sanction is formulated and issued by the community. It will always be difficult for unfair entrepreneurs to hire honest and skilled workers. Their recruiting potential is substantially lowered to the point that they will be forced to operate with low-skilled workers whom nobody else is willing to hire.

Sanctions are significant also for workers unwilling to commit themselves to the job. As their careers progress, they will find it increasingly difficult to obtain a challenging job, will find no professional growth opportunities and will not be respected by their fellows.

A policy for cooperation and participation

In the previous pages we asked ourselves why industrial districts are characterized by the co-presence of strong competition and cooperation among firms; we also questioned why there is an attitude of participation within the firms, despite the presence of conflicts. We attempted to explain these situations by referring to a complex structure of cautious behaviour, recognized rules and sanctions.

At this point, given that the objective is no longer to observe, but rather to plan efficient intervention, we need to provide more precise answers to the questions at hand. To this end, it could be useful to categorize what happens within districts using the metaphor of the prisoner's dilemma. Relationships that link together actors within the district often reflect the characteristics of this classic example.

- Loss of trust, occurring in firms involved in an exchange or between workers and entrepreneurs, leads to the worst possible results, since in spite of the resources and energies dedicated to the effort, nothing is gained.
- Cooperation, pursued thanks to the mutual interest in a relationship, ensures that positive results are obtained for both parties.
- Isolated defection guarantees maximum success. The subcontractor who receives a model to produce, produces it on his own and sells it

with his own trademark, realizing the maximum profit. The same happens to the contractor who either pays the minimum price on the market or sets up as many payment instalments as possible. The same is also true for the entrepreneur who, having received maximum commitment from his workers, refuses to meet the implicit contractual agreements that were the basis of worker participation.

If this is the picture, and if goodwill and the positive influence from the genes in the chromosomal legacy of people in Emilia-Romagna or Veneto are exploitable, then what constellation of interests can guarantee their participation?

The first and most comprehensible explanation is that the game is played not once but many times over. Betraying the trust of another person means losing future opportunities from the client, the supplier, or losing the chance to get the best out of one's workers, or the chance to work under better conditions and with higher remuneration. In the case of the game played only once, the player has gained more than with cooperation; the same is not true with the repeated game where prices and earnings refer to a longer period of time in which neither of the two parties knows the date of expiry.

In this connection, the simplest case is when the delivery price is fixed. A very low price, that in certain market conditions cannot cover the subcontractor's fixed costs, represents a significant profit for the contractor firm. If, on the other hand, the calculation on convenience is based on an ongoing relationship, there will be awareness that: 'a dead supplier is worthless to anyone'; and the price paid to the subcontractor must be such as not only to guarantee adequate remuneration for the skills provided, but also sufficient to enable investment to keep up with available technology.

At the same time, anyone requesting workers' participation can decline a significant wage increase when the firm is doing well. This can only be done once though. In an ongoing relationship, entrepreneurs must keep their promises or surrender and lose all competitive advantage stemming from their workers' extra commitment.

In several cases, then, the district's productivity can be explained as above, and cooperation can simply be considered the result of a continuity of relationships that leaves no room for opportunism. After all, in analytical patterns such as those just described, the clarifying variable is reputation and the great need for reputation that marks the life of the actors within the district.

What was argued in the previous sections seems to confirm this hypothesis. The cautions described obviously represent a way to reduce the risk of unilateral defection. When one's contracts or orders are divided up among several suppliers or clients, no defection can be so significant as to put the future of the firm at risk. That said, this behaviour has its own costs, but it also encourages a framework of trust.

Another example of protection from risk is provided by the district norms that regulate production mistakes; the risk in this case does not depend on bad faith or unfairness, but on communication problems. When the subcontractor makes buttonholes that are too big, the contractor will have to pay for the material wasted and the supplier will only have wasted his labour, if the product cannot be recycled. Rules are designed to protect both parties equally, with an equal sharing of the losses. In any case, given that the rules assume frequent plant visits and deliveries in small lots, even when the order itself is large, the danger of something like this happening is quite small. Despite the low risk, it does occasionally happen, given the widespread informality of the contracts and the lack of definition of details. Since mutual plant visits are expensive in terms of costs and time, the increase in costs is appreciable; but visits encourage trust and the costs are eventually recovered by the future increase in collaboration.

The risk of individual defection is different compared to a 'normal' situation and, likewise, the incentives for mutual cooperation are also different.

First of all, incentives are carefully graded, based on the efforts made. Take for example the case when the artisan asks the tile factory owner to utilize his plant to work on his prototype. The gain the artisan realizes by cooperating, if he meets his objectives, is not just the profit he would enjoy in selling the new machine to the owner who allowed him to test it at his plant. Given that it is agreed that the commitment that the artisan has put into his research is greater than the costs incurred by the tile factory in hosting him, the rules of the game presume that the firm where the artisan tested his machine merely enjoys the right of first use. The tile factory owner will be the first to use the machine, thus taking advantage of the know-how acquired during the testing phase. But his market advantage is only temporary, and the artisan will be able to sell the machine to others, on a better market, therefore increasing his profits.

At the same time, the bonus given to a worker in recognition of his commitment may vary in size and significance. There are bonuses ranging from opportunities to attend advanced training courses and professional conferences, to financial ones, to offers of a partnership in the firm or, in a newly created firm, the opportunity to carry through a specific idea or project during favourable market conditions.

In addition to the careful and graded definition of bonuses, the district's situation—as already mentioned—ensures that cooperation brings with it particularly fruitful results. Workers' participation calls for a reinvestment of the profits: this is the way the firm will achieve success, which in turn will guarantee higher wages and larger profits as compared to those firms that do not rely on collaboration and high technology. Cooperation among firms enables stability in prices, the guarantee of a minimum number of orders and timely deliveries: all these are positive aspects in the good management of the firm. Having several suppliers and several clients is also a positively recognized practice: it allows one to use the know-how acquired through a broad base while allowing, among other things, ample distribution of the learning costs. It is important to remember the norm by which it is unfair to reveal secrets or talk about practices that represent a competitive advantage for one's suppliers or clients. In any case, the numerous opportunities for technological convergence within the district often ensure that this occurs without any problems.

The district's institutions and rules increase the amount of sanctions, compared to a 'normal' situation. The stronger the commitment 'to learn to work together', the greater the loss that both parties will incur in the case of failure of trust. In more general terms, one can say that the more incentives, the more sanctions—given that the failure of trust indicated by a defection, besides leading to the loss of even larger incentives, presumes an even larger sanction.

In even more general terms, referring to the amounts of the bonus and the sanctions, it is worth recalling Russo's (1996b) reminder that in the district, each actor 'plays several games simultaneously'. Each supplier has several clients, and at times several subcontractors who work for him/her—located further away from the market of the finished product—and each client has several suppliers, and often even several clients. Each actor basically plays on various tables at the same time. The point here is that the style of the game that each actor plays on each different table is known to all the other actors as well. The style of the game on one table, fairness or unfairness on another table, reflect on all tables, in something like a domino effect both in space and time. The physical proximity of the players, the frequent role changes (from end firm to subcontractor and vice versa), the lack of class divisions, and the significant social mobility, all foster an environment where information travels fast (as we have already discussed). The community is asked to give a reasonable opinion on contro- versial cases. Manipulation of information becomes quite difficult and in the end the consequences of a certain act, whether positive or negative, are far reaching. With respect to a 'non-district' environment, the pay-off structure is thus greatly modified in the way described, and the chances of successful cooperation are consequently higher. For, in cases like this, one is not necessarily faced with a repetitive game but, rather, with a change in the relative values of the pay-offs of the game. This enables serious prob- lems to be tackled more efficiently, both in terms of operative and industrial politics.

Everyone knows that a social game brings with it advantages for all involved—if played in the long term; but if this is so, why is this style of game not applied everywhere? Why are social games not diffused through all economic structures? To argue that the rules of the game in industrial districts have been written by history is not sufficient: analytically, it is an unsatisfactory answer. We need to explain why cooperation is so successful in some circumstance and not in others. If only implicitly, this line of

reasoning suggests that the codes written by history in the district communities are not replicable, to the point that no community can choose to
apply them today if it has not applied them in the past. This leaves no
room for political initiative. As Sabel writes jokingly, there is absolutely no
independence 'in the choice of one's ancestors'. On the other hand, asking
where the different structure of pay-offs comes from provides a point of
departure for several interesting interpretations. Specifically, our attention
should focus on two different aspects.

The first, already discussed above, is that cooperation is encouraged by
two conditions, namely the rapid diffusion of information and the rich
network of relationships that each of us has with others. As we have shown,
this situation not only facilitates the acknowledgment of opportunistic
behaviours, but also extends the outcomes of loyalty-based or unfair choices
made by any of us, thus affecting the pay-offs associated with the chosen
course of action. The more the agents' behaviours are known—and the
more visible their changes—the more are the chances of cooperation.

It is important to keep in mind that a tight network of communication is
the result of a concentration of activity within a specific territory, of the
fragmentation of productivity (which inevitably increases the number of
contracts to which a firm is committed), and also of a concentration of
institutions operating in the area. Active and democratic associations of
entrepreneurs offer several opportunities for meetings and discussions in
which opinions and news circulate quickly and freely. Political parties and
various associations (cultural, religious, volunteer-based, or even social) are
nothing but a set of exchanges and personal relationships in which the
professional ethics of an individual can be quickly confirmed or modified.
All those institutions committed to improving the professional ethics of
their agents (schools, service centres) ensure that case-by-case evaluations
are more accurate, are performed by a wider audience of judges, and are
quickly communicated across the community.

The second aspect inducing a change in the pay-off structure is the
behavioural code enforced within the district. The rules of this code have
indeed been written in the past—they are reflected in the nation's law—
even though they continue to be changed. However, it is not useful to claim
that they have been indiscriminately written *by history*, since this leads to
one, and only one, political conclusion: as Bufalino said (1996) in
agreement with Sabel, 'anyone entering this world should be very careful in
choosing place, year and parents'. Here again it is worth recalling the
relevant role played by institutions in working out these rules. From time to
time the very powerful associations of artisans have publicized and diffused
rules of caution. The '20 per cent rule' by Lorenz (1988) ('never agree on
more than 20 per cent of contracts from the same supplier if you do not
want to become a hostage') was a discussion item at several meetings and
was later proposed and advertised as a blind management rule.

In general, the authoritativeness of the majority of the community is legitimized by some institutions that have a non-relevant role. The loan consortia, for example, preferentially assign the ability to grant loans to expert artisans with good reputations; the loans have low interest rates and depend on the amount of the loan requested irrespective of the capital of the applicant and without the need to check his honesty and professional track record. In other cases, cooperative behaviours are induced and proposed as a model to be imitated by political structures within the community. During an industry crisis, for example, the mediation work done by local institutions and the citizens' efforts in favour of the firm facing the crisis have always been subordinate to an attitude of reasonable willingness by both parties. The mayor would put pressure on local banks or on other entrepreneurs who could get the firm out of trouble, only if the workers and the entrepreneur of the firm in difficulty agreed to 'do their share' with a display of strong commitment. In the history of industries in Emilia-Romagna, several turnarounds of firms have received a lot of attention, to the point where they have become local myths. These turnarounds have been possible thanks to a guarantee from City Hall in support of a loan granted by local banks to the workers who had formed a cooperative and had re-routed their severance pay into the firm's capital. This is another example of incentive, and in favour of participation.

Fairs and locally organized competitions contribute to the increase in transparency and visibility of behaviours; these activities are usually small-scale (the small town celebrating the arrival of the new priest) but they reflect esteem and consideration—suffice it to think of a firm producing good wine, or an efficient harvesting machine, or a stunning copy of a Tiffany lampshade—all of which will be sold at good prices around the world. Various initiatives organized by the regions also work towards this goal: for example, the certification of agricultural and food products, or the certification of firms using the ISO 9000 standards.

Even work contracts and national laws play an important role in the perspective examined here. In Central Italy labour unions and artisans' associations have signed regional and local contracts much earlier than in the rest of the country, guaranteeing wages and working conditions almost equal to those granted in large firms. From the analysis previously made, this outcome can be interpreted as cancelling the risk of unilateral defection by the entrepreneur. The possible range of actions still open to the entrepreneur is less wide than previously and the temptation for maximum exploitation is reduced.

All we have said so far helps to explain the way in which history has written the rules of the districts. Laws and contracts have constructed a framework of reference. A more detailed regulation, based on norms only apparently less reasonable, has set unwritten standards that have been wisely enforced by the community in order to govern a matter as difficult to administer as participation and cooperation amongst firms. Unwritten contracts have therefore gained in importance and have been widely used;

their regulation is managed by a community of competent individuals who are aware of what is going on around them. We have analysed the content, structure and processes of formation and enforcement of the norms and rules—written and unwritten—governing the industrial district in Emilia-Romagna. We hope that this contribution can help the institutions concerned create or encourage cooperation in other contexts as well.

Bibliography

Bufalino, G. (1996) *L'Unità*, March 10.

Brusco, S. (1992) 'Small firms and the provision of real services', in F.Pyke and W. Sengenberger (eds) *Industrial District and Local Economic Regeneration*, Geneva: International Institute for Labour Studies.

Brusco, S. (1995) 'Concorrenza tacita, sapere locale ed innovazione' (Unpublished paper) *Dipartimento di Economia Politica*, University of Modena.

Brusco, S. and Fiorani, G. (1995) 'Competitività, partecipazione econdizione operaia', in P. Bartolozzi and F. Garibaldo (eds) *Lavoro creativo e impresa efficiente*, Roma: Ediesse.

Brusco, S. and Sabel, C. (1981) 'Artisan production and economic growth', in F. Wilkinson *The Dynamics of Labour Market Segmentation*, London: Academic Press.

Gallino, L. (1978) *Dizionario di Sociologia*, Torino: Utet.

Lorenz, E. H. (1988) 'Neither friend nor strangers: Informal networks of sub-contracting in French industry', in D. Gambetta (ed.) *Trust*, New York: Blackwell.

Russo, M. (1985) 'Technical change and industrial districts', *Research Policy*, n. 3.

Russo, M. (1996a) *Cambiamento tecnico e relazioni tra imprese*, Torino: Rosenberg & Seller.

Russo, M. (1996b) 'Units of investigation for local economic deveploment policies', *Economie Appliquee*, n. 1.

Solimas, G. (1996) *I processi di Formazione*, la crescita e la soprevvivenzo delle piccole imprese, Milano: Angeli.

2 The fairness properties of interfirm networks

Anna Grandori and Massimo Neri

Reasons for fairness rules in networks

The properties and outcomes of interfirm networks in terms of effectiveness and efficiency have been fairly well analysed. Alliances among different firms have been shown to be superior to both an integrated firm and market contracting when there are contrasting production and transaction cost functions for all the parties involved, such as high coordination costs deriving from asset specificities and uncertainty favouring integration, and economies of specialization and scale favouring deverticalization (Eccles 1981; Mariotti and Cainarca 1986). Other studies have shed light on the advantages of alliances for pooling complementary and co-specialized resources and for generating successful innovations (Richardson 1971; Teece 1986; Ouchi and Bolton 1988). The dynamic efficiency properties of interfirm networking in terms of increasing the learning capacities of economic systems, lowering the costs of adaptation to market demands and decreasing the difficulties of organizational change, have also been analyzed (Pfeffer and Salancik 1978; Colombo, forthcoming; Cantwell, forthcoming).

There are a number of reasons why these effectiveness and efficiency assessments and explanations of the wide set of institutional arrangements classified as networks should be complemented by assessments and explanations in terms of fairness and justice. The following four reasons, at least, seem particularly important and corroborated by existing research.

1 Many interfirm organization problems are mixed-motive games with multiple Pareto-superior solutions. Therefore the design or prediction of a network arrangement 'adequate' for governing a given relationship is *under-determined* if only effectiveness and efficiency criteria are used (Grandori 1991). For example, in a cooperative relationship among different firms for realizing a complex industrial project—say an 'intelligent building'—all partners usually agree that a network structure is beneficial (Pareto-superior) for everybody. However, their preferences usually diverge as to which network structure is better:

construction firms, on the basis of the value of the activities they perform, often prefer and request subcontracting arrangements with other parties; while those parties often prefer and request a more paritarian contract such as a consortium or a joint venture (Grandori 1989a).

2 If parties perceive many possible acceptable points of agreement, the process leading to an agreement may be very long and costly, in the absence of any cognitive anchoring. As pointed out by Schelling (1960) long ago and recently reproposed by negotiation theorists with a cognitive orientation (Pruitt 1981), the perception of *focal points*, which have some property of symmetry, uniqueness and simplicity that differentiate them from other possible points, can quickly lead to a satisfactory solution, thereby allowing information processing economies. In this respect, the use of fairness rules, even the most naive ones such as the rule of equal shares, has properties of information cost reduction.

3 It can be hypothesized that the use of fairness criteria in the process of searching for possible points of agreement enhances the likelihood of finding Pareto-superior contracts, thereby contributing to increasing contract efficiency as well. Indeed, empirical research on negotiation has shown that the nature of heuristic trial and error rules employed for generating possible agreements does have an influence on the achievement of 'integrative' Pareto-superior solutions. Examples are practices such as 'bridging' among unilaterally generated alternatives, and exchange among matters that are valued differently by the different partners (Pruitt 1981). In these processes, parties' attention is focused on a 'central' zone of their possible area of agreement; that is, at least implicitly, search is *fairness-bounded*.

4 Cognitivist researchers have empirically shown that fairness criteria are applied by decision-makers even in structured problems where market exchange and unilateral profit maximization criteria were applicable in principle, and even at the price of renouncing part of their pay-off when they have no obligation or compensation for doing so (Kahneman, Knetsch and Thaler 1986a, 1986b). The critical laboratory experiment used for this purpose is an 'ultimatum game', where one player (the allocator) is asked to propose a division of a sum of money between him/herself and another player (the recipient) who in turn can either accept the offer or reject it, in which case both players receive nothing. The game theory, profit-maximizing solution to this game would be for the allocator to propose a 'token' payment to the recipient, who should accept any positive offer. However, the empirical evidence is that many allocators offer much more than a minimal positive payment, and that recipients sometime reject positive but small offers.

This argument is similar to the one raised by the Behavioural Decision Theory also regarding risk and the framing of decisions: rather than simply describing practical deviations from rational behaviour, it implies that the utility functions of actors include preferences and weights assigned to such things as uncertainty of positive or negative consequences, or fairness; in particular, it suggests that in subjective utility terms, economic actors are often not *fairness-neutral* as much as they are not risk-neutral.

The first three points are prescriptive arguments. They do not imply that fairness criteria will always be used, as much as efficiency or effectiveness criteria are not always used. The first three arguments imply that fairness criteria can generate solutions, and solutions that can be defined superior in some interesting respects, where other criteria do not suffice.

The fourth argument is descriptive, asserting that economic actors will 'often' use fairness rules in practice. Then, it would be desirable to complement the argument with a specification of the circumstances in which we expect that fairness judgements will actually be important. In connection with the relevant empirical research available as well as with the above arguments about when fairness rules are useful, we can advance the following predictions, that will find support in the empirical material reported later in the paper.

Fairness rules will be used in defining network and other organizational arrangements, independently of any individual propensity towards being fair, when:

- the sets of possible effective and efficient solutions are wide (in general in cooperative games with many matters of exchange);
- parties are free to exit even though it is convenient to reach a negotiated agreement (they are not 'locked in', there are alternative partners);
- there is uncertainty on the value of the best alternatives to a negotiated agreement so that reservation prices are not known for sure to either party and it would be cognitively difficult to push a counterpart 'close' to its walkaway price (such as in joint ventures, consortia and complex agreements);
- the exchange relationship is multilateral rather than bilateral, so that the 'comparable others' that invite and sustain equity judgements are available both in cognitive and bargaining power terms (such as in franchising);
- the relationship is repeated and expected to be long-lasting, so that the incentives to adopt rules that can be accepted independently of one party's particular position in one single exchange (i.e. just procedures) are increased.

44 *A. Grandori and M. Neri*

Definition of Fairness Rules for Network Analysis and Design

Concern for justice plays an important role in many fields of social science. Philosophers and social psychologists (Homans 1961; Adams 1965; Rawls 1971; Deutsch 1975), mathematicians (Raiffa 1982), economists and management researchers (Greenberg 1990) and legal scholars (Thibaut and Walker 1975), have confronted the topics in question, rendering the notion of justice interdisciplinary. The term 'justice' is usually considered more general and is referred to the philosophical and moral foundations of statements such as 'all men are equal in the eyes of law'. The notion of fairness is usually intended to be more operationalizable and is meant to contextualize the justice principle in specific situations, conflicts and negotiations, through concrete rules and norms. We shall privilege the concept and the term of fairness in this study, in the first place because our interests are not philosophical but consist in increasing our ability to explain and predict observable economic behaviours; and in the second place because we are also interested in increasing our ability to evaluate these behaviours in terms of the distribution of the benefits they generate. For these purposes, the concept of justice seems too general. In particular, in spite of the wide use made in this paper of interesting contributions from 'organizational justice' literature, we prefer to restrict the concept in order to avoid a purely subjective definition, by which anything that *looks* fair to involved actors *is* fair. The problems and drawbacks of such a conception have been pointed out (Pillutla and Murnighan 1995), and they are especially important if the aims of analysis are prescriptive as well as descriptive. Although we are aware that efficiency and effectiveness criteria may conflict with fairness criteria, and indeed precisely because of this, we shall privilege a notion of fairness as an additional criterion that helps in choosing acceptable solutions among the many efficient and effective ones that are often available in multiple-actor, multiple-issues problems, or in defining some sensible solution in the first place when the structure of the problem (alternatives, consequences and preferences) is ill-defined. In addition, we shall retain the distinction, employed in organizational justice theory, between *substantive* and *procedural fairness*. For, particularly when problems are ill-structured and preferences themselves not very clear, judgements about the rationality of processes and procedures may be more important (and more accessible) than judgements about the entity of consequences (Simon 1976). The notion of 'distributive justice', as it is called in organizational justice literature, or, as we prefer to say, of 'substantive fairness', refers to rules or criteria capable of dividing or determining shares of resources considered to be valuable (in the case of interfirm relations: money, bundles of property rights, organizational structures and procedures) which are to be attributed or allocated to different actors (in our case, firms). By contrast, the procedural dimension is represented by the processes and the rules used to reach that specific outcome, as well as with the system of interaction and communications which develop in the decision-making process. In the analysis of interfirm agreements, decisions about the organizational and contractual architecture—e.g. the choice between a joint venture and consortium—represent the substantive aspect (even if it is a choice among possible organizational procedures that will regulate interfirm cooperation); while the procedural dimension refers to the characteristics of the negotiation process of the agreement.

Fairness criteria

We are concerned here with identifying a typology of criteria of substantive fairness that helps in predicting the structure of interfirm agreements. This aim implies that we are interested in distinguishing among fairness rules that are not strictly functional equivalents and can generate different outcomes. For example, in a negotiation of an equity joint venture between two firms, if ownership shares are allocated according to an equality rule we should observe a 50–50 division of property rights irrespective of the value of the conferred assets; while a division based on the proportionality of outcomes to contributions should lead to symmetrical shares only in the case of equally valuable contributions. To this end, we can distinguish among the following different types of fairness rules.

Input–output criteria

Among the most widely applied and analysed fairness criteria, especially in economic activities, are those based on rules of correspondence between the pay-off received by each party and the contribution it gives to the achievement of the total output or 'pie' to be divided. This logic has often been defined as an 'equity' principle, especially in the literature with a sociological orientation, with reference to the 'equity theory' developed by Adams (1965) and others, maintaining that a widely accepted social norm is that returns to the various members of a society should be proportional to their contributions. In a first scholarly formulation this justice principle has been operationalized in the following fair division rule (Walster and Walster 1975):

> (Output–Input)/Input (for the actor) should be equal to (Output–Input)/Input (for comparable others)

In a first classic interpretation, this principle of equal returns on investments was supposed to be so strong as to be applied even against one's own interest: that is, actors try to modify the elements of the equation in order to restore balance both in the case they are 'underpaid' and in the case they are 'overpaid'. Some empirical support has been found for this contention, but some judge the results questionable, and in any case those results were bound up with the particular problem of work contributions and pay rates (Mowday 1987). It may well be that in labour problems equity concerns are greater than in economic action more generally. So we shall here follow a second interpretation of the principle of equal returns on contributions, implying that interdependent actors, who can observe each other's contributions and outcomes, would react to their own underpayment and to others' overpayment.

Among the limits of applicability of this rule, one should observe that it implies *interpersonal comparisons of utility, the measurability of both inputs and outputs and their expression in the same measurement unit*. If applied to economic coalitions among firms, it equalizes the returns on investment of the partner firms, thereby being insensitive to the differences in normal rates of return in different sectors—a frequently debated issue in the negotiation of interfirm agreements. Less pretentious (in terms of information require-ments) rules of proportionality of outcomes to contributions could, however, be constructed, and are widely observed in practice; they do not involve such direct comparisons between inputs and outputs, but rather compare contributions among themselves and apportion pay-offs according to the same proportion. For example, in interfirm associations governed through voting systems, important contributions are financial fees and other monetizable resources; while one of the main matters qualifying the governance system, and subject to division, is the allocation of voting rights. It has been observed that egalitarian principles such as 'one firm, one vote' are perceived as unfair by the participating firms, and that there is a tendency to assign a firm a percentage of voting rights that is equal to the percentage of the total resources it contributes (Lammers 1993).

It should be noted that this rule, like any rule based on inputs or contributions, still implies that individual contributions to the total result are identifiable and measurable. Therefore, the *measurability of contributions as well as of outcomes* stands out as an important contingency condition for the application of this class of fairness rules and of the organizational structures based on it.

Outcome-based criteria

The criteria for fair division proposed by game theory and economic analysts are based on outcomes evaluated according to parties' utility or preferences rather than on the value of contributions. In addition, the number and value of the available alternative agreements with other counterparts are directly taken into account in the calculation of fair solutions. Therefore, these fairness rules generate solutions that depend on the relative strength or replaceability of the partners, as well as on the strength of their preferences in the matters under negotiation. Actually, the different fair division rules that have been proposed give weight, more or less, to those two elements or treat them in different ways. Fairness criteria elaborated by games theoreticians usually share some basic properties—namely, a fair division rule should select a contract that belongs to the Pareto frontier (it should not lead to a dominated solution), it should not rest upon interpersonal comparisons of utility, and it should be acceptable, *ex ante*, 'behind a veil of ignorance', without knowing what one's own final position will be (Nash 1950; Rawls 1971).

The most used criterion is the Nash principle, or the *maximum product* of the parties' utility. If negotiating parties adopted this criterion, they would reach contracts characterized by those possible, additional, interesting and distinctive features. First, if from the set of contracts from which the Nash solution was selected some of the other rejected forms of agreement disappear (e.g. it turns out that they are no longer legal or technically feasible), the parties would continue to rank the formerly selected contract as their preferred solution. In practical terms, the agreement would have some stability property with respect to external changes that may reduce the originally available 'pie', which may be an interesting thing for the much-complained-of 'instability' of interfirm cooperative agreements. Second, a Nash solution could be devised even if solutions are 'discrete' rather than continuous and if many of the goods exchanged cannot be easily translated into money equivalents (Nash 1950). This is also an interesting property for bargaining over interorganizational agreements, as we have shown in previous work on how efficient and fair organization structures can be designed or assessed with the use of ordinal utilities over discrete organizational alternatives (Grandori 1991). On the other hand, it may happen that if the pie widens and new Pareto-superior agreements become feasible, the maximum product of utilities may select on the new frontier an agreement in which the position of one party worsens with respect to the previous contract (Raiffa 1982). In practical terms, the Nash fairness criterion is not very sensitive to the differences in the parties' relative strength as reflected in the maximum gain that each party could realize if all the pie were allocated to it, i.e. to the structure of the Pareto frontier in the extreme (unilateral gain) regions.

Alternative rules have been proposed that are more sensitive to these differences in the bargaining power of parties, such as the *equal proportion rule* and rules based on *balanced increments* or *concessions* (Raiffa 1982). The equal proportion rule states that each party gets the same percentage of the maximum utility it can hope for in the case where the total surplus is allocated to their side, and is consequently very sensitive to any improvement in the unilateral position and best alternatives of each party. A balanced concession rule is similarly based on a logic of proportional division, in that it prescribes that the frontier of Pareto-efficient agreements be followed through small incremental concessions representing an equal proportion (say one tenth or one hundredth of the difference between one's walkaway value and one's maximum attainable pay-off) of sacrifice for each side, until the two converging offers meet. In this way, the final point is influenced not only by the maximum values, but also by how many attractive alternatives each party is renouncing in order to approach a middle zone.

In the case of many players, we find a similar competition between fairness rules assigning more weight to the relative replaceability of each party and to the amount of resources it controls, and fairness rules that do not reflect the possibility of excluding one or more partner in order to achieve a larger share of a smaller pie. Raiffa (1982) discusses this problem of coalition analysis, starting precisely with an application to an interfirm negotiation about possible governance structures (How should three cement companies who can form a cartel split the synergies they would create? If two-way or three-way mergers generate synergies that increase total earnings, how should they divide them?). As the empirical studies that follow will illustrate, this problem is quite relevant in the formation of joint-venture and consortia agreements. Each partner should make an offer to other interesting (synergistic) partners that cannot easily be surpassed by other parties' offers. Larger coalitions may increase the total amount of gains or the likelihood of obtaining them, but may require some sacrifice in the individual shares of gain obtained by the single firms. If the synergies generated by the different possible coalitions are significantly different, the application of different fairness rules may lead to quite different allocations of reward and property rights among firms. For example, suppose that no company by itself would get a contract for the construction of a tunnel, and that three companies together would obtain a large contract, but that companies A and B together would still get a fairly large contract, companies B and C an average contract, and companies C and D a small contract. It has been shown, both analytically and empirically, that if the process of network formation is competitive, with each firm free to make any offer of fair division to any other player, the shares obtained by each firm would be proportional to the differences in the surpluses generated by the different parties in the various two-way coalitions even in the case in which an all-ways coalition were formed (Raiffa 1982). By contrast, if the three parties assume that it would be rational to form a coalition that does not exclude one of them, they can treat all contributions as unreplaceable. For example, fairness rules that calculate shares as averages of the marginal increases in the total pay-offs that each firm would bring about in joining the total coalition in all positions and order of arrival, would eliminate first-mover advantages and bargaining-power effects. These rules would produce much more paritarian allocations than the former rules.

An implication of this outline of alternative fairness rules is that partners in different positions of strength have interests in endorsing fairness rules that are relatively more advantageous for their side ('stronger' parties would prefer proportional rules and 'weaker' parties would prefer rules that construct some sort of joint utility function to be maximized). Which of these two types of rules prevails in practice, and when, is an interesting research question. We are inclined to hypothesize that, in spite of the less favourable position, structurally 'weaker' firms will on average get more than their 'fair-as-proportional' share. This prediction would imply that interfirm networks have some wealth redistribution properties. Among its reasons, there are the following. The allocation of resources according to the intensity of preferences may end by giving more resources to the 'rich' (one who assigns less utility to a marginal increase in them) and less to the 'poor' (one who assigns high value to even a small improvement in his position), thereby reinforcing the initial differences in contribution capacities. More 'egalitarian' utility-based fairness rules are closer to other important and basic notions of fairness such as equality and needs. In addition, asymmetric allocations need more justification, discussion, calculation and bargaining. Therefore, more egalitarian solutions may often be preferred by all parties for reducing information and negotiation costs, at least up to a certain level of importance of the pay-offs. Lastly, utility-based criteria, even though not requiring a precise measurement of contributions or inputs, do require *a precise measurement of outcomes and a clear assessment of preferences and interests*. Therefore, in many situations these rules will be substituted for less demanding decision criteria. In the words of Raiffa himself (1982: 274):

> To some extent, the complexity of the real situation softens the intensity of the bargaining dynamics. The parties are not clear about what is in their own interest, and their knowledge about the interests of others is likewise vague. Compromise is often easier to arrange in a situation of ambiguity [. . .]: many real-world negotiations are happily not as divisive as starkly simple laboratory games, because in the real world it is difficullt to see clearly what is in one's own best interest.

Need-based norms

A different way to assess interests and preferences, rather than ordering all possible outcomes according to preferences, is to consider one's own needs and aspirations. A need is considered to arise for matters the lack of which would threaten balanced existence, a vector of 'acquisitions' that can vary from elementary things such as being adequately nurtured, being in good health, escaping avoidable morbidity and premature death, to more complex acquisitions such as being happy, having self-esteem, participating in the life of the community (Sen 1992). The assessment of needs may be less difficult and ambiguous than the assessment of the value of contributions and outcomes (Albin 1993), even though there has been considerable debate and differentiation among perspectives on needs ranging from universalistic, innatist and objectivist models (Maslow 1954) to perceptual and learned models (March and Simon 1958; McClelland 1971). On the other hand, if not for their clarity and objectivity, needs may be easier to assess because they are rooted in the actors themselves rather than in what the environment can offer as reward. Needs and aspiration levels call for 'being satisfied' rather than for maximizing pay-offs. Fairness judgements based on need satisfaction, therefore, require less information-processing than fairness judgements based on the maximization of parties' returns on contributions or parties' utility. Since need is socially and culturally constructed, and need-driven allocations are independent of contributions or outcome intensities, needs should be legitimized by the players' mutual acknowledgment of what is essential to the existence of the relationship in order to provide the basis for fair division rules in multi-actor games as networks. As Pruitt (1972) puts it, need-based equity is 'a norm of mutual responsiveness, which requires that the party with the stronger needs achieve the greater benefit'.

In the case of interfirm networks, there should be a reciprocal acknow-ledgement of the existence of elements that influence the ability of a firm (usually the weaker one) to function and which are taken by the parties to be legitimate in the relationship. For example, in the case of a sub-contracting company that has a particularly weak financial structure, the application of a need-based norm would lead to a division of pay-offs in such a way that the latter need not suffer problems of liquidity. In this way, the parties rank higher the Pareto-efficient allocative solution that gives more resources to the most disadvantaged party.

Fairness heuristics

In complex and ambiguous situations, heuristic shortcuts can substitute for too costly or cognitively complex calculations, either of the 'optimizing' or of the 'satisfying' kind (March 1978; Kahnemann, Slovic and Tversky 1982). Decisions about fair division of resources are no exception. Two kinds of fairness rules that have the nature of 'blind' heuristics are especially important in practice, and they also exemplify two different major sources of legitimation of the use of heuristics: the reduction of information processing costs and the availability of applicable past experience.

The *equal share* norm represents the expression of an absolute equality principle between partners: in this case the partners receive rewards of the same (comparable) value, regardless of their utilities, contributions and needs. Two possible variants of the equal share norm, particularly useful in more complex bargaining situations, are *equal concession* and *equal sacrifice*. While the equal concession norm requires that parties split the difference between their current positions, the equal sacrifice one states that they must suffer equally in making concessions, in terms of their subjective disutility. In addition to the generic ability to foster a climate of harmony and trust between the partners, the use of an equal shares criterion appears to respond to requisites of reduction of information costs and process complexity.

The same blind or automatic approach is observable in the use of *anchored equity* (Tversky and Kahneman 1974). In this case the decision is made by anchoring to historical precedents (Pruitt 1981) and making adjustments from status-quo situations. This method appears to be frequently practised in long-lasting relationships (for instance in sub-contracting networks), in which partners use customs or past agreements for solving their negotiations, adjusting the solution incrementally if needed.

To conclude our operationalization and classification of fairness rules, it is worth noting that we have grouped rules on the basis of the type of rationality involved—from value maximizing to satisfying to 'blind' and automatic. This option responds to the aim of being able to predict when, in economic activities, the regulation of relationships is more likely to obey the different rules, generating structures that are, for example, more parity-based or more proportional to contributions. This does not imply that actors are always 'meta-rational' and capable of choosing the best decision strategy according to the state of information and conflict. The use of different types of fairness rules may be learned or inherited and 'socially selected' as an adequate practice in certain domains of activity (Simon 1990). Irrespectively of the fact that they are designed, learned or selected, what we have found and shall illustrate in the next paragraphs is that problem complexity and the number of conflicting actors do matter for the type of fairness rules that can be effectively applied in the system.

Procedural Fairness

When judgement is formed under uncertainty, and the best alternatives to a negotiated agreement are not clear or cannot be discovered through a reasonable effort, actors sensibly shift from substantive to procedural rationality (Simon 1976). In addition, actors often assign positive valence to procedural justice on its own merits (Greenberg 1987).

According to studies on organizational justice (Leventhal 1980; Gray 1989; Bies, Tripp and Neale 1993), in order for any decision-making process to be defined as fair it must feature procedures that: *are consistent over parties and time* (rules of the game remain the same during the process), *represent concerns of all parties, provide opportunities for 'voice' and the revision of decisions, and are based on accurate information*.

If firms apply procedural fairness criteria, they will give weight to the process through which a contract is achieved rather than merely to the costs and benefits brought by the contract itself. For example, they may agree to bargain item by item, as often occurs in technical contracts with a myriad of matters that cannot be negotiated all at once, but on the basis of bilateral technical information and analyses and taking turns in the role of first offerer.

Unintended and perverse consequences of fairness judgements

Before moving into the analysis of several cases in which the concrete role of fairness in interfirm networks is discussed, it is necessary to emphasize the limits of the concept of fairness and the dangers that the use of fairness criteria in decision-making may entail.

First of all, a limiting feature of the concept of fairness itself is that, in most problems, there are many possible rules operationalizing the idea of reaching a just distribution of resources; even in the case in which the concept is not merely a perceived construct and even if it is restricted to the criteria for discriminating among Pareto-efficient solutions. Although fairness criteria help in reducing the set of undominated solutions, they may not lead straightforwardly to one. In addition, given that different parties are more or less advantaged under different fairness rules, conflict of interest is re-created about which rule is best. Therefore, since justice is not a unitary concept, fairness concerns might cause impasses, working as an 'additional barrier to conflict resolution' (Arrow et al. 1995), even when parties would be better off by reaching an agreement than not. In the second place, some attributes of fair solutions—especially of solutions generated by procedural justice concerns and by criteria other than outcome-based ones—may contrast with attributes of efficient solution. For example (as shown later by the analysis of franchising agreements), the attribute of equal treatment to clients (or suppliers) in equivalent positions and providing similar contributions, may contrast with the search for partner-specific, Pareto-superior exchanges of resources and other contractual items.

Moreover, the use of fair procedures is prone to manipulative biases. It has been noted that high commitment to procedural fairness may grant to some parties a sort of 'license for expoitation': procedures which are legitimized as fair may create a sort of 'illusion of fairness', convincing the parties to eliminate the concern for substantive fairness (Bies, Tripp and Neale 1993). For example, a subcontractor who defines explicit and clear procedures with a subcontractee in order to define a fair process, may feel that any type of substantive outcome is good, independently of the relative shares.

Lastly, the use of fairness norms may have costs which, instead of being absorbed by the coalition parties, may be shifted outside of the relationship, thereby creating negative externalities. For example, inside a subcontracting system, surplus allocations made as a function of the needs of weaker firms may create efficiency problems at the economic system level, sustaining inefficient firms. More commonly, the desire to accomodate the partners' needs and preferences in a coalition may lead to 'enlarging the pie' to be divided—say the final price on the market or the amount of staff in a joint venture—far beyond its sustainable size in terms of the efficiency of the wider system.

It is not impossible, however, to take these concerns into account in designing agreements, as the case studies in this and other chapters in this book hopefully show.

Empirical studies of network negotiation processes: the role of fairness

In this section we shall analyse the role of fairness in the formation of interfirm agreements, presenting the relevant empirical data among those that have been gathered in a series of researches on networks as negotiated arrangements. The studies from which we shall draw the evidence on the use of fairness rules presented here have considered four types of network, initially defined in broad contractual terms: joint ventures, consortia, franchising and subcontracting (Cadoni 1989; Bonfanti 1990; Ioannilli 1990; Coppola 1993; Bergonzini 1996).[1] We shall connect the data from different studies where it is useful for illustrating the role of fairness judgements in the choice *between* these different network contracts, rather than merely for choosing one particular package of rights allocations within the same contractual scheme. In addition, *ad hoc* longitudinal case studies have been constructed for examining some issues of comparison and integration between different network forms that were left uncovered in the above-mentioned studies. The material and the discussion are grouped in the three sections which follow, and which focus on the different types of fair judgements and procedures that emerge in different types of interfirm networks. The first section focuses on networks designed *ad hoc* in a negotiated fashion for the governance of complex and innovative undertakings. There, the forms of alliance typically considered are joint ventures, consortia and subcontracting agreements, and fairness rules are predominantly based on outcomes and/or contributions or on an equality principle. In the second section, more cost reduction-oriented networks are examined, such as franchising and commercial agreements. The negotiation of these forms is heavily concerned with finding a balance between fairness—as equal treatment and acceptability of offers on the part of the franchisee—and the efficiency gains that could be obtained through specific negotiations between the central firm and individual partners. The third section reports the main findings on the definition of contractual clauses in subcontracting relations in traditional mature industrial district activities (textile-clothing), showing the importance—and limits—of routinized and anchored equity.

The negotiated design of fair governance structures: joint ventures, consortia and subcontracting in innovative large-scale industrial projects

In the negotiation of *equity joint ventures* the pooling of complementary resources is usually the core integrative matter, while the allocation of property rights (division of shares) and decision rights (division of management roles in the joint venture) typically represents the distributive side of the game. According to the analytic framework developed above, we would predict that whereas joint ventures are formed for cooperation in R&D and, more generally, for carrying out informationally complex and interdependent activities in which it is difficult to discern the input contributions of the different partners, highly paritarian arrangements will be formed. This outcome is to be expected for reasons of information costs and ambiguity leading to the application of equality-based fairness rules, as well as of the perception of symmetrical coalition power of the partners as long as each contribution appears to be critical in its specific or co-specialized combination with the other contributions, and its value to the coalition appears to be largely independent of its market value.

This contention seems to be consistent with the observed abundance of equal shares agreements in high-technology sectors. The actual application of the expected egalitarian fairness rules has been also documented in in-depth longitudinal case studies. Two cases of formation of joint ventures between Italian and Japanese firms for the joint development and production of high-technology products are briefly recalled here (Cadoni 1989; Grandori and Perrone 1986). The former study concerns a joint venture established between two large multinational corporations in the electronic sector for the development, production and commercialization of laser printers and xerox machines. The Japanese company was world leader in the technology for optical products for office automation and was interested in collaborating with firms based in foreign countries who could contribute in organizing production and sales close to the final markets. The Italian group strategy was more finance-oriented, although its activities were mainly related to the electronic sector, and it had a solid productive structure in Italy. The two parties were in total agreement as to the option of governing their cooperation through a joint-venture and regarding the opportunness of locating production in Italy (with the Italian company conferring a plant); but their interests were quite opposed in the following matters qualifying the joint-venture structure: how the ownership of shares should be divided, how the positions on the board of directors should be divided, to what extent the research into the development of the laser printer should be assigned to the joint venture (with the Italian firm preferring more joint research and the Japanese firm preferring less). The agreement achieved has turned out highly symmetric, but not blind to the possibilities of Pareto-improvement through an exchange between the items most valued by the different parties; actually, the details of the discussion process show that it was generated by a mix of an equal share rule and a principle of allocation as a function of the intensity of preferences. Precisely three representatives of each mother firm were sitting on the board of directors; the focal point for an agreement on the ownership structure had been a fifty-fifty split throughout the negotiation process, but the Italian firm finally obtained a 50 per cent plus one share in response to its strong interest in a formal integration of the joint venture in the financial group, while the Japanese firm obtained 1 per cent of the operation management positions in the production plant in order to support and control the introduction of production methods consistent with its quality and R&D requirements. As a resource commitment symmetrical with its contribution in the production and commercialization of the new product on the Italian market, the Italian firm obtained an allocation of the relevant R&D activities to the joint venture.

An application of a mix of fairness rules more sensitive to the differences in the values of parties' contributions should be expected, where these differences were more measurable and important. Evidence for this prediction was obtained in the other study on the negotiation of a research and production joint venture between two small–medium enterprises. In this case, the Italian firm was one of the world leaders in void technologies and gas purification techniques. The Japanese firm had the productive structure for realizing the new type of large gas purifiers in which the small but critical and sophisticated parts ('getters') produced by the Italian firm could be included, as well as controlling the access to the Japanese market. The structure of the joint venture formed for assembling and commercializing the new gas purifiers was based on an equal shares principle as to shareholding and directorship appointments. However, the two mother firms were to continue to produce separately the two types of components (the structure of the machine and the 'getter' component), whose costs and prices were quite different in spite of the fact that the getter was technologically critical. Thus the two firms engaged in a distributive bargaining over the transfer prices that should regulate the exchange of these goods between the mother firms and the joint venture. The minimum acceptable prices (reservation prices) were set by both sides at the levels of the production costs of the component, i.e. according to the principle of satisfying their structural constraints or needs. They then negotiatied an external price of the purifier sustainable on the final market, and planned to divide the available surplus in shares proportional to the usual mark-ups realized by the two firms in their respective markets.

When the contributions of different actors are substantially separable and measurable, both efficiency and fairness criteria would lead to the adoption of governance structures that allocate property, reward and decision rights, taking into account the amount and criticality of these contributions. In the case of interfirm cooperative relationships, a type of contract suitable for achieving this proportionality is a *consortium contract* that creates common responsibility towards a client regarding the final goods or services to be provided, but internally makes a clear and contractual division between which activities are to be performed by what firm, and divides the total income among the partners according to the value of these activities. Subtle negotiation and coalition analysis problems arise in the determination of these shares. They have been explored in a study on a series of cases of formation of alliances in international construction and engineering activities (Bonfanti 1990). In this study, it was decided to consider also the most relevant contiguous contractual forms that firms can and do evaluate as an alternative to consortia for regulating their cooperation, i.e. joint ventures and subcontracting arrangements.

The importance of fairness considerations in *the choice between a joint venture and a consortium contract* was shown in the 'Maracaibo' case study. An Italian firm, present in a Latin American country through a subsidiary currently engaged in road construction projects, timely obtained information on the imminent opening of a bidding auction for the construction of a hydroelectric power plant in that country and on the characteristics of the project requested. On the basis of this critical information, the Italian firm first contacted another firm with the required competence in civil engineering in the hydroelectric sector and concluded a preliminary agreement about participating in the endeavour through an equal shares joint venture. Then this sub-coalition contacted another local civil engineering firm, because it transpired that the inclusion of a local firm seemed substantially to enhance the chances of winning. The competences of and possible contributions by the three firms overlapped greatly in the construction activities, whereas the firms contributed quite different and complementary resources in other areas: first-mover advantages and local commercial relationships and experience on one side, hydroelectric know-how on another, and image and political advantages on the third. The choice of forming a joint venture for conducting and profiting jointly from construction activities, rather than forming a consortium, responded at least to the two fair-play considerations: given that all firms could participate in construction activities, there were no clear technical competence criteria for assigning parts of them, and bargaining over that type of division would have created a very competitive game, with likely losses of 'atmosphere'; if an attempt had been made to define the firms' shares on the basis of the values of the goods and services provided—as in a consortium—the two smaller firms, providing more commercial and non-material advantages would have been under-represented. The three civil engineering firms then formed a joint venture, which, in turn, formed a consortium with a firm providing the more clearly separable electro-mechanical components of the plant.

Firms contributing assets of different nature and amount typically rank the two contractual forms of *consortia and subcontracting* according to preference in different ways. Those partners who contribute to generating larger shares of income (typically construction firms) often prefer to assume the role of main contractor for themselves, and to procure the necessary contributions from other firms through subcontracting. Under a subcontracting arrangement, the main contractor can appropriate a larger share of the quasi-rent created by the cooperation, owing to the information advantages of its central position as well as the more substitutable position of its counterparts. On the other hand, if the risks involved in the project are large (in the sense of the probability and amount of possible losses), then these preferences may be reversed, because 'smaller' contributors may prefer not to share the responsibilities and risks that a consortium contract would involve, while the 'larger' contributors would prefer to find partners with whom to share those risks. The case of the 'passante ferroviario' of Milan shows evidence of both situations and of the two different emerging contractual solutions. The Metropolitana Milanese opened a bidding process to assign the job of constructing a stretch of railway line. About thirty firms participated in the pre-qualification phase, among which coalitions were formed in order to be able to carry out the project defined by the client.

In a first phase, the construction firms with general competence qualifying them for the project sought to form coalitions among themselves— that is, among partners with similar rather than different technical and economic profiles. This option stemmed from two main objectives: to enlarge the production capacity and to share the risks. The project was, indeed, a very large one and the activities quite hazardous. The group analysed in the Bonfanti's study was formed by three firms and regulated by a 'consortiated company', a legal institution contemplated in Italian law, intermediate between a consortium and a joint venture: a new company is created, on which central administrative and technical resources are conferred for conducting joint activity, the partners participate directly through a limited liability contract as to the ownership and reward rights (rather than indirectly through equities) and through 'democratic' councils in which the partners are formally represented as to decision rights (rather than through appointment of persons in a hierarchy). This choice can be interpreted as being efficient for all participants given the similarity of competences, the presence of interdependences and economies of scale in productive and administrative activities, and the need for risk sharing. More controversial and subject to negotiation was the choice of a governance structure for the relationship between the consortiated activities of tunnel and railway construction, and the complementary activities of soil consolidation. These activities are clearly identifiable and technically different, but they are interdependent in the sense that they can only proceed hand-in-hand with the entire subway construction activity. However, the main sources of variance and risk pertain to the construction activities rather than to the soil consolidation activities. The firm contacted by the consortiated company to perform the soil consolidation activities thus faced a trade-off. It could accept the offer to join the consortiated company that the construction firms initially set up with the idea of further reducing risk. In this way, on the other hand, it would end up bearing significant risk while having little influence on the activities generating it and being probably a more risk-averse actor than the larger construction firms. The fourth firm judged that this would squeeze its expected profits too much, and therefore asked for a very high participation share as a condition for its participation in the consortiated company. The other firms, in turn, were faced with the dilemma of substantially reducing their own shares in order to offset the additional transfer of risk to the fourth firm or to increase the final bidding price with the likely result of losing the job. The solution was to resort to a subcontracting agreement, under which the fourth firm would receive smaller but more certain rewards.

If a consortium contract is adopted, shares of income are defined in monetary values, so activities should be turned to account by using prices. If the participant firms set high, 'cost-plus' prices they can increase their share but they contribute to decreasing the likelihood of winning as a coalition (and in bids for the realization of big industrial construction projects, not winning means losing all the resources consumed by the preparation process). Therefore, firms should typically find a fair procedure for down-adjusting the sum of their cost-plus or usual market prices towards the 'target price' that can be competitive in the bidding auction with other coalitions. For example, in the 'Calaveras' consortium case, three European firms combined their complementary expertise and production capacities to obtain the assignment of a hydroelectric plant construction project from a regional utilities company in the US: one of the firms operated in the electro-mechanical sector, the second in the civil engineering sector, the third was an engineerng firm with a strong trading and business development record, commercial orientation, and diversified experience as general contractor. The three firms decided to follow an equal proportion rule in the negotiation of prices: they agreed to start with an offer to the client at the level of the sum of the usual market prices of the different firms for their products and activities, to negotiate an acceptable discount with the client, and then reduce the parties' prices all by the same percentage.

In addition to the division of shares, many other features of the consortium governance structure cannot be defined without applying fairness rules which serve to allocate risks and rights in efficient and equitable ways: they typically include the distribution of voting rights, the compensation to be paid to the firm performing the leader function, the definition of internal penalty systems for distributing the costs of delays and other uncompliance events. Drawing on all the case studies mentioned on consortia, we can observe that the voting scheme typically adopted for all major decisions in the various councils is a unanimity scheme, that is the least efficient in terms of decision process costs but the fairest in terms of representation of all interests. In some cases, small superior arbitration units were constituted, but always including at least one president or CEO for each firm, as an efficient and fair alternative to eventual resort to external justice systems. On the other side, the needs for efficient technical day-to-day coordination and communication with the client are met by appointing a leader firm. The fee paid for these governance activities is determined with reference to the fair practices specific to the sector (around 2.5 per cent). Lastly, the internal penalty system incorporates rules for distributing the eventual negative consequences deriving from unforeseen events among the partners. At least two competing fair division principles are considered. One possibility is to establish who is responsible for the delay or other shortcoming and make the firm in question pay the entire indemnity due to the client for that contingency. This would represent a contribution-based criterion, and would eventually come up against the costs and difficulties in detecting and measuring the (negative in this case) contributions. In addition, firms clearly perceive the problem that partners may not be equally able to absorb negative cash flows of significant amount. Thus a 'mutual insurance' scheme is often adopted, whereas the total penalty due to the client is divided in proportion to the shares held by the different firms in the consortium. This rule, based on an equal proportion principle irrespective of who contributed what to the negative outcome, seems to be especially relevant if the core problem to be solved is not one of disincentivating opportunism but, rather, of insuring against the possibility that something going wrong in a complex system independently of the goodwill of the parties.

Fairness without negotiation: the ultimatum game of franchising

The 'negotiation' of the franchise relationship has been analysed, in aggregate terms, on a sample of 183 Italian businesses and services, production and distribution (Ioannilli 1990). In this example we shall refer to franchising as the situation in which the franchisor grants the franchisee a licence for the sale of his own goods or services and provides for transfer of technical know-how, management assistance and support of various kinds (material and otherwise). In exchange, the franchisee pays an initial fee and some type of ongoing fee to the franchisor. Given the 'package' of resources that are the object of the relationship, it is conceivable that the reciprocal preferences will be distributed as follows: the parties jointly consider as a positive utility the transfer, from the franchisor to the franchisee, of technical know-how and management competence through training and instruction, locating and setting up the sales outlet, as well as consultation and management assistance carried out by the franchisor. The preferences relative to the payment of fees and royalties from the franchisee to the franchisor are clearly divergent, as are those regarding the interests relative to an exclusive right in the zone which might be granted to the franchisee. While it is plausible to assume that the franchisee assigns a positive utility to the right to an exclusive right in a certain zone, it is possible that the limitation of competition and thus the reduction of competitive incentives could be viewed in a negative manner by the franchisor, whose profits are, however, influenced by the behaviour of the franchisee.

Therefore, it can be expected that interests are substantially convergent about management systems (training, assistance, setting up the sales outlet), as they tend to make the chain effective and efficient in operation, while interests relative to the allocation of rewards (fee, royalties) are likely to be divergent. Although franchising involves complex exchanges, the concrete negotiation of the agreements is often reduced to a minimum, with the franchisor drawing up the whole text of the affiliation contract and setting out an offer of apportionment of the surplus, leaving the franchisee with the mere decision either to take it or leave it (Ioannilli 1990). This feature of franchising negotiation can be attributed to the fact that the relationship between the franchisor and the individual franchisee is part of the network of relations that binds the franchisor to all the members of the chain.

We can say that the application to all the franchisees of the same contract is an application of the principle of fairness over the network (*equal* treatment from the procedural and substantive point of view) as well as a device for reducing negotiation costs in the presence of many players.

If on one side it is possible to explain the adoption of a last offer procedure within the 'ultimatum game' framework, in the real case of franchising, unlike most of the experiments carried out on the ultimatum game (Guth, Schmittberger and Schwarze 1982), the offerer (franchisor) is led to consider the receivers' (franchisees) interests by the fact that this last offer does not occur in the context of a one-shot negotiation, but is only the start of a long-term relationship: for this reason, the desire to be fair with the future partner could be added to the need to make an offer that will be accepted.

A good example of this attitude is often emerging on the issue of geographic area exclusive right. In 75 per cent of the agreements included in Ioannilli's sample, a zone exclusive right was accorded to the franchisee. A reason for this might be found in the franchisor's wish to avoid competitive behaviour among franchisees in a single area; moreover, in the early development of the network, the cost of the area exclusive right concession is likely to be not relevant, since the area is 'unexploited'. Nonetheless, the framing of this evidence in fairness terms seems reasonable: the concession should then be considered as a unilateral acknowledgement that the item ranks very high in the franchisees' preference function.

The option to negotiate by means of a last offer, however, sacrifices the possibility of increasing efficiency and fairness in the relationship with the individual franchisee, in relation to his individual preferences that are only potentially similar to the 'average'. It is possible to hypothesize that Pareto-superior solutions could therefore be achieved by exploiting the interaction with the individual franchisees. In one case (franchising production in the garment sector) the area agents who are responsible for the relations with the franchisees, within the framework of a standard contract that regulates entrance fee, royalties and quality standards, negotiate the other elements of the relationship according to the specific needs and preferences of the individual franchisee. These items usually concern the establisment of the sales outlet, local advertising policies and *ad hoc* training activities.

These hypotheses have been further supported by an *ad hoc* study recently conducted on the *International Delivering*[2] network. ID is an international company providing door-to-door express delivery service in almost 200 countries. In order to serve its clientele, by handling distribution of parcels and documents in almost every part of the world, the company created a network of locally owned branches, as well as agencies, indirect units, cooperatives and agents. It should be pointed out that, as ID operates on an international level with a long-standing and consolidated image of reliability, it imposes quality standards that are identical throughout the world. One example of this is overnight delivery guaranteed practically anywhere in the world. To achieve its declared objectives of quality, ID requires substantial organizational integration with its suppliers (agencies, indirect units, co-operatives), considered as partners. None of these partners, however, works exclusively for ID and therefore part of their turnover is independent of their relationship with ID.

The current solution is a commercial agreement between ID and partners. The commercial agreement is drawn up by headquarters but some margin of negotiability is left to the district managers. In fact, the standards of quality required are uniform throughout the ID network, but within each district there are different problems, particular operating conditions that necessitate negotiation: the relationship is constantly negotiated through a task force named 'fair costs'. The team's goal is the analysis of the ID-partner exchange in terms of *fairness*, determining, area by area, what is the actual contribution of the partners and of ID to the relationship and to the creation of the final value of the service, in terms of costs and investments, but also in terms of quality. As the output is measurable (delivery in the required time at the level of the service requested) and the ratio existing between inputs and outputs of the parties can be determined, it is possible to apply a criterion of rewards proportional to contributions. As from 1994, ID compensates partners on the basis of the number of parcels handled by each employee.

ID asks its partners to make specific investments (managerial investments and physical assets) and to respond to its needs, but at the same time it makes a number of concessions: on the one hand these are standardized contributions for the use of cellular phones, uniforms and logos on the vans, on the other hand they are, instead, partners-specific (special rates, material support, incentives) and conditions regulating the right to conduct independent local delivery activities.

Therefore, a fair contract that seems to be superior to a standard franchising contract, in this case, would be—so to speak—a 'tempered franchising', in which a greater organizational integration is associated with *ad hoc* contractual provisions tailored to the specific needs and preferences of local partners.

Anchored equity in long-term subcontracting inside industrial districts

The empirical evidence considered here is drawn from case studies research on subcontracting in the fashion industry (Coppola 1993). From cases studies in different areas and industries, it is apparent that while at the beginning of the relationship there is a high propensity to find solutions that are mutually acceptable and therefore creative in the generation of alternatives, the parties tend later on to perpetuate the relationship in a stable manner over time. The relationship, therefore, becomes more and more habitual and routine-based by an implicit standard of *anchored equity*, utilizing as the basis of the relationship the contract initially stipulated between the parties, to which additions are made from time to time often in an informal manner, dealing with timing, prices and the technical specifications of the product, but rarely renegotiating the overall contractual framework. However, using historical precedents, while reducing negotiation costs and making the process rapid and cooperative, also reduces the consideration of superior alternatives. Parties do not develop all the integrative potential latent in the subcontracting system, and are content with solutions that could be improved for both sides.

For example, in the studied Italian fashion subcontracting systems, a recurrent inherited problem, along with the habitually adopted, loosely coupled relational contract system, is the compression of time for raw material orders that must be made by the producer, typically a subcontractor. The subcontractor often receives the technical specifications from the main contractor at the last minute, and is unable to program purchases of raw materials in time, so that there is an increase in time and costs that is carried over to the final consumer (Coppola 1993). A more integrated agreement form, including interfirm programming, could lead to important savings. In one successful case, the parties, in addition to programmed product exchange, enlarge their agreement to include the opening of an outlet for their products, the management and revenues of which are attributed to the subcontractee who also feeds into the system useful market information in this way.

Conclusions

We have shown that fairness is an important dimension in the analysis of interfirm governance structures—as much as and probably more than it is generally relevant in organizational analysis (Grandori 1991; Neri 1994, and forthcoming). It improves the capacity to explain and predict adopted organization forms, as well as to design or choose an agreement. We have also shown that fairness criteria are actually applied in forming interfirm networks. The general implication of these findings for research and design is that the outcomes of network organizational forms (as well as of other multi-actor, multi-preference governance structures in general) can and should be evaluated not only in terms of efficiency and effectiveness but also in terms of fairness and justice.

Intermediate and 'mixed' forms are rated as superior more often if a criterion of fairness is used in addition to others. We think that this is desirable, given that organizational arrangements that are hybrid mixtures of a variety of coordination and governance mechanisms seem actually to be much more common in practice with respect to what would have been predicted by existing theoretical frameworks, leaving aside the problem of fair division among actors with different interests.

Moreover, the classification of fairness rules proposed here enables specific predictions to be formulated about which types of rule are more likely to be employed in different situations. The complexity and interdependence characterizing activities, and specifically the possibility of measuring contributions/inputs and outcomes/outputs, accounts for the possibility of using fairness criteria based on those parameters. The longevity and stability of relationships enhance the likelihood of effective use of anchored equity and needs-based criteria. The experiences described are consistent with the general information-processing theory propositions that the relative amount and importance of the resources involved for the partners would justify more investment in analysis and therefore more calculative fairness judgements; and that the higher the difficulties/costs of information gathering, processing and communication, or the time constraints, the more heuristic the decision rules will be.

Notes

1 These studies were researches conducted for degree dissertations under the supervision of Anna Grandori using the theoretical framework developed in Grandori (1989, 1990, 1991).
2 Invented name to maintain privacy.

Bibliography

Adams, J. S. (1965) 'Inequity in Social Exchange', in L. Berkovitz (ed.) *Advances in Experimental Social Psychology*, New York: Academic Press.

Albin, C. (1993) 'The role of fairness in negotiation', *Negotiation Journal*, July: 223–44.

Arrow, K., Mnookin, R., Ross, L., Tversky, A. and Wilson, R. (1995) *Barriers to Conflict Resolution*, Stanford: Norton.

Austin, W. and Hatfield, E. (1980) 'Equity Theory, Power, and Social Justice', in G.Mikula (ed.) *Justice and Social Interaction*, New York: Springer Verlag.

Bazerman, M. H. (1985) 'Norms of distributive justice in interest arbitration', *Industrial and Labour Relations Review*, 38(4): 558–70.

Bergonzini, E. (1996) 'Relazioni interorganizzative nel settore delle spedizioni: un caso di studio', tesi di laurea, Facolta' di Economia, University of Modena.

Bies, J. R. and Moag, J. S. (1986) 'Interactional justice: communication criteria of fairness', in R. J. Lewicki, B. H. Sheppard and M. H. Bazerman, (eds), *Research on Negotiations in Organizations*, vol. 1: 43–55, Greenwich CT: JAI Press.

Bies, R. J., Tripp, T. M. and Neale, M. A. (1993) 'Procedural Fairness and Profit Seeking: The Perceived Legitimacy of Market Expolitation', *Journal of Behavioral Decision Making*, 6: 243–56.

Bonfanti, F. (1990) 'Analisi dei negoziati a più parti nelle reti di imprese: il caso dei consorzi', tesi di laurea, University L. Bocconi, Milano.

Burton, J. (1969) *Conflict and Communication: the use of controlled communication in international relations*, London: Macmillan.

Cadoni, L. (1989) 'Analisi dei processi negoziali nelle relazioni interoganizzative', tesi di laurea, University L. Bocconi, Milano.

Cantwell, J. (ed.) (forthcoming) 'Technology and the Theory of the Firm', *Journal of Economic Behavior and Organization*, special issue.

Colombo, M. (ed.) (forthcoming) *The Changing Boundaries of the Firm*, London: Routledge.

Coppola, A. (1993) 'Negoziazione e interazione nel sub-contracting: il settore moda', tesi di laurea, University L. Bocconi, Milano.

Deutsch, M. (1975) 'Equity, equality and needs: what determines which value will be used as the basis of distributive justice?', *Journal of Social Issues*, 31: 137–50.

Eccles, R. J. (1981) 'The quasi firm in the construction industry', *Journal of Economic Behaviour and Organizations*, 2: 335–57.

Fisher, R. and Ury, W. L. (1981) *Getting to Yes: Negotiating Agreements Without Giving In*, Boston: Houghton Mifflin.

Grandori, A. (1984) 'A prescriptive contingency view of organizational decision making', *Administrative Science Quarterly*, 29: 192–208.

—— (1989a) 'Efficienza ed equità delle reti interorganizzative: una prospettiva negoziale', *Economia e politica industriale*, no. 64.

—— (1989b) 'Reti interorganizzative progettazione e negoziazione'; *Economia e Management*, 7: 28–40.

—— (1991) 'Negotiating efficient organization forms', *Journal of Economic Behavior and Organization*, 16: 319–40.

—— (1992) 'Processi e tecniche di negoziazione nelle organizzazioni', in G. Costa (ed.), *Manuale di Gestione del Personale*, Torino: UTET.

Grandori, A. and Perrone, V. (1986) *Il caso AIV-TANYO*, Milano: SDA Bocconi.

Grandori, A. and Soda, G. (1995) 'Inter-firm networks: antecedents, mechanisms and forms', *Organization Studies*, 16(2): 183–214.

Gray, B. (1989) *Collaborating*, San Francisco: Jossey Bass.

Greenberg, J. (1987) 'A Taxonomy of Organizational Justice Theories', *Academy of Management Review*, 12 (1).

—— (1990) 'Organizational justice: yesterday, today and tomorrow'. *Journal of Management*, 2(6): 399–432.

Greenberg, J. and Cohen, R. L. (1982) 'Why justice? Normative and instrumental interpretations', in J. Greenebrg and R. L. Cohen (eds) *Equity and Justice in Social Behavior*, New York: Academic Press.

Guth, W., Schmittberger, R. and Schwarze, B. (1982) 'An experimental analysis of ultimatum bargaining', *Journal of Economic Behavior and Organization*, 3: 367–88.

Homans, G. (1961), *Social Behavior*, New York: Harcourt, Brace, Jovanovich.

Ioannilli, A. (1990) 'Analisi negoziale delle reti inter-organizzative: gli accordi di franchising', tesi di laurea, University L. Bocconi, Milano.

Kahneman, D., Knetsch, J. and Thaler, R. (1986a) 'Fairness and the Assumption of Economics', *Journal of Business*, 59(4): 284–300.

—— (1986b) 'Fairness as a constraint of profit seeking:entitlements of the market', *The American Economic Review*, 76(4): 728–41.

Kahneman, D., Slovic, P. and Tversky, A. (1982) *Judgement under uncertainty: heuristics and biases*. New York: Cambridge University Press.

Lammers, C. (1993) 'Interorganizational Democracy', in S. Lindenberg and H. Schreuder (eds), *Interdisciplinary Perspectives on Organization Studies*, Oxford: Pergamon Press.

Leventhal, G. S. (1980) 'What should be done with equity theory?', in K. Gergen, M. Greenberg and R. Willis (eds), *Social Exchange Theory*, New York: Plenum.

McClelland, D. C. (1971) *Assessing Human Motivation*, New York: General Learning Press.

March, J. G. (1978) 'Bounded rationality, ambiguity, and the engineering of choice', *Bell Journal of Economics*, 9.

March, J. G. and Simon, H. A. (1958) *Organizations*, New York: Wiley.

Mariotti, S. and Cainarca, G. C. (1986) 'The evolution of transaction governance in the textile-clothing industry', *Journal of Economic Behavior and Organization*, 7: 351–74.

Maslow, A. H. (1954) *Motivation and Personality*, New York: Harper & Row.

Mowday, R. T. (1987) 'Equity theory predictions of behavior in organizations', in R. M. Steers and L. W. Porter (eds), *Motivation and Work Behavior* (fourth ed.), New York: McGraw-Hill.

Nash, J. F. Jr. (1950) 'The bargaining problem', *Econometrica*, 18: 155–62.

Nelson, R. R. and Winter, S. G. (1982) *An Evolutionary Theory of Economic Change*, Cambridge Mass.: Harvard University Press.

Neri, M. (1994) 'L'Equità nelle Organizzazioni', *Sviluppo & Organizzazione*, 145: 33–44.

—— (forthcoming) 'L'Equità procedurale nella progettazione delle politiche del personale', *Sviluppo & Organizzazione*.

Ouchi, W. G. and Bolton, M. K. (1988) 'The logic of joint research and development', *California Management Review*, vol. XXX, no.3: 9–33.

Pfeffer, J. and Salancik, G. R. (1978) *The External Control of Organizations: A Resource Dependence Perspective*, New York: Harper & Row.

Pillutla, M. and Murnighan, J. K. (1995) 'Being fair or appearing fair: strategic behavior in ultimatum bargaining', *Academy of Management Journal*, 35(5): 1408–26.

Pruitt, D. G. (1972) 'Methods for resolving differences of interests: a theoretical analysis'. *Journal of Social Issues*, 28.

—— (1981) *Negotiation Behavior*, New York: Academic Press.

Raiffa, H. (1982) *The Art and Science of Negotiation*, Cambridge: Cambridge University Press.

Rawls, J. (1971) *A Theory of Justice*, Cambridge, Mass.: Belknap Press.

Richardson, G. B. (1971) 'The organization of industry', *Economic Journal*, 82: 883–96.

Schelling, T.C. (1960) *Strategy of Conflict*, Cambridge, Mass.: Harvard University Press.

Sen, A. K. (1992) *Inequality Reexamined*, Oxford: Oxford University Press.

Simon, H. (1955) *Models of Man. Social and Rational: Mathematical Essays on Human Behavior in a Social Setting*, New York: Wiley.

—— (1976) 'From substantive to procedural rationality'. In J. S. Latsis, *Method and Appraisal in Economics*, Cambridge: Cambridge University Press.

—— (1990) 'A mechanism for social selection and successful altruism', *Science*, 250: 1665–8.

Teece, D. J. (1986) 'Profitting from technological innovation: implication for integration, collaboration, licensing and public policy', *Research Policy*, 15(6): 286–305.

Thibaut, J. and Walker, L. (1975) *Procedural Justice*, Hillsdale NJ: Erlbaum.

Tversky, A. and Kahneman, D. (1974) 'Judgment under uncertainty: heuristics and biases', *Science*, 185: 1124–31.

Walster, E. and Walster, G. W. (1975) 'Equity and social justice', *Journal of Social Issues*, 31: 21–43.

3 Inside partnership

Trust, opportunism and cooperation in the European automobile industry

Erhard Friedberg and Jean-Philippe Neuville

In itself, interfirm cooperation and governance in the industrial sector is not a new phenomenon. As classic studies on districts, quasi-integration and cooperation (Houssiaux 1957, Phillips 1960, Macauley 1963, Blois 1972, Richardson 1972, Becattini 1978) already suggest, it is in fact a traditional, independent and stable form of coordination which can be seen as a permanent alternative to other forms, like market or hierarchy. The reason why it has attracted increased attention in a rapidly growing literature is therefore to be sought elsewhere; first, in its quantitative and qualitative development (Contractor and Lorange 1988), and second, in its growing visibility which is linked to its deliberate use by management as a strategic and formalized device to structure, i.e. steer, relationships with suppliers, competitors and clients.

'Industrial partnership' is an example of these efforts to develop a new and formalized governance form for subcontracting. Based on the Japanese industrial model (Aoki 1988, Helper 1993, Sako 1992, Baudry 1995), it aims to go beyond the traditional 'make' or 'buy' alternative which firms face when developing a new product, in order to develop a lasting cooperative relationship of 'making with' some specific selected subcontractors which become 'partners' for the contracting firm.

As a new and lasting form of interfirm cooperation and because of its distinctive features which we will go into in more detail shortly, 'industrial partnership', like any other form of cooperative action, is of course vulnerable to opportunistic behaviour by any one of the 'partners'. It is therefore not surprising that the main focus of the growing literature on 'industrial partnership' has been on the means used to cope with this risk.

Institutions for creating and guaranteeing information about potential partners, trust understood as a mechanism enabling one of the partners to subjectively reduce the risk of opportunistic behaviours by the other, contracts and their incentive-structure, and long-term committment seen to produce long-term benefits for everyone involved in the relation have been used as four functional equivalents for explaining the emergence of interfirm cooperation through the reduction and control, if not the disappearance, of the risk of opportunism. The first does so by producing reliable quality labels, the second by involving social mechanisms which are based on moral resources (norms, interpersonal relations and commitments, identity, experience), the third by providing instruments for coordination which rely on positive and negative monetary incentives (Tirole 1989), and the fourth by sharing a rational calculation in advance.

These explanations of interfirm cooperation, which are of course complementary, carry considerable new insights for our understanding of the structure of economic action. In particular, they have helped overcome overly cynical and utilitarian models whose focalization on short-sighted opportunistic behaviour made them not only blind to the phenomenon, but also unable to explain it. However, they also have their shortcomings.

The most important of these seems to us to lie in their purely synchronic perspective, which seems to overestimate the capacity of contractual arrangements and of the procedures which monitor their implementation, to block and control, if not completely eliminate opportunism. Industrial partnership is seen to found what Sabel has called a 'constitutional order' where the problem has in fact disappeared because partners have agreed to monitor one another's behaviour and to follow certain procedures for the re-evaluation of the situation in the light of the results of this monitoring. With a few notable exceptions (in particular, Nooteboom 1996), these analyses tell us little indeed about the process of cooperation, about what is going on inside industrial partnerships, or how and to what extent opportunism is really checked on a day-to-day basis. They seem to consider that once the decision to cooperate has been taken and the institutional framework set up, problems will disappear.

Such a strictly game-theoretical conception of cooperation, which in fact reduces cooperation to a once and for all decision to prefer collective benefits to individual profits, seems to us to be too reductionist to come to grips with the behavioural and process dimensions which are inherent in all relations, be they conflictual or cooperative, may they link individual or collective actors. This is why we have tried to open up the 'black box' of interfirm cooperation in our research by putting greater emphasis on a process perspective, where interfirm cooperation is defined as *a common coordinated action which brings into contact and interaction employees of two organizations linked by a long-term contract.* (Smith Ring and Van de Ven 1994; Nooteboom 1996; Neuville 1997a) and where, therefore, the interaction processes by which 'industrial pertnership' is actually implemented, are the basic focus of analysis.

Such a perspective yields a more complex, diverse and surprising picture, where trust and opportunism do not exclude each other but co-exist, where, in other words, cooperation can and should be analysed as a mix of bounded trust and bounded opportunism, where trust and time not only reduce opportunism, but can be understood also as incentives for (bounded) opportunism, and where, last but not least, the actual functioning of that mix not only directly conditions the evolution of interfirm cooperation but also introduces strong biaises into the procedures designed to monitor the 'partners'.

Industrial partnership as an 'agency relation': the relevance of qualitative uncertainty

In the car industry, 'partnership' is a pattern of interfirm cooperation based on one main exchange : economic resources (market/order shares) on the part of the buyers against something like a polymorphic product and/or service (design, development, production and delivery of components and/ or units) on the part of the suppliers. As a specific form of interfirm cooperation, it has four main characteristics.

First, interfirm relations and contractual commitments are located within a long-term contractual framework for cooperation. This situation differs from markets with spot transactions (subcontracting) as well as from organizations with hierarchic integration (Weberian bureaucracy). In industrial partnership, car manufacturers are committed to cooperate with their chosen suppliers over several years ; however, the possibility of breaking the contractual link remains. Such a pattern of organized action, which mixes the stability of hierarchy with the threat of a potential return to the market, theoretically allows both of them to benefit from an interorganizational learning process (Aoki 1988; Asanuma 1989), without suffering from bureaucratic dysfunction (Merton 1952; Gouldner 1954; Crozier 1964) and from free-riding (Olson 1965).

The second distinctive feature of industrial partnership is the nature of the 'product': the principal's economic decision concerns a complex, expensive and potential process. Complex because a car manufacturer buys not only a set of specific skills covering a broad range of activities from design to mass-production and delivery of a component, but also a process, i.e. the way these skills are organized. Expensive in as much as it involves the creation of specific assets over a longer period of time. Potential because at the time the buyer signs the contract, the product has yet to be produced : like the market for rubber (Siamwalla 1978; Popkin 1981) or for used cars (Akerlof 1970), asymmetric information between partners creates a situation in which the quality of 'product' cannot be determined at the time of sale but months later. These are the reasons why the investment decision depends on the perceived quality of the firms instead of the product. In other words, and on a more general level, industrial partnership switches exchange from markets of products to markets of organizations (Favereau 1989): products do not compete, but organizations and their reputations.

Third, the just-in-time co-production system increases interfirm interdependence. All the basic principles of the Japanese production model (Monden 1983; Ohno 1988) tend to make the production system more complex and vulnerable to failure or partial disturbances. On the one hand, we have a wide range of different components (economy of variety) and a fractionating of delivery-lots which goes hand in hand with the growing sophistication of logistics and delivery systems. On the other hand, inventories have been reduced to the strict minimum and therefore cannot be called upon to compensate for temporary shortages : in such a system, any failure by the supplier, or any disturbance in the delivery system has dramatic repercussions on the car manufacturer who very quickly will have to stop production.

Fourth, because of their long-term commitments towards their suppliers, car producers have an interest in accepting considerable investments in training, in financial support and in technological as well as organizational development in order to increase the performance of the cooperation. These investments in turn produce specific outputs such as intra- and interorganizational learning (Aoki 1988; Asanuma 1989) or collective know-how and skills for cooperation. In short, it generates what can be called a relational rent and, linked to it, a common interest in the relationship. As a consequence, breaking the cooperation becomes parti-cularly expensive. This explains why partnership is a contractual relation where under normal conditions 'voice' will prevail over 'exit' (Hirschman 1970; Helper 1993), or, in other words, where partners prefer informal negotiations to legal conflicts. Although the discontinuation of a 'partner-ship' is never completely excluded, supplier firms do benefit from a larger room for manoeuvre than would be the case in a traditional subcontracting relationship: the cost of the decision to change partners is too high to be taken lightly by the car manufacturer.

All this, of course, should not have us forget that behind the common interest which is produced by, and at the same cements, interfirm coopera-tion, individual divergent interests do persist. Despite words like 'partner-ship', 'partners' and 'cooperation', and within the limits they impose, each actor has own individual interests to pursue: car manufacturers seek to get the lowest possible prices for supplier services, while suppliers, of course, seek to increase earnings through either higher prices or bigger orders.

Putting all this together, one can easily see that for the car manufacturer, partnership as a special kind of interfirm purchasing agreement is a risky cooperation form which resembles very much an intra-firm labour contract: on the basis of contractual commitments (purchasing agreement=labour contract), a car manufacturer establishes a binding relationship with a set of specific skills (supplier=worker), and pays for it with a share in the overall purchase (market shares=salary) according to the quality of the supplier's performance (i.e. the respect of the terms of the contract= minimal work requirements). Like any such pattern of cooperation, partnership therefore fits perfectly the principal-agent model (Pratt and Zeckhauser 1985). On the one hand, we face a status asymmetry between the two 'partners': one chooses (the principal—car manufacturer) whereas the other is chosen (the supplier—agent). On the other hand, the principal (like the employer) faces a double qualitative uncertainty relating to the potential (adverse selection) and effective (moral hazard) quality of the supplier. Indeed, all of the characteristics of 'partnership' in the car industry emphasize the extreme imbalance between the two 'partners' as well as express and illustrate the critical nature of this qualitative uncertainty. No wonder, then, that car manufacturers have gone out of their way in developing rational tools with a view to reducing it.

A first reduction of that uncertainty is of course the contract between the partners. But signing a contract implies having selected partners, i.e. having faced and tried to control the risk of adverse selection. And having to sign an irreducibly incomplete contract means facing and having to control the risk of moral hazard on the part of the selected suppliers. Contracts, therefore, are only a small part of the solution. They have to be complemented by the assessment of suppliers, both before and after the signing of the contract.

The function of the *ex ante* evaluation is to control the risk of adverse selection of suppliers by trying to assess their respective quality-potential, i.e. their capability of keeping up with their contractual commitments. This evaluation relies first of all on a set of exogenous institutional information bearing on the trustworthiness of the potential suppliers: quality-insurance, quality-awards, certification, ISO 9000, standards, labels and total quality management are generally considered to be institutional trust-signals which reduce qualitative uncertainty and have been introduced and analysed as such in the literature (Zucker 1986; Eymard-Duvernay 1989; Baudry 1994, Benezech 1996). Being able to provide these trust-signals, however, is a necessary but not a sufficient condition for a supplier to be selected. All car manufacturers will add to them direct assessments made by their own Purchasing Departments, through what could generically be called 'qualification procedures'. These procedures always amount to sending a body of auditors to inspect the prospective suppliers' production sites in order to try and assess their structural capacity (industrial process, logistics, personnel training, financial health, quality of the management, R&D potential, . . .) to satisfy the car manufacturer's qualitative and quantitative demands.

The *ex post* evaluation is meant to control the risk of moral hazard on the part of the selected suppliers. It bears on the effective quality of the components delivered, i.e. the suppliers' conformity with contractual commitments. This evaluation is actually and to some extent exclusively in the hands of the car manufacturers' assembly-line operators and managers who are the direct customers of the components delivered by the suppliers. It is essentially based on a set of procedures for declaring the respective supplier's quantitative and qualitative failures and defects to the Purchasing Department.

Both *ex ante* and *ex post* evaluations thus produce a great number of reports and indicators which the Purchasing Departments centralize and manage, and on which its members, the individual buyers, will base their decisions as to which supplier will get what share of the overall order. In other words, the car manufacturer's purchasing strategy thus essentially depends on the way the necessary information and indicators are being generated, processed and passed on by those in contact with suppliers, i.e. the car manufacturer's auditors and the assembly-line operators and managers.

Industrial partnership in action

Understanding the actual working of 'partnerships' within the car-industry therefore calls for close scrutiny and analysis of the empirical interaction processes through which operational actors within the car manufacturers and their respective counterparts within the different supplier-firms actually manage the co-development and co-production of a car and implement the various procedures designed for the qualitative and quantitative evaluation of suppliers' performance. It is this analysis which we shall turn to now.[1]

Ex ante *evaluation of the supplier's capability*

When a new vehicle is to be developed, the Purchasing Department uses its qualification procedures in order to select its 'partners'. Before signing any new contract, the prospective partners' (suppliers') production sites and technical services are being inspected in order to evaluate their quality-potential.

The auditors in charge of this mission easily and willingly admit the difficulty of the task, for several reasons. First they recognize that they do not have the skills and competencies to seriously evaluate the prospective supplier's technology: as a rule, the rate of technological innovation in the different subsectors is too high. Second, they feel vulnerable to what they call the 'mask syndrome'. When an auditor visits a supplier, the latter has always been forewarned and can therefore show a process which differs from the one which is normally implemented.

Offhand, one would be tempted to argue that both problems could be easily handled. In order to fill some of the information gap, for instance, auditors' technical competencies would only have to be increased through training. However, there was no attempt to do so within the two car makers we studied : indeed, we found only one auditor who on his own initiative had taken it upon himself to increase and keep up his technical skills.[2]

Thus, one could easily imagine ways in which an auditor could avoid being deceived by a show case which some suppliers could be tempted to put on in order to convey a favourable impression. He or she could, for instance, visit a supplier by surprise in order to observe the gap between the way the process has been officially evaluated and the way it is actually run when looked at unexpectedly. Although rules do not forbid this kind of behaviour, none of the auditors we met actually made use of such an opportunity. According to them, an unannounced control would not only have been unfair, it would also have been counter-productive. Indeed, they argued that such controls would institute an atmosphere of tension and confrontation which would in fact prevent them from obtaining what they wanted from suppliers, i.e. a minimum of transparency about the way they actually managed their production process.[3] In other words, they were afraid that in the case of a showdown, the suppliers had the stronger hand.

The actual solution which the auditors developed empirically was much simpler, but apparently very effective. It consisted in constructing a cooperative relationship with one or two key actors within the suppliers' Quality and/or Design and Production Engineering Departments. In order to construct such a relationship, however, they had to have something useful to exchange. And indeed they had, namely strategic information on two issues which were of interest to the supplier : on the one hand, knowledge about the suppliers' competitors (regarding product, process, organization, and so on) ; on the other hand, information about the car manufacturer's purchasing policy and future cars. That was, to some extent, the price they had to pay in order to obtain in exchange an increase in the suppliers' transparency concerning their process and organization.

Thanks to this relationship, the auditors were able to re-equilibrate somewhat their bargaining position in face of the prospective suppliers, who now had an interest in limiting their potentially opportunistic use of the information asymmetry. Lest they lost the auditors' trust and coopera- tion, they could not take too much advantage of their good faith.

If the auditors did not succeed in constructing such a relationship, then the suppliers' evaluation was a less positive one. If they succeeded, however, the objectives of their audits would implicitly have been modified. The auditors' mission would no longer be the control of the conformity of the suppliers' process and organization to whatever level was specified for qualification. Much rather, it would be to assess the suppliers' capacity to reach that specified level by the time the car, for which the supplier was being selected, was ready for mass-production, and also to form an assessment of the risk generated by residual failures on the part of the prospective supplier.

Ex post *evaluation of suppliers' qualitative performance*

During the phase of mass-production of a car, whether that production started one or five years earlier, we have observed two overall results that we can generalize to all the assembly lines (Neuville 1997a) : (i) the quality of the suppliers' parts or components was still variable (despite *ex ante* evaluation, ISO standards and qualification procedures, there remained considerable uncertainty about quality) and (ii) assembly-line operators, as well as managers, only very exceptionally accepted the need to stop the production (the rhetoric of total quality management notwithstanding, quantity still was the superordinate goal on the production sites).

When there is an *ex ante* evaluation, the quality of parts delivered by the suppliers is no longer controlled by a specific department: parts are directly delivered to the assembly lines. Thus, the final assembly lines do not only have to put together all the parts of a car, they also have to check the parts first. Every time they find a defect, the rules say that they have to rework it at the cost of the supplier. If this cannot be done, then they have to put it aside. At the same time, the assembly lines have to declare all the defects in order to inform the Purchasing Department on the various suppliers' qualitative performance. This is the formal story. Our observations, however, showed it to be quite different, with the Purchasing Departments being all but systematically informed about suppliers' quantitative and/or qualitative failures. Let us again sum up our findings.

If the defect concerned only one isolated part, the assembly line repaired it as well as possible and did not declare anything. If repairing the part was impossible, the defective part would be put aside and assembly-line managers would try and negotiate a way for charging the supplier, without informing the Purchasing Department.

If two or three parts came up with the same defect once in a while, the assembly line would still rework the parts without informing anyone. But the supplier responsible would be called in and clearly told by the assembly-line managers that although the Purchasing Department should be informed about this, they were willing to keep things at their level if they could be sure that quality would be held steady in the future. As to the incriminated supplier, he or she would try and explain the reasons for this incident as well as assess the risk of it occurring in the future, and would promise to control 100 per cent of the production before delivering it.

If the defective components turned up two or three times in a delivery-lot, this meant trouble. Even then, however, assembly-line managers would not systematically declare the incidents to the Purchasing Department. They would threaten the supplier that unless he or she sent someone for on-site inspection and, if necessary, for reworking the defective parts on the line, they would declare the defects and/or would have to stop the line. Suppliers would generally agree to do so, because this solution had at least two possible benefits for them. On the one hand, their presence would avoid defect-declaration to the Purchasing Department. On the other hand, it would allow them to secretly inspect the way their parts were actually handled and assembled on the line and to find out whether the defect could not be due to the non-respect of operating procedures by assembly-line operators, in which case they would be able to transfer the responsibility of the defect onto the car manufacturer.

If a defect occurred even more regularly in each delivery-lot, then this would be interpreted by the assembly-line management as the sign of a real dysfunction in the supplier's process. When such an ultimate situation was reached, assembly-line managers would, as a last resort, declare the incident to the Purchasing Department, and would have to stop production if they ran out of parts because of the frequency of the defects. The supplier who was unable to get his process back under control sooner, would be considered responsible for his or her failure and would be fully and officially sanctioned.

Ex post *evaluation of suppliers' quantitative performance*

The second post-contractual evaluation concerns the suppliers' quantitative and logistic performance, i.e. the way they respected, or not, their just-in-time delivery commitments.

Because of tight flow process and inventories reduction, the logistics technicians on the car manufacturer's production sites are also under pressure. They have to see to it that they do not lack components in order that production is not halted, while simultaneously keeping inventories of parts inside the factory as low as possible. This contradiction in objectives is all the more difficult for them to manage as, due to both exogenous and endogenous disturbances, there is always a gap between actual consumption of parts and pre-established production programs.

The logistics technicians can only get some hold on that dilemma if they are able to establish a cooperative relationship based on mutually beneficial exchange with the supplier or more specifically with their counterparts (the suppliers' logistics technicians). Such a relationship will provide them with the necessary flexibility, a flexibility, however, which comes neither from physical flows nor from procedures.

What are the elements of the situation. In order to avoid running out of parts and being responsible for a stop in production, the car maker's logistics technicians must anticipate all the various disturbances which might alter the even flow of parts, such as a component's overconsumption (endogenous trouble) or a supplier's delivery delay (exogenous trouble). The suppliers' logistics technicians, on the other hand, have an interest in hiding actual delays, with the hope that their failure to deliver exactly on time will go unnoticed and will therefore not deteriorate their ratings on the evaluation of their logistics performance. While the car manufacturers' logistics technician needs transparency and just-in-time information, the supplier has an interest in opacity. And the car manufacturers' technicians are clearly in trouble, as they cannot force their counterparts within the suppliers to inform them in due time.

They are, therefore, the driving force behind the search for some sort of a deal which would make it worthwhile for their counterparts to inform them and cooperate with them. And we observed that they were able to strike a bargain around an exchange of some tolerance on their part against some more transparency on the part of their counterparts within the suppliers. Here are two examples of this kind of exchange.

First, the suppliers' technicians would forewarn their counterparts on the production site that the delivery of the part would be one hour late, thus giving them time to organize and face up to the situation. In exchange, this non-respect of contractual commitments would not be declared to the Purchasing Department. Second, when the car manufacturers' logistics technicians needed supplementary parts because of overconsumption or an inventory error, the suppliers would deliver them without arguing that it was not written on the official order. In exchange they would be informed ahead of time about planned production increases or decreases, enabling them to adjust in time their resources and production-flow.

Thus, the suppliers of the defective part who had been able to offer some transparency to their logistics counterparts on the production sites, did not have to fear that their failures, at least as long as they did not cause a stop in production, would be declared to the Purchasing Department. The car manufacturer's logistics technicians, on the other hand, succeeded in quietly managing their inventories and in minimizing their risk of leaving the assembly line without the necessary parts and of being held responsible for a halt in production.

From economic contract to local orders

The preceding examples are not the result of theoretical considerations. They are based on the empirical observations and findings collected in intensive qualitative field-studies in the factories and purchasing departments of two major European car manufacturers and with a great number of their suppliers. They point to major, and in our eyes, decisive discrepancies between the theory of the new philosophy and management of subcontracting summed up in 'industrial partnership' and the practice of actors in the field.

When looked at from some distance, the patterns of behaviour and interaction which can be observed, seem to have one common denominator, i.e. 'restraint'. The actors involved in the day-to-day management of partnership both within the car manufacturers and the supplier firms seem unwilling to use whatever means for coercion or negative sanction the formal organization of the 'partnership' might provide them with. On the part of the suppliers, one can observe restraint in actually profiting fully from the information asymmetries which are inherent in the relation with the car manufacturer : they do show their process and they do forewarn their clients when something is wrong or when unexpected and unforeseen delays occur. And the same can be said of the representatives of the car manufacturer : the auditor conspicuously refrains from unannounced inspection tours, and the assembly-line managers indeed go out of their way not to declare the actual inadequacies of suppliers to the Purchasing Department nor to stop production, both of which would have devastating effects on the respective suppliers' performance records within the Purchasing Department and on subsequent orders from the car manufacturer.

All our observations definitely point in the same direction: to the existence of a basic complicity and solidarity transforming into allies what at a formal level would look like opposing parties. Instead of fighting each other in order to maximize whatever short-term profits they expect from the relationship, they cooperate within the framework of mutually des-tructive, 'last-resort' sanctions which may frequently be invoked as threats[4] but which are rarely put into effect.

In order to last, however, such a cooperative relationship needs a common stake, and, more important still, something to exchange. The common stake is avoiding the equally disruptive effects of non-cooperation for both sides: lost orders, decreased market-share and deteriorating reputation for the supplier, difficult and potentially unreliable *ex ante* evaluations and production losses on the side of the car manufacturer.

The commodity which is exchanged is, of course, different in *ex ante* and *ex post* evaluations. In the relations involved in *ex ante* evaluations, the transaction is based mostly on the exchange of mutually interesting information:[5] the auditor will provide information on future cars as well as on competitors, and in exchange will get a better and more realistic picture of the suppliers' real capability and thus will gain a better position for a realistic evaluation. In the *ex post* evaluation situation, whether it concerns the qualitative and quantitative performance of suppliers, the good to be exchanged is mostly the car manufacturers' tolerance of suppliers' inade-quacies against more transparency and supplementary service (help) on the part of the latter.

In fact, the interactions involved here can be conceptualized as a quasi-market for 'non-quality', i.e. performance by the supplier which does not live up to contractual commitments. There is a supply: the supplier who tries and for whom the production sites of the car manufacturer tolerate inadequate performance (non-conformity to contractual quality require-ments concerning the design of parts and/or delivery conditions). There is a demand: assembly-line and production-site operators and managers who are willing to accept (indeed have no choice but to accept) such inadequate performance if they want to avoid having to stop production and thus incur production losses. And there is a price, namely the conditions under which the latter are willing to accept such inadequate performance, i.e. the supplementary, non-contractual service which suppliers will have to deliver in order to 'get away' with it.

To give just a few examples, such service may range from minor changes in the design of parts which are non-contractual but which will help assembly-line operators in their task, to giving a hand to assembly-line operators in checking components in order to select the 'good' ones, to accepting to take back parts which were true to design but which have been impaired by incorrect usage on the assembly line and even to providing 'extra parts' as a substitute for these, which are now missing from the inventories.

Indeed, it could include anything that will help their counterparts in the production sites of the car manufacturers in doing what they are paid to do: assemble a fixed number of cars which satisfy ever-rising quality requirements, despite all the unplanned qualitative and quantitative disturbances which are all the more threatening to an even production flow today as reserves and slack have been eaten up by lean-management techniques. One could almost say that within limits, of course, lesser quality in the productive and logistic performance of any supplier can be made up by his or her reactiveness and efficiency in bringing solutions to problems arising in the work-flow of the car manufacturers' production sites.

Our journey inside partnership thus brings to light the existence of tight-knit, boundary-spanning arrays of social exchange relations at all the interfaces between car manufacturers and their suppliers. Based on cooperative arrangements, complicity and trust, these relations are the basic tools and mediators for the implementation of the contractual framework of partnership, the mediators through which the economic exchange of contract is translated into a series of 'rules of the game' able to establish 'local orders' (Friedberg 1993), stabilizing and regulating the actual behaviour of operational actors while enabling them to manage the day-to-day contingencies of their job.

The significance of these local orders should not be analysed in purely negative terms as mere impediments to the improvement of actual quality or to the attainment of official goals. Quite to the contrary : indeed, all the recent amelioration of the quality of the cars produced has been managed through precisely such arrays of social exchange and the informal processes of negotiation and transaction they are based on. The significance of our observations is therefore to be seen elsewhere : it lies in the gap that they show to exist between the theory and practice of the new (Japanese) style for the management of subcontracting. Quality may have been improved, but this has been obtained in ways quite different from those that the new management philosophy would have us believe or would prescribe. And these ways have important theoretical as well as practical implications, some of which we should like to briefly sketch out below.

Some implications for theory

At least four themes with direct implications for the theory of interfirm cooperation and more generally of the structuring of fields of collective action can be drawn from our observations based on a process-view of partnership.

The first has to do with the intricate link between formal and informal characteristics of these local orders which make it impossible to oppose these two levels of action or to attribute actual performance to either of them (Friedberg 1993, 1996). Formal and informal dimensions of cooperation in these local orders not only cannot be separated, but have to be seen as interdependent and equally important components which rely on and produce each other. One is not more rational or more efficient than the other, one is not an impediment to the other. Quite the contrary: one is the condition for the efficiency and performance of the other.

Without the legal contractual framework and the possibilities of sanction as well as negotiation that it offers to operational actors, the transactions at the operational level would simply not be possible. If, to take just one example, assembly-line managers did not have the possibility of hiding suppliers' inadequacies or, on the contrary, of declaring them or even simply making them visible to all through production stops, and if suppliers did not have the possibility of invoking formal prescriptions (the design and contractual quality requirements) by threatening to respect them again,[6] they would not be able to start any negotiation. But at the same time, the same legal framework without the liberties that operational actors take with it, would only paralyse action as it would be unable to actually guarantee an even production flow of reasonably 'good' cars, i.e. cars satisfying ever-increasing quality requirements.

The reason is simple: no *ex ante* qualification, however sophisticated and well instrumented, can prevent uneven quality and unforeseen disturbances during the mass-production phase. The apparent paradox around ISO quality standards or other certification or qualification procedures is a case in point. Certification and qualification, as a trust-signal, is supposed to inform the buyer about the quality and capability of the seller's organization and production process and therefore theoretically becomes an indicator of the seller's reliability to develop, produce and deliver components as promised and codified in contract. However, we were not able to observe any significant difference in the actual performance of the supplier-firms. Whether certified or not, all of them were victims of failures and thus unreliable to a certain extent. Thus, ISO and similar procedures for the qualification of potential suppliers have more to do with providing legitimate decision criteria for buyers than insurance against seller's failures. Such insurance is beyond reach.

And such inevitable variation in the quality of supplies has to be managed on a day-to-day basis without interrupting production. In order to do so, operational actors will actually use their role in the implementation of this framework in such a way as to transform its legal and contractual dispositions into instruments for creating the conditions of negotiations which, when durably successful, may easily produce a very solid cooperative relationship based on interpersonal trust. In turn, such a relationship will reintroduce flexibility into an otherwise very cumbersome and top-heavy structure.

More generally, we could say that economic interfirm contract, incomplete by nature like any formal device in organizational life, with time becomes institutionalized, i.e. loaded with social interpersonal contracts that 'complete' the terms of the economic contract and make possible its implementation. In other words, local commitments based on mutually beneficial exchange, reciprocity and trust are made possible by global information-based commitments, and, by progressively becoming autonomous from the latter and taking on a life of their own, will increasingly mediate, i.e. modify, its impact. The question then becomes : which one is the relevant contract for understanding the actual functioning and dynamics of interfirm cooperation, the economic or the social one ? In the light of our findings, the answer can only be both, an answer which in turn clearly underscores that contract and decision-making wih regard to make or buy decisions alone cannot provide a satisfactory entry into the study of interfirm cooperation.

A second worthwhile aspect to be stressed is the co-existence in these local orders of both trust and opportunism. On the one hand, our results corroborate the hypothesis that durable cooperative arrangements generate and are based on trust (Axelrod 1984), as well as other empirical results, especially in Swedish studies (Ford, Hakansson and Johanson 1986; Johanson and Mattsson 1987; Hallén, Johanson and Seyed-Mohamed 1991), which have demonstrated that repeated exchanges lead to mutual adaptation and interpersonal bonding that enable interfirm cooperation to digest most of the turbulence. This systemic flexibility based on specific interpersonal relations goes beyond any formal agreement, that is to say without any legal assurance for both parties, as it is based on something like a 'moral contract'. From this point of view, trust is really a moral resource (Hirschman 1984), socially constructed by a cross-learning process.

On the other hand, however, our results also go to show that this does not exclude opportunistic behaviour. For example, when assembly-line managers and operators tolerate suppliers' failures because they trust the promises their counterparts in these firms have made, the latter can and do take advantage of the situation: they can and actually do reintroduce defective products selectively into the delivery-lots, with the hope that this will not be detected by the assembly line; they can and actually do transfer some quality control operations and some reworking of defective components onto the assembly line.

What this co-existence of trust and opportunism indicates is that opportunism should not be studied as a decision problem, but as a relational problem, like trust and power in social-exchange theories. This is to say, that the presence or absence of opportunism and trust in a relation is not a matter of decision at one moment, but rather one of process where (i) trust and opportunism flow easily one into the other and where (ii) opportunism is not so much a question of one of the partners choosing to betray, but a question of the other detecting unexpected behaviour and interpreting it as betrayal (Sabel 1993). Opportunism matters if we consider subjective perceptions of actors instead of objective descriptions of an external observer. In this perspective, one of the partners may betray with the chance that the other does not perceive a thing, that is to say without any damage to his trust capital. And the more cooperation is based on trust (less control and more autonomy), the more each of the partners can take the risk of bounded opportunism.

In a way, this indicates that we have to go beyond the either/or conception which one frequently encounters in regard to trust. Whether it is based on a norm of reciprocity (Dore 1987; Berger *et al.* 1993), on interpersonal relations (Granovetter 1985; Karpik 1989), on membership in a community (Ben-Porath 1980) or on the experience of past cooperation (Ford *et al.* 1986; Johanson and Mattsson 1987; Hallén *et al.* 1991), trust, in the long run, will be analysed as something which exists or not in a given relation or in a given context. Reality seems to be much more complex. Empirical exchange relations are neither based on power, bargaining and opportunism, nor on trust: they include all of these dimensions. And if in numerous works (Lorenz 1988; Aoki 1989; Bradach and Eccles 1989; Grabher 1993; Baudry 1994), the introduction of time in interfirm relations is seen to allow cooperation because it reduces information asymmetry, builds up trust and interpersonal bonding and therefore drastically reduces or even excludes the risk of opportunism, deeper analysis of the empirical exchange relations opens up the possibility of a causality going the other way: trust reduces control and thus becomes vulnerable to bounded opportunism. Much more, it cannot be denied that trust is built in a strategic way : i.e. in order to be opportunistic, a given supplier firm has to appear trustworthy and therefore has a stake in investing time and resources into building up trust (Neuville 1997b, 1998).

The third theoretical theme that can be drawn from our findings on the process of interfirm cooperation has to do with the socially constructed nature of 'quality'. Looked at from the operational level, quality is not just something 'objective' in the sense that it could be defined in purely technical terms and that its attainment could be ascertained unequivocally. It is also socially constructed as it depends in part on the outcomes of the various negotiations and transactions without which it would not exist. Indeed, the emergence and satisfactory functioning of these boundary-spanning local orders are unthinkable without the basic indeterminacy of what the 'quality' of a vehicle or a part (component) really is. This basic indeterminacy entails the fact that quality requirements cannot be un-equivocally codified in contractual terms. The contractual framework of the industrial partnership is thus basically incomplete : it leaves blanks to be filled through action, it leaves ambiguities which operational actors can put to use as resources in bargaining and exchange processes. And it provides assembly-line management with one basic weapon: they are the ones who in the last resort will be defining the quality, i.e. the acceptability of a part.

The final quality of a car is thus the product of the rules of the game which have prevailed in the bargaining and exchange processes between partly internal, partly external actors and which have led to the acceptance or the refusal as well as to the (official or unofficial) modification of this or that part or component. These ongoing bargaining processes on what definition of quality will prevail at any time are not unlimited, but subject to certain modes of regulation which will prevent them getting out of hand. The technical instrumentation of quality is a first constraint which limits the leeway of operational actors in their day-to-day dealings.[7] But the short-term regulation of these processes is elsewhere: it is located in the final evaluation of the quality of a vehicle which is situated at the end of the assembly line and which marks a sort of internal demarcation line between manufacturing and sales. The local department of quality control which is in charge of this final evaluation is not completely external to these processes, as it may—and frequently does—participate in the bargaining. But it is sufficiently distanced from it to be able to act as a sort of justice of peace whose decisions call actors back to order. It does so by arbitrarily varying the quality requirements which it enforces, thus indirectly steering the level of attention, vigilance and mutual tolerance of the members of the quality-producing networks.[8]

One final theme flowing from our process-view on partnership should be mentioned, namely the convergence of our findings concerning two car manufacturers in two European countries. This convergence is remarkable, even troubling, as one could and would have expected national or 'cultural' variation (Dore 1987; d'Iribarne 1989; Fukuyama 1995). Without sustaining technological determinism as a satisfactory explanation, we must stress the extreme resemblance between our two car manufacturers as far as their production and coordination systems are concerned : both are inspired by the Japanese model of industrial partnership and both have drawn the same prescriptive conclusions from this model. It may well be that this mimetic process which is being funneled by the spread of ISO procedures and certifications leads to very similar technological and organizational problems and to a convergence in the actual functioning of European car manufacturers, but more and deeper research should be done on that question.

However, there is another 'cultural' issue which could be raised in relation to our findings. The locals orders we observed come close to what has been seen as characteristic of social exchange in industrial districts (inter-individual trust based on reciprocity). But this is obtained without all the other ingredients that are usually mentioned in explaining 'industrial districts': partnership links national and international firms, and variables such as identity, proximity, community or local norms seem to be 'catalysts' or 'boosters' rather than structural mechanisms. Maybe time more than space, is the key variable to understanding the process of interfirm cooperation.[9]

Some implications for practice

Last, but not least, we should like to draw attention to the practical implications which the structure and functioning of these local orders entails for the management of this new philosophy of subcontracting called 'industrial partnership'. Two levels of analysis have to be distinguished here.

First of all, the way these social networks are structured and function, directly influences supplier evaluation by the Purchasing Department and thus its purchasing strategies and decisions. The *ex ante* and *ex post* evaluation procedures which are at the basis of its purchasing decisions are definitely biased. They do not provide a faithful picture of the gap between the suppliers' contractual commitments and their effective performance. They reflect instead the auditors' and/or assembly-line managers' and operators' estimation of the suppliers' capacity to manage and keep under control the inevitable gaps between their contractual commitments and their real performance, an estimation which is considerably influenced, as we have seen, by the level of trust and cooperation which in the field characterizes their day-to-day relationship to this or that supplier.

In other words, and to put it more bluntly, the evaluation procedure only indirectly sanctions the suppliers' industrial process. As a consequence, the car manufacturers do not necessarily contract with the best possible suppliers (in an absolute sense, whatever that would be), but with those whose representatives have been able to establish a relationship of trust and cooperation with their own technicians and operational managers. What the evaluation procedures really measure, then, is the suppliers' capacity to cooperate and to find solutions for the day-to-day disturbances which threaten the even flow of production of good cars. And that means that *ex post* evaluation finally is more important than the *ex ante* evaluations. One can even ask the question : what is the use of the *ex ante* evaluation, if finally the only thing that really counts is the suppliers' aptitude to manage his failures?

From there flows another practical implication for the governance of the supply relationship: the structure and functioning of these boundary-spanning local orders can and must be interpreted as enabling suppliers to re-equilibrate the balance of power in their relations with the car manufacturers. Indeed, on the operational level, it seems to us that the balance of power definitely tilts in favour of the suppliers. Of course, operational managers always have the resource to threaten with a stop of the assembly line and a declaration of suppliers' failures. However, this is a self-defeating weapon, which punishes production just as much as it does suppliers. It is therefore only used as last resort, even if it remains a threat frequently used to obtain cooperative behaviour on the part of the suppliers.

Suppliers offer the one thing that is irreplaceable: reactivity and flexibility in an otherwise more and more tightly coupled production process which, however, continues to be threatened by a great number of potential qualitative and quantitative disturbances. They have the short-term solutions which help production sites to respect production programmes, to find better and more comfortable ways of assembling, and to overcome a temporary shortage of this or that component. And, in exchange, they are able to externalize some of their non-quality and some of their production costs onto the car manufacturers.

One could say that the suppliers slowly win back what they had to concede during the initial negotiation of the deal with the Purchasing Department. By progressively emptying the contractual commitments of their content, they partially or completely win back during mass-production what they had to offer in order to get the deal. Short-term earnings by the car manufacturer in his contractual arrangements may well be eroded by medium- and long-term losses due to the governance and/or implementation costs of the partnership relations.

Notes

1 The following developments are based on a comparative empirical investigation in the course of which we interviewed, between 1993 and 1994, 230 managers and employees of two big European car manufacturers and twenty-five supplier-firms. Moreover, we spent six months observing the actual day-to-day functioning of the plants both the car manufacturers (five assembly-lines) and the suppliers (fifteen companies). In addition, we collected all written material relative to interfirm cooperation between our car manufacturers and their suppliers (commercial contracts, technical descriptions, delivery procedures, quality insurance dossier, indicators, and so on).
2 The solution he used was to entertain informal relations with machine-makers and raw-material companies of the suppliers he was in charge of.
3 The reasoning behind this argument is quite paradoxical: something which logically should allow the auditor to reduce moral hazard is presented as though it actually increased this same moral hazard.
4 This would be the case for instance with the assembly-line managers' prerogative to stop the assembly line if incoming components are not of the required quality: this possibility is often introduced in the discussion with the suppliers' representatives and thus used as a threat, but hardly ever is it really put into practice. This possibility is a sort of atomic bomb which defines a common interest in avoiding what both consider as a mutually destructive and therefore undesirable outcome.
5 Although some tolerance on the part of auditors will always be involved also.
6 A supplier threatening to again deliver parts true to design is of course paradoxical since this is what he is supposed to do in the first place. However, it happens all the time, as the suppliers, as a service to his or her partners on the assembly line, often have accepted to slightly modify contractual design in order to make a part easier to assemble. They have done so, however, without any formal change in the contractual dispositions and/or the design, and these changes are therefore revocable, if necessary, and can become a commodity to be exchanged against some tolerance and comprehension on the part of the assembly-line managers for the (temporary) difficulties of their suppliers.
7 But one should not forget that this instrumentation can also be used in the negotiations going on between the involved actors, and that they can and will be transformed by this use.

8 It has been noticed, and we have observed, that the level of quality in any factory will go up mechanically when there is a control of every car, and will go down again when the control is made on statistical grounds (one car out of n cars is subject to control). This is, of course, just another element which goes to show how 'arbitrary' and variable the prevailing level of acceptatbility and 'quality' is.

9 It may be said, however, that proximity still may have its importance. It is not the common belonging to a community, but the interpersonal knowledge and direct interaction between assembly-line managers and operators and the various suppliers' representatives which do seem to make a difference.

Bibliography

Akerlof, G. (1970), 'The market for lemons: quality uncertainty and the market mechanism', *The Quarterly Journal of Economics*, 84: 488–500.

Angel, D. P. (1991), 'High-technology agglomeration and the labor market : the case of Silicon Valley', *Environment and Planning*, 23: 1501–16.

Aoki, M. (1988), *Information, Incentives and Bargaining in the Japanese Economy*, Cambridge: Cambridge University Press.

Asanuma, B. (1985), 'The organization of parts purchases in the Japanese automotive industry', *Japanese Economic Studies*, 13: 32–53.

Asanuma, B. (1989), 'Manufacturer–supplier relationships in Japan and the concept of relation specific skill', *Journal of the Japanese and International Economies*, 3: 1–30.

Axelrod, R. (1984), *The Evolution of Cooperation*, New York: Basic Books.

Baudry, B. (1994), 'De la confiance dans la relation d'emploi ou de sous-traitance', *Sociologie du Travail*, 1/94: 43–61.

Baudry, B. (1995), *L'économie des relations interentreprise*, Paris: La Découverte.

Becattini, G. (1978), 'The development of light industry in Tuscany: an interpretation', *Economic Notes*, 2: 107–23.

Benezech, D. (1996), 'La norme: une convention structurant les interrelations technologiques et industrielles', *Revue d'Economie Industrielle*, 75: 27–43.

Ben-Porath, Y. (1980), 'The F-connection: families, friends, and firms in the organization of exchange', *Population and Development Review*, 6: 1–30.

Berger, H., Noorderhaven, N., Nooteboom, B. and Pennink, B. (1993), 'Understanding the subcontracting relationship: the limitations of transaction cost economics', in J. Child, M. Crozier, R. Mayntz *et al.* (eds), *Societal Change Between Market and Organization*, Vienne: Avebury.

Blois, K. J. (1972), 'Vertical quasi-integration', *Journal of Industrial Economics*, 20: 253–72.

Bradach, J. L. and Eccles, R. G. (1989), 'Price, authority and trust: from ideal types to plural forms', *Annual Review of Sociology*, 15: 97–118.

Brousseau, E. (1993), *L'économie des contrats*, Paris: PUF.

Brusco, S. (1982), 'The Emilian Model: productive decentralization and social integration', *Cambridge Journal of Economics*, 6: 167–84.

Clark, P. and Staunton, N. (1989), *Innovation in Technology and Organization*, London: Routledge.

Contractor, F. J. and Lorange, P. (eds) (1988), *Cooperative Strategies in International Business*, Lexington: Lexington Books.

Crozier, M. (1964), *The Bureaucratic Phenomenon*, Chicago: University of Chicago Press.

Dore, R. (1987), *Taking Japan Seriously*, Stanford: Stanford University Press.

Drucker, P. (1990), *The New Realities*, New York: Harper and Row.

Eymard-Duvernay, F. (1989), 'Conventions de qualité et formes de coordination', *Revue Economique*, 40: 329–59.

Favereau, O. (1989), 'Marchés externes, marchés internes', *Revue Economique*, 40: 273–328.

Ford, D., Hakansson, H. and Johanson, J. (1986), 'How do companies interact?', *Industrial Marketing and Purchasing*, 1: 26–41.

Friedberg, E. (1996), 'The relativization of formal organization', in M. Warglien and M. Masuch (eds), *The Logic of Organizational Disorder*, New York: Walter de Gruyter.

Friedberg, E. (1997), *Local Orders*, Greenwich: JAI Press.

Fukuyama, F. (1995), *Trust*, New York: The Free Press.

Gouldner, A. (1954), *Patterns of Industrial Bureaucracy*, Glencoe/New York: The Free Press.

Grabher, G. (ed.) (1993), *The Embedded Firm. The Socio-Economics of Industrial Networks*, London: Routledge.

Grandori, A. and Soda, G. (1995), 'Interfirm networks : antecedents, mechanisms and forms', *Organization Studies*, 16/2: 183–214.

Granovetter, M.S. (1985), 'Economic action and social structure: the problem of embeddedness', *American Journal of Sociology*, 91/3: 481–510.

Hallén, L., Johanson, J. and Seyed-Mohamed, N. (1991), 'Interfirm adaptation in business relationships', *Journal of Marketing*, 55: 29–37.

Hart, O.D. and Holmstrom, B. (1987), 'The theory of contracts', in Bewley (ed.), *Advance in Economic Theory*, Cambridge: Cambridge University Press.

Helper, S. (1993), 'An exit-voice analysis of supplier relations : the case of the U.S. automobile industry', in G. Grabher (ed.), *The Embedded Firm: On the Socio-economics of Industrial Networks*, London: Routledge.

Hirschman, A. O. (1970), *Exit, Voice and Loyalty*, Cambridge, Mass: Harvard University Press.

Hirschman, A. O. (1984), 'Against parsimony: three easy ways of complicating some categories of economic discourse', *American Economic Review Proceedings*, 74: 88–96.

Houssiaux, J. (1957), 'Le concept de quasi-integration et le rôle des sous-traitants dans l'industrie', *Revue Economique*, 2: 221–47.

Iribarne, (d') P. (1989), *La logique de l'honneur*, Paris: Seuil.

Johanson, J. and Mattsson, L.-G. (1987), 'Interorganizational relations in industrial systems', *International Studies of Management & Organization*, 17: 34–48.

Karpik, L. (1989), 'L'économie de la qualité', *Revue Française de Sociologie*, 30: 187–210.

Kreps, D.M. (1990), *A Course in Microeconomic Theory*, New York: Harvester Wheatsheaf.

Lamming, R. (1993), *Beyond Partnership*, New York: Prentice Hall.

Lane, C. and Bachmann, R. (1996), 'The social constitution of trust: supplier relations in Britain and Germany', *Organization Studies*, 17/3: 365–95

Lomi, A. (1991), *Reti Organizzative*, Bologna: Il Mulino.

Lorenz, E. H. (1988), 'Neither friends nor strangers: informal networks of subcontracting in French industry', in D. Gambetta (ed.), *Trust: Making and Breaking Cooperative Relations*, Oxford: Basil Blackwell.

Macauley, S. (1963), 'Non-contractual relations in business: a preliminary study', *American Sociological Review*, 28: 55–66.

Macneil, I. R. (1987), 'Relational contract theory as sociology: a reply to Professors Lindenberg and de Vos', *Journal of Institutional and Theoretical Economics*, 143: 272–90.

Merton, R.K. (ed.) (1952), *Reader in Bureaucracy*, Glencoe, N.J.: Free Press.

Miles, R. E. and Snow, C. C. (1986), 'Network organizations: new concepts for new forms', *California Management Review*, 28: 62–73.

Monden, Y. (1983), *Toyota Production System*, Atlanta: Institute of Industrial Engineering and Management Press.

Neuville, J. Ph. (1997a), *Le modèle japonais à l'épreuve des faits*, Paris: Economica.

Neuville, J. Ph. (1997b), 'La stratégie de la confiance', *Sociologie du Travail*, 3/97: 297–319.

Neuville, J. Ph. (1998), 'La tentation opportuniste. Figures et dynamique de la coopération inter-individuelle dans le partenariat industriel', *Revue Française de Sociologie*, 39–1: 71–103.

Nooteboom, B. (1992), 'A postmodern philosophy of markets', *International Studies of Management and Organization*, 22: 53–76.

Nooteboom, B. (1996), 'Trust, opportunism and governance : a process and control model', *Organization Studies*, 17/6: 985–1010.

Ohno, T. (1988), *Toyota Production System*, Cambridge, Mass.: Productivity Press.

Olson, M. (1965), *The Logic of Collective Action*, Cambridge, Mass: Harvard University Press.

Phillips, A. (1960), 'A theory of interfirm organization', *Quarterly Journal of Economics*, 74: 602–13.

Piore, M. and Sabel, C. (1984), *The Second Industrial Divide*, New York: Basic Books.

Popkin, S. (1981), 'Public choice and rural development. Free riders, lemons, and institutional design', in C. Russel and N. Nicholson (eds), *Public Choice and Rural Development*, Washington, D.C.: Resources for the Future.

Powell, W. W. (1990), 'Neither market nor hierarchy: network forms of organization', *Research in Organizational Behavior*, 12: 295–336.

Powell, W. W. and Smith-Doerr L. (1994), 'Networks and economic life', in N. J. Smelser and R. Swedberg (eds), *The Handbook of Economic Sociology*, Princeton: Princeton University Press.

Pratt, J. and Zeckhauser, R. (eds) (1985), *Principals and Agents : The Structure of Business*, Boston: Harvard Business School Press.

Richardson, G. (1972), 'The organization of industry', *Economic Journal*, 82: 883–96.

Sabel, C. (1993), 'Constitutional ordering in historical context', in F. W. Scharpf (ed.), *Games in Hierarchies and Networks*, Frankfurt am Main: Campus Verlag.

Sako, M. (1992), *Prices, Quality and Trust. Interfirm Relations in Britain and Japan*, Cambridge: Cambridge University Press.

Saxenian, A.L. (1994), *Regional Networks: Industrial Adaptation in Silicon Valley and Route 128*, Cambridge, Mass.: Harvard University Press.

Shapiro, C. (1982), 'Consumer information, product quality and seller reputation', *Bell Journal of Economics*, 13: 20–35.

Siamwalla, A. (1978), 'Farmers and middlemen: aspects of agricultural marketing in Thailand', *Economic Bulletin for Asia and the Pacific*, June: 38–50.

Smith Ring, P. and Van de Ven, A. H. (1994), 'Developmental processes of cooperative interorganizational relationships', *Academy of Management Review*, 19/1: 90–118.

Thorelli, H. B. (1986), 'Networks: between markets and hierarchies', *Strategic Management Journal*, 7: 37–51.

Tirole, J. (1989), *The Theory of Industrial Organization*, Cambridge, Mass.: MIT Press.

Warren, R. (1967), 'The Interorganizational field as a focus of investigation', *Administrative Science Quarterly*, 12: 396–419.

Williamson, O. E. (1975), *Markets and Hierarchies: Analysis and Anti-Trust Implications*, New York: Free Press.

Williamson, O. E. (1985), *The Economic Institutions of Capitalism*, New York: Free Press.

Wilson, R. (1985), 'Reputations in games and markets', in A. Roth (ed.), *Game-Theoretic Models of Bargaining*, Cambridge, Mass.: Cambridge University Press.

Zucker, L. (1986), 'Production of trust: institutional sources of economic structure, 1840–1920', *Research in Organizational Behavior*, 8: 53–111.

Part 2

Differentiated competences, coordination mechanisms and learning outcomes

4 The dynamic efficiency of networks

Bart Nooteboom

Introduction

We take the competence/resource-based view of firms for granted (Penrose 1959): the firm is made up from a number of competencies, based on resources, embodied in a configuration of various forms of capital (financial, human, social), which to a greater or lesser extent is idiosyncratic to the firm. It is such unique capabilities of firms that allow them a basis for profit.

Step by step we will develop a number of propositions (P), on the basis of which a trade-off will be made between more and less integrated forms of organization. Some principles apply generally, under all conditions, others only under certain conditions (C). For an introduction, we consider the strategic context in which firms operate, and specify the notion of integrated and disintegrated forms of organization.

Several causes are yielding radical product differentiation. Technological development yields flexible methods of production and acts as an enabling cause.[1] Individualization of consumer behaviour provides a market opportunity. Globalization of markets provides an incentive, to reduce pressures of price competition by product differentiation. But radical product differentiation greatly increases the complexity of both input and output markets, and to be 'sustainable' (Zuscovitch 1994), it requires that firms concentrate on 'core competencies' (Prahalad and Hamel 1990). That implies a first principle (P1) under the condition (C) of complex and changing markets and technology:

C: Complex and rapidly changing markets and technology.

P1:   One must outsource as many activities as possible, outside of core competencies, even if that entails 'transaction specific investments', in the sense treated in transaction cost economics (TCE).

In particular, rather than claiming to have full competence in all dimensions of their products and production processes, firms should make use of the specific competencies of suppliers not only in production, but also in the process of research and development. Rather than making blueprints of required inputs that are 'thrown over the wall' to suppliers, there should be 'early supplier involvement' in the design process (Helper

1991; Lamming 1993). This further increases the specificity of investments in the transaction relation. As indicated in TCE, this yields dependencies and risks of 'hold-up', which raise complicated issues of 'governance' of relations between formally independent but materially dependent firms, in forms of organization 'between market and hierarchy' (Williamson 1985; Nooteboom 1996).

Innovation and learning form a crucial dimension of the problem, but traditional TCE does not deal with that (Nooteboom 1992). How one deals with that dimension depends on one's theory of knowledge and learning. In Nooteboom (1992, 1999b) it was argued that the implicit epistemology of mainstream economics is inadequate, and the use of a constructivist perspective is proposed (see also Berger and Luckmann 1966). According to that perspective, perception, interpretation and evaluation are conducted on the basis of cognitive categories which are in turn developed from experience in employing such categories, in interaction with the physical and social environment. As a result, knowledge is path-dependent, and people (and firms) with different trajectories of development, in different markets and technologies, perceive things differently. As a result:

C: Complex and rapidly changing markets and technology.
P2:   Outside sources are needed not only for static efficiency, but also for dynamic efficiency: for learning (complementary cognitive competence).

Networks are in fashion. The underlying idea in the strategic context indicated here is that central control is often not efficient, and that disintegration is often better. But networks of firms, such as industrial districts, obviously are not always better than large, integrated firms; small is not always beautiful. What exactly are the comparative advantages of integration and disintegration? When should activities be integrated under unified ownership, by merger and acquisition (MA), when should they be brought under shared ownership (equity joint ventures), when should they be more loosely connected by means of alliances, and when should they interact only by arms-length transactions? These are the questions we seek to answer in this chapter.

We define a network as a pattern of more or less lasting linkages between nodes, where the nodes represent different organizational units. These units may be firms or divisions within firms (departments, subsidiaries). According to this definition, we can have networks within a firm, between firms, and combinations of them. The linkages may be uni- or bidirectional, representing flows of products (goods and services), sharing of resources, relations of ownership or other forms of control, lines of cooperation and communication.

More precisely, linkages can be 'vertical', constituting flows of products (goods or services) from suppliers to users, in intrafirm value chains or interfirm value systems (Porter 1985). The linkages may also be 'horizontal', where similar, competing products (substitutes in consumption) are pooled to share a common resource of production or distribution, in a scale strategy. The linkages may also be 'diagonal' or diversified, where dissimilar products, which may be complementary in research, marketing, distribution or service are pooled to share a common resource (an R&D facility, production facility, distribution channel, service facility, brand name), in a scope strategy. All these linkages can have different strengths, in terms of size (volume), type, frequency, and durability of exchange, and in terms of force of control.

From the literature on incomplete contracts (Hart 1995) we take the following principle:

P3:   There are two main dimensions of integration: centralization of decision rights and centralization of rights to profits.

We define (dis)integration as (de)centralization of decison rights and/or rights to profits. One can have one without the other. For example: in a centralized firm with dispersed shareholding there is decentralization of rights to profits with centralization of decision rights. In a single-owner holding company we have the opposite: centralized rights to profits and decentralized decision rights. A balanced equity joint venture (JV) yields an intermediate case: rights to profits and decision rights are shared equally between parent companies (which usually will have some degree of centralization of profit and decision rights). A graph of organizational forms along these two dimensions was proposed by Nooteboom (1999a): see Figure 4.1.

The scheme includes the perhaps unfamiliar notion of a 'virtual firm': a firm with an 'umbrella' (brand name; limited but strategically crucial central coordination) covering dispersed, decentralized activities and considerable dispersion of profit rights. An example is Benetton, which provides a brand name and an ICT network for mutual coordination and adaptation for fast local response to differentiated and highly variable demand. It is close to networks of differentiated, independent firms with mutual adaptation and coordination ('flexible specialization', cf. Piore and Sabel 1983), but entails more central coordination and more concentration of ownership. A 'federated firm' has a somewhat higher level of centralization of decision rights and profit rights. An example is the recent federalization of IBM, which was instituted to compete with more flexible, specialized and independent firms.

Governance

First we summarize some general principles of governance (Grandori 1997; Nooteboom 1999a). Governance aims to achieve goals and contain risks:

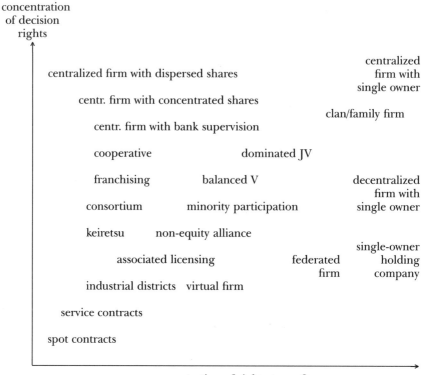

Figure 4.1 Degree of integration

Source: Nooteboom 1999a

P4:   One can govern by control, on the basis of decision rights, or by motivation. Control can be bureaucratic (by administrative fiat) or contractual (legal). Motivation can be based on material incentives (profit rights) or ethical norms and values or bonds of friend- or kinship.

We can distinguish between behavioural and technical governance. Behavioural governance deals with the alignment of interests, incentives, opportunism, loyalty. Technical governance refers to the control of spillover (unintended outward flow) of knowledge, and the alignment of technical specifications. The latter may be needed to ensure appropriate connections in vertical linkages, and to ensure common usage of resources in horizontal and diagonal linkages. This is the case to the extent that a technology is systemic rather than stand-alone (Teece 1988), and there control needs to be close to the extent that no standards across interfaces between component technology have been established (Teece 1986; Langlois and Robertson 1995).

There are well-known motivational advantages in the decentralization of profit rights, with independent firms striving for efficiency and innovation for the sake of their own survival and profit (unless motivation is damped by mono- or oligopoly and entry barriers):

P5:   In principle, decentralized profit rights are good for motivation.

Integration may be impossible simply for technical reasons:

C: The resources that need to be integrated are not separable from other resources.
P6:   One has to either integrate more than is desired (with a view to core competencies) or renounce integration.

Cooperation between competitors (substitute products in the same market) yields much more of a behavioural governance problem than the use of networks for pooling complementary products or competencies. In the first case there is a zero-sum and in the letter case a positive sum game. On the other hand, the integration of different firms is costly and risky, due to possible incompatibilities between different firm-specific cultures and ways of doing things. This risk is greater to the extent that the firms are engaged in different technologies and markets. This confirms the argument in favour of concentration on core competencies. Thus:

P7:   In case of cooperation between substitute activities (competitors) integration (MA) has an advantage of behavioural control and may be feasible in terms of the costs and risks of integration;
      On the other hand, in case of cooperation between complementary activities, alliances in networks may be feasible concerning behavioural control, and costs and risks of full integration (MA) would be higher.

Another argument for integration can arise when for technical reasons (systemic technology) coordination is required, and this is difficult to achieve between separate firms. Let us first consider the disintegrated form as the base case. Contingent contracting between independent firms is possible when monitoring of performance (output) or effort (input) is possible and contingencies are not uncertain (one knows what relevant contingencies can occur), and their complexity and variability is not excessive. When complexity and variability increase, some central coordination may be needed, by some form of bureaucratic supervision and coordination. This typically applies to a building consortium, with some centralized bureaucratic coordination by one of the participants (Grandori 1997). Thus:

C: Monitoring is possible and there is no (radical) uncertainty, so that contingent contracting is possible.

P8:   Contracts between firms are preferable, with some centralized bureaucratic control to the extent that contingencies are complex or variable.

However, when monitoring is possible but contingent contracting is not, due to uncertainty, then integration has advantages, as is well known from TCE: within a firm, decisions and conflict resolution do not have to be upheld in court, but can be based on administrative fiat, and information needed for monitoring can be demanded far beyond what can be demanded from an outside firm. Thus:

C: Monitoring is technically possible but contingent contracting is not, and control is important (e.g. because technology is systemic).

P9:   The integrated firm is preferable for its advantages of administrative fiat.

These advantages of integration need some qualification: inside a firm, administrative fiat and monitoring can have adverse effects on motivation. It can lead to 'influence costs' (Milgrom and Roberts 1989): counter-productive meddling and jockeying for position to enhance careers. But within firms control *can* be relaxed to yield more autonomous units. And, on the other hand, there *can* be durable linkages between firms without formal control of ownership or contract, on the basis of mutual interest, or loyalty based on institutions, habituation or bonds of kinship or friendship (Nooteboom 1996). That is the basis for Figure 4.1.

Another reason for integration is that it yields better means to control spillover. This is particularly important when knowledge is documented. When knowledge is tacit (Polanyi 1962, 1966, 1969), its transfer requires close interaction and development of mutual understanding (Kogut 1988; Choi and Lee 1997; Brown and Duguid 1991), so that spillover does not occur easily. The risk of spillover of documented knowledge is greater to the extent that partners in cooperation have direct or indirect links to competitors. Control of spillover of documented knowledge does not require integration if the partner is able to prevent it and one can monitor either whether spillover through the partner occurs or his efforts to control it. When this condition is not satisfied, and therefore control does require integration, a JV in which the pooled activities are brought together may suffice. Thus:

C: Knowledge is not tacit, partners have direct or indirect links with competitors, and spillover or efforts to control it cannot be monitored.

P10:   Some degree of integration is needed, but a JV may suffice. But when knowledge is tacit, this blocks spillover and integration for spillover control is not needed.

However, governance by any form of control becomes impossible when outputs and inputs of effort cannot be measured. This may be the case for several reasons. One reason is that production necessarily takes place outside the observational reach of the firm (for example: driving a taxi). Another reason is that the effort cannot be judged by its very nature (for example: abstract professional activity). As is known from the principal-agent literature, then bureaucratic and contractual control both break down, and recourse to self-motivation by decentralization of profit rights is often required. We say 'often', because in contrast to what most economists would say, it is possible that agents have an internal drive, apart from profit, towards loyalty and effort.

Thus taxi drivers and professionals performing abstract work should preferably be claimants of residual profits: independent entrepreneurs or members of a legal partnership. In case of independent firms, behavioural governance is needed when there is cooperation on the basis of specific assets, which create exit barriers, which create vulnerability to 'hold-up', as analysed in TCE. How can governance be tackled in this situation? Instruments for governance are the following: bureaucratic or legal control (to the extent that it is still possible), switching costs due to ownership of specific assets, incentives on the basis of value relative to alternatives that partners offer each other, hostages, reputation mechanisms, and trust on the basis of values/norms, habituation, bonds of family, kinship, friendship, clan (Nooteboom 1996). The optimal mixing of these instruments is a complicated affair which goes beyond the scope of the present chapter. To summarize:

C: Monitoring of performance and effort is impossible and cooperation yields exit barriers.

P11:   Decentralization of profit rights is needed, with governance consisting of a mix of: control, incentive alignment and trust generating forms of bonding.

An important remaining question is how to choose between different forms of more or less decentralized profit rights; in particular the choice between a JV and a non-equity alliance. Generally, the set-up costs of a JV are higher: one needs to set up a new firm, with its own management and staff, and there is more risk involved in the integration into a joint operation of staff from the different parent companies, with their idiosyncratic cultures, systems of remuneration and ways of doing things. The higher set-up costs reduce flexibility to the extent that they raise exit barriers. Setting up a new firm is not feasible if its purpose is not clear. A non-equity alliance gives more flexibility of exploring, reducing and extending areas of cooperation. The advantage is that when it is relevant, spillover as well as conflicts of interest are more easily controlled (see P10). As a matter of general principle:

P12:   The choice between a JV and a non-equity alliance depends on a trade-off between on the one hand the greater grip of behavioural and spillover control of the former and the lower set-up costs and greater flexibility of the latter.

Having established definitions and ground rules, we now proceed to an analysis of efficiency.

Static efficiency

Here we do not discuss allocative efficiency, and focus on efficiency in production, marketing and distribution (static efficiency). Efficiency in innovation (dynamic efficiency) is discussed in a later section. Two central dimensions of static efficiency are economies of scope and scale. Economies of scale have become less in some areas of production; particularly in information and communication technology (ICT): hardware has become small and cheap, and software easy to use. In other areas of production they remain unchanged: the scale effect of physical capacity.[2] As argued by Ohmae (1989), in many industries the importance of fixed costs has greatly increased. Due to automation, variable labour costs have declined relative to fixed costs of investment in technology. Up to a point, one can make costs of equipment variable by leasing, but increasingly, due to increased product differentiation, installations need to have a dedicated architecture. Ohmae applies this also to IT: while in the past one could have access to outside computing capacity by means of timesharing, now firms typically need dedicated architectures of IT networks. A criticism of this view is that it is valid only to the extent that the technology is not modular. When one can configure dedicated architectures from standardized elements the problem largely disappears. Nevertheless, the point is clear that in many respects fixed costs have indeed increased. This applies not only to physical assets of production, but also to R&D, brand name, distribution and sales force. For sales, one may employ outsiders on a commission basis, but then one still needs to provide the requisite training, manuals and other facilities.

There are economies of scale also in transaction costs (Nooteboom 1993). Transaction costs are higher for small firms: both for themselves and for their partners in transactions or networks. This is due to the following characteristics that are typical of small firms:[3] limited resources of specialized staff support; a practical and short-term, improvisational approach, rather than an explicit and long-term strategic policy; practical and tacit knowledge, with limited documentation and few formal procedures. These characteristics can be explained on the basis of dis-economies of small scale (high set-up costs of information systems and procedures) and the limited need for them due to direct supervision. As a result, transaction costs of search, evaluation, contract design and monitoring of contract execution are high, both for the firm itself and its partners. Due to lack of a spread of risks, the risk of default is higher, which also increases the risk for partners. In an attempt to compensate for this, small firms rely more on reputation mechanisms (rather than detailed contracting), and on network contacts to support reputation mechanisms and to compensate for lack of staff services. Particularly for small firms it is useful to seek economy of scale and scope in sharing fixed costs in general, and in staff or information facilities in particular, in some form of cooperation with other firms. Thus:

P13:   An important objective, particularly for small firms, is to achieve economies of scope and scale by increased utilization of fixed assets, including assets for the reduction of transaction costs.

Thus the question concerning the productive efficiency of networks, from a static perspective, in large part is a question to what extent networks can contribute to the coverage of fixed costs, when those obtain. To the extent that networks go together with more fragmentation in the sense of fewer shared assets, and duplication of fixed costs, they are productively less efficient.

Scale can be increased in two ways: by further penetration in a given market (increased market share), or by expansion into new markets.

We established before (P7) that for reasons of behavioural governance increase of share by pooling the same products in the same market requires integration by MA. Expansion into new markets can be achieved by own investment or by riding piggy-back on existing local resources (of production, marketing and distribution). The first will often take too much time, and tends to generate additional fixed costs. Thus the second is generally to be preferred, from the perspective of productive efficiency. Here, if the products brought into the market compete with those in existing local systems, sale of property rights (licensing) or MA is the best for reasons of governance (P7). However, costs and risks of MA can be high, due to the difference between partners. Then a decentralized form of organizing the firm is to be preferred (e.g: holding company). When the products are complementary, in distribution or marketing, there is less conflict of interest, and scale can be achieved by the more decentralized means of an (equity or non-equity) alliance. But then we are really talking about scope rather than scale.

P14:   Scale strategy: integration under unified ownership, in an intrafirm network, by means of MA, of competing producers in a given market. One may also consider integration of competing products from different markets, by MA, but to the extent that the markets are different this may conflict with the focus on core competence in the areas of marketing, distribution and sourcing. Then it seems preferable to sell or buy a licence. When integration under unified ownership does take place, a large degree of autonomy should be allowed to units in different markets.

When products are differentiated, opportunities for economy of scope are determined by the flexibility of the resource (in R&D, production, IT, marketing, distribution): to what extent can it be employed for different products? Typically, resources of brand name and distribution can be used for different products if those have some complementarity in distribution, which implies complementarity in transportation, perception/image, purchase or consumption. Thus one can combine different types of car in a distribution channel, and different fashion goods (watches, shoes, clothing) under the umbrella of a brand name (Swatch, Benetton, etc.). In a service network, efficiency can be increased by combining different products that can utilize the same service competence. Production machinery is typically more dedicated, but due to novel ICT flexibility has increased in some areas (flexible production automation): flexible prototyping by representation and simulation in a computer; programmable general purpose machinery for working metal, wood, textiles; programmable extrusion and moulding machinery for plastics.

Scope can be increased either by product diversification or by adding complementary products from other producers. The condition then is that the existing resources are sufficiently flexible to accommodate the novel products. Product diversification should be consistent with core competence, and building one's own new products can be too slow. Pooling complementary products with others is feasible by means of alliances, and desirable if the products fall outside core competence. The choice between equity or non-equity alliance was discussed before (P12).

P15:   Scope strategy: economy of scope requires that resources are sufficiently flexible to accommodate different products. If it fits in core competence, diversification can be achieved by building one's own new products or by MA, but the first may be too slow and the second may carry too much cost and risk of integration. The alternative that is generally to be preferred is to pool complementary products from different producers in an alliance.

The reciprocal adoption of each other's complementary products by two producers, in an alliance, is particularly attractive, because then both sides possess a hostage from the partner. If in the course of an alliance one partner were to absorb the competence to produce the partner's product,[4]

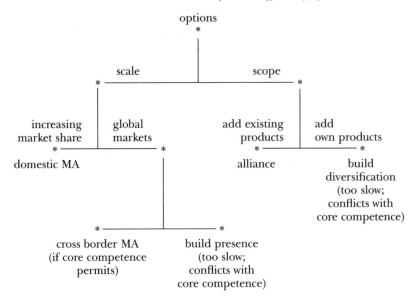

Figure 4.2 Options for covering fixed costs

or to enter the partner's market, and thereby expropriate the partner's contribution, the other partner could reciprocate. The preferred options are represented in Figure 4.2.

These conclusions are in accordance with evidence that MA tends to be more successful when dealing with similar activities, within core competence, while alliances tend to be more successful when dealing with complementary activities, from different areas of core competence, in different markets. On the basis of a sample of alliances and acquisitions of each of the top fifty companies in the US, Europe and Japan, Bleeke and Ernst (1991) found that of all acquisitions in existing geographical markets 94 per cent succeeded, while of acquisitions across different geographical markets only 8 per cent succeeded. Of alliances across different geographical markets 62 per cent succeeded, while of alliances within existing markets only 25 per cent succeeded.

Thus, from the static perspective of efficiency, in governance and the utilization of fixed costs, interfirm networks are less efficient than integration in intrafirm networks in a scale strategy, and more efficient in a scope strategy. This yields an important element in our dynamic theory of network efficiency.

A cycle of learning

For a study of dynamic efficiency we require a theory of innovation, and for this we require a theory of organizational learning (for a survey, see Cohen and Sproull 1996). One of the greatest challenges here is to explain the relation between 'exploitation and exploration' (March 1991; Holland 1975), which have alternatively been called 'single vs. double loop' (Argyris and Schön 1978), or 'first order vs. second order' learning (Fiol and Lyles 1985; Hedberg, Nystrom and Starbuck 1976). For this, we employ the theory set out in Nooteboom (1999b), which was inspired by the 'genetic epistemology' of Jean Piaget (1970, 1974).

Learning and innovation are reconstructed as a process with different stages. Nooteboom (1999b) uses the notion of a script to model cognitive as well as productive practices. A script has an 'architecture', consisting of a sequence of nodes that represent activities. A node is like a variable in a mathematical formula, allowing for different 'substitutions', which represent different ways of performing an activity. This notion allows for different levels of innovation. There is 'radical' architectural innovation, in which nodes from different previous practices are brought into novel scripts, comparable to Schumpeter's 'novel combinations'. There is incremental 'parametric' innovation by novel substitutions: within the practice of a script, activities are performed in novel ways while maintaining the architecture of the script.

At first the result of radical innovation is unsettled: the novel practice is as yet indeterminate, and must be 'consolidated', very much by trial and error, into a 'dominant design'. Novel practice is messed up with encumbrances from past practice, that are redundant or ill-fitting in the novel practice. For example, in the transition from wood to iron construction (of bridges, etc.), principles of wood construction (wedges for connections) were retained that for iron did not make sense (connections by means of nails or welding were more appropriate).

These redundancies and misfits have to be teased out in experimentation with variations. One finds a novel way of doing things, but it is not yet understood precisely how or why it works. In other words: knowledge is procedural rather than declarative (Cohen and Bacdayan 1994; Cohen 1991), and tacit rather than documented. It is important not to let consolidation set in too early, before alternative reconfigurations have been sufficiently explored to yield an optimal dominant design. As this process proceeds, the novel practice gets better understood, as to how and why it works, and knowledge tends to develop from procedural to declarative, and from tacit to documented, although tacit elements are likely to remain to a greater or lesser extent.[5] The architecture of the script becomes determinate and can be specified. This allows for more rationalization and systematization, a grip for scientific analysis, and formal procedures and training, which in turn allow for specialization and division of work, and the development of standards for the interfaces between different segments of the script.

The next stage is that this design is applied to novel use contexts, in a process of 'generalization', which goes together with increase of scale, which yields further efficiency. As experience accrues, efficiency further increases by 'learning by doing', along 'experience curves' (Yelle 1979).

The stages of consolidation and generalization can be seen to support 'exploitation' or 'first-order learning', which yields a narrowing down of substitutions in nodes and sequences of nodes, down to an optimal practice, in a given context, and a widening of contexts ('generalization') to reap the benefits.

Next is the stage of 'differentiation': as application is generalized in different contexts, differences in appropriate application are required and may be recognized and allowed, in incremental innovation, with different substitutions into nodes and some alterations in the sequencing of nodes. However, as the practice becomes normal, it may be taken for granted, and may become routine. This can provide an obstacle to the recognition of the need and of opportunities for differentiation and reciprocation. Then failures of the practice in novel contexts may yield the pressure for opening up to adjustments, but this may not suffice. Painful misfits trigger action only if the pain is felt.

Next, as the architecture becomes less fixed and more messy, with branches extending in different directions, there emerges a motivation for 'cleaning up', in a more parsimonious structure. There also arise hints for the direction in which such a novel synthesis might be sought, for regrouping substitutions into novel nodes, novel combinations and architectures of nodes. This occurs as in their branching out scripts come into contact with each other, on the basis of common substitutions into nodes in the different scripts, which suggests that it may be worth trying a recollection of substitutions into novel nodes or a swap of nodes.

In this stage of 'reciprocation', in a confusion of loosened connections and experiments of novel combinations, we wind up at the beginning: an indeterminate architecture of indeterminate nodes, in a radical innovation of 'novel combinations'. The stages of differentiation and reciprocation can be seen to yield the earlier notion of 'exploration'. The theory indicates how exploitation and exploration are connected in an overall process of development.

In this theory there are two types of variety which are necessary for innovation: variety of exploitation in the stage of generalization, as a precondition for variety of exploration in the stages of differentiation, reciprocation and the trial of novel combinations. In other words: a variety of context is required to generate a variety of content. The theory is illustrated in Figure 4.3.

In this stage theory, the question arises how rigid the stages are: can a stage be skipped, and can reversals of order occur? For example, could one go straight from consolidation to differentiation, i.e. expand the area of application of a novel script while allowing for differentiation from the start? This appears possible in principle. But other modifications seem difficult. Consolidation seems a logical condition for expansion of

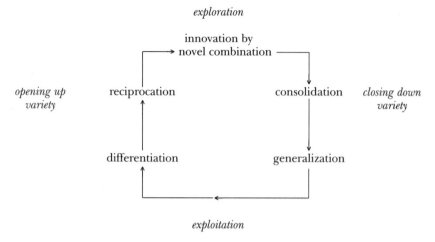

Figure 4.3 Cycle of learning

application. Variety of exploitation seems a precondition for variety of exploration.

The cycle applies to a given technology, and a firm may be simultaneously involved in different technologies in different stages of development. The question then is how a firm deals with such differences. One stage is likely to require other attitudes, skills and procedures than another stage. As indicated: consolidation requires a narrowing of focus, to exploit the potential of the innovation, while differentiation and reciprocation requires a loosening and opening up to novel needs and opportunities. How can these be combined in one culture, strategy and structure?

We now proceed to apply the theory for an analysis of dynamic efficiency.

Dynamic efficiency

It is a long-standing issue in the (neo)schumpeterian, geographical and organizational literatures whether integrated structures of large firms or disintegrated structures of small firms are dynamically more efficient. Some extoll the dynamic capabilities of disintegrated structures of small, independent firms (Piore and Sabel 1983), while others point to their limitations in view of the advantages of large, integrated firms (Amin 1989). A survey of the literature (Nooteboom 1994) indicates that while small, independent firms tend to engage less in R&D, when they do, they tend to do so more intensively and more efficiently (Nooteboom 1991; Nooteboom and Vossen 1995). Part of the explanation is that there are fixed set-up costs in R&D, which constitute an economy of scale and create an entry barrier especially for small firms. On the other hand, small firms tend to be faster, more flexible and more daring with respect to radical change, partly due to lack of vested interests and lack of rational evaluation.

The finding should be refined by taking into account differences in stage of development, and type of technology. For lack of specialized researchers and due to a more practical, short-term orientation, small firms tend to be weaker in systemic, fundamental research, while they are better at applying and commercializing the results of fundamental innovations produced elsewhere. While they have fewer and less specialized resources, in the execution of R&D they tend to be more motivated and less bureaucratic. Thus there is 'dynamic complementarity': small firms tend to be good where large ones are weak, and vice versa. The advantages of large firms are material and the advantages of small firms are behavioural (Rothwell 1989). Thus:

P16:   Small independent firms in disintegrated structures tend to engage less in R&D, but when they do they tend to do so more intensively and more efficiently. There is dynamic complementarity: large integrated firms tend to to better in systemic and fundamental research, while small firms tend to be better at novel combinations in application and commercialization.

Related to this, there are differences in 'dynamic transaction costs': the costs of transferring knowledge or competence. Inside the small firm, researchers encounter fewer problems of internal acceptance and implementation of novelty, partly because the developers and users are often the same people. However, small firms are weaker at incremental innovation in systemic technology: this requires that during innovation systemic linkages between a sufficient range of component technologies are coordinated and kept in pace, so that they move together in harmony (Teece 1986). They can try to achieve such harmony by cooperating in innovation networks, but that is more complicated than coordination within a firm. It becomes easier, however, as technology settles down sufficiently to yield industry standards on the basis of the dominant designs that emerge from the stage of consolidation.

It has often been claimed that small firms have a disadvantage in appropriation: it is relatively costly for small firms to protect innovation by patents, and they have fewer resources to make patent protection feasible. But this applies only when knowledge is documented. We noted before that, in general, small firms engage more in tacit knowledge: in small firms documentation of knowledge is relatively expensive and less needed. An additional benefit here is that tacit knowledge facilitates appropriation. As noted before (P10), more integrated structures have an advantage in the control of spillover, but this is relevant only when knowledge is not tacit. When knowledge is tacit, then for the purpose of control one need not bring possible recipients of the knowledge under unified ownership, because control can be exercised in the very process of close interaction that is needed for the exchange or pooling of knowledge. And contrary to what some researchers say (Hennart 1988; Osborn and Baughn 1990), integration under unified ownership is not needed, under those conditions, in order to enable communication. Independent firms can undoubtedly interact closely on the basis of tacit knowledge in the early stages of technological development.

A further consideration derives from the theory of product/technology lifecycles. That theory is close to our theory of cycles developed in the previous section. A 'fundamental' innovation, in the form of a new function or a radically new way of performing an existing function, yields an initial phase of consolidation, with the development of a dominant design, followed by a stage in which attention shifts to greater efficiency by means of process innovation, and in which the market for the new product is expanded. This goes together with a wearing out of initial innovation monopoly, due to imitation by new entrants, lapse of patents or invention around them, and a resulting pressure on price, and pressure to reduce costs. One opportunity to be derived from this is to employ the expansion of the market to utilize economies of scale. Recall that earlier (P7) we found that utilization of economy of scale tends to require integration. This goes together with either fast growth to large size or the takeover of successful entrepreneurs surviving from the innovation stage. The basic technology has become standard, with a consolidation of tacit knowledge into documented and more easily diffusible knowledge. Next, due to ongoing pressure on price, there is a tendency to differentiate products, in order to escape from pure price competition, to the extent that the market offers a potential for it. Whether the industry integrates or disintegrates in these stages depends on the possibility of separating different steps in the overall production process, by modularity on the basis of diffused know-how and standards for interfaces (Langlois and Robertson 1995), and on opportunities for product differention. Generally, at this stage of development technology has settled down and uncertainty has decreased, which yields better opportunities for contracting between firms (P8, P9). At the end of the lifecycle, the next innovation forms a substitute, and only small residual 'niche' markets remain, which tend to be exploited by small firms who do not innovate radically, but who in that stage no longer face the disadvantage of diseconomy of small scale, since the large volume demand has shifted to the novel innovation (Nooteboom 1984). Thus:

C: Stage of consolidation or generalization (so that knowledge is no longer tacit, and there are pressures to reduce costs), and there are economies of scale and/or technology is systemic, or:
The stage of incremental innovation for differentiation, and technology is systemic.

P17a: Large, integrated firms have the advantage from the perspectives of behavioural and technical control (including control of spillover).

C: The same stages, but economy of scale is limited and technology is stand-alone and industry standards have developed and uncertainty has subsided sufficiently to enable contractual associations between firms.

P17b: Small firms can keep up, by utilizing forms of cooperation (industrial districts, associations, consortia).

On the other hand, in the novel combinations of radical innovation and creative destruction, as analysed before, disintegrated structures of differentiated units have the advantage in the stages of reciprocation and exploration of novel combinations. There are many reasons for this. One reason is that systemic coherence breaks down, and the advantage in that of integrated firms falls away. Having built up their size and success on the exploitation of incumbent technology, they have more vested interests in maintaining it (not to cannibalize existing products). They are likely to suffer more from routinization that blinds one to novel needs and opportunities in novel contexts. Radically novel combinations would cause too much break-up of existing integrated and often path-dependent structures. Their advantage in systemic coherence during the stages of generalization and incremental innovation during differentiation turn into disadvantages in the 'creative destruction' of reciprocation and novel combinations. Disintegrated structures of differentiated units in the form of constellations of different small firms also allow for more flexibility of changing patterns of interaction to explore novel combinations: trying one combination and breaking it up to team up with others if it fails.

Further reasons derive from our earlier analysis. Under the conditions of change and uncertainty of this stage, it is more urgent to utilize a variety of outside sources, rather than exploit internal knowledge (P2). Under these conditions, existing knowledge and standards no longer apply, and knowledge tends to be tacit. As a result, monitoring of activities is difficult, which also favours disintegration (P11). Furthermore, the tacitness of knowledge in these stages blocks spillover so that integration for spillover control is less needed (P10). Markets are still emerging and small, and novelty is still monopolistic, so that there are neither pressures nor opportunities for utilizing economy of scale (P13, P14). Complementarity of assets and competence is crucial for the speedy and flexible exploration required here, so that economy of scope prevails over economy of scale, and this favours more disintegrated structures in the form of alliances (P15). In the choice between a JV and a non-equity alliance the advantage goes to the latter, because uncertainty is too great to pin down exactly what would need to belong to the novel firm to be set up in the equity joint venture (P12). Thus:

C: Stage of reciprocation or exploration of novel combinations so that:

knowledge is still tacit and integration for spillover control is not needed, there is great need for a variety of outside sources to cope with uncertainty, and flexibility of shifting alliances is needed for the exploration of novel combinations. Then the advantages of integration in systemic technology break down and turn into disadvantages.

P18:   Disintegrated structures of differentiated units have the advantage. Scope dominates scale, and scope favours alliances rather than integration.

By disintegrated structures we think primarily of networks of small firms, but one can also think of disintegrated structures within a large firm: the federated firm or the virtual firm (Figure 4.1), with highly independent units with a large share in profit rights, to allow for and promote 'intrapreneurship' for exploring novel combinations. We propose that the latter structures are arising as the large firm's answer to the comparative advantage of industrial districts under the presently prevailing conditions of creative destruction. Such structures have an advantage in providing central coordination or a brand name, but a disadvantage is that with the diversity required to provide a seedbed for novel combinations, the building of a joint culture or way of doing things becomes more difficult. Large firms can also get along in radical innovation by letting small innovative firms do the exploration and taking them over when they are succesful. But that will succeed, and the entrepreneurial success of the acquired firm will survive, only if integration is not too tight: the large firm should have a disintegrated structure. On the other side, small firms may achieve economies of scope by sharing fixed resources, and may also develop a joint brand name, but then a problem of free-riding may arise, which would yield the need for some central monitoring and control.

It is important to note that the claims cannot be reversed. Industrial districts are not always the engines of creative destruction indicated here. Disintegrated structures are needed for radical innovation, but that does not imply that disintegrated structures always produce radical innovation. Next to disintegration, a necessary condition is differentiation, to provide a seedbed for novel combinations. There are several types of industrial districts. The openings for this are present in the qualifications in the various principles analysed above. See, in particular, P17a. Economy of scale does not obtain if the market is too small (as in residual markets, indicated above), products are highly differentiated and the corresponding technology is inflexible, or the nature of the technology does not entail much effect of scale (P7). It can happen that knowledge remains tacit after consolidation, thus eliminating the need to integrate for spillover control (P10). A number of technologies are stand-alone rather than systemic (P16). Turbulence, generating uncertainty, may remain after consolidation, as in high-tech industries with ongoing radical innovation, or in fashion industries where ongoing rapid adjustments in differentiated products are required. Under ongoing uncertainty the needs for a variety of outside sources (P2), economy of scope in complementary competencies or resources (P15) and the need for flexible associations (P12) remain. Monitoring effort may remain impossible, thus favouring decentralized profit rights (P11).

C: Economy of scope keeps dominating scale, technology is stand-alone, knowledge remains tacit even after consolidation, monitoring even within firms is difficult even after consolidation, uncertainty remains, with the ongoing need for rapid adjustments, a variety of outside sources and flexibility of association.

P19: Disintegrated structures can have a prolonged existence.

Thus:

P20: There are different types of industrial districts: those that offer differentiation and utilize their potential to produce radical innovation and those that exploit niches where the need to integrate is absent or advantages of disintegration remain when there is no radical innovation.

Discussion

Some of the results of our analysis (P17, P18) indicate that corresponding to the cycle of learning (Figure 4.3) there is a cycle of integration and disintegration (Figure 4.4):

*   A stage of loosening and subsequent disintegration of intrafirm networks, with more autonomy of units, or a transition to interfirm networks, by alliances between firms, to allow for reciprocation and the exploration of novel combinations.
*   A tightening of linkages, to establish a 'dominant design', or optimal architecture, in a given context (market), and to utilize it in reaping the rewards, by means of generalization, i.e. extension to different contexts (markets).

In other words: disintegration is dynamically efficient, to generate 'exploration', while integration into tighter intrafirm networks is needed to achieve productive efficiency in 'exploitation'. From a dynamic perspective, integrated and disintegrated structures are not substitutes but complements, in a dialectic of disintegration and integration. The argument is summarized below.

Depending on how systemic the incumbent technology is, some loosening of control within an MNE (multinational firm) may already be needed at the stage of differentiation. Subsidiaries in different markets need to have more freedom, first to modify the marketing, distribution and

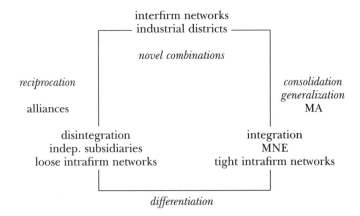

Figure 4.4 Cycle of (dis)integration

servicing of products, and subsequently to modify the products, with variations in design, engineering, production and sourcing. When the technology is systemic, central technical control in developing new products and processes must be maintained. In reciprocation, subsidiaries need to be allowed to establish novel network connections across the boundaries of the MNE; even with subsidiaries of competing firms. One reaches a point where the trade-off between productive and dynamic efficiency of continuing integration within the MNE switches in favour of the dynamic efficiency of disintegration. Zanfei (1996) implicitly recognized this, and proposed that the only remaining function of the MNE head office would be to supply *ex post* rewards for innovative conduct of subsidiaries. But it is likely that capital markets supplying rewards in terms of capital gains to independent firms is much more efficient at this.[6]

In the exploration of novel combinations novel tacit knowledge arises, but it is feasible for separate firms to interact in tacit knowledge, and the autonomy of units is needed to provide sufficient variety and flexibility of experimenting with novel combinations, before consolidation sets in. For joint production on the basis of complementary tacit knowledge, close interaction is required, and here the risk of spillover is limited and can be controlled in the process of interaction. It is feasible from the perspective of technical control, in spite of the fact that the novel technology is not sufficiently developed to yield standards that enable modularization, because at this stage systematicity of the novel technology is still limited (connections are still exploratory), and there is not yet pressure of competition to achieve productive efficiency by means of scale. And, in any case, such standards are not in sight before a dominant design emerges. Of course, this does make the process messy, confused and inefficient from a static perspective, with lots of misunderstanding, trial and error and shifting linkages in the loose network. That is precisely what makes that type of network useful from a dynamic perspective, at this stage of development.

But if disintegration is dynamically more efficient, why the subsequent integration in the stages of consolidation and generalization? Why not maintain the flexibility of interfirm networks? The main reason for integration into larger, multinational firms lies in their productive efficiency, competitive pressure and ability to offer a wider scope of markets (for generalization). We noted that in the stage of consolidation, knowledge tends to proceed from procedural and tacit to declarative and documented. This makes it more easily diffusible. One reason to integrate is to control spillover. When spillover cannot be stopped, the innovator's temporary monopoly is eroded, and competitive pressure increases, and thus the pressure increases to utilize opportunities for greater productive efficiency by means of scale and scope. The development towards declarative knowledge and documentation not only creates the incentive but also the means to do so: because knowledge becomes more documented, there is a possibility for formalization, systematization and scientification and for the division of labour. The transition from procedural and tacit knowledge to declarative and documented knowledge also implies a lessening of the importance of spatial distance. Tacit knowledge can be transferred only by imitation on the basis of direct observation and interaction, which requires proximity. When knowledge has become declarative and documented, it can be transferred over large distances. These effects form a technical enabler for the spread over more distant markets (generalization), and economy of scale. A further cause lies in governance, as discussed previously. Problems of behavioural control give an advantage to integration, in order to achieve economy of scale by combining competing activities. Especially when the new technology is systemic integration yields an advantage in technical control.

This expansion is needed as a basis for the subsequent stage of differentiation, which, however, requires a loosening of control within the MNE, as indicated. The technical enabler for this is that meanwhile, in the consolidation in the larger firm, standards are developed for interfaces, which allows more 'modularization' (Langlois and Robertson 1995), and thereby more independence for a foreign subsidiary. Ongoing integration in technical control is needed in this stage to the extent that the technology is systemic.

Abernathy and Utterback advanced a similar hypothesis that the nature of innovation changes in the course of development, with first a 'fluid' state, characterized by many radical product innovations by often smaller, flexible production units or enterprises, followed by a 'specific' state with emphasis on efficient production of given products, with incremental innovation in more inflexible, larger, integrated units (Abernathy 1978). Similar ideas were also advanced by Freeman, Clarke and Soete (1982) and Davis, Hills and Laforge (1985).

The analysis suggests that at the moment the interest in interfirm networks is so large (networks are in fashion), because in many areas we are at a stage of exploration, with turmoil in novel combinations of technologies and practices, while this can be expected to shift to a renewed interest in the integrative function of multinational enterprises (MNEs) for the purpose of exploitation.

But, of course, although there may be Schumpeterian 'swarming' of innovations, we should not expect all developments to be in synchrony: in some areas we may be in the stage of disintegration and in others in the stage of integration. This particularly complicates matters when a single large firm is engaged in several developments in different stages. In one activity the firm may need to integrate for the consolidation and generalization of recent innovations, while in another activity in a further stage of development it may need to loosen its ties to allow for differentiation and reciprocation.

The literature yields ample empirical evidence. For a survey see Nooteboom (1994). Jewkes, Sawyers and Stillerman (1958) reported that of sixty-one inventions during the first half of this century only sixteen could be ascribed to large firms. Mansfield (1969) later reported an empirical investigation that the productivity of R&D in the largest firms is lower than in medium sized and large firms. A study by Schmookler (quoted in Blair 1972) showed that inventions by operating staff took place almost entirely in smaller businesses. An American report on the 'State of small business' in 1983 reported that small firms (less than ten people employed) produced two-and-a-half as many innovations per employee as large firms (Davis, Hills and Laforge 1985). On the basis of the innovation database of the Science Policy Research Unit (SPRU) in Brighton, Wyatt (1985) claimed that the relative innovative efficiency (innovative output divided by innovative input) of small firms is much higher than in large firms. In a study of innovation data in the US Small Business Administration database, Acs and Audretsch (1990) found a higher average rate of innovation among small than among large firms. The tendency of large firms to hold back on the innovations that they do produce (to protect stakes in existing markets) is reflected in a study by George Washington University, which showed that firms with more than $100 million sales or more than 100 patents actually applied only 51 per cent percent of their patents, compared with 71 per cent for smaller firms (quoted in Weinberg 1990).

Individual cases are electrical light (Thomas Edison), the telephone (Bell), assembly line production of cars (Henry Ford), airplanes (the Wright brothers), microcomputers (Silicon Valley), computer-aided design (see Rothwell and Zegveld 1985), self-service retailing (see Nooteboom 1984). The latter study gives a unique illustration of a series of lifecycles of retail forms, that were inititated by small firms, who were bypassed by large firms, which subsequently moved on to the next innovation, while small firms stayed on to occupy residual niches in the older form.

We noted before that it is conceivable that the stage of generalization is skipped, and the expanded exploitation of a novelty is directly combined with differentiation. Typically, what we might expect is generalization (scale strategy) in a domestic market (or some homogeneous part of such a market), by means of MA, followed, perhaps quite rapidly, by a differentiated globalization (or extension across heterogeneous domestic markets) by means of alliances. We could also expect global extension under integration, by means of MA, but this is likely to be successful only when either the product by its nature does not require much differentiation, or the competitive pressure to differentiate is limited.

We also noted that the cycle is not universal; there are exceptions, depending on the conditions. When effects of scale are small, technology is stand-alone, knowledge remains tacit even after consolidation, monitoring is always difficult, and uncertainty remains, with the ongoing need for rapid adjustments and a variety of outside sources and flexibility of association, disintegrated structures can have a prolonged existence and maintain their advantage (P19). Thus there are several types of industrial districts (P20).

The literature has indicated several of such districts that seem to be pretty much 'ticking over';[7] continuing their existence without much evidence of radical innovation. The renowned districts of clothing and shoes in Italy come to mind (Piore and Sabel 1983; Amin 1989). One recently studied example is the Danish industrial district of furniture producers (Malmberg and Maskell 1996). These cases satisfy the conditions specified for their occurrence (P19).

Examples of large firms that have emulated the dynamic advantages of networks of differentiated firms by decentralized forms (federations, virtual firms) are the 3M company, Benetton and the Swedish Bank Scandia. In the 3M company emerging novelty is set aside in the organization, in autonomous units ('skunk works'), that can operate outside the strictures of established procedures for developed products. This sidesteps some of the obstacles for innovation in large firms. But note that in terms of our theory this is achieved by an intrafirm network with very loose control and large autonomy of units at appropriate stages of development. In other words: flexible networking is achieved within the firm.

Appendix: summary of propositions

C denotes conditions (contingencies), and P denotes propositions concerning principles of strategy, organizational design, contracting or 'governance'.

C: Complex and rapidly changing markets and technology.

P1:   One must outsource as many activities as possible, outside of core competencies, even if that entails 'transaction specific investments', in the sense treated in transaction cost economics (TCE).

C: Complex and rapidly changing markets and technology.

P2:   Outside sources are needed not only for static efficiency, but also for dynamic efficiency: for learning (complementary cognitive competence).

P3:   There are two main dimensions of integration: centralization of decision rights and centralization of profit rights.

P4:   One can govern by control, on the basis of decision rights, or by motivation. Control can be bureaucratic (by administrative fiat) or contractual (legal). Motivation can be based on material incentives (profit rights) or ethical norms and values or bonds of friend- or kinship.

P5:   In principle, decentralized profit rights are good for motivation.

C: The resources that need to be integrated are not separable from other resources.

P6:   One has to either integrate more than is desired (with a view to core competencies) or renounce integration.

P7:   In case of cooperation between substitute activities (competitors) integration (MA) has an advantage of behavioural control and may be feasible in terms of the costs and risks of integration.
        On the other hand, in case of cooperation between complementary activities, alliances in networks may be feasible concerning behavioural control, and costs and risks of full integration (MA) would be higher.

C: Monitoring is possible and there is no (radical) uncertainty, so that contingent contracting is possible.

P8:   Contracts between firms are preferable, with some centralized bureaucratic control to the extent that contingencies are complex or variable.

C: Monitoring is technically possible but contingent contracting is not, and control is important (e.g. because technology is systemic).

P9:   The integrated firm is preferable for its advantages of administrative fiat.

C: Knowledge is not tacit, partners have direct or indirect links with competitors, and spillover or efforts to control it cannot be monitored.

P10:   Some degree of integration is needed, but a JV may suffice. But when knowledge is tacit, this blocks spillover and integration for spillover control is not needed.

C: Monitoring of performance and effort is impossible and cooperation yields exit barriers.

P11:   Decentralization of profit rights is needed, with governance consisting of a mix of: control, incentive alignment and trust generating forms of bonding.

P12:   The choice between a JV and a non-equity alliance depends on a trade-off between, on the one hand, the greater grip of behavioural and spillover control of the former and the lower set-up costs and greater flexibility of the latter.

P13:   An important objective, particularly for small firms, is to achieve economies of scope and scale by increased utilization of fixed assets, including assets for the reduction of transaction costs.

P14:   Scale strategy: integration under unified ownership, in an intrafirm network, by means of MA, of competing producers in a given market. One may also consider integration of competing products from different markets, by MA, but to the extent that the markets are different this may conflict with the focus on core competence in the areas of marketing, distribution and sourcing. Then it seems preferable to sell or buy a licence. When integration under unified ownership does take place, a large degree of autonomy should be allowed to units in different markets.

P15:   Scope strategy: economy of scope requires that resources are sufficiently flexible to accommodate different products. If it fits in core competence, diversification can be achieved by building one's own new products or by MA, but the first may be too slow and the second may carry too much cost and risk of integration. The alternative that is generally to be preferred is to pool complementary products from different producers in an alliance.

P16:   Small independent firms in disintegrated structures tend to engage less in R&D, but when they do they tend to do so more intensively and more efficiently. There is dynamic complementarity: large integrated firms tend to to better in systemic and fundamental research, while small firms tend to be better at novel combinations in application and commercialization.

C: Stage of consolidation or generalization (so that knowledge is no longer tacit, and there are pressures to reduce costs), and there are economies of scale and/or technology is systemic, or:
The stage of incremental innovation for differentiation, and technology is systemic.

P17a: Large, integrated firms have the advantage from the perspectives of behavioural and technical control (including control of spillover).

C: The same stages, but economy of scale is limited and technology is stand-alone and industry standards have developed and uncertainty has subsided sufficiently to enable contractual associations between firms.

P17b: Small firms can keep up, by utilizing forms of cooperation (industrial districts, associations, consortia).

C: Stage of reciprocation or exploration of novel combinations so that: knowledge is still tacit and integration for spillover control is not needed, there is great need for a variety of outside sources to cope with uncertainty, and flexibility of shifting alliances is needed for the exploration of novel combinations. Then the advantages of integration in systemic technology break down and turn into disadvantages.

P18: Disintegrated structures of differentiated units have the advantage. Scope dominates scale, and scope favours alliances rather than integration.

C: Economy of scope keeps dominating scale, technology is stand-alone, knowledge remains tacit even after consolidation, monitoring even within firms is difficult even after consolidation, uncertainty remains, with the ongoing need for rapid adjustments, a variety of outside sources and flexibility of association.

P19: Disintegrated structures can have a prolonged existence.

P20: There are different types of industrial districts: those that offer differentiation and utilize their potential to produce radical innovation and those that exploit niches where the need to integrate is absent or advantages of disintegration remain when there is no radical innovation.

Notes

1 In particular information technology: programmable machines, computer-aided design, simulating rather than building prototypes, etc.
2 The fact that for a sphere the content increases with the cube and the surface with the square of the radius, while content determines capacity and surface costs (of material, transport, cleaning, heat loss through radiation), which continues to create economies of scale in process industries, transport, accommodation.
3 For several reasons, small business is more differentiated than large firms (Nooteboom 1993), so that generalization is difficult. Nevertheless, some characteristics can be identified that occur generally, to a greater or lesser extent, and that are typical for small business compared to large business.
4 This has often happened in alliances between Western and Japanese companies, where the Western company supplied an innovative product or a new technology, and the Japanese company supplied access to the Japanese market (which is hard to obtain other than by such an alliance). In time, the Japanese company

caught up in the technology, by imitation, and in the end bought the partner out (Jones and Shill 1993).

5 In an explanation, one cannot keep on explaining the terms of explanation, in infinite regress. At some point terms must be taken for granted, in unexplained and tacit knowledge.

6 I do not mean to say that capital markets are completely efficient at this, but only that they are likely to be more efficient than financial divisons of corporate headquarters.

7 I adopt this apt expression from Ash Amin, in his contribution to a discussion at an EMOT workshop in Durham, June 1996.

Bibliography

Abernathy, W. J. (1978) *The Productivity Dilemma*, London: Johns Hopkins University Press.

Acs, Z. and Audretsch, D. (1990) *Innovation and Small Firms*, Cambridge MA: MIT Press.

Amin, A. (1989) 'Flexible specialisation and small firms in Italy: myths and realities', *Antipode* 21: 13–34.

Argyris, C. and Schön, D. (1978) *Organizational Learning*, Reading, Mass.: Addison-Wesley.

Berger, P. L. and Luckmann, T. (1966) *The Social Construction of Reality*, New York: Doubleday.

Blair, J. M. (1972) *Economic Concentration*, New York: Harcourt, Brace Jovanovitch.

Bleeke, J. and Ernst, D. (1991) 'The way to win in cross-border alliances', *Harvard Business Review*, November/December: 127–35.

Brown, J. S. and Duguid, P. (1991) 'Organizational learning and communities of practice', *Organization Science*, 2, 1, reprinted in M. D. Cohen and L. S. Sproull (eds) (1996), *Organizational Learning*, London: Sage: 58–82.

Choi, C. J. and Lee, S. (1997) 'A knowledge based view of cooperative arrangements', in P. Beamish and P. Killing (eds), *Cooperative Strategies: European Perspectives*, Jossey, MA: Bass.

Cohen, M. D. (1991) 'Individual learning and organizational routine', *Organization Science*, 2, 1, reprinted in M. D. Cohen and L. S. Sproull (eds), 1996, *Organizational Learning*, London: Sage: 188–229.

Cohen, M. D. and Bacdayan, P. (1994) 'Organizational routines are stored as procedural memory', *Organization Science*, 5, 4, reprinted in M. D. Cohen and L. S. Sproull (eds), 1996, *Organizational Learning*, London: Sage: 403–30.

Cohen, M. D. and Sproull, L. S. (eds) (1996) *Organizational Learning*, London: Sage.

Cohen, W. M. and Levinthal, D. A. (1990) 'Absorptive capacity: a new perspective on learning and innovation', *Administrative Science Quarterly* 35: 128–52.

Davis, C. D., Hills, G. E. and Laforge, W. (1985) 'The marketing/small enterprise paradox', a research agenda, *International Small Business Journal*, 3, 3: 31–42.

Fiol, C. M. and Lyles, M. A. (1985) 'Organizational learning', *Academy of Management Review*, 10, 4: 803–13.

Freeman, C., Clark, J. and Soete, L. (1982) *Unemployment and Technical Innovation*, London: Pinter.

Grandori, A. (1997) 'An organizational assessment of interfirm coordination modes', *Organization Studies* 18/6: 897–925.

Hart, O. (1995) *Firms, Contracts and Financial Structure*, Oxford: Clarendon Press.

Hedberg, B. L. T., Nystrom, P .C. and Starbuck, W. H. (1976) 'Camping on seesaws: prescriptions for a self-designing organization', *Administrative Science Quarterly*, 21: 41–65.

Helper, S. (1991) 'Strategy and irreversibility in supplier relations: the case of the U.S. automobile industry', *Business History Review*, 65, Winter: 781–824.

Hennart, J. (1988) 'A transaction costs theory of equity joint ventures', *Strategic Management Journal*, 9: 361–74.

Holland, J.H. (1975) *Adaptation in Natural and Artificial Systems*, Ann Arbor: University of Michigan.

Jewkes, J., Sawyers, D. and Stillerman, R. (1958) *The Sources of Invention*, Macmillan.

Jones, K. K. and Shill, W. E. (1993) 'Japan: allying for advantage', in J. Bleeke and D. Ernst (eds), *Collaborating to Compete*, New York: Wiley, 115–44.

Kogut, B. (1988) 'A study of the life cycle of joint ventures', in Contractor and Lorange (eds), *Cooperative Strategies in International Business*, Lexington Books: 169–93.

Lamming, R. (1993) *Beyond Partnership*, New York: Prentice Hall.

Langlois, R. N. and Robertson, P. L. (1995) *Firms, Markets and Economic Change*, London: Routledge.

Malmberg, A., and Maskell, P. (1996) 'Proximity, institutions and learning, towards an explanation of regional specialization and industry agglomeration', EMOT workshop, Durham, 28–29 June.

Mansfield, E. (1969) *Industrial Research and Technological Innovation*, London: Longmans, Green and Co.

March, J. (1991) 'Exploration and exploitation in organizational learning, *Organization Science* 2,1.

Milgrom, P. and Roberts, J. (1989) 'Bargaining costs, influence costs and the organization of economic activity', in J. Alt and K. Shepsle (eds), *The Foundations of Political Economy*, Cambridge Mass: Harvard U. Press.

Nooteboom, B. (1984) 'Innovation, life cycle and the share of independents: cases from retailing', *International Small Business Journal*, 3, 1: 21–33.

Nooteboom, B. (1991) 'Entry, spending and firm size in a stochastic R&D race', *Small Business Economics*, 3: 103–20.

Nooteboom, B. (1992) 'Towards a dynamic theory of transactions', *Journal of Evolutionary Economics*, 2: 281–99.

Nooteboom, B. (1993) 'Firm size effects on transaction costs', *Small Business Economics*, 5: 283–95.

Nooteboom, B. (1994) 'Innovation and diffusion in small firms: theory and empirical evidence', *Small Business Economics*, 6: 327–47.

Nooteboom, B. (1996) 'Trust, opportunism and governance: a process and control model', *Organization Studies*, 17, 6: 985–1010.

Nooteboom, B. (1999a) *Inter-firm Alliances; Analysis and Design*, London: Routledge.

Nooteboom, B. (1999b) 'Innovation, learning and industrial organisation', *Cambridge Journal of Economics*, 23: 127–50.

Nooteboom, B., and Vossen, R. W. (1995) 'Firm size and efficiency in R&D spending', in A. van Witteloostuijn (ed.): *Market Evolution; Competition and Cooperation*, Deventer Netherlands: Kluwer.

Ohmae, K. (1989) 'Global logic of strategic alliances', *Harvard Business Review*, March–April.

Osborn, R. N. and Baughn, C. C. (1990) 'Forms of interorganizational governance for multinational alliances', *Academy of Management Journal*, 33, 3: 503–19.

Penrose, E. (1959) *The Theory of the Growth of the Firm*, New York: Wiley.

Piaget, J. (1970) *Psychologie et epistémologie*, Paris: Denoël.

Piaget, J. (1974) *Introduction a l'épistémologie génétique*, Paris: Presses Universitaires de France.

Piore, M. and Sabel, C. (1983) 'Italian small business development: lessons for US industrial policy', in J. Zysman and L. Tyson (eds), *American Industry in International Competition*, Government Policies and Corporate Strategies, Ithaca: Cornell University Press.

Polanyi, M. (1962) *Personal Knowledge*, London: Routledge.

Polanyi, M. (1966) *The Tacit Dimension*, London: Routledge.

Polanyi, M. (1969) *Knowing and Being*, London: Routledge.

Porter, M. E. (1985) *Competitive Advantage*, New York: The Free Press.

Prahalad, C. and Hamel, G. (1990) 'The core competences of the corporation', *Harvard Business Review*, May–June.

Rothwell, R. (1989) 'Small firms, innovation and industrial change', *Small Business Economics*, 1: 51–64.

Rothwell, R. and Zegveld, W. (1985) *Innovation and the Small and Medium Sized Firm*, London: Francis Pinter.

Scherer, F .M. (1980) *Industrial Market Structure and Economic Performance*, Chicago: Rand McNally.

Shank, R. and Abelson, R. (1977) *Scripts, Plans, Goals and Understanding*, Hillsdale: Lawrence Erlbaum.

Teece, D. J. (1986) Profiting from technological innovation: implications for integration, collaboration, licensing and public policy, *Research Policy*, 15: 285–305.

Teece, D. J. (1988) 'Technological change and the nature of the firm', in G. Dosi, C. Freeman, R. Nelson, G. Silverberg and L. Soete (eds), *Technical Change and Economic Theory*, London: Pinter.

Weinberg, N.M. (1990) 'Innovation, competition and small business', PhD dissertation, Erasmus University Rotterdam, Alblasserdam, Netherlands: Haveka.

Williamson, O.E. (1985) *The Economic Institutions of Capitalism; Firms, Markets, Relational Contracting*, New York: The Free Press.

Wyatt, S. (1985) 'The role of small business in innovative activity', *Economia and Politica Industriale*.

Yelle, L.E. (1979) 'The learning curve: historical review and comprehensive survey', *Decision Sciences*, 10: 302–28.

Zanfei, A. (1996) 'Technology and the changing organization of transnational firms', paper EMOT workshop, Durham, 28–30 June.

Zuscovitch, E. (1994) 'Sustainable differentiation; Economic dynamism and social norms', paper J. A. Schumpeter conference, Münster, 19–21 August.

5 Interorganizational relations in the Modena biomedical industry

A case study in local economic development[1]

Andrea Lipparini and Alessandro Lomi

Introduction

Over the last decade, the study of business strategy and policy has witnessed a relatively quiet revolution loosely organized around the belief that competitive advantage—and the persistence of economic rents—may have relational components that are neither industry nor firm specific (Dyer 1996; Hansen *et al.* 1997). The effects of this gradual reorientation have remained largely unnoticed because of the (i) rapid diffusion and managerial appeal of resource-based approaches to firm behaviour and performance (Rumelt 1984; Wernefelt 1984); (ii) solid economic roots and indisputable value of more traditional industry-based approaches to competitive strategy (Porter 1980); and (iii) lack of an integrated—let alone coherent—framework for exploring the relational basis of organizational structures and processes.

In spite of the strong hold of mainstream theories of strategy, evidence from the study of traditional (Sabel *et al.* 1986) and emergent industries (Powell *et al.* 1996), and small (Lipparini 1995) and large companies (Lorenzoni and Baden-Fuller 1991), both in Europe (Herrigel 1996) as well as in the United States (Saxenian 1994) and Japan (Gerlach 1992), is gradually accumulating, which suggests that some of the most fundamental organizational and economic outcomes—such as learning (Powell *et al.* 1996), knowledge transfer (Storper 1996), job creation (Piore and Sabel 1984), technological innovation (Podolny and Stuart 1995), entrepreneurship (Freeman 1996) and performance (Uzzi 1996)—can be usefully characterized *as emergent properties of networks of companies* rather *than attributes of individual organizations*. Despite its obvious heterogeneity, this gradual shift in the locus of action from individual companies to communities of interdependent organizations implies a basic reorientation of the unit of analysis in the study of the firm from the definition of dyadic transactions to the governance of networks of relations (Lomi 1997).

But if core processes (such as, for example, innovation and learning) that are traditionally associated with specific dimensions of organizational structures (such as, for example, decentralization and formalization) really are emergent properties induced by patterns of interaction among the members of an interorganizational community, then questions arise about the nature of the link between (i) environmental uncertainty and organizational structure, and (ii) organizational structure and performance.

The relationship between uncertainty and organizational structure—theoretically rooted in behavioural and cognitive theories of bounded rationality developed by Simon (1947) and March and Simon (1958)—has been at the centre of the debate on organizational economics during the last twenty years (Williamson 1975, 1991). One of the main tenets of this line of inquiry is that organizations react to key uncertainties and dependencies in their environments by removing transactions from the market and placing them in more hierarchical contexts (Williamson and Ouchi 1980; Ouchi 1980). Since the work of Thompson (1967), this has been regarded as one of the most widely shared principle of organizational design (Pfeffer and Salancik 1978).

However, more recent research is beginning to question the generality of this principle by showing that—when market uncertainty increases—individual companies tend to interact *more*, rather than less with other organizations, therefore increasing their overall volume of market transactions (Podolny 1994). This research shows that the main effect of market uncertainty in *not* the enclosure of the sources of uncertainty within corporate boundaries, but the increased reliance on external partners that are *known* and *trusted* to be *reliable* (Podolny 1994; Baker 1992). Under conditions of market uncertainty and volatility, factors typically considered as 'non economic' such as, for example, status, reputation, role and position (Burt 1992; Faulkner 1987; Podolny 1993) define and sustain entire networks of transactions across corporate boundaries as individual organizations attempt to stabilize their mutual dependencies.

Questions about the link between organizational structure and performance—the second 'problem area' identified above—probably define the field of business strategy as a distinctive intellectual enterprise (Porter 1996; Rumelt *et al.* 1994), and have been central to the development of theories of organizational design and contingency theories of organizations (Burns and Stalker 1961; Lawrence and Lorsch 1967; Galbraith 1973). In these perspectives, differences in performance across companies are assumed to reflect a differential degree of fit to their environments, while, in more modern formulations, are seen as the consequences of differential rates of return on heterogeneous firm-specific assets and resources (Barney 1991).

However, recent research suggests that the value of idiosyncratic resources may be contingent upon the position occupied by the firm in a multiplex relational system, on the role set of the organization, and on its 'niche' width (Di Maggio 1986; Burt 1992; Podolny *et al.* 1996). But if differential rewards for individual managerial choices are associated with positions occupied in a multiplex exchange topology—i.e. in networks of direct and indirect relationships among corporate actors—then the strength of the conceptual link between individual strategies and performance needs to be closely scrutinized.

Against this broad theoretical background, in this chapter we report preliminary results from an empirical study on the relationships among companies involved in the production and commercialization of biomedical devices located in and around the northern Italian city of Modena. Italy is the fifth largest market in the world for biomedical products with a global share of 4 per cent in terms of sales. In Italy, we estimate that over 90 per cent of the total number of companies involved in the production of biomedical devices is concentrated in well-bounded geographical areas around the city of Modena. We chose the members of this interorganizational community for study for pragmatic reasons related to the fact that spatial proximity greatly simplifies the collection of relational data. Also we expect the study of this specific community of organizations to have at least some theoretical value related to the fact that the production and commercialization of biomedical devices is characterized by an intense vertical and horizontal division of labour among organizations, and therefore lends itself particularly well to network analytic approaches.

In the limited empirical context of the study, we try to address some of the general theoretical problems mentioned in this introduction by concentrating on the relational aspects of firms' production activities, and by documenting how heterogeneity in individual relational profiles simultaneously induces—and is sustained by—articulated interorganizational roles. While our data collection and analysis work is still in progress, we believe that the preliminary results reported here clearly indicate the need and the value of developing a more complete relational perspective on economic activities in order to understand the organization and division of labour both within as well as between organizations.

The paper is organized as following. In the next section we provide some information on the Modena biomedical industry. We discuss significant events which triggered the progressive formation of the relational structures in one of the most important agglomeration of production units in the world. Then we offer a provisional taxonomy of the actors involved on the basis of their role in the community. The central section is devoted to the presentation of the research design, the methodology, and the structure of the datasets. Finally, we provide a representation of the relational structures as well as measures of centrality. We close the paper with a discussion of results and implications for future research on this industry.

The biomedical industry in Modena

The biomedical industry includes a wide range of product categories. In Italy, the National Council for Research (CNR 1987) defines the industry in terms of the set of technologies and products for sanitary uses, excluding drugs. At least six different branches can be identified according to this classification,: (1) materials and equipment for 'scanning' techniques; (2) equipment for functional evaluation; (3) artificial organs and prothesis; (4) equipment and material for laboratory analysis; (5) instruments for therapeutic use; and (6) instruments for rehabilitation. The recent classification of economic activities provided by the ISTAT, the National Statistics Institute, includes biomedical products in categories 33.10.1 and 33.10.2, which refers to the manufacturing of medical and surgery devices.

In the US, the medical device industry is described in terms of the Standard Industrial Classification (SIC). In the revised classification of 1987, the old SIC 3693 is now divided into the categories labeled SIC 3844 and SIC 3845. This group of sectors is involved mainly in the production of high-quality medical apparatuses, electromedical equipment, and surgical instruments.

The origins and development of the world biomedical industry date back to the 1950s, with the application of electronics and materials science to medicine. In the following decades, the industry benefited enormously from the technological interdependencies with other sectors (microelectronics, mechanics, biochemistry, biotechnologies, physics-biophysics, optics, aerospace, nuclear). The rapid growth of the industry and the use of complementary knowledge to develop different applications led to a variety of products.

Prior studies have shown that companies in this industry have a tendency to locational agglomeration (Gibson 1970; Oakey 1983; Malecki 1985; de Vet and Scott 1992). Among the most important countries producing biomedical products, the United States and Italy show the highest concentration of production units. In the US, the first market for biomedical devices with a share of over 40 per cent of the world market, the production of medical instruments is concentrated in five states: California, Florida, Illinois, Massachusetts and New York. Out of these five, California is by far the most important. The majority of Californian biomedical producers are located in the southern part of the State (US Department of Commerce 1989). Three counties alone (Los Angeles, Orange and San Diego) account for over 57 per cent of establishments and 68 per cent of employment in the region. The high-technology segment of the industry tends to agglomerate in the Irvine area of Orange County.

In Italy, the fifth world market for biomedical products in terms of sales, the locational agglomeration is so apparent that some areas in the northern province of Modena are labelled as the 'biomedical valley'. More precisely, this is identified with the district of Mirandola, the dynamic core of the industry and the place of origin of all the main technological innovations. The biomedical industry represents a relatively recent development within the historical industrial texture of the city, but it has grown at an extremely rapid pace over the last three decades. Now, Modena's biomedical industry is the most important European centre for the production of (1) sterilized disposables for extra-body blood circulation (dialysis, oxygenization, transfusion of blood, plasmapheresys, filtering), (2) disposables for the administration of injectable sterilized solutions (defluxion devices and nutritional membranous pouches), (3) sterilized disposables for respiratory use in reanimation and anaesthesia, and (4) equipment for the use of the disposables mentioned above. At the international level, Italian producers rank at top positions in terms of product quality and innovation.

As we discuss below, the population of firms in Modena's biomedical industry represents a unique opportunity for exploring the key role played by smaller and younger firms, and for studying the formation of networks of interfirm relationship to access complementary resources and capabilities. This community of firms generates innovative products and applications which allows Italy to be positioned at the technological forefront in this sector; it also represents an organizational community with distinctive organizational structures and processes.

A case study in regional economic development

In his study of semiconductor firms in California, J. Freeman (1984) suggested that entrepreneurs come from organizations, but not all organizations produce entrepreneurs. We take this observation as our point of departure to describe the entrepreneurial origins of the biomedical industry in Italy.

The pharmacist Mario Veronesi was the first entrepreneur in Italy to introduce and distribute sterilized disposables to hospitals and, more importantly, he developed the first Italian artificial rein and its accessories. During the last three decades, most of the organizational entries into and exits from the community can somehow be traced back to something that Mario Veronesi did. Not only did he establish the community in 1963, but he also experimented with an unconventional pattern of growth (for Italy) by selling his companies to larger international corporations. In this sense the entrepreneur is pleased with the capital gains resulting from the sale of the companies (Freeman 1984), the new subsidiaries having been profitable before the sale and having experienced a fast growth. This pattern of growth is considered the only viable option to overcome the constraints related to the critical size needed to be competitive on a global scale.

In 1963 Dr Veronesi founded his first organization in the district of Mirandola, MIRASTET. With only five employees, the firm aimed at satisfying hospitals' demand for ready-to-use disposables for the circulation of blood and other fluids. This type of product would allow the healthcare system to abandon the traditional rubber tubes which needed careful sterilization before use.

The demand grew so rapidly (from millions to hundreds of million units) that Doctor Veronesi was forced to rename the firm (STERILPLAST) and reorganize its production system, increasing the number of employees from five to thirty, and outsourcing production stages such as the extrusion and moulding of connectors to two small firms located nearby. In 1965 a professor at the Padova Hospital was looking for a product suitable for the extra-body blood circulation used to connect a patient to an artificial rein. Thus, STERILPLAST began the production and export of tubes for extra-body circulation. Using an unpatented artificial rein manufactured by an American company as a basis, the firm developed the first Italian artificial rein, and in 1966 an internal division—DASCO—was created and exclusively devoted to this line of products.

Despite or perhaps because of its rapid growth (over 1,000 artificial reins installed in three years of activity), in 1970 DASCO was sold to SANDOZ, the Swiss multinational operating in the pharmaceutical industry. The opportunities of being small and flexible turned into constraints. Among them, the need for financial and human resources, the long time requested by public institutions (such as hospitals in Italy) in which to pay small manufacturers, the need of a managerial culture to confront strategic moves of multinational rivals that were connected to university hospitals, and ownership of technologies developed in the US and Sweden. The injection of competencies was not sufficient to avoid an internal crisis at DASCO. In this period, many technicians and employees 'spun-off', and several firms were established in the area, contributing to the formation of a relational texture based on manufacturing capabilities on circuits and accessories for emodialysis. Through a joint venture with the French company Rhone Poulenc, owner of a patent for the development of a special membrane for short therapeutic treatments, HOSPAL DASCO gained relevant market positions in Europe, expecially in Italy and France. In 1988, the firm was sold to GAMBRO (Volvo Group).

Following the process suggested by Freeman (1984) entrepreneurs in the Italian biomedical industry spun-off from the few clearly identified incubator companies, because the organizational crises induced by rapid growth forced technicians to abandon their existing jobs. In this way, the multinational companies played an important role in the creation of the relational structure of the industry, by making the founders aware of their capabilities.

In 1973 Dr Veronesi, together with a number of technicians, founded BELLCO, which rapidly developed an innovative set of disposables. It is in this period that product innovation replaced the practice of imitating American devices not protected by patents. The quest for capital to sustain growth, and the twenty months (on average) credit requested by the hospitals, forced BELLCO to find a partner. In 1975, ENI, the national oil company, entered with 60 per cent of the proprietary asset, and in 1982 acquired the remaining 40 per cent. ENI was not able to manage this small organization which faced problems that were very different from those of the chemical industry. In 1990, SORIN Biomedica, part of the FIAT

Group, became the sole owner of the company. SORIN Biomedica also has the majority share in CORTEK, a firm operating in cardiosurgery which was founded by technicians from BELLCO and DIDECO.

In 1980, Dr Veronesi created DIDECO, a manufacturer of oxygenizators for cardiosurgery, the only Italian firm—and one of only two European producers—to specialize in equipment for oxygenization, self-transfusion and separation of haematic components. Five years later, net sales reached $20 million. In 1988, the firm was sold to the Canadian multinational PFIZER, and in particular to its biomedical division, SHILEY. The latter began to produce the products once manufactured in California at the DIDECO factory, thanks to lower costs and distinctive competencies at the local level. Three years later, DIDECO more than doubled its net sales and in 1990 it was sold to SORIN BIOMEDICA.

In 1986, Dr Veronesi and some of his collaborators from previous ventures founded DAR, which in 1997 employed over 200 people and realized $40 million net sales in Italy and Europe. The firm is involved in the production of respiratory circuits for the connection of patient ventilators in the operating room and in intensive care. In 1993, the American multinational MALLINCKRODT, operating in the same sector, acquired DAR. In the same year, the German multinational BRAUN Melsungen acquired the CAREX European Group, a merger of three small firms in the area. In 1990, the American multinational BAXTER entered the district with the acquisition of MIRAMED.

The industry structure: actors' typologies and interfirm basic connections

The development of the organizational community is consistent with prior research (Scott and Angel 1987; Scott 1988) suggesting that innovative producers within certain industrial sectors tend to agglomerate if active 'spin-offs' are taking place, and entrepreneurs are, at least to some degree, residentially stable. However, infrastructural investments and limited mobility are only two of the possible factors underlying the geographical concentration of economic activities.[2]

This organizational community is characterized by an internal structure of relationships whereby distinctive competencies in the labour market induce a tightly connected network of organizational interdependencies. The community is also characterized by dense horizontal and vertical linkages with subcontractors, service providers and other manufacturers. These connections create a relational-intensive system of production that puts pressure on the decision of entrepreneurs on how to locate their business (de Vet and Scott 1992). In our case, agglomeration has been accentuated because existing firms are constantly innovating: frequent changes in processes and products require closeness to a constellation of specialized suppliers and firms offering complementary products.

The industry structure and the presence of relational multiplexity allow a marked division of labour among the members of the community along the seven main vertical stages of the production process: design, working phases, moulding, assembling, sterilization, commercialization and distribution. With regard to their specific competencies and positions within the system, we identified six typologies of actors.

1 The biomedical firms with a direct access to the market

These firms are the most prominent actors in the community. Here we include the companies founded by Doctor Veronesi, such as BELLCO, HOSPAL DASCO, DIDECO, DAR, and others like HAEMOTRONIC and MIRAMED. These are the largest in terms of employees (more than 200, on average), net sales, and a remarkable export orientation. These six firms, mostly owned by multinationals, represent 75 per cent of the entire community in terms of employees and net sales. They generally focus on the internal production of disposables and on the use of subcontracting or external alliances for the production of equipment. The 'strategic activities', such as final assembly and testing are performed in-house. This restricted number of actors is able to interact directly with the market—mostly public and private hospitals—using its network of distributors and internal representatives.

2 The biomedical firms not directly linked to the market

These smaller firms, sometimes linked to multinationals through commercialization agreements, do not have direct access to the market. They rely on an interface—i.e. a distributor—to communicate with hospitals and therapeutic centres. These companies operate in market niches, offering customized products realized in small batches. For this reason, they are sheltered from competitive attacks from larger companies, from which they have often generated as spin-offs. Some of these firms are subcontractors to the larger companies, but have been able to evolve by developing their own brands. The use of external actors is crucial for these firms to survive: they extensively resort to complementary competencies in the supply of standard components, laboratory analysis and moulding. They generally concentrate on assembly, but this is not always the case for all the actors in this category.

3 The producers of components

These companies concentrate on the production of plastic components for the two categories of firms mentioned above and for the 'assemblers'. For the production of components, technical creativity and competencies are needed. This explains why most of these companies acted as engineering workshops for the production of moulds for biomedical components, and only later became manufacturers of intermediate products. In some cases, these firms perform some assembly. In some cases, the development of their technical competencies allow them not only to meet high quality standards, but also to design and produce innovative components on the basis of the requirements of the biomedical firms directly or indirectly linked to the market.

4 The assemblers

Within this category, we find small and very small units acting as assemblers for the disposables and components producers. The assembler receives the components and the blueprints, and performs the assembly under the supervision of the Quality Control staff of the lead manufacturer. Sometimes, these units are linked to the biomedical firms by family relationships. A common behavioural path is the creation of long-lasting relationships with a limited number of important clients. Having automated the assembly phase, larger companies in the local community tend to use the assemblers when demand from the market is particularly high. In other cases, the assembly is outsourced for those products with low technological content. An important competitive leverage is represented by the reduction of time to delivery of assembled subsystems or products.

5 The producer of moulds and the moulders

Members of this category are manufacturers of moulds for leading biomedical manufacturers. The relationships with the biomedical firms are very close. The mould is typically built according to client specifications. While in the past it was the lead manufacturer who bought the raw materials on the market, now it is the small firm involved in moulding who is in charge of purchasing them, sometimes collaborating with its client for the choice of the most appropriate granule.

6 The equipment producers

There are other important firms active in the production of equipment for assembly, expecially for the larger companies; others are involved in the manufacturing of equipment for the assembly of sterilized disposables. We also found engineering workshops providing components for biomedical equipment, circuits for cardiosurgery, components for assembly equipment, and so forth. Figure 5.1 reports the basic connection among these six typologies according to a partitioning based on a firm's age and competencies at the manufacturing and design level.

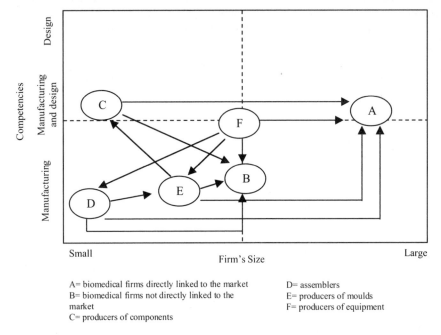

Figure 5.1 Competencies, size and basic connections among players in the Modena biomedical industry

Methodology

The organizational community boundaries

The number of firms operating in Modena's biomedical industry cannot be determined accurately because of the different criteria adopted by the statistical system in the classification of economic activities. In our study we cross-checked information on membership in the population by relying on different sources: agencies and institutions (ISTAT and U.S.L.15, the Local Health Authority), specialized catalogues and reports, and offices (Camere di Commercio) where firms have to register themselves and update their records.

A preliminary list of firms was compiled using CERVED, the computerized system that stores and retrieves organizational data within and across regions, which is based on the classification codes provided by ISTAT. Within the categories 33.10.1 and 33.10.2, which refer to the manufacturing of medical and surgery devices, we found ninety firms. With the aid of phone calls and direct interviews with a small number of prominent firms, we elaborated a more accurate definition of existing firms producing disposables, devices and related services that could be labelled

as 'biomedical'. On the basis of the different sources of information mentioned above, some firms were cancelled and new ones added. We decided
to drop those firms whose activity in the biomedical industry was labelled as
'marginal' or 'not prevalent'.

At the end of this preliminary stage, we identified ninety-six firms,
localized in the province of Modena, and primarily involved in this type of
activity. More precisely, firms were mainly concentrated in the town of
Mirandola (40), Medolla (15), Modena (10), Carpi (8), Concordia (7),
Cavezzo (5), and others (11). This organizational community includes the
firm's typologies outlined in the previous section. In particular, we have a
small number of large firms relying upon a consistent number of smaller
units for design, manufacturing, and services.

If compared with the 2,600 textile firms in Prato, or the over 200
ceramic-tile producers in Sassuolo, this may appear a population of limited
interest. However, the biomedical valley represents the highest concentration of Italian firms in this industry and one of the most significant
agglomeration of innovative units in the world of biomedical devices. With
$350 million of sales and over 3,000 employees the Mirandola district
alone contributes one-fifth of the entire domestic market for biomedical
products.

The collection of relational data

We collected the data through questionnaires and direct interviews. The
research program which started in 1995 was articulated in five steps: (1) the
definition of the interorganizational field; (2) the fine-tuning of the list of
actors in the community; (3) the delivery of a questionnaire, with
methodological notes, after a preliminary phone check; (4) additional
phone calls to solve problems in the interpretation of relational data; (5)
personal interviews with eleven prominent actors to support our interpretation of empirical evidences. Points 1 to 3 refer to the period September–
December 1995; points 4 and 5 are relative to January–May 1996.

The questionnaire was mailed to the ninety-six members of our final list.
Considering that the aim of this preliminary study was to provide insights
into the relational structure of an organizational community, we designed
and administered a very simple questionnaire. In a first section, firms were
asked to provide basic data such as: age, number of employees, net sales,
export rate, production typology, and modes of formation—to check
whether or not they had spun-off from others in the community. The
second section of the questionnaire was specifically designed to elicit
relational data. On the basis of the preliminary list, the firms were asked to
indicate those actors with whom they entertained working relationships at
the end of 1995. If a relation did exist, firms had to specify: (a) if they 'buy
from' or 'sell to' the actor indicated; and (b) the specific content of the
relationship. The former allowed us to orient the relational graph

connecting the actors in the community; the latter, allowed the construction of relational subsets based on a different relational content. We supplied a complete list of actors to respondents.

We differentiated the relational content with the aid of previous research and interviews with prominent informants in the community. Companies may depend on others for the supply of: raw materials (e.g. plastics for extrusion); subcontracting (e.g. they provide the blueprint to an external supplier, who is asked to return a finished product or component); components and parts (e.g. parts of a disposable, assembled or not); finished products or services (e.g. assembled disposable sets, transportation, design, final testing). We collected and coded data on thirty-nine members of the community who were producing biomedical devices and/or disposables. In the empirical part of the research we concentrated on this set of thirty-nine firms, which we found to be highly representative of the community in terms of sales, employees, competencies and reputations. However, five of the thirty-nine firms were finally disqualified.

In our multirelational dataset, we utilized a dichotomous rating scheme to indicate whether or not a tie existed. The relational data collected were arranged within five square matrices of size 39×39. The matrix named TOT_REL refers the totality of exchanges connecting the thirty-nine sampled firms. In this matrix, an entry is 1 if at least one relationship among the 'row'-company and the 'column'-company is present. We also coded four matrices based on the relational contents mentioned above (RAW_MAT; SUB_CONT; COM_PART; FIN_PROD).

Measurement issues

We used the software UCINET IV (Borgatti, Everett and Freeman 1992) to analyse the data. Given the preliminary nature of this study, we adopted relational rather than positional techniques for the analysis. A first group of measures is used to explore the proposition that centrality is not necessarily an attribute of the larger and older firms.

We adopted the category of prominence identified by Knoke and Burt (1983), according to which an actor is prominent if he is visible to others in the social network. There are two classes of prominence measures: centrality and status or prestige. An actor is central if extensively involved in relationships with others, and is prestigious to the extent to which he is recipient of many choices or citations from prestigious alters.

In directed networks, degree centrality comes in two forms: indegree and outdegree. The first indicates the number of other actors who choose that firm in the particular relationship (e.g. the number of relations 'received'). The second is the number of actors chosen by the firm (e.g. the number of relations 'sent'). These are good indicators of the informal status that the individual has in the community. A high centrality score based on degree indicates 'where the action is' in the network (Wasserman and Faust

1994). This measure is also an expression of the communication potential of an actor: central firms tend to have greater access to information, more power, status or influence.

Some authors consider central the organization which is in some way close to the others in the network (Sabidussi 1966; Bonacich 1972; Nieminen 1973; Burt 1982). Other contributions see centrality as related to positioning on the communicational paths connecting pairs of actors (betweeness). The 'actors in the middle' are supposed to have more inter-personal authority and thus greater control over the community (Friedkin 1991). These actors may facilitate or inhibit the communication in the network, acting like filters for the access to information. The central actors benefit from a higher social integration, and a greater control of raw materials, financial resources and relevant information. Furthermore, prominent actors tend to adopt technological innovation earlier when compared with peripheral units (Coleman *et al.* 1966; Rogers and Kincaid 1981).

At this stage, the measure of centrality based on the number of direct ties (degree) is sufficient to show how the role of 'key player' tends to change when considering different relational contents. This measure is normalized to permit comparisons of degree-centrality across networks of different size. We also provide for each relational subset centralization indexes and more simple measures of centralization, such as density and variance. The graphic representation—obtained with the software KRACK-PLOT—of the positioning or the members of the community will help in the interpretation of the structures related to the different relational contents.

Preliminary results

Table 5.1 reports a number of descriptive network statistics. The density of the matrix TOT_REL indicates that 9 per cent of the possible relationships among members of the community are taking place. The number of direct ties (degree) is particularly high and suggests the existence of an intense relational activity. The Freeman's outdegree centralization index (Freeman 1977) is rather high. The high variability between the centrality indexes of the individual actors in the sample indicates the existence of a 'centre' and a 'periphery' defined in terms of raw relational activity. The Table also reports centralization measures based on closeness and betweeness. The relatively low value of the latter, indicates that many actors are able to get information from others, being positioned on the communicational path between pairs of firms.

With regards to matrices based on different relational contents, we observe the importance of relationships based on exchange of components and parts. This is consistent with the idea of a community with actors manufacturing final products resorting to external highly skilled suppliers

Table 5.1 The relational subsets: preliminary data

	TOT_REL (n=39)	RAW_MAT (n=39)	SUB_CONT (n=39)	COM_PART (n=39)	FIN_PROD (n=39)
Density (%)	0.09	0.02	0.01	0.06	0.01
Number of ties (degree)					
outdegree	126	32	19	82	21
indegree	126	32	19	82	21
Centralization (Freeman index)					
outdegree	38.19%	39.33%	6.97%	41.32%	6.83%
indegree	18.78%	8.82%	12.52%	16.36%	9.60%
Variance S^2D: on normalized					
outdegree	136.89	62.10	5.28	96.88	4.56
on normalized indegree	59.12	6.70	7.06	32.60	5.98
Centralization (Sabidussi index):	5.44%	2.67%	2.17%	4.07%	1.91%
Variance S^2C: on closeness	15.95	1.61	0.75	6.58	0.48
Centralization (on betweeness):	12.80%	0.35%	8.32%	20.03%	9.53%
Variance S^2B: on normalized betweenness	12.03	0.00	8.81	14.99	4.87

to provide parts to be assembled. This matrix has a density of 0.06, a higher outdegree centralization index (41.32 per cent), and a high value of the variance based on normalized outdegree (14.99), when compared with other datasets. The relevance of the use of suppliers of components and parts in the biomedical industry is also signalled by the high value of centralization based on normalized betweeness (20.03 per cent).

The raw materials represent both an opportunity as well as a constraint for the biomedical firm. The severe limitations imposed by international standards of quality are forcing the firms to resort to skilled suppliers, offering high-quality products. Due to the social impact of biomedical products and the low tolerance for error, quality and reliability are of crucial importance to the business. For these reasons, skilled suppliers of raw materials in the area gain recognition and are positioned at a centre of a network of relationships. These suppliers sometimes offer components and not simply raw materials (i.e. plastics for extrusion in the production of disposables). The density of the subset RAW_MAT is 0.02 but the out-degree centralization index (39.33 per cent) is close to that of the matrix COMP_PART. The indegree measure of centralization is the lowest in the multirelational dataset (8.82 per cent). The centralization based on betweeness is very low (0.35 per cent), indicating that almost all the connected actors may have access to the suppliers of raw materials in the area.

The contracting out of working hours (subcontracting) and the acquisition of finished products (or completed functional groups of products) do not seem to represent significant relational contents. In both cases, density is low (0.01 per cent). Prior research on this industry has considered the use of subcontracting as a viable option for improving efficiency and growth. The low centrality and centralization scores in the matrix SUB_CONT can be explained by the interpretation that the firms gave to the term 'subcontracting'. In fact, operators in this industry tend to include traditional subcontracting[3] in the 'components and parts' category. Often, they buy components or parts externally manufactured on the basis of a blueprint or at least informal communication about the basic requirements of components or subassemblies. For these subsets, the indegree measure of centralization is low but higher than their respective outdegree, and the variance based on normalized degree (both in and out) is very low.

Table 5.2 reports the measures of centrality computed for the individual actors across the five datasets. We concentrated on twenty firms sorted by their respective score on normalized outdegree in the matrix TOT_REL. The use of degree to rank the firms in the population is useful when arguing the proposition that central positions are not a prerogative of the larger organizations. For each firm, we indicate their respective classes of age, size, net sales and export rate, in order to facilitate the interpretation of preliminary results. As to age and size, for instance, categories range from 1 (smaller and younger firms) to 4 (larger and older units). At the bottom of the Table are reported the mean and the standard deviation for normalized outdegree and indegree in each relational subset. Figures 5.2 to 5.6 are useful for a better interpretation of central positions.

When considering the normalized outdegree for the dataset TOT_REL, the larger organizations are not positioned at the top (Table 5.2). The role of 'central firm' is played by the smaller firms, like MACO, INCO, and LUCO, with a number of employees ranging from ten to twenty. Eleven firms reported a score higher that the mean value. Among them, we found only one firm of class 4 in terms of size (HAEM), and two firms of class 4 in terms of age (SAGE and EURO). As to normalized indegree, a large firm (BELL) has the highest score. This firm is followed by two small firms (classes 1 and 2 respectively), positioned at the bottom of the list based on outdegree. Twenty firms out of the thirty-nine are positioned above the mean value. The firm INCO, ranking in second position, did not report any data. Figure 5.2 offers a first picture of the relational structure in the biomedical industry in Modena, with the smaller firms as key players in supplying others in the community, and the larger as recipient of many connections. This confirms the idea of larger firms as orchestrators of

Table 5.2 Centrality measures for each relational subset (top twenty firms sorted by scores in normalized outdegree in the network TOT_REL)

	Firms	Size Ctg.	Age Ctg.	Sale Ctg.	Exp. Ctg.	TOT_REL		RAW_MAT		SUB_CONT		COMPART		FIN_PROD	
						NrmOutDeg	NrmInDeg	NrmOutDeg	NrmInDeg	NrmOutDeg	NrmInDeg	NrmOutDeg	NrmInDeg	NrmOutDeg	NrmInDeg
1	MACO	2	3	2	3	44.74	13.16	2.63	2.63	5.26	–	44.74	10.53	5.26	2.63
2	INCO	2	3	3	1	42.11	–	39.47	–	–	–	2.63	15.79	2.63	–
3	LUCO	2	1	3	2	36.84	18.42	31.58	2.63	–	–	18.42	7.89	–	2.63
4	MEDI	3	2	2	2	34.21	10.53	2.63	2.63	2.63	2.63	34.21	7.89	5.26	–
5	SAGE	2	4	2	4	18.42	10.53	–	2.63	–	–	21.05	7.89	2.63	5.26
6	HAEM	4	3	4	4	17.79	18.42	–	5.26	–	–	13.16	–	–	–
7	BIEX	2	3	2	2	15.79	–	–	–	–	–	15.79	7.89	–	–
8	PLAS	2	2	3	3	13.46	10.53	–	2.63	2.63	2.63	18.42	10.53	–	–
9	BIOS	3	1	3	2	13.16	15.79	5.26	5.26	5.26	7.89	7.89	7.89	–	–
10	EURO	3	4	3	3	13.16	7.89	–	–	7.89	–	7.89	–	–	–
11	EMOT	1	3	1	1	10.53	–	–	–	5.26	–	5.26	–	5.26	–
12	DROP	2	3	1	1	7.89	–	–	5.26	2.63	–	–	10.53	7.89	–
13	DIAL	2	2	2	1	7.89	13.16	–	–	7.89	–	2.63	2.63	–	–
14	BOCL	2	3	1	1	7.89	2.63	–	5.26	–	13.16	–	12.16	2.63	10.53
15	BELL	4	4	4	3	5.26	26.32	–	5.26	5.26	2.63	5.26	5.26	–	–
16	CMGA	2	2	2	1	5.26	10.53	–	5.26	–	2.63	2.63	7.89	5.26	–
17	GALL	3	3	2	3	5.26	13.16	–	5.26	–	–	–	2.63	5.26	–
18	MBME	3	1	3	1	5.26	2.63	–	–	–	–	2.63	–	2.63	–
19	LASE	1	1	3	1	5.26	2.63	–	2.63	–	–	2.63	–	2.63	–
20	DOCT	1	1	1	1	2.63	–	–	–	–	–	2.63	–	2.63	–
	MEAN (n=39)					8.50	8.50	2.16	2.16	1.28	1.28	5.53	5.53	1.42	1.42
	S.D. (n=39)					11.70	7.69	7.88	2.59	2.30	2.66	9.84	5.71	2.14	2.45

Legend:

Ctg.	Size (Employees)	Ctg.	Age (years)	Ctg.	Net Sales (,000 $)	Ctg.	Export (%)
1	n<=10	1	n<=5	1	n<=500	1	n=0
2	10<n<=20	2	5<n<=10	2	500<n<=1,000	2	0<n<=25
3	20<n<=100	3	10<n<=20	3	1,000<n<=10,000	3	25<n<=50
4	n>100	4	n>20	4	n>10,000	4	n>50

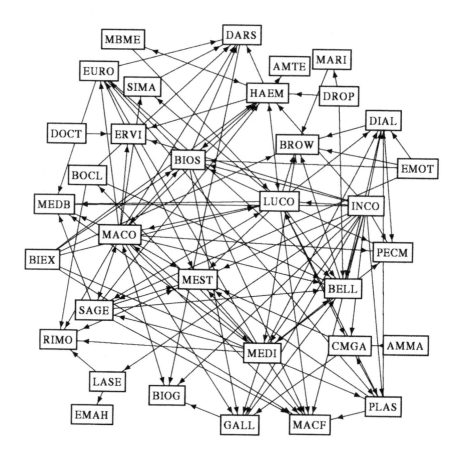

Figure 5.2 The Modena biomedical industry: total relationships (n=39)

different relationships in the community which they have helped to develop.

In the network based on the exchange of raw materials (Table 5.2 and Figure 5.3) we appreciate the central role played by INCO and LUCO, with high values in the outdegree measure of centrality. In this dataset, only six firms reported positive outdegree values. The scores in the indegree measure of centrality indicate that firms are being approached by small and young key actors for the supply of plastics and other raw materials for biomedical use.

The limited use of subcontracting relationships confirms the role of smaller firms in supplying the larger and older ones with working capacity.

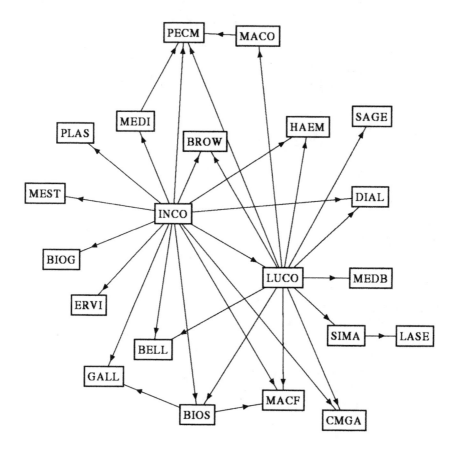

Figure 5.3 The Modena biomedical industry: exchange of raw materials (n=39)

Smaller firms like MACO, EMOT and BOCL have the highest outdegree score. Classes of size and age increase when considering the indegree index. Here, EURO, BELL and DARS, among the older firms in the community, received the highest score. Even smaller units are able to enter the relational texture of the pioneers in the industry. The subcontractors work for more than a single client, and sometimes act as a bridge connecting central firms as recipients of many choices (Figure 5.4). For instance, BOCL works for DARS and BELL (class 4); MACO supplies BELL and EURO (class 4).

The exchange of components and parts is the most relevant relational content in this industry. The prominent role of smaller firms emerged in

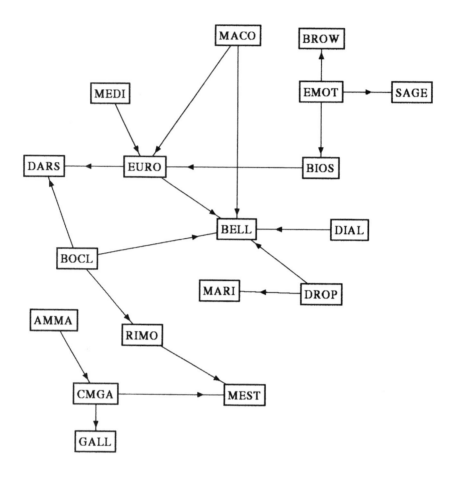

Figure 5.4 The Modena biomedical industry: the use of subcontracting (n=39)

the subset COM_PART. Suppliers like MACO and MEDI are important sources of flexibility for the larger biomedical firms. Many firms have a high value both for outdegree and indegree, indicating an intense activity of transformation and adaptation of components to the specific requirements of their clients. Larger firms like BROW and BELL are important clients for firms in the area, being able to interact with many suppliers (Figure 5.5). At the same time, even the smaller firms seem to be able to interact with actors of different size and age, representing strategic interfaces between biomedical firms offering complete lines and specialized suppliers with complementary capabilities. The influence of these smaller

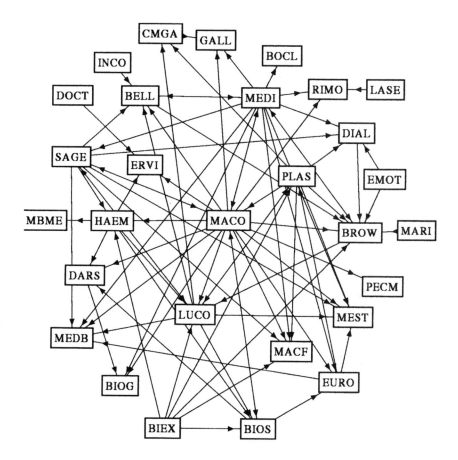

Figure 5.5 The Modena biomedical industry: exchange of components and parts (n=39)

units working as key actors may be increased via links with powerful firms in the community. Connections to powerful firms may provide useful information in a communication network, but may be dangerous in negotiating within a bargaining network (Brass and Burkhardt 1992).

With regards to the exchange of finished products of functional sub-assembled groups, the larger firms receive the highest indegree score (HAEM, BELL and BROW). The smaller firms are able to produce finished groups that will be assembled as an integrated unit. Firms are connected along a chain that has as final recipient a large firm. This is the case of DARS, the last of a series of five actors (Figure 5.6). Larger firms tend to

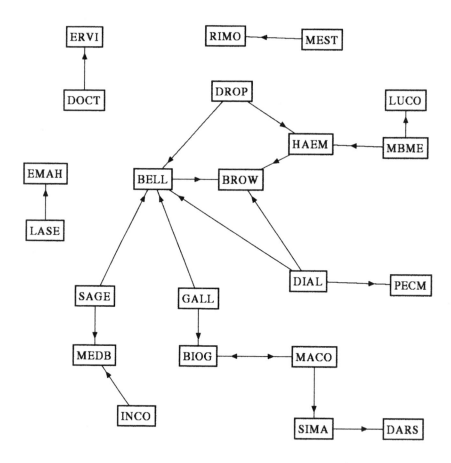

Figure 5.6 The Modena biomedical industry: exchange of finished products
(n=39)

sell their product directly to the market but also to other producers in the
area (i.e. BELL to BROW, or HAEM to BROW).

The proposition that the relational capability is not necessarily related to
size and age if firms are part of a spatially located community could be
supported by studying some of the preliminary results. The environment
could accelerate the formation and development of a relational texture
where the different actors soon know the rules of the game. To be part of a
community spatially located with a common background and entrepreneurial formulas may represent a way of accelerating knowledge on
'who' can do 'what'. The presence of relational multiplexity allows the
establishment of a learning-by-interacting mechanism, where a firm's age

and size matter, but is not decisive in explaining the relational structure of the community.

Figures 5.7 to 5.12 illustrate three relational subsets (TOT_REL, RAW_MAT, COM_PART) and, for various classes of age and size, the mean outdegree and indegree measure of centrality. As to the network of total relationships (TOT_REL) taking place among the actors, it is easy to note that there are no significant differences among classes of firms in terms of age. The older actors in the community have the higher indegree (Figure 5.7), but all the different classes fall around the mean value (8.50 for the normalized outdegree). Things are different when considering the firm's size (Figure 5.8). Here, the firms with more than 100 employees are central

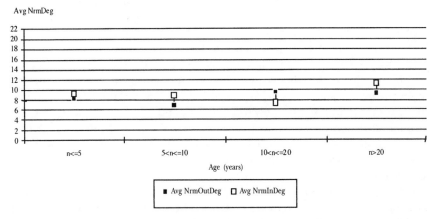

Figure 5.7 Average degree centrality by classes of firms' age (dataset: TOT_REL)

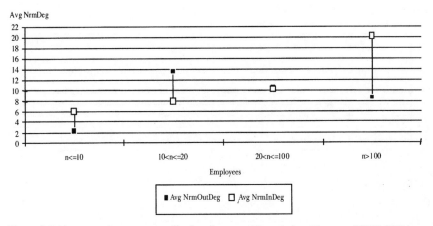

Figure 5.8 Average degree centrality by classes of firms' size (dataset: TOT_REL)

actors if we choose the indegree in the identification of prominent organizations, but they are not the key players if the focus is on the outdegree centrality. In this case, key players have to be found among those firms ranging from ten to twenty employees.

If we consider the network of relationships defined by exchanges of raw materials (RAW_MAT), whose critical role is related to constraints in the quality standards imposed by the international community, the age of the firm is important in explaining the relational structure. On the basis of this relational content, younger firms supplying others with materials of high quality are visible and prominent actors (Figure 5.9). The firms in this class also register the highest value in the indegree centrality, stressing the fact that the need to internalize raw materials is a fundamental one despite organizational age.

Size is also useful in capturing the central role in this type of network. The firms in class 1 (less than ten employees) and those in class 4 (more than 100) have low scores in outdegree (Figure 5.10). The first are not able to produce raw materials because this requires a critical mass in order to benefit from economies of scale. On the other hand, larger organizations are focused on design, assembly, final testing and distribution. They are the recipients of many choices in the sense that they buy from many actors when compared to others in this specific relational content. The mid-sized firms (for this specific industry) are those with the highest number of connections.

A first glance at the network of exchange relationships of components and parts reveals how older firms are obtaining the highest score in outdegree centrality (Figure 5.11). They supply components to others in

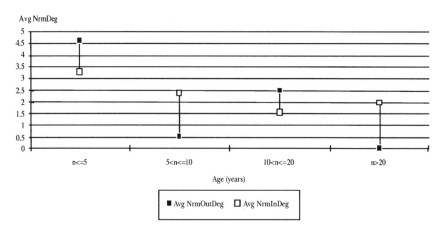

Figure 5.9 Average degree centrality by classes of firms' age (dataset: RAW_MAT)

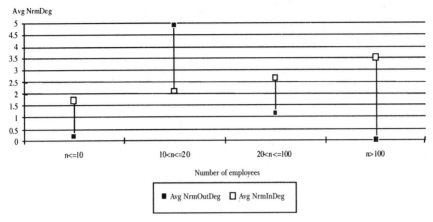

Figure 5.10 Average degree centrality by classes of firms' size (dataset: RAW_MAT)

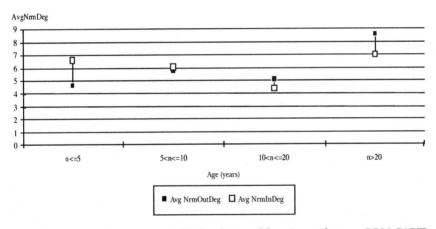

Figure 5.11 Average degree centrality by classes of firms' age (dataset: COM_PART)

the community, and at the same time internalize components and parts. This seems to confirm their central role as workflow orchestrators adding value to components which they will return to their clients. The very young firms have an indegree centrality close to that of the larger in class 4. The size is interesting when observing the high use of relationships by smaller firms for their needs of components and parts. These are mostly supplied by firms falling in classes with more than ten employees (Figure 5.12). The

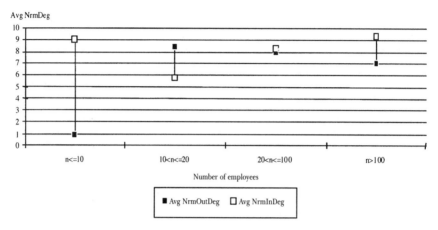

Figure 5.12 Average degree centrality by classes of firms' size (dataset: COM_PART)

larger ones are central actors when considering indegree as the measure of centrality consistent with their role as final assemblers.

With respect to classes of net sales, not reported in this study, the maximum integer value is for firms with more than $10 million. Smaller firms, with the exception of those realizing less than $500 thousand, have a better score in outdegree centrality. The centrality indexes by classes of export report the low score of those firms selling their products exclusively on the internal market (class 1) and those with more than half of their net sales realized abroad (class 4).

Discussion and conclusion

This study shows that shared knowledge and the network-like structuring of interfirm relationships do seem to matter for the performance of the system under study. Entering into close relations with other organizations is a means of accessing and leveraging resources and complementary capabilities which small firms generally lack. Small-firm network membership emphasizes geographically-located distinctive competencies that combine to allow firms to undertake organizational tasks that no one of them could accomplish individually. The large-scale reliance on interfirm collaborations in the biomedical industry reflects a fundamental concern with access to knowledge and resources.

What is known about which relational structures work best and what outcomes are derived from network participation is often limited. Our basic research question was centered on how small and medium-sized firms are structured within an organizational community. A relevant outcome is the access to resources. As a result of their network involvement, actors in the community can achieve positive transactional and relational advantages. The rationales offered to explain the increasing reliance on collaboration involve risk-sharing, access to new markets and technologies, and the pooling of complementary skills.

Two main implications seem to emerge from the study. The first is about the different roles played by participants in the network. The second refers to the functioning of interorganizational networks with distributed knowledge and specialized tasks. The key factor affecting industry growth was the formation of different types of organizations. The new organizational forms seem to have an important role in helping larger and older organizations reduce their weaknesses. Decoupling strategies such as subcontracting and outsourcing create new forms which may improve the viability of entire populations of firms. The information conveyed through the network is influenced by the network structure and, consequently, by each participant's position in the industry structure. Traditionally, firms with more experience are recognized to be better able to locate themselves in a benefits-rich position. Firms with more experience are also supposed to have more ties and these ties provide more reach into their respective resource environments. However, evidence from the study presents a rather different picture. Limited size and age do not reduce the propensity to form external ties. Age, per se, appears to be unimportant in the context of network experience and density. Size can be considered an outcome of interfirm structures rather than a determinant of partnerships.

Our preliminary results confirm the central role of the larger firms—the final assemblers or generalists—and their contribution to creating the industry, but they also support the proposition that smaller and younger organizations—the specialists—are vital to the organizational community. This can be found in the high scores reported in measures of outdegree centrality.

The generalists are crucial to the smaller units for their survival and growth, being visible actors, recipient of many relationships, and acting as knowledge-transfer facilitators for the entire business community. The injection of new competencies into the system is sometimes realized by encouraging the mobility of technicians across firms. As to the specialists, being positioned on the communication path connecting larger generalist firms, they provide complementary capabilities derived from their differentiated roles within the organizational community.

Specialists could then be considered as connecting actors, catalysts in the learning process occurring within the context of membership. Organizational characteristics such as age and size appear to be ancillary when accounting for patterns of collaboration.

The second relevant implication emerging from the study is the need of appropriate governance mechanisms to integrate into the overall system of relationships diverse sources of knowledge and providers of resources, such as sterilized disposables or high-quality raw materials. In fast-growing high-tech industries characterized by intense and frequent changing technologies, the investigation of how the different actors are linked and how they integrate into a network of relationships is of the utmost importance. This bears similarities to the idea of connecting and integrating roles that an organization should activate in order to solve its potential problems of coordination. One may easily observe from the biomedical experience in Modena that when relevant knowledge is widely distributed and not easily produced within the firm boundaries, relational activity increases.

When knowledge is distributed and responsible for the competitive advantage of an entire system, the locus of innovation lies in the network of interorganizational relationships (Powell *et al.* 1996). Price, power, or trust should then be combined into an architecture of governance mechanisms, and considered as drivers of a system in which many diverse firms work together in efforts to keep pace in high-growth industries. Horizontal modes of interfirm integration are used as substitutes of more conventional ways of structuring, such as the joint venture form of alliances. Rather than using external relations as a short-term mechanism to integrate a capability a firm has not yet acquired, organizations use networking to expand all their bases of knowlege, promoting their sense of community-level mutualism.

The structure of interfirm relationships among the new and smaller firms in the community may represent an interesting topic for further investigation aimed at confirming the apparently reduced liability of newness and smallness in organization systems similar to the one presented in this study. Theorists claim that firms are supposed to be vulnerable to the liabilities of newness (Aldrich and Auster 1986), and that these pressures are particularly severe when an industry is in its formative years (Aldrich and Fiol 1994). How organizations try to avoid the lack of legitimacy and resources is often related to their use of close working relationships with proximate organizations.

In our study, disconnected firms are rare, supporting the idea that unconnectedness is a liability (Baum and Oliver 1992). The study of the evolution of this localized system of production reveals how entrepreneurship is crucial for a correct interpretation of the relational structures within a community. Future researches will investigate how the networks of relations among existing units affect the entrepreneurship as the driving force of the founding process that gives form to the population. Another promising area for further research is the relationship between social structures of production and organizational dynamics.

Notes

1 A preliminary version of this paper was presented at the EMOT Workshop, Interfirm Networks: Outcomes and Policy Implications, Modena, September 5–8, 1996.
Thanks are due to Raffaele Corrado for assistance in the preparation of this paper. Authors also wish to thank Anna Grandori, for encouragement and valuable suggestions.
2 The local infrastructures for instance, are one of the main constraints to viability, for the actors in the community. No highways or railways cross the 'core' of the biomedical valley. Therefore, products have to circulate by trucks, and it often takes one hour to cover 25 miles.
3 The leading assembler supplies the external firm with a blueprint and sometimes with raw materials. The supplier adds value to the component or part and delivers it back to the leading firm.

Bibliography

Aldrich, H. E. and Auster, E. R. (1986) 'Even dwarfs started small: liabilities of age and size and their strategic implications', *Research in Organizational Behavior*, 8: 165–98.

Aldrich, H. E. and Fiol, C. M. (1994) 'Fool rush in? The institutional context of industry creation', *Academy of Management Review*, 19 (4): 645–70.

Baker, W. E. (1992) 'The network organization in theory and practice', in N. Nohria and R. Eccles (eds), *Networks and Organization: Structure, Form, and Action*, Cambridge, MA: Harvard Business School Press, pp. 397–429.

Barney, J. B. (1991) 'Firm resources and sustained competitive advantage', *Journal of Management*, 17: 99–120.

Baum, J. and Oliver, C. (1992) 'Institutional embeddedness and the dynamics of organizational populations', *American Sociological Review*, 57: 540–59.

Bonacich, P. (1972) 'Factoring and weighting approaches to status scores and clique identification', *Journal of Mathematical Sociology*, 2: 113–20.

Borgatti, S. P., Everett, M. G. and Freeman, L. C. (1992) *UCINET IV Version 1.00*, Columbia Analytic Technologies.

Brass, D. J. and Burkhardt, M. E. (1992) 'Centrality and power in organizations', in N. Nohria and R. Eccles (eds), *Networks and Organizations*, Boston, MA: Harvard Business School Press.

Burns, T. and Stalker, G.M. (1961) *The Management of Innovation*, London: Tavistock.

Burt, R. (1982) *Toward a Structural Theory of Action*, New York: Academic Press.

Burt, R. S. (1992) *Structural Holes. The Social Structure of Competition*, Cambridge, MA: Harvard University Press.

Consiglio Nazionale delle Ricerche (CNR) (1987) *Analisi di mercato delle tecnologie biomediche*, vol. 1, section 1, Progetto Finalizzato tecnologie biomediche e sanitarie.

Coleman, J. S., Katz, E. and Menzel, H. (1966) 'Medical innovation: a diffusion of an innovation among physicians', *Sociometry*, 20: 253–70.

de Vet, J. M. and Scott, A. J. (1992) 'The southern californian medical device industry: innovation, new firm formation, and location', *Research Policy*, 21: 145–61.

Di Maggio, P. (1986) 'Structural analysis of organizational fields', in B. Staw and Cummings, L. (eds), *Research in Organizational Behavior*, Conn.: JAI Press, 8: 335–70.

Dyer, J.H. (1996) 'Specialized supplier networks as a source of competitive advantage: evidence from the Auto Industry', *Strategic Management Journal*, 17: 271–91.

Faulkner (1987) *Music on Demand*, New York: Transaction Books.

Freeman, L. (1977) 'A set of measures of centrality based on betweenness', *Sociometry*, 40: 35–41.

Freeman, J. (1984) 'Entrepreneurs as organizational products. semiconductor firms and venture capital firms', *Working Paper*, Berkley: University of California.

Freeman, J. (1996) 'Entrepreneurship and the infrastructural community', *Working Paper*. Berkeley: University of California.

Friedkin, N. E. (1991) 'Theoretical foundations for centrality measures', *American Journal of Sociology*, 96: 1478–504.

Galbraith, J. (1973) *Designing Complex Organizations*, Reading, MA: Addison-Wesley.

Gerlach, M. (1992) *Alliance Capitalism: The Social Organization of Japanese Business*, Berkeley: University of California Press.

Gibson, L. J. (1970). 'An analysis of the location of instrument manufacturers in the United States', *Annals of the Association of American Geographers*, 60: 335–67.

Hansen, M. H., Hoskisson, R., Lorenzoni, G. and P. Smith Ring (1997) 'Strategic capabilities of the transactionally-intense firm: leveraging interfirm relationships', *Working Paper*, Texas A&M University.

Herrigel, G. 1996. *Industrial Constructions. The sources of German industrial power.* New York: Cambridge University Press.

ISTAT, Istituto Nazionale di Statistica (1995) 7^ *Censimento generale dell'Industria e dei Servizi*, Roma.

Knoke, D. and Burt, R. S. (1983) 'Prominence', in R. S. Burt and M. J. Minor, (eds), *Appled Network Analysis*, Newbury Park, CA: Sage, pp. 195–222.

Lawrence, P. and Lorsch, J. L. (1967) *Organization and Environment. Managing Differentiation and Integration*, Cambridge, Mass: Harvard University Press.

Lipparini, A. (1995) *Imprese, relazioni tra imprese e posizionamento competitivo*, Milano: Etas Libri.

Lomi, A. (ed.) (1997) *L'analisi relazionale delle organizzazioni. Riflessioni teoriche ed esperienze empiriche*, Bologna: Il Mulino.

Lorenzoni, G. and Baden Fuller, C. (1995) 'Creating a strategic center to manage a web of partners', *California Management Review*, 37, 3: 146–63.

Malecki, E. J. (1985) 'Industrial location and corporate organization in high technology industries', *Economic Geography*, 61, 4: 345–69.

March, J. G. and Simon, H. A. (1958) *Organizations*, New York: Wiley.

Nieminen, J. (1973) 'On centrality in a graph', *Scandinavian Journal of Psychology*, 15: 322–36.

Oakey, R. (1983) 'High-technology industry, industrial location, and regional development: the British case', in F .E. I. Hamilton and G .J. R. Linge (eds), *Spatial Analysis, Industry, and the Industrial Environment*, Chichester: John Wiley, vol. III, pp. 179–296.

Ouchi, W. G. (1980) Markets, Bureaucraties, and Clans, *Administrative Science Quarterly*, 25: 124–41.

Pfeffer, J. and Salancik, G. R. (1978) *The External Control of Organization*, New York: Harper & Row.

Piore, M. J. and Sabel, C. (1984) *The Second Industrial Divide*, New York: Basic Books.

Podolny, J. and Stuart, T. E. (1995) 'A role-based ecology of technical change', *American Journal of Sociology*, 100: 1224–60.

Podolny, J. (1993) 'A status-based model of market competition', *American Journal of Sociology*, 98: 829–72.

Podolny, J. (1994) 'Market uncertainty and the social character of economic exchange', *Administrative Science Quarterly*, 39: 458–83.

Podolny, J. M., Stuart, T. E. and Hannan, M. T. (1996) 'Networks, knowledge, and niches: competition in the worldwide semiconductor industry, 1984–1991', *American Journal of Sociology*, 102, 3: 659–89.

Porter, M. (1980) *Competitive Strategy*, New York: The Free Press.

Porter, M. E. (1996) 'What is strategy', *Harvard Business Review*.

Powell, W. W., Koput, K. W. and Smith-Doerr, L. (1996) 'Interorganizational collaboration and the locus of innovation: networks of learning in bio-technology', *Administrative Science Quarterly*, 41: 116–45.

Rogers, E. M. and Kincaid D. L. (1981) *Communication Networks: Toward a New Paradigm for Research*, New York: Macmillan.

Rumelt, R. (1984) 'Towards a strategic theory of the firm', in R. Lamb (ed.), *Competitive Strategic Management*, NJ: Englewood Cliff, Prentice Hall.

Rumelt, R., Schendel, D. and Teece, D. (1994) *Fundamental Issues in Strategy*, Boston, MA: Harvard Business School Press.

Sabel, *et al.* (1986) 'How to keep mature industry innovative', *Technology Review*.

Sabidussi, G. (1966) 'The centrality index of a graph', *Psycometrika*, 31: 581–603.

Saxenian, A. (1994) *Regional Advantage. Culture and Competition in Silicon Valley and Route 128*, Cambridge, MA: Harvard University Press.

Scott, A. J. and Angel, D. P. (1987) 'The U.S. semiconductor industry: a locational analysis', *Environment and Planning*, 19: 875–912.

Scott, A. J. (1988) *New Industrial Spaces: Flexible Production Organization and Regional Development in North America and Western Europe*, London: Pion.

Simon, H. A. (1947) *Administrative Behavior*, New York: The Free Press.

Storper, M. (1996) 'Innovation as collective action', *Industrial and Corporate Change*, 5: 761–90.

Thompson, J. D. (1967) *Organizations in Actions*, New York: McGraw-Hill.

US Department of Commerce (1989) *US Industrial Outlook*, Washington D.C.: Government Printing Office.

U.S.L.n.15, (1994) 'Resoconto attività produttive', Mirandola.

Uzzi, B. (1996) 'The sources and consequences of embeddedness for the economic performance of organizations: the network effect,' *American Sociological Review*, forthcoming.

Wasserman, S. and Faust, K. (1994) *Social Network Analysis: Methods and Applications*, Cambridge University Press.

Wernerfelt, B. (1984) 'A resource-based view of the firm', *Strategic Management Journal*, 5: 171–80.

Williamson, O. (1975) *Markets and Hierarchies: Analysis and Antitrust Implications*, New York: The Free Press.

Williamson, O. (1991) 'Comparative economic organization: the analysis of discrete structural alternatives', *Administrative Science Quarterly*, 36.

Williamson, O. and Ouchi, W. (1981) 'The markets and hierarchies and visible hand perspectives', in A. Van de Ven and W. Joyce (eds), *Perspective on Organizational Design and Behavior*, New York: Wiley.

6   Industry clusters as commercial, knowledge and institutional networks

Opto-electronics in six regions in the UK, USA and Germany[1]

Chris Hendry, James Brown, Robert DeFillippi and Robert Hassink

Introduction

Industry clusters are defined as geographically localized concentrations of firms in the same industry (Swann and Prevezer 1997) or in closely related industries (Porter 1990). Academic research on industry clusters suggests that the strength and dynamism of such clusters are facilitated by university, commercial and governmental relations (Biggiero 1998). Moreover, these relations may be located within local, national and international networks. Industry clusters may thus vary by both the extent to which they are supported by university, commercial and governmental cooperative ties, and by the extent to which these ties are locally, nationally or internationally patterned.

Each of these relationship types offers distinctive advantages to participating cluster firms. First, university relations provide access to advanced technical knowledge that may be commercialized by member firms in cooperation with their university partners. Second, universities may serve as incubators for cluster firm formation by former university employees or students. Third, universities provide highly talented human capital to manage and staff cluster firms. Commercial relations between firms in the form of joint ventures, strategic alliances, subcontracting partnerships and outsourcing relations provide cluster firms with access to complementary resources required for product development, manufacturing or marketing and distribution activities. Finally, governmental relations can benefit cluster firms through subsidies and procurement contracts, by facilitating cooperation amongst cluster firms, and through investment tax credits, regulatory protection or regulatory relief.

Successful industry clusters do not necessarily manifest the full range of commercial, university and governmental relations. Some clusters are more richly networked with commercial firms and have few if any linkages with either governmental or university institutions (e.g. Hollywood's film-making cluster). Others have commercial and governmental ties, but lack close linkages to universities (e.g. Italy's furniture, footwear, textiles and clothing districts). Yet others have commercial and university ties, but weak governmental linkages (e.g. Seattle's software cluster). These examples suggest that clusters may arise with distinctive networks of university, commercial and governmental relations.

Industry clusters whose relations are primarily local are classified as industrial districts. Locally concentrated networks have been extensively studied within central and north-eastern Italy (Bagnasco 1977; Brusco 1982; Becattini 1989; Bellandi 1992). Industry clusters whose relations are primarily within the nation-state, but are non-local, are conceptualized as manifestations of national systems of innovation (Porter 1990; Lundvall 1992; Nelson 1993). Finally, industry clusters whose networks are primarily international in character are conceptualized as nodes within international networks of production and distribution (Amin and Thrift 1992; Kaounides 1995).

Against this background of possibilities, this chapter examines regional clusters in the UK, USA and Germany in a modern high-tech sector—opto-electronics—with the intent of answering the following questions:

1   To what extent are clusters of firms in opto-electronics participating in governmental, commercial and university cooperative relations?
2   To what extent are clusters of opto-electronics firms embedded in primarily local, national or international networks of cooperation and mutual support?

The focus is thus initially on understanding the evolution of different clusters, the form they take, and why particular sets of relations have come about. This gives some insight into the strengths and weaknesses of the configurations we see—explaining, for example, why growth has happened in the form it has in terms of numbers and size of firms. However, the prime focus here is to differentiate descriptively among different types of network. A fuller assessment of growth and innovation, using more quantifiable measures of performance, will come later.

Opto-electronics

In less than a quarter of a century, the electronics industry has been responsible for transforming every aspect of commercial and industrial life. In a report published in 1988 in the UK, the Advisory Council On Science and Technology (ACOST) claimed that opto-electronics has the potential to make a similar impact on society in the next twenty-five years.

The ACOST report defines opto-electronics as 'the integration of optical and electronic techniques in the acquisition, processing, communication, storage, and display of information' (ACOST 1988). Thus, an important defining characteristic of the industry is the concept of 'technology fusion'

(Dubarle and Verie 1993). This is the principle that combining two or more complementary technologies leads to the creation of new products with functionality and capability that were previously not considered possible. In the case of opto-electronics the point at which technologies come together is often at the level of basic science, and involves disciplines such as traditional optics, solid-state physics, materials science and information technology, with the consequence that the industry is heavily reliant on scientific research and the ability to envisage the commercial potential of a discovery, when used in conjunction with other results (Kodama 1995).

Opto-electronics technologies have emerged from a period of laboratory-based R&D in the 1960s and 1970s, into an applications and diffusion phase in the 1980s and 1990s. In the initial phase, the organizational studies research question has been, how existing large firms absorb these new technologies into their set of core competencies. Miyazaki (1995) traces this process in relation to a number of leading Japanese and European firms, and concludes that 'in-house development has been the primary mode of competence building, especially in the early and middle phases of development' (Miyazaki 1995: 203). Miyazaki (1995) argues for the critical importance of establishing competence in core technological disciplines as representing a more effective long-term strategy, than the alternative approach of buying in components and devices whose underlying scientific operating principles are not fully understood.

So, at this initial stage of evolution, much of the developmental and applications activity is typically buried within large firms having other interests. Eventually divisions form within large firms, as technologies coalesce and product opportunities emerge. Dosi describes these patterns of technological development as 'technological paradigms' (Dosi 1984). 'Pure', independent firms also begin to appear through spin-off activity, either inside the large company or through employees leaving to form their own enterprises, or from individuals with an entrepreneurial streak coming out of the university research environment. Accelerated rates of change in the industry bring increased complexity of products and a more extensive range of end-user applications. Firms begin to appreciate their inability to encompass the complete set of skills required for successful commercialization of this technology and create external linkages in order to gain leverage from retained core competencies (Rothwell 1992).

At this point, the relationships between firms and infrastructure elements such as universities, the labour market, research institutions and government agencies become more critical, as R&D activity and skills are externalized into markets rather than hierarchies (Williamson 1975), and as the industry becomes characterized by the presence of large numbers of SMEs, often in the form of agglomerated networks surrounding the original players.

A critical question then arises, concerned with how these relationships operate in defined localities, and how key players such as large commercial enterprises, government agencies and universities influence the evolution of the industry. This chapter is concerned with this question, and with the local, national and international character of networking relations enjoyed by cluster firms in each locality.

Research objectives and analytical framework

The findings reported here arise out of a wider comparative study, involving researchers in the UK, Germany and the USA, which addresses a number of general objectives through the specific example of the opto-electronics industry. Foremost among these is testing and developing a model of 'industry clusters' in which national competitive advantage accrues where there are concentrations of firms in the same and related sectors in the same locality. Opto-electronics provides a good test of this and other general themes related to high technology industry in that it:

• is concentrated in particular localities in the UK, Germany and the USA;
• has followed a different trajectory in each country through the pursuit of different end-markets, levels of infrastructure support and governmental policy;
• is an important strategic sector with applications in many high-technology products and markets; and,
• comprises a number of subsectors at different stages of technological maturity and organization, which are subject to different levels of market fragmentation through regulation and public procurement;

The phenomenon of 'industrial districts' (or regional clusters) excited renewed interest during the 1980s (Goodman, Bamford and Saynor 1989) and added impetus from Michael Porter's (1990) wide-ranging study of comparative national advantage. It is possible, however, that the importance of industry clusters as regional concentrations is overstated by failing to take account of other forms of networking in which firms engage, extending beyond their locality. These include national and international supply-chain relationships and strategic alliances. As Kaounides (1995) has observed, there now exists a very complex web of such alliances in advanced materials sectors, including opto-electronics. From the outset, therefore, the study sought to establish empirically the extent of local, national and international linkages.

To explore these network relationships among firms, and the influences upon them affecting their growth and performance, we used a broad framework comprising factors from the network and strategic management literatures (see Figure 6.1), namely:

1   The networks of related firms and the nature of cooperative and

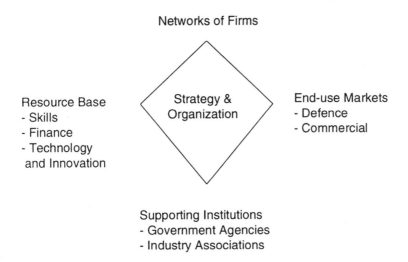

Networks of Firms

Resource Base
- Skills
- Finance
- Technology
  and Innovation

Strategy &
Organization

End-use Markets
- Defence
- Commercial

Supporting Institutions
- Government Agencies
- Industry Associations

Figure 6.1 Five sets of factors for analysing the emergence and role of clusters in opto-electronics

competitive relationships between them, including the role of large firms in organizing the sector (Florida and Kenney 1990).

2   The available resource base, in terms of skills, knowledge, technology and finance.

3   The network of supporting institutions, such as industry associations, for promoting trade, skills and R&D, and the role of public authorities at local and national level—the proper role of which is a matter of some controversy (Porter 1990; Walker 1993; Kaounides 1995).

4   The nature of the end-markets served (which in opto-electronics initially comprised particularly defence and telecommunications, but now include quite disparate commercial markets), and the extent to which these have had beneficial or detrimental effects on the long-term development of the industry in the different regions (see Kaldor 1984; Stoneman 1987; McKinsey 1988; Walker 1993; but also ACOST 1988).

5   Internal organizational factors and company strategies pursued over time, including investment patterns and attitudes to risk (ACOST 1988; Campbell, Sorge and Warner 1989; Freeman 1991), which make the difference between successful and unsuccessful firms (Florida and Kenney 1991).

A feature of this five-factor model is that it incorporates Porter's attention to end-use markets, which is relatively absent from the more inward-looking European representation of industrial districts, while also giving attention to supporting institutions which are a feature of the European tradition, but which Porter tends to disparage.

In addition to these factors, the underlying technological structure of the industry is of considerable importance in fostering network relationships. Because opto-electronics depends on 'technology fusion' (Dubarle and Verie 1993), the industry gives rise to a structure whereby end-use products evolve from a combination of a number of intermediary products and underlying generic technologies. Thus, Miyazaki (1995) characterizes the industry in terms of a three-level model comprising *generic technologies*, *key components* and *products and systems* with end-user applications. The need to combine these in specific and precisely defined ways has implications for networking, from R&D through to production.

The concept of network, loosely defined as a collection of agents and the set of interconnecting relations between them, is a wide ranging one, and as DeBresson (1991) points out, many different types can exist, each one lending itself to a different analytical framework. Consequently, how the network phenomenon facilitates the growth and development of a specific high-technology industry such as opto-electronics involves making a choice on the perspective to be adopted. The five-factor model taken as the general underlying framework for studying such an industry, and the work of Van de Ven and Garud (1993), suggest three network relations that are especially interesting: (1) the network of commercial organizations and the trading patterns between them (since the nature of business relationships between operational actors is central to any industry); (2) the network of relationships between firms and government agencies (since government authorities have a distinctive role in supporting economic development within their jurisdictions); and (3) the network of cluster-firm relations with universities (since these are the source of important developmental resources such as knowledge, skilled labour and complementary support services). In this chapter we use the terms 'commercial network', 'governmental network' and 'university network' to distinguish between these three types of networks.

Networks in six regions

An earlier study (Hendry, Arthur and Jones 1995) had identified the fact that firms in opto-electronics are concentrated in certain localities in the UK, Germany and the USA. The project therefore sought to evaluate the relative importance of the above five sets of factors in the development of the opto-electronics sector in six regions in these three countries, in three stages—an initial mapping involving extensive interviews, a series of case studies, and a final survey. This chapter draws upon findings from the first two stages of the study, focusing specifically on the networking phenomena.

In the course of the qualitative phase of the research, comprising stages 1 and 2, in-depth interviews were conducted in 100 firms during 1996–97 (in some cases with a number of employees) in six regions in the UK, USA and Germany. These were supplemented by a wide range of interviews with companies in other regions (including Scotland and Florida), government officials, senior university researchers and industry experts, and active participation in the Welsh Opto-electronics Forum, to broaden background understanding and gain insight into network relationships from different perspectives. Public documents were also accessed. However, the inadequacy of statistics (deriving partly from the emerging character of the industry, partly from widely differing practices of governments in the three countries) meant that the companies themselves were an essential source of primary data.

The six regions featured are Wales and East Anglia in the UK, Arizona and Massachusetts in the USA, and Bavaria (primarily Munich) and East Thuringia in Germany. Apart from each of these being prime centres of opto-electronics activity, they also provide a series of contrasts. Wales and East Anglia were selected to provide a contrast between an old industrial region and a region which has seen the most dramatic development of high-tech industry in the UK. Arizona and East Thuringia are both like Wales, insofar as all three have struggled to emerge from depression; each sees opto-electronics as a key industry to help lift the local economy; and all three have active regional development agencies which are spearheading this. On the other hand, Massachusetts and Munich are (like East Anglia) vibrant centres of high-tech industry which have enjoyed relatively uninterrupted growth. Other features, such as the role of universities in the regions, became more evident in the course of the study. The prime criterion for selection, however, was the presence of a significant concentration of opto-electronics firms in each area.

Table 6.1 provides some basic facts about the 100 firms. The data is current at 1997 and is derived from interviews, company documents and other published sources. All figures are percentages, with the total number of firms in the region and the sample shown at the foot of the table.

We now review the origins and development of the opto-electronics industry in these six regions, the role of government and universities in stimulating it, and the resulting characteristics of firms, as background to understanding the network relationships that have developed.

Wales

Wales is a principality in the UK with a strong sense of identity and a history that goes back to the beginnings of society in Great Britain. In more modern times it has suffered from a decline in traditional industries such as coal and steel, and this has been coupled with initiatives at regional and national level aimed at economic regeneration. Some of these initiatives go back to the 1930s, the most lasting manifestations of which are the industrial estates developed to attract industries to the area under the Special Areas Act (1934).

In 1964 the Welsh Office was created to be responsible for public

Table 6.1 Firms by size, age, industry level, ownership and start-up pattern in six regions, expressed as percentages of firms in sample

	Wales	EA	AZ	MA	Bavaria	Thuringia
Employees[a]						
<10	24	19	35	20	10	30
10–100	38	73	47	35	70	50
100–500	38	8	18	25	20	20
>500	0	0	0	20	0	0
Years in operation in the region[b]						
<5	14	0	30	10	20	70
5–10	24	27	30	20	10	30
10–20	24	50	30	25	30	0
>20	38	23	10	45	40	0
Level in three-level model[c]						
Generic	33	16	4	17	6	0
Component	37	52	43	50	55	53
End-product	30	32	53	33	39	47
Ownership[d]						
Independent Private	44	46	76	35	50	40
Quoted	0	4	0	15	0	0
National subsidiary	22	12	12	40	20	60
Foreign subsidiary	34	38	12	10	30	0
Start-up pattern[e]						
Company spin-off	57	61	29	50	70	80
University spin-off	5	23	41	35	0	20
National investment	29	8	18	5	0	0
Foreign investment	9	8	12	10	30	0
Sample firms	18	23	19	20	10	10
Est. firms in region[f]	25	53	125	370	152 in Germany	

Notes

a.   Total number of full-time employees at location.
b.   Number of years the company has been operating in the region with its current identity and function.
c.   Position in three-layer model (firms operating at more than one level are accounted at each one).
d.   Independent private, publicly quoted company, subsidiary of own-national, or foreign subsidiary.
e.   Origin as either a spin-off from a company or university faculty/student start-up, or investment by an own-national company or foreign inward investment.
f.   Sources—Photonics Spectra, trade publications, WDA, Arizona Optics Industry Directory.

administration in Wales, followed in 1976 by the Welsh Development Agency (WDA) with a directive to bring new companies and new industries into Wales, to create jobs and stimulate entrepreneurship. This has had some considerable success to the extent that in recent years, despite having just 4 per cent of the UK workforce, Wales has attracted over 20 per cent of foreign inward investment in the UK.

As well as the accepted value of inward investment, bringing jobs and income to the region, an additional consequence of the inward investment policy can be seen in the number of company spin-offs that have arisen from firms initially entering the region through inward investment. This is exemplified in the north where the development of the opto-electronics industry has relied heavily on the growth trajectory of one company, Pilkington plc (the largest manufacturer of flat and safety glass in the world for the automotive and construction sectors). In 1957, Pilkington plc took the decision to establish a new division in North Wales specializing in the production of high-quality ophthalmic glass (Barker 1994). From this initial investment, augmented by a deliberate policy of diversification into new business areas, Pilkington plc spawned a number of independent enterprises, each of which has developed an identity and a growth trajectory of its own.

Table 6.1 reflects this long-standing policy emphasis on inward invest-ment, with Wales enjoying the greatest percentage of firms in the categories with 100–500 employees among the six regions. Wales shares with Massachusetts and Bavaria a high percentage of firms established for more than twenty years. It is possible also that the more even spread of firms across Miyazaki's (1995) three-level model of the industry is due to the fact that inward investment has been encouraged over a number of technologies and industry sectors.

What is missing from this picture is the start-up company originating from a university research department. This may be to do with the university presence in Wales being dispersed around a number of centres in the region, and no single one having sufficient critical mass. It does not mean that such institutions dissociate themselves from commercial opera-tions—in fact, the reverse is the case, particularly in recent years, as university research departments have built up research contract revenues to bolster other sources of funding. So far, though, this has not been trans-formed into the creation of independent commercial ventures.

East Anglia

East Anglia is formally defined as comprising the counties of Norfolk, Suffolk and Cambridgeshire. It has never been a heavy industrial area. Indeed, the most famous institution in the region has always been the University of Cambridge with its formidable reputation for scientific research, which in optics goes right back to Isaac Newton. In terms of numbers of firms, opto-electronics activity in this region centres around Cambridge, where there is a concentration of opto-electronics companies. But an important and historically significant commercial presence is also found in BT Laboratories at Martlesham, and, bordering on the region, in GEC-Marconi and NORTEL (formerly STC) in Essex.

The 'Cambridge Phenomenon' refers to the explosive growth of high-technology companies in and around the Cambridge area during the

1980s, which followed the creation of the Cambridge Science Park in 1973. This has been extensively studied and documented (Segal, Quince and Wickstead 1985; Keeble 1989; Saxenian 1989; Garnsey and Cannon-Brookes 1993). The resulting pattern in Cambridge is of a large number of small companies, a focus on software and services, no development of large-scale manufacturing, and small companies becoming integrated into global supply chains (rather than building up a significant manufacturing presence locally themselves).

However, Cambridge has a history of high-technology industry going back well before the science park, to the Cambridge Scientific Instrument Company in the 1890s. This spawned numerous companies which, when combined with new entrants spinning out of the university environment, resulted in a complex picture of commercial and technological development in scientific instruments, aeronautics and communications (Cattermole and Wolfe 1987). In the course of time, these went through successive episodes of expansion and contraction. Consequently, opto-electronics activity in East Anglia is characterized by an agglomeration of firms in and around the city of Cambridge, consisting of start-ups originating in the University of Cambridge and the fall-out from older established firms in scientific instrument manufacture. The number of new firms in opto-electronics started during the 1980s growth period was around thirty (out of 900 new firms), and many of these grew out of older firms in the locality that were restructuring and downsizing. Opto-electronics thus stands somewhat apart from the 'Cambridge Phenomenon'.

An explanation for this lack of concerted effort and focus on opto-electronics may be that university research in this field is fragmented across the departments of Astronomy, Engineering and Materials Science. This contrasts with the growth of biotechnology and computer software firms in Cambridge where the university has a single external research focus (through the Medical Research Centre and Computer Aided Design Centre).

Keeble (1989) suggests that the impetus behind the recent growth of high-technology firms in Cambridge is a combination of macroeconomic and technological changes, and certain local factors, which have created new market and product opportunities ideally suited to the development of small-to-medium-sized high-technology enterprises (SMEs). Consequently, as Keeble (1989) notes, Cambridge is a centre for high R&D content firms staffed by highly qualified technical people who like living in the area. There is very little interaction between firms and not much evidence of an inclination for, or drive towards, dramatic company and business growth.

One further paradox in the region is that no cluster of opto-electronics companies emerged in the vicinity of British Telecom's research centre at Martlesham, despite the fact that BT was at the heart of developments in optical fibres for carrying telecommunications traffic. A different development trajectory is evident in that locality (some 60 miles from Cambridge), with the creation of only one major opto-electronics manufacturer spinning off from BT (initially as a joint venture and then as a wholly-owned part of Hewlett Packard), and nothing in the way of a cluster of small firms.

Reflecting this history, Table 6.1 shows that East Anglia has the highest percentage of firms across the six regions in the 10–100 size bracket (closely followed by Bavaria), and of firms in the 10–20 years age bracket. As with Wales and Bavaria, it has a very high proportion of firms that are now owned by larger foreign companies. In common with Massachusetts, East Anglia has a small but non-trivial percentage of firms involved in generic materials supplied to the opto-electronics industry.

Arizona

Arizona is in the top ten of US states for population growth. This has not always been the case. After many years of continual growth, based on the 5Cs (Copper, Citrus, Cattle, Climate and Cotton) the bottom fell out of the Arizona economy in the mid-1980s when the savings and loans industry declined, the flow of people coming into the state reduced and property prices collapsed.

To address these fundamental problems in Arizona's economy, a state-wide public/private partnership was initiated to develop the Arizona Strategic Plan for Economic Development (ASPED). This was completed in 1992, and in the implementation that followed, the idea of promoting industry cluster development became a central policy objective. Opto-electronics was one of ten industry clusters identified by the ASPED coalition. The subsequent Governor's Strategic Partnership for Economic Development (GSPED) encouraged each cluster to develop a wide array of collaborative activities to stimulate information sharing, joint marketing and production activities, and the development of stronger educational, financial and governmental infrastructure foundations (Waits 1996).

The basis for opto-electronics activity in Arizona was the creation of the Optical Sciences Center (OSC) at the University of Arizona in 1970. The University of Arizona itself was established in 1885 as a land grant university by the Arizona State Legislature.

In the early 1960s, the 'Needs in Optics Committee' of the Optical Society of America identified a requirement for additional programmes to provide graduate-level education in optics, at a time when there was only the one centre at Rochester, New York. Under the leadership of Aden Meinel, who was in Tucson establishing the Kitt Peak National Observatory, and with the financial support of the University of Arizona Foundation and the promise of a US Air Force contract for academic research, plans were made for an Optical Sciences Centre, to be established at the University of Arizona. This came into existence in 1970.

The objectives of the centre, set out by Aden Meinel (Powell 1996), show that this was outward-looking from the beginning:

The laboratory is designed to fill three purposes; (1) the establishment of a research centre for experimental and theoretical optical physics that is responsive to the national needs at the limits of state-of-the-art. (2) the establishment of a strong graduate curriculum in optical physics and technology to produce Ph.D. graduates with a solid theoretical background and a knowledge of technology at an advanced level. (3) the establishment of a centre where the emergence of new technology can be translated into industrial competence through frequent contact with visiting personnel from the optics area in industry.

(Powell 1996)

When the OSC started there were very few companies in Arizona based on optics technology. There are now over 125 such companies, concentrated in Tucson and Phoenix (the principal towns in Arizona, separated by a distance of around 100 miles). These firms have total revenues estimated at more than $340 million a year (Catts, Johnson and Gibson 1996). This pattern of many very small firms is borne out by Table 6.1 which shows that Arizona (among all the regions investigated) has the highest percentage of firms with fewer than ten employees (closely followed by Thuringia). Moreover, Arizona (and Tucson in particular) lead all six regions with the highest percentage of firms spun off from a university and the highest percentage of firms under independent private ownership. These patterns are consistent with the role of the University of Arizona Optical Science Center as a major source of new firm formation in the cluster.

Massachusetts

In its annual census of opto-electronics related companies, the Photonics Spectra's corporate guide consistently ranks Massachusetts second in the USA (after California) in terms of the number of firms. For example, in 1995 Massachusetts is recorded as having 374 opto-electronics related firms to California's 744 firms, and New York State's 360 (Spectra 1995). The vast majority of opto-electronics firms in Massachusetts are SMEs, but the state also features the largest opto-electronics firm in the USA (EG&G) and opto-electronics subsidiaries of very substantial corporate parents (for example, Lockheed Martin). Moreover, Massachusetts is the headquarters for some of the leading and largest firms in selected opto-electronics industry segments (for example, Optical Corporation of America in thin film optical coatings). Table 6.1 bears out this picture, with a greater bias than the other regions investigated towards established large firms (that is, firms with more than 500 employees that have been in the area for more than twenty years).

Two key factors have been significant to the development of the industry in Massachusetts. First, there is the pre-eminent role played by the universities; and second, the influence of opto-electronics firms (in many cases, formed by engineers and scientists coming out of the university environment) that were created specifically to exploit the opportunities presented by government spending on defence.

The role of universities in firm formation and growth in Massachusetts cannot be overstated. Among the half dozen universities associated with opto-electronics technology and industry development in Massachusetts, MIT is the pre-eminent contributor to the region's intellectual and entrepreneurial human capital. Many of the largest, most innovative and dynamic opto-electronics firms in Massachusetts were either founded or staffed by MIT faculty or graduates. MIT's involvement with opto-electronics goes back to Ali Javan, the originator of the Helium Neon gas laser in 1960 who subsequently joined the faculty at MIT (Hecht 1992). At MIT, he started the development of the school which has since expanded to over 200 research faculty working in opto-electronics. MIT has also earned a reputation as *the* school for technology-based entrepreneurs, through its institutional support for research commercialization (aided by its Technology Liaison Office), its many centres for technology research (for example, Lincoln Laboratories), and its entrepreneurially-oriented Sloan School of Management.

However, MIT is not alone in supporting the development of opto-electronics in the region. Other universities include Boston University, which was the source of the technology and the people that became ITEK, one of the leading firms in space-based military reconnaissance systems; Tufts University, which has an opto-electronics centre that works closely with local entrepreneurs in the commercialization of research (where the founder of the American Optical Corporation studied in the 1950s); Northeastern University; and the University of Massachusetts at Lowell (which has a research centre specializing in electrical engineering with opto-electronics applications).

The second most obvious factor in the development of opto-electronics in Massachusetts is the impact of defence expenditure. In the post-war period of the late 1940s and 1950s, the initial formation of defence-oriented Massachusetts firms drew considerable strength from the existence of founders and key engineering personnel coming out of the area's major universities. Subsequent growth of the Massachusetts opto-electronics industry in the 1960s through to the mid-1980s was also spurred by similar dynamics of federal government military procurement, university-based military research, and commercial spin-offs started by university faculty and graduating students.

Table 6.1 indicates that Massachusetts is second only to Arizona in the percentage of opto-electronic firms started as university spin-offs. However, Massachusetts leads all regions in the percentage of largest and oldest opto-electronics firms. This reflects the area's long-standing participation in opto-electronics and the continuing presence of large, mature opto-electronics firms as well as younger, smaller firms in the region.

Bavaria

Munich (the capital of Bavaria) and its eight surrounding counties comprise some 2.4 million inhabitants, with Munich having the highest economic growth rate of all German cities, the highest GDP per capita, the highest employment growth and the lowest unemployment rate (Sternberg 1997). It also has the highest proportion of employment in high-tech industries and research and development functions, and the highest proportion of start-ups in high-tech industries. Munich's particular strengths are in electronics and microelectronics, the space and aircraft industry (mostly defence oriented), and to a lesser extent the automobile industry (Sternberg 1997).

The largest companies in the electronics sector are Siemens, Siemens-Nixdorf, Digital, Motorola, Hitachi, Texas Instruments, Fairchild and IBM. The pivotal role of Siemens in the Munich economy is illustrated by the fact that Siemens employs over 12,000 persons in R&D in Munich and that more than four-fifths of electrical engineering companies in the area have business relations with Siemens (Sternberg 1997). Munich also is Germany's leading defence industry city (Deutsche Aerospace, Siemens and Krauss-Maffei). It also boasts a significant concentration of company headquarters, and business and financial consultancies, software companies and insurance firms.

Munich's opto-electronics cluster is based primarily on the presence of a large number of subsidiaries of large, internationally-owned electronics companies (such as AT&T Opto-electronics, Motorola and General Instruments), as well as large German-owned companies such as Siemens, and a number of smaller firms. Among these smaller firms are a large number of laser firms which are primarily distributors of laser products manufactured in Japan and America.

The main impetus for the development of laser technology in Munich came from two companies. In the 1960s, Siemens was the first German manufacturer of small helium/neon gas lasers in Munich. Also during the 1960s, Laser Optronics, having started as a distributor of an American company, built the first high-performance gas and solid-state lasers for material processors. Subsequent laser company growth in the area was stimulated by the presence of many potential users of laser technology among high-tech firms, and helped by Germany's most important laser trade fair being held there annually.

Table 6.1 shows Bavaria second only to East Anglia in the percentage of firms in the 10–100 size bracket, and second to Massachusetts in firms older than twenty years. The age of its opto-electronics firms reflects their earlier origins and subsequent relocation from Berlin after the Second World War. As with Wales and East Anglia, Bavaria also has a high percentage of opto-electronics firms owned and established by foreign companies, which reflects the large number of laser distributor companies acting for US and Japanese manufacturers. Finally, it shares with Thuringia and Arizona a very low representation of firms involved in generic materials supply for the opto-electronics industry.

Thuringia

Thuringia is the most south-western of the new Laender in eastern Germany. The region has a long tradition of manufacturing, with approximately 40 per cent of the workforce involved in manufacturing in 1990.

The university city of Jena (population 100,000) is the acknowledged centre of the opto-electronics cluster in Thuringia. The city is home to Carl Zeiss, the world-renowned optics company, founded in 1846 as a result of a collaboration between the optics practitioner Carl Zeiss and University of Jena optics professor Ernst Abbee. This collaboration established a company tradition of close cooperation between industrial production and scientific research over the next one hundred years, as Zeiss diversified from microscopes to optical measurement instruments. However, the company suffered severe losses of technology, equipment and personnel after World War Two to both Western and Soviet occupational forces. By the mid-1960s, Carl Zeiss had diversified into laser applications and laser measurement technologies for defence. In the 1970s, the GDR semiconductor industry became part of Carl Zeiss Jena and the company began to manufacture cameras and navigation systems for use in satellites and high-altitude military aircraft.

During this period, the development of opto-electronics involved collaborations between Carl Zeiss, the universities in Jena and Ilmenau (Thuringia), and research institutes belonging to the Academy of Sciences based in Jena. Additionally, the GDR viewed Zeiss Jena as a strong partner to Comecon countries in microelectronics and optics/fine mechanics during the 1970s and 1980s. Although defence played a role in subsidizing research facilities in Zeiss and the research institutes, the main impetus was originally for scientific and civilian applications in fibre optics. Defence research played a more decisive role in efforts by Comecon countries to develop countermeasures to the Strategic Defence Initiative's (Star Wars) research in the West.

After German re-unification (1991), Carl Zeiss was reorganized into two companies—Carl Zeiss Jena GmbH (microscopes and scientific instruments) and Jenoptik (owned by the State of Thuringia, with operations in lasers, optics and laser diodes.) Reunification produced a dramatic decline in manufacturing employment in Thuringia, from 400,000 in January 1991 to 118,000 by December 1993 (DIW 1994). While employment in manufacturing has shrunk to one-third of its former size, employment in private R&D in the region has shrunk to one-seventh of its size before reunification (SFTT 1994). The remaining R&D employees primarily work in semi-public research centres (Forschungs-GmbHs), not in private firms. Much of

Thuringian public and private research is heavily concentrated in Jena (Hessinger 1995), where the only two large companies which survived reunification are located—Carl Zeiss Jena (2,800 employees, with 400 in R&D) and Jenoptik Jena (1,270 employees, with 350 in R&D).

Before 1991, Carl Zeiss Jena employed a total of 23,000 people. As part of the fall-out from its dismemberment, some 200 business start-ups (not all in opto-electronics) have been established since reunification by Zeiss employees, often by former department directors (Grunenberg 1996). Other small opto-electronics firms established in and around Jena since 1991 have their roots in the university or research institutes. Downsizing at the University of Jena itself encouraged members of the engineering faculties to start up new businesses, some of which are in areas of opto-electronics such as optical sensors, optical coatings, precision optics and laser displays. Contributing to these processes of new firm formation, the Thuringian state funds business incubator centres—one of which, the Technologie-und-Innovationspark Jena (TIP), houses thirty small firms, including some active in laser and spectral image processing (Scherzinger 1996).

As Table 6.1 shows, it is not surprising then that Thuringia has the largest percentage of new firms (less than five years of age). The region (Jena in particular) also boasts the largest percentage of company spin-offs of any of the six regions. These features attest to the consequences of the post-reunification downsizing of Carl Zeiss and of the University of Jena, and the efforts by the State of Thuringia to facilitate the formation of small spin-off companies from their corporate and university parents.

The commercial network and the role of the large firm

The overview of the six regions shows how each cluster has evolved and why particular sets of network relations have come about. The characterization of the regions is not dependent on the statistical representativeness of the case sample, which varies in coverage between regions, but, rather, draws on the case profiles to show the consequences of the regional histories and how the case profiles are consonant with this.

We turn now to specific features of the networks found in and across the regions. The caveat about statistical representativeness continues to apply. This could be considered strongest in relation to the analysis of commercial networks that follows, were it not for the fact that the evidence is consistent across all six regions.

The relative importance of local, national and international commercial networks

The company interviews had two principal objectives: (1) to establish what commercial networks opto-electronics firms engage in, and where these are located (to get a measure of the density of the commercial network and configure a mapping of the region); and (2) to understand how these, and other, networks contribute to the development of the company. Network ties with other firms include customers, suppliers, partners and collaborators. Since the proximity of competitors is also considered a stimulus to innovation (Porter 1990) and add to the pattern of commercial relationships between firms in the sector, they are also included in the analysis below.

From interview data we have constructed the bar charts in Figure 6.2 as a representation of the strength of the different connections, differentiating between the local, national and international geographic sub-networks. The figures are based on a relative assessment of the importance to the individual company of the three different geographic spaces, expressed as a percentage. For customers and suppliers this is effectively equivalent to the proportions of business transacted in local, national and international markets. For collaborators and competitors a more subjective assessment is made based on who firms perceive as their collaborators and competitors, and where these are. The figures for each relationship are then averaged to represent the result for an 'average' firm in the region. (The figures for sales and purchases are thus not the average of the aggregate sales/ purchases for all firms. Since this would reflect the activities of larger firms to a greater extent, the charts below can be assumed to be biased towards how smaller firms behave. The fact that they point consistently towards the national and international arenas being more important reinforces the significance of this finding.)

Analysis of the data shows that the commercial network splits into three clear divisions made by the boundaries of the region, the nation-state, and the international arena, so that at a preliminary level of analysis, a broad comparison can be made about the contributions of each of these sub-networks. In the following paragraphs, we interpret these bar charts in the light of the regional histories and the general character of the industry.

The outstanding feature from Figure 6.2, which is consistent across all regions, is the low importance attached to local *customer* markets. As the data presented in Table 6.1 confirms, most of the opto-electronics activity carried out by SMEs is at the components level and this places the great majority of firms we interviewed into the niche market category. In general, the local market is not large enough to sustain development for firms in specialized products, and their search is for customers on a national basis (where the size of the market permits) or internationally. Specific regional factors play a part, however. Thus, Bavarian firms have a more local orientation, because they are there as distributors to sell to large firms around Munich.

Relationships with *suppliers* show a similar pattern, with the exception of Thuringia and Massachusetts. The general pattern is probably a consequence of the nature of the technology. Opto-electronics is a complex

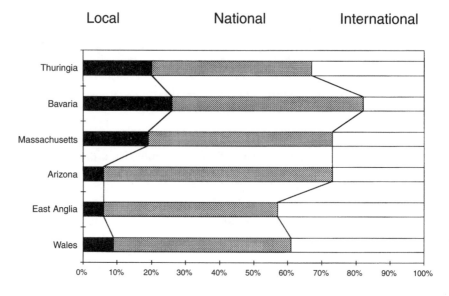

Figure 6.2.1: Customers

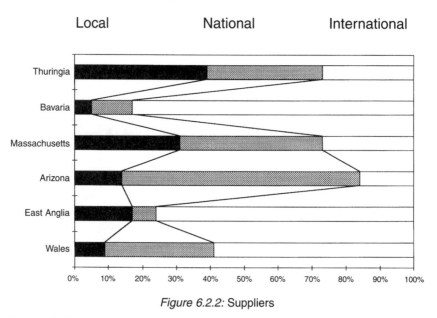

Figure 6.2.2: Suppliers

Figure 6.2 Relative importance of the local, national and international networks, expressed as a percentage for each of four types of business connection

industry that operates on three vertical levels in the production chain, across a horizontal spectrum of different materials and generic technologies. The physical properties of the materials and components are

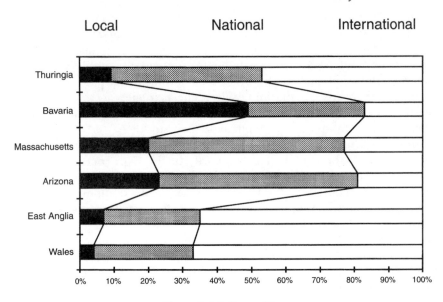

Figure 6.2.3: Competitors

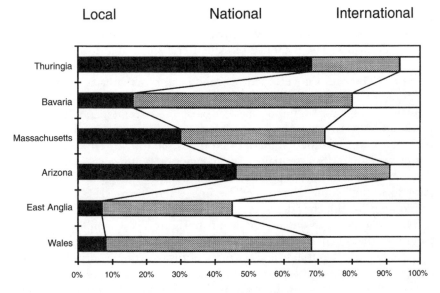

Figure 6.2.4: Collaborators

Figure 6.2 (continued)

very narrowly defined and will only contribute towards the desired effect in the end-user product when combined with a restricted number of alternatives. In other words, the choice of possible combinations is bounded by the physical properties of the elements and by the desirable features of the end-user product. Add to this the market pressure for products that are 'smaller, lighter, cheaper', and the consequence is that small firms looking for externally sourced items are unlikely to find precisely the right one in the immediate locality. This pattern is most pronounced in East Anglia and Wales. The extreme case of Bavaria is because the firms there are distributors acting for large international manufacturers, from whom they purchase their stock.

In the two regions where there is most local sourcing—Thuringia and Massachusetts—the explanation lies partly in the high concentration of firms in the region, but more especially in the fact that both of these are long-established optics regions where there has been a tradition of drawing upon local suppliers of optical-quality glass crafted into lenses, prisms and mirrors for inclusion in optical instruments. However, while it is true that some Massachusetts firms began their businesses with an emphasis on local supply sources, these have been greatly diversified (especially in the complex, scientific components and materials area) as the technology has become more sophisticated. In some respects, therefore, Massachusetts may be hollowing out and becoming more of a regional node for a national value-chain.

The case of Arizona offers a precedent for this process. In Tucson—the main centre for opto-electronics activity in Arizona—there is a history of large-scale optics. The presence of skilled craftsmen able to manufacture these optical elements derives almost totally from spin-offs from the Optical Sciences Center and government astronomical observatories in the area, resulting in a labour force that is highly skilled in this work. Optical elements still remain an important part of opto-electronics, and Tucson has a tradition of collaborating, work sharing, and competition in optics technology, which is the hallmark of an industrial district. However, as one moves away from this essentially craft activity to recently developed production processes that have a greater scientific and technological content, the local focus fades and is replaced by one where firms seek commercial connections in a much wider geographic and technological space.

The network of *competitors* depicted in Figure 6.2.3 exhibits a similar pattern to that of customers, with very limited localized competitive activity. The exception is Bavaria, where a cluster of firms, acting as distributors for foreign-owned manufacturers of lasers, has been attracted to the area because of its image as a high-technology region with strong economic growth prospects (Sternberg 1997). Here the competition is not so much between rival manufacturers, as between rival distributors competing to become agents for the highest-quality foreign suppliers. Bavaria aside, the general picture is one of national and international competition. Where there is local competition, it is often the result of a company breaking up because of internal disagreements about its future strategic direction, and the resulting separate companies coming to occupy adjoining, but slightly different positions in the market. In these cases, although there may be a sense of local rivalry and even bitterness, respondents generally indicated that the competitive effect was quite small in comparison with the global factor.

In summary, then, from Figure 6.2 it is apparent that extra-regional commercial linkages are more important than intraregional ones. Our hypothesis is that this is a consequence of the highly diversified nature of the end-user markets, combined with the complex scientific and techno-logical rules that determine how products are put together. Figure 6.2 suggests that the German and UK regions have a slightly greater recourse to global suppliers and customers than the US regions, and this presum-ably reflects the relative size of the industry in the three countries. The fact that a local focus is least pronounced in the two UK regions may be due to the fact that some 50 per cent of the firms interviewed in Wales and East Anglia are owned by larger organizations domiciled externally, including major multinational companies. In these instances, the local enterprise takes on the role of a centre of expertise for the group as whole, while it benefits from internal access to central research and development laboratories, established distribution channels to global markets, and more favourable conditions of financial support than might be found on the open market.

The large firm as a coordinating force through the supply chain

Up until the late 1980s, the growth of the opto-electronics industry in the UK was largely driven by the telecommunications and military markets, led by British Telecommunications (BT), the Ministry of Defence (MOD), and associated large UK-based defence contractors. Together, they fostered research and development in universities and private industry, and success-fully commercialized this work by bringing products into effective use. In the USA, a similar pattern was evident, with the addition of space applica-tions and at one time a huge investment in 'Star Wars' technology. Opto-electronics in Thuringia was also stimulated by defence R&D. However, the collapse of the Soviet Union in 1989 and the decline in spending on laser weapons and military equipment, plus deregulation of telecommunications and the opening up of the telecoms market to new entrants, has produced a degree of fragmentation in the industry. Changes in end-use markets—on the one hand, greater competition and a move away from centrally-funded programmes in defence; on the other, technological differentiation in telecommunications products—have given a stimulus to SMEs, and encouraged collaboration between large and small firms.

Having initially dominated the major opto-electronics industry sectors, large firms have thus gone on to shape the commercial networks we now see (a pattern of development observed elsewhere by Storper and Harrison (1991), and Florida and Kenney (1991)). Fragmentation paradoxically puts a premium on large firms to act as 'system integrators' (Lorenzoni and

Ornati 1988; Lorenzoni and Baden-Fuller 1995), and, as customers, they are a major source of strength to a network. Many of our respondents in SMEs are thus very clear that part of their growth strategy is to develop links with large, influential, globally represented companies. This is most noticeable in the defence market served by firms in Wales and Massachusetts, where the end-user requirements are complex and demanding, and are best satisfied by major international defence contractors and systems houses. As the defence market gets more sophisticated in respect of advanced technical products, the need to collaborate becomes more insistent. A similar pattern is emerging in markets outside the defence sector, as opto-electronics firms increase their focus on end-user applications and target such industries as automobiles, aviation, information technology and telecommunications. An aspect of this large firm/small firm cooperation is customer-funded product development, where the opto-electronics firm delivers a product or service to its funding source under an exclusive or preferred customer contract. The customer as a major source of ideas for new product development is a theme that emerges consistently from our interview data.

The importance of the 'system integrator' helps to explain the patterns of local, national and international collaborations in Figure 6.2.4. In Wales and East Anglia, opto-electronics firms serve large contractors in other industries located elsewhere (such as defence and telecommunications) with whom they collaborate to develop refined components and materials. The high proportion of firms in these two regions at the generic (basic materials and technologies) end of the value-chain reflects this subordinate relationship. Massachusetts, however, is home to large firms in major high-tech industries which use opto-electronics products, so collaborators are to a greater extent local. Arizona has, among other sectors, the more narrowly focused space observatory industry. The customer is therefore local, but also the value chain is shorter with reliance on the sophisticated production of lenses, so (small) component and (small) end-product firms predominate. Thuringia, which has the greatest extent of local collaboration, is a collection of firms which have largely spun out of from the break-up of Carl Zeiss Jena Kombinat. These firms retain close links, not least through the personal affiliations of staff and the rich infrastructure of research institutions which support a collaborative ethos. In this case, the role of systems integration can be said to be embedded much more in the network itself, supported by a strong regional development policy.

Connections along the value chain are a crucial part of any firm's network. But while customers are an important source of new product ideas, the supply base has to do with improving product quality, by using advanced materials and better quality optical, electronic or mechanical elements. A substantial proportion of our sample firms operate at the middle of the value chain, in key component and end-use product manufacturing. Product inputs at this point are fabricated crystals, optical elements, commodity diode lasers, sensors and optical fibres that are extensively checked for conformance to specification. The component they form a part of usually depends critically on the material input from these generic inputs for its own performance, functionality and durability. Supplies are therefore sourced on the basis of the best available, and because the significant parts of their supply chain are outside the region, component- and system-level firms in the region do not act as an integrating force locally for suppliers (other than for low-value items).

This points to the fact that the shape of the supply chain is a critical factor in the extent to which networks are locally focused. Where the supply chain pyramid has a small base, in which many firms depend on a few basic materials and components of a rarefied and uniform nature (as is also the case with silicon chips), few companies will be capable of this, and most regional concentrations will be imperfect industrial districts. The technological characteristics of the industry are therefore a major determinant of the network form it takes.

At the other end of chain, the shape of the commercial network is largely determined by the activities of large, or otherwise powerful, players, rather than by the collective action of numbers of small firms. This can take many forms, with large firms as important customers, as collaborators on new product development, and as the means to market entry. In opto-electronics, these relationships tend to have a national or international perspective, because many of the markets involve national champions (defence, telecoms), or involve international consumer markets (IT, consumer electronics). Of course, one of the most powerful forms of global integration through the supply chain is where a local facility is part of a parent firm's global network. Large firms such as these may act as a coordinating force from outside the area to connect a regional node into their global network (Amin and Thrift 1992).

In general, though, intraregional connections are not as important as those outside the region, and they are mainly directed at large firms. Our conclusion, then, is that networks in opto-electronics are more of the 'core' type, where one (or more) firms have the ability to determine the existence of others, rather than a 'ring' where power is distributed symmetrically (Storper and Harrison 1991), and the centre of this 'core' often lies outside the region.

The large firm as an incubator and source of interfirm relationships

A further instance of this 'core' pattern is the role of the large firm as an incubator for spin-offs. Table 6.1 shows that in every region except Arizona, over 50 per cent of the firms sampled originated from within other companies in a spin-off process, and even in Arizona where the influence of the Optical Sciences Center is strong, the figure is nearly 30 per cent. This is rather striking evidence of a second large firm phenomenon—the role of the large firm as an incubator for new spin-offs. In many cases, this has been essentially a process whereby large firms have restructured their business, creating small firms with umbilical links often of a social and professional kind.

There appear to be many reasons for this spin-off activity, and almost none are based on a deliberate strategic intent by a parent company to create new enterprises. Rather, the creation of a new company comes about as a by-product of some other strategic activity. The classic case is the diversification policy that turns into a divestment policy when the economic climate worsens and the parent company reverts to its perceived core business (e.g. Pilkington in North Wales in the late 1980s, and Cambridge over a longer time period). A second cause of spin-offs is the change in strategic direction by a parent company, because of changes in the market or regulatory framework. An example of this is BT in East Anglia, which divested itself of much of its technical expertise in opto-electronics hardware (into Hewlett Packard), when market and regulatory changes reinforced the logic that its main business is in service provision and network operations. The third pattern is that familiar from Silicon Valley, where entrepreneurs leave a founder company to develop alternative approaches to technological development and niche products as a new industry takes off. The American Optical Corporation, founded in the 1950s in Massachusetts, produced a dozen spin-off firms in this way (causing some commentators to refer to the area as the birthplace of fibre optics). The fourth way spin-offs have originated, and the one that shows the most strategic intent, is in Thuringia where the federal Government restructured Carl Zeiss Jena.

The process of spinning out from large companies is a positive dynamic for the expansion of the opto-electronics industry. In the first place, much of the existence of the industry is due to large firms withdrawing from non-core activities and creating space for SMEs. In the second place, spin-off activity can lead to a greater variety of firms in a locality, with consequent opportunity for expansion and growth into new market areas the larger firm would have ignored.

University–firm networks and the process of technology transfer

All six regions have a considerable university presence, turning out highly qualified scientists and engineers to work in the opto-electronics industry, and conducting basic research into the underlying scientific questions that in due course form the basis for new commercial products.

While companies are broadly satisfied with the education of scientists and engineers, the bigger problem lies with the university transferring technology to the commercial sector. The problem here stems from the fundamentally different aspirations of academics and industrialists. On the one hand, university scientists are driven by intellectual curiosity, a desire to extend the frontiers of scientific knowledge, and a career system that rewards prowess in achieving it. Industry, on the other hand is interested in discoveries that have commercial potential which can be taken from the laboratory environment through the laborious process of transforming them into practical products. Of course, not all new product ideas originate from the very latest discoveries in the laboratory. In fact, the converse is often the case, as industry searches for solutions to problems posed by the marketplace in a technological domain within which they have experience and the necessary productive capability to turn ideas into products. Such solutions may well be from already established scientific results.

There are two distinct ways in which ideas are transferred to industry in opto-electronics in our sample. The first is the entrepreneurial start-up, where one or more scientists (faculty or graduate student) take the results of their research into the marketplace to form a new venture. The six regions differ dramatically in the role of the regional university as a source of entrepreneurial start-up. On the basis of a simple league table suggested by Table 6.1, Arizona comes out top of the six regions with 41 per cent of firms in the sample having begun in this way, followed by Massachusetts (35 per cent), East Anglia (23 per cent), Thuringia (20 per cent), Wales (5 per cent) and Bavaria (0 per cent). These figures reflect the relative emphasis of the universities in these areas on encouraging start-up, and the strengths of the local universities themselves.

A key area of the ACOST (1988) recommendations in the UK was for support for research, and the proposal to establish interdisciplinary centres of expertise to concentrate resources and avoid dilution of effort. This led to the establishment of the Opto-electronics Research Centre (ORC) at the University of Southampton in 1989. The ORC has established itself not only as a centre of high-quality research, but also as a source of commercial innovation, spawning a number of SMEs in the area and developing links with large manufacturing organizations. This centre has arguably had more immediate success in stimulating a regional cluster in opto-electronics through start-ups originating from a university, than any other research centre in the UK, although it is as yet small. In contrast, a substantial amount of all basic government research funding in opto-electronics within the UK has gone into five universities in the central region of Scotland, but the effect in stimulating commercialization and local industrial develop-ment has been uncertain. This model for achieving technology transfer has, therefore, still to show its value in the UK, and the existence of one or many universities may itself be insufficient to stimulate cluster develop-ment, unless wider cultural and institutional issues are addressed.

The second means of fostering innovation—collaboration between universities and industry to transfer ideas rather than people, through R&D partnerships—is where much of the policy effort has gone, and continues to go. It is this, in particular, that reflects the efficacy of network support.

Links between universities and industry in the UK go back to the origins of the technology and its early stages of commercialization. The successful development and introduction of the fibre-optic network in the UK, for example, owes much to the collaborative efforts between BT and a number of university research centres. An examination of the UK government-funded Joint OptoElectronics Research Scheme (JOERS) and LINK contracts awarded also reveals extensive collaboration between university departments and industrial enterprises since the early 1980s. Industry–university collaborations also have a long history in Thuringia and in the two US regions. The downside, in the UK at least, is that arguably too little of this collaborative activity has resulted in successful products—the case of liquid crystal displays, invented in the UK and commercialized by the Japanese being a prime example (ACOST 1988).

A consequence of the ACOST (1988) review was a change in emphasis in public research funding from pure research to the application of techno-logy. The LINK programme, started in 1987 as a pan-governmental collaborative R&D initiative covering a number of new technologies (but with specific reference to opto-electronics), supports research into the integration of opto-electronic devices and techniques into systems with market potential. A specific condition of financial support is that proposed projects should involve one or more companies and one or more science-based partners. SMEs are actively encouraged to participate and the involvement of an end-user is also considered desirable, thus building large firm–small firm links. This principle continues in the LINK Photonics programme and the wider Technology Foresight initiative. The LINK programme, however, makes no attempt to encourage specific regional clustering, unlike the German scheme, Laser 2000, which is allied to the goals of regional development with a strong bias towards Bavaria, where much of the high-power laser industry is located. That is not to say, how-ever, that strengthening opto-electronics firms in their local environment may not have knock-on effects on the locality and on other firms.

In a high-technology-based company, keeping up to date with relevant scientific and technological advances and assessing their commercial poten-tial is a key competence, and one that is typically left to the engineering group of employees. Having a network of contacts is crucial to this role, and this means having access to university research centres, trade con-ferences and exhibitions, and (where applicable) parent-company research departments. All this is highly individualistic and has an industry-wide, rather than a regional inclination. All six regions are well served by an educational infrastructure in opto-electronics, but this is no guarantee that it will be utilized in this way, as the linkages are likely to follow individual intellectual preferences and have a specialized industry focus.

In conclusion, then, all six regions contain a vibrant university research community and firms with good track records and established market presence. Moreover, a network of contacts exists, within the region and beyond, that includes multinational corporations, universities, and government research centres. However, much of the interaction between academia and industry can best be described as universities playing a supportive role in response to industrial initiatives. Intellectual exchanges regarding technological issues and problems, training and educational support, use by industry of specialized equipment, provision of graduates and post-graduates as potential employees, and contract research, all take place, but to a highly variable degree. The reasons for this are examined elsewhere (Hendry, Brown, DeFillippi and Hassink 1997), but one of the fundamental issues is the nature of the dialogue between industry and academia in each country.

The institutional network and the role of development agencies

As the above discussion shows, making technology transfer happen from universities to firms is problematic, and central governments in all three countries have had active policies to facilitate this. With the exception of Thuringia in Germany, however, such policies have not been specifically designed to foster local regional networks (other than in an unintended, incidental fashion). Technology transfer is only one aspect of the relationships among the actors in a network, however, and central government is only one type of institution facilitating such relationships. Local government and its regional development agencies, and trade associations (both those relating to a technology and those representing customer markets), are other principal institutions.

The institutional network differs from the commercial one in that firms are not compelled to engage with it. The institutional network can be a source of complementary or additive knowledge which provides the impetus for a new direction, stimulates some other change in company strategy, creates a sense of regional identity, lobbies on behalf of firms, and (in the case of end-user industry associations) provides a meeting-place and 'clearing-house' for products and services.

Whereas the locality was relatively less important in firms' commercial networks, companies saw local agencies giving more significant support than did those outside the region. Moreover, the absence of local infrastructure support was regarded as the biggest gap in institutional support. Equally notable, however, is that firms tend to participate in trade associations related to their end-markets, rather than in relation to their technology. This ties in with the dearth of local ties, and firms' orientation towards links outside the region. From a network perspective, the relative lack of interest in formal associations based on a common technology, compared with those related to products, reflects the difficulty in establishing common interests and regulating the behaviour of members who are likely to be competitors (Zan 1992). Market motivations prevail.

However, affiliation-based networks which can lead to cooperation may develop with time, and as they are perceived to offer market opportunities. The absence of supportive local institutions can lead to a search for that capability outside the region, or the creation of an organization to deliver it. In the first case, firms will look outside the region for scientists, engineers, venture capital and industry knowledge. In the second, we observe the emergence of industry cluster institutions such as the Arizona Industry Optics Association (AIOA) and the Welsh Opto-Electronics Forum (WOF).

The Welsh Opto-electronics Forum (WOF) was launched in January 1996 as an association of Welsh companies, universities and governmental institutions to build an informal network of partners to create a sense of mutual identity which could aid promotional activity, and provide information on market opportunities, technical developments and funding. The WOF aims to promote the growth of a regional opto-electronics industry in Wales by supporting industry–academic cooperation, improvements in opto-electronics education, and stimulation of collaborative research, co-marketing and technology transfer among its members. One key output achieved already is a contribution to the Regional Technology Plan for Wales (WDA 1996).

In Arizona, the situation was somewhat different. The crisis of economic decline occurred almost overnight and urgent action was necessary at the end of the 1980s. The result of a joint study, which included consultation with over 1,000 Arizonans, was the Arizona Strategic Plan for Economic Development (ASPED) published in October 1992. It was out of this positive consultation experience that the optics representatives decided to institutionalize their cluster and form the Arizona Optics Industry Association (AOIA) as a non-profit corporation, independent of government, in August 1992 (Lake 1996).

In Thuringia, the Science Ministry funds collaborative research projects that require the participation of at least one Thuringian company and one state university. Since 1995, the Science Ministry has spent about 35 million DM on opto-electronics and optical research projects. In addition, the Thuringia State supports a dense infrastructure of technology-transfer agencies which are both free-standing (e.g. the Thuringian Agency for Technology Transfer and Innovation Promotion) and affiliated with regional universities, such as the University of Jena.

There is, thus, a difference of emphasis between Arizona industry cluster associations and those of Wales and Thuringia. Although in each the underlying objective is to improve the prospects for, and the visibility of, the local opto-electronics industry, in Wales and Thuringia there is a strong emphasis on technology transfer and facilitating links between industry and academia, whereas in Arizona the focus is more on creating networks among firms and acting as a pressure group at local, state and national levels. One might infer that this is because technology transfer between the Optical Sciences Center in Arizona and local firms already works well.

Although a key objective in the Arizona sectoral clusters is to improve the resource 'foundations' for firms (including human resources, technology, capital, physical infrastructure and information infrastructure), what many firms value the Arizona Industry Optics Association for is its lobbying efforts on such matters as favourable tax legislation. In other words, it operates like other industry bodies, such as the UK's Defence Manufacturers' Association, which offer the possibility of immediate and direct economic benefits.

Conclusions and issues arising

Based on our findings from the 'mapping' of these six regions and interviews with executives in one hundred opto-electronics firms across the regions, we can begin to answer the questions posed at the beginning of this chapter. The two questions were:

1 To what extent are clusters of firms in opto-electronics participating in governmental, commercial and university cooperative relations?
2 To what extent are clusters of opto-electronics firms embedded in primarily local, national or international networks of cooperation and mutual support?

Regarding the first of these, our findings suggest the importance of such relations. However, the depth and extent of these is highly variable. Patterns of cooperation vary considerably across the regions. Government fostering of cluster firm development is much more salient in Wales, Arizona and Thuringia, than in East Anglia, Massachusetts and Bavaria. These differences defy national cultural explanations and instead reflect local historical experiences of each region. The three regions with significant government involvement in cluster development have all suffered economic set-backs in which local (state) and even federal government leadership and resources were mobilized to assist in economic development and renewal. By contrast, the three regions with less significant government involvement have enjoyed more stable economic development spurred by private investment initiatives, and have had less reason to seek governmental assistance or leadership.

Commercial relations have primarily involved vertical value-chain transactions, including collaborative development of new and improved products or processes with major customers, and outsourcing of components, complementary systems or materials from suppliers. Relatively little horizontal collaboration among direct competitors, to create a common product or develop generic technology, seems evident in any of the regions (compare this with evidence of consortia relationships generally in the USA and Japan reported by Bolton, Aldrich and Sasaki 1994). These findings reinforce the image of a highly vertically structured industry, as conceptualized by Miyazaki (1995). The role of large firms as sources of corporate spin-offs is pervasive across all regions except Arizona, where the absence of mature and large opto-electronics firms restricts opportunities for corporate spin-offs. A common phenomena is for corporate spin-offs to arise from adverse economic conditions facing large mature firms in each of the regions.

University cooperative relations are abundantly evident in case histories from all the regions. However, the impact of these university ties on commercial growth and development varies widely across regions. On one measure (the stimulus to start-up firms), Massachusetts appears to lead all regions both in the number of university start-ups originating in its universities, and in the growth of these into large and productive enterprises. This largely reflects the extraordinary success of MIT in fostering high-technology commercialization and entrepreneurial start-ups among its faculty and students. Arizona has also fostered a high rate of such start-ups, but the resulting enterprises have tended to remain small, niche firms. East Anglia and Thuringia have produced a moderate level of university start-ups under quite different circumstances. Whereas East Anglia has generated high-technology start-ups as a result of perceived commercial opportunities, Thuringia has done so out of the financial adversity affecting its universities and the region in general.

Whether these differing economic conditions produce different long-term cluster development trajectories must await further research, although the evidence points to strong 'path-dependency' effects. Secondly, whether particular configurations of these sets of relationships, or factors—that is, networks of firms, the presence of universities, and institutional support from government—makes a difference to long-term performance, must await analysis of our forthcoming survey research.

On the second question—whether firms are embedded in primarily local, national or global networks—our data provides scant support for the industrial district model of intense local cooperation among regional firms. Proximity without intimacy or interaction seems the more common circumstance of the opto-electronics firms in each region (although Thuringia may be the exception due to the pervasive networks of personal relations among former Zeiss employees who have founded spin-off firms in the region). Local ties appear most focused on sharing public infrastructure goods, such as a skilled pool of human capital, convenient transportation facilities, and quality of life amenities. The university offers the most localized of institutional resources, but its contribution is most often indirect, as a source of engineering, scientific and management talent rather than as a direct provider of technology. Commercial ties among firms are primarily national and international with respect to both end-user markets and factor markets. The exception tends to be low-value-added commodity inputs that are generically available and therefore more conveniently sourced locally. Where there are embedded local ties, these tend not to involve extensive, pervasive, overlapping networks ('dense' ties), so much as a series of fragmented networks among sub-sets of firms and people in the whole cluster.

This raises questions about the reality of a 'cluster', and what opto-electronic firms really derive from proximity. Many are more oriented to customer industries outside their region, than they are to thinking of themselves as sharing a common technology. If customer industries are more significant to their development, how are opto-electronics firms disadvantaged if user industries are locally weak or absent? If they are disadvantaged, it might imply that government policy and local agencies should be concerned with stimulating and building related industries, rather than with the R&D diffusion process, technology transfer, and commercialization as a 'supply side' factor. Indirectly, government policy in the UK in the early stages of the sector's development involved both tracks, through defence spending and targeted support for defence-related R&D. With the decline in defence spending and a more cost-conscious environment following the mid-1980s competitiveness initiative, this twin-track has disappeared.

In summary, our findings suggest that opto-electronics industry clusters within the three countries commonly function as localized nodes of national and international networks of technology development, production and distribution. Some regional clusters have a more central role in technology development (e.g. East Anglia and Massachusetts); others are more focused on manufacturing (e.g. Arizona, Wales and Thuringia); and still others are major loci for distribution (e.g. Bavaria). However, these are somewhat forced distinctions. It is more accurate to portray each regional cluster as simultaneously participating in multiple networks and for individual firms within each cluster to enjoy either more central or peripheral roles in each of these networks, based upon their distinctive capabilities, scale and geographic scope of their activities. Findings from our forthcoming survey will shed additional light on the consequences of these differences in patterns of network affiliation on firm-level revenue, employee growth and employee productivity.

From a network-theoretical perspective, among the various possible mechanisms of interfirm coordination (Grandori and Soda 1995), examples can be found of such phenomena as personal networks, formal associations and joint R&D. But what they term 'interfirm authorities'—leadership by a central firm over clusters of firms—seems to be the prevailing solution, especially if firm-to-firm relations are considered. In addition, that mechanism tends to be employed on a national and international basis, rather than purely local. In the relations between firms and universities and technology centres the mechanism of common infrastructure and the sharing of physical and human resources seems to have often prevailed over a systematic and region-wide dense web of knowledge-exchange ties.

Considering that the USA, Germany and the UK are (behind Japan) the major players in opto-electronics, this is all the more surprising. We do not know if Japan's comparative success is built on greater recourse to networking. But if this is also not the case, our evidence requires that the role of networking behaviour needs to be re-evaluated in relation to purely market forms of coordination.

But if this is also not the case, our evidence suggests that proximity and the local clustering of firms may be associated with different types of network structures. In particular, in our case it is associated with hub coordination and commensality-based cooperation rather than necessarily with interactive teaming and intimacy.

Notes

1 The authors gratefully acknowledge the support of The Leverhulme Trust in funding the project, and of the Welsh Development Agency in providing additional support and research access.

Bibliography

ACOST (1988) *Opto Electronics: Building on our Investment*, London, HMSO.

Amin, A. and Thrift, N. (1992) 'Neo-Marshallian nodes in global networks', *International Journal of Urban and Regional Research*, 16, 4: 571–87.

Barker, T. C. (1994) *Pilkington: An Age of Glass*, London: Boxtree.

Bagnasco, A. (1977) *Tre Italie. La problematica territoriale dello sviluppo italiano*, Bologna: IL Mulino.

Becattini, G. (1989) *Modelli locali di sviluppo*, Bologna: IL Mulino.

Bellandi, M. (1992) 'The incentives to decentralized industrial creativity in local systems of small firms', *Revue d'Economie Industrielle*, 59: 99–110.

Biggiero, L. (1998) 'Italian industrial districts: an evolutionary and institutionalist view', Presented at Conference on The Future Location of Research in a Triple Helix of University–Industry, Government Relations, New York, 7–10 January 1998.

Bolton, M. K., Aldrich, H. E. and Sasaki, T. (1994) 'Information exchange and governance structure in US and Japanese R&D consortia', Working paper, April.

Brusco, S. (1982) 'The Emilian model: productive decentralization and social integration', *Cambridge Journal of Economics*, 6: 167–84.

Campbell, A., Sorge, A. and Warner, M. (1989) *Microelectronic Applications in Great Britain and West Germany*, London, Policy Studies Institute/Anglo-German Foundation.

Cattermole, M. J. G. and Wolfe, A. F. (1987) *Horace Darwin's Shop: A History of the Cambridge Scientific Instrument Company 1878 to 1968*, Bristol: Adam Hilger.

Catts, B. C., Johnson, L. and Gibson, J. A. (1996) *Arizona Optic Industry Resource Directory and Industry Analysis*, Tucson, University of Arizona.

Cooke, P. and Morgan, K. (1993) 'The network paradigm—new departures in corporate and regional development', *Environment And Planning D: Society & Space*, 11, 5: 543–64.

DeBresson, C. and Amesse, F. (1991) 'Networks of innovators—a review and introduction to the issue', *Research Policy*, 20, 5: 363–79.

DIW (1994) *Standortanalyse fur den Wirtschaftsraum Thuringen. Gutachten im Auftrag des Thuringer,* Ministeriums fur Wirtschaft und Verkehr, Deutsches Institut fur Wirtschaftsforschung *et al.*: Berlin.

Dosi, G. (1984) *Technical Change and Industrial Transformation,* London: Macmillan Press Ltd.

Dubarle, P. and Verie, C. (1993) *Technology Fusion: A Path to Innovation. The Case of Opto-electronics,* Paris: OECD.

Florida, R. and Kenney, M. (1990) 'High-technology restructuring in the USA and Japan', *Environment and Planning A,* 22: 232–52.

Florida, R. and Kenney, M. (1991) 'Organizational factors and technology-intensive industry: the US and Japan', *New Technology, Work and Employment,* 6, 1: 28–42.

Freeman, C. (ed.) (1991) *Technology and the Future of Europe,* London: Pinter.

Garnsey, E. and Cannon-Brookes, A. (1993) 'The 'Cambridge phenomenon' revisited: aggregate change among cambridge high-technology companies since 1985', *Entrepreneurship & Regional Development,* 5, 2: 179–207.

Goodman, E., Bamford, J. and Saynor, P. (eds) (1989) *Small Firms and Industrial Districts in Italy,* London: Routledge.

Grandori, A. and Soda, G. (1995) 'Interfirm networks: antecedents, mechanisms and forms', *Organisation Studies,* 16, 2: 183–214.

Grunenberg, N. (1996) 'Wir sind eure Minenhunde, Wie sich Beschaftigte des einstigen Kombinats VES Carl Zeiss Jena in der Markwirtschaft zurechtfinden', *Die Zeit,* 44: 33–4.

Hecht, J. (1992) *Laser Pioneers,* London: Academic Press.

Hendry, C., Brown, J., DeFillippi, R. and Hassink, R. (1997) 'The role of government, universities and research centres in fostering innovation in SMEs: a three-country study of opto-electronics', Presented at 27th European Small Business Seminar, Rhodes, 17–19 September.

Hendry, C., Arthur, M. B. and Jones, A. M. (1995) *Strategy Through People: Adaptation and Learning in the Small-Medium Firm,* London: Routledge.

Hessinger, P. (1995) 'Aufbau Ost als Nachbau West bei der industriellen Restrukturierung Ostdeutschlands? Eine netzwerktheoretische Perspektive', in H. Rudolph (ed.) *Geplanter Wandel, ungeplante Wirkungen. Handlungslogiken und -resourcen im Prozess der Transformation,* WZB Jahrbuch, Berlin: edition sigma: 266–84.

Kaldor, M. (1984) *Military R&D.* A Report for the Swedish Group of the UK Government Expert Study on Military R&D, SPRU, University of Sussex.

Kanter, R. M. (1995) *World Class: Thriving Locally in the Global Economy,* New York: Simon and Schuster.

Kaounides, L. C. (1995) *Advanced Materials,* London: Financial Times.

Keeble, D. E. (1989) 'High-technology industry and regional development in Britain. The case of the Cambridge phenomenon', *Environment and Planning C: Government and Policy,* 7: 153–72.

Kodama, F. (1995) *Emerging Patterns of Innovation.* Boston: Harvard Business School Press.

Lake, A. A. (1996) *The History of the Arizona Optics Industry Association,* Global Networking of Regional Optics Clusters, Denver, SPIE—The International Society for Optical Engineering.

Lorenzoni, G. and Baden-Fuller, C. (1995) 'Creating a strategic center to manage a web of partners', *California Management Review,* 37, 3: 146–63.

Lorenzoni, G. and Ornati, O. A. (1988) 'Constellations of firms and new ventures', *Journal of Business Venturing*, 3: 41–57.

Lundvall, B. A. (ed.) (1992) *National Systems of Innovation*, London: Pinter.

McKinsey, C. (1988) *Performance and Competitive Success: Strengthening Competitiveness in UK Electronics*, London: NEDO.

Miyazaki, K. (1995) *Building Competences in the Firm: Lessons from Japanese and European Opto-electronics*, London: Macmillan Press Ltd.

Nelson, R. (ed.) (1993) *National Innovation Systems*, Oxford: Oxford University Press.

Porter, M. E. (1990) *The Competitive Advantage of Nations*, London: Macmillan.

Powell, R. C. (1996) *Optical Science Center*, Tucson AZ: University of Arizona.

Rothwell, R. (1992) 'Successful industrial innovation: critical factors for the 1990s', *R&D Management*, 22, 3: 221–39.

Saxenian, A. (1989). 'The Cheshire Cat's grin: innovation, regional development and the Cambridge case', *Economy and Society*, 18, 4: 448–75.

Scherzinger, A. (1996) 'Forschung und Entwicklung (FuE) in den Ostdeutschen Agglomerationen Jena and Dresden', *DIW-Vierteljahreshefte zur Wirtschaftsforschung*, 2: 172–89.

Segal, Quince and Wickstead (1985) *The Cambridge Phenomenon: The Growth of High Technology Industry in a University Town*, Cambridge: Segal Quince & Partners.

SFTT (1994) *Forschung und Technologie in Thuringen*, Abschlu bericht der Strategiekommission fur Forschung und Technologie in Thuringen (Fassung 3.0), Thuringer Ministerium fur Wissenschaft und Kunst, Erfurt.

Sieppel, G. (1981) *Opto-electronics*. Reston, Virginia: Prentice-Hall.

Spectra, P. (1995) *The Photonics Spectra Corporate Guide*. Pittsfield, MA: Photonics Spectra.

Steedman, H. and Wagner, K. (1987) 'A second look at productivity, machinery and skills in Britain and Germany', *National Institute Economic Review*.

Sternberg, R. (1997) *Technologiepolitik und High-Tech Regionen-ein internationaler Vergleich*, Munster, Hamburg: Lit-Verlag.

Stoneham, P. (1987) *The Economic Analysis of Technology Policy*, Oxford: Oxford University Press.

Storper, M. (1995) 'The resurgence of regional economies, ten years later: the region as a nexus of untraded interdependencies', *European Urban and Regional Studies*, 2, 3: 191–221.

Storper, M. and Harrison, B. (1991) 'Flexibility, hierarchy and regional development: the changing structure of industrial production systems and their forms of governance in the 1990's', *Research Policy*, 20: 407–22.

Swann, P. and Prevezer, M. (1997) 'A comparison of the dynamics of industrial clustering in computing and biotechnology', *Research Policy*, 25: 1139–57.

Van de Ven, A. H. and Garud, R. (1993) 'The development of an infrastructure for entrepreneurship', *Journal of Business Venturing*, 8.

Waits, M. J. (1996) State of Cluster-based Economic Development in Arizona. Global Networking of Regional Optics Clusters, Denver, SPIE.

Walker, W. (1993) 'National innovation systems: Britain', In R. Nelson (ed.) National Innovation Systems; A Comparative Analysis, Oxford: Oxford University Press.

WDA (1996) 'Wales regional technology plan: an innovation and technology Strategy for Wales'. Cardiff: Welsh Development Agency.

Williamson, O. (1975) Markets and Hierarchies. New York: Free Press.

Zan, S. (1992) Organizzazione e rappresentanza, Roma: NIS.

7 Organizational learning and the role of the network broker in small-firm manufacturing networks[1]

Keith G. Provan and Sherrie E. Human

In recent years, small- and medium-sized manufacturing enterprises (SMEs) have joined or formed cooperative interorganizational relationships, such as networks, to access resources for organizational growth without the constraints of vertical integration. Recent publications describe how 'networks help small companies think and act big' (Selz 1992) thus allowing SMEs to gain knowledge, resources, and customers that might only be available to much larger firms. Modelled after European network successes, US networks have focused on increasing member competitiveness through joint activities such as design, production and marketing. Since SMEs in the US have not traditionally formed ongoing, cooperative interfirm relationships, especially with competitors, the recent SME network phenomenon has spawned considerable interest in the US among researchers and practitioners alike. However, much of this work has served only to document the phenomenon, while describing some basic network characteristics and expected outcomes.

One underexplored issue that is theoretically interesting and important for both US and European industrial policy is the role played by networks for enhancing organizational learning. When firms become involved in networks, they must interact on a regular basis with network members, presumably learning more about these other firms and gaining knowledge about markets, resources, customers, production, and the like. In addition, as part of the cooperative interaction process, firms and their members are able to learn more about themselves and their own competitiveness, including strengths and weaknesses.

The study reported here examines the extent to which SME networks serve as a learning mechanism, and the role of the network broker in facilitating this process. Learning is defined as the capacity of network member firms to enhance their awareness of both competition and their own competitiveness. This definition of organization learning emphasizes observable behaviours and attempts to capture changes in organizational beliefs and knowledge (Levitt and March 1988). We examine organizational awareness of competition and competitiveness through the comparative study of two SME networks in the secondary wood processing industry. The concurrent appearance of SME networks across the US provides a unique opportunity to compare exchange patterns across networks at similar points in their development and to draw inferences about what firms learn from their network participation.

Organizational learning in networks

Learning has been recognized as a fundamental organizational process at least since the work of Cyert and March (1963), and is a concept that has attracted significant recent attention as well (c.f. *Organization Science*, vol. 2, 1991; Powell, Koput and Smith-Doerr 1996). The basic idea is that organizations can and do learn, through a process of knowledge acquisition, information distribution, information interpretation and organizational memory (Huber 1991). While it is important not to anthropomorphize, it seems clear that learning can go well beyond the individual, such that knowledge learned by organizational members is retained by the organization and passed on to future members, often through changes in organizational routines or beliefs (Levitt and March 1988). Thus, it is the organization itself that benefits from the learning of its individual members.

While learning may be stimulated by a variety of factors, scholars have suggested that interfirm relationships, such as networks and joint ventures, result in organizational learning, facilitating adoption of new processes and procedures (Hamel 1991; Lyles 1988). In a similar manner, network participation can allow members to learn more about themselves and each other, thereby enhancing competitiveness in dealing with firms outside the network.

Where networks have a particular advantage over more traditional interorganizational relationships (IORs) for stimulating learning is that networks are based on norms of trust and long-term commitment (Jarillo 1988; Powell 1990; Larson 1992). In traditional IORs like supplier–buyer relationships, linked firms are hesitant to divulge much about their operations and strategies for fear that others will take advantage of this knowledge and they will lose competitive advantage. This is the problem of opportunism that Williamson (1985) discusses as a major transaction cost in vertical contractual relationships between organizations. Competitor firms will be reluctant to develop any types of links because the incentives for opportunism are so high, with competitors behaving in ways that maximize their self-interest.

In contrast, when firms commit themselves to a long-term network relationship, they implicitly agree that greater strategic advantage can be attained through cooperation than through competition. Information begins to flow more freely among network members and opportunism is drastically reduced, in part because of the advantages of cooperation and in part because of the potential of sanctions and damaged reputation that are likely as a result of social embeddedness (Granovetter 1985; Provan 1993). This free flow of information thus allows significant learning to take place, as network firms acquire knowledge they can trust about themselves, about their network members, and about non-network competitors through their network contacts.

Small- and medium-sized firms in networks have an additional advantage in that their small size, and the small size of other network members, facilitates learning. Large firms tend to compartmentalize their activities and may have several sets of interfirm ties built around their various division and product structures. While organizational learning is still possible, it may be slowed or stopped by the difficulties of dissemination in a large organization. In addition, it is likely to take many years for ideas and knowledge to pervade the organization as a whole. For these reasons, it seems likely that firms in SME networks are especially well-suited to learn from their interactions with other firms in the network. Support for this contention has recently been demonstrated in a study of biotechnology industry firms by Powell *et al.* (1996).

Even though firms should learn as a result of their SME network involvement, it seems likely that different types of network structures will result in different amounts of learning. For instance, some networks may have considerable interaction among member firms while others may have very little or may interact only through a central coordinating body. It is here that the role of the network broker may be critical since it is the broker that often determines, or at least guides, network composition and interactions. Lorenzoni and Ornati (1988) described how the lead, or broker, firm in their interorganizational constellations ensured that members took advantage of dyadic opportunities with each other. However, the broker did not facilitate group meetings for constellation members, thereby limiting full interaction among member firms. In this case, network firms would no doubt learn something about one another through their individual broker-sponsored dyadic ties but broader learning might be limited.

The role of the network broker seems particularly important for encouraging learning among firms that are, for the most part, competitors. On the one hand, it seems likely that firms in competitor networks would be hesitant to break down the barriers that kept them competitive in the first place, preferring only minimal network involvement, and hence, less learning than their counterparts in networks of complementary firms. On the other hand, it is these competitor firms that have the most to gain from their network involvement. A strong network broker may be critical for ensuring that cooperative network links are developed and maintained, thereby encouraging a network climate that is supportive of the open flow of information needed for successful learning.

Based on these ideas and the lack of empirical research on SME networks and organizational learning from network involvement, we conducted an exploratory study addressing two primary research questions.

First, does organizational learning take place as a result of involvement in an SME network? Second, to what extent does organizational learning vary across networks with differing broker roles?[2]

Methods

A two-stage exploratory research design was used, incorporating multiple data sources such as in-depth interviews, surveys and archival documents (Eisenhardt 1989; Jick 1979). Data collection occurred from mid-1994 to early 1995.

Network and market sampling

Two manufacturing networks in the secondary wood products industry were selected from a national US directory (Lichtenstein 1992) after preliminary interviews with network consultants, administrators and member firms. Secondary wood products represented one of three primary industries in the national network directory and comprised ten of the twenty-seven networks profiled. Both networks selected included an administrative or broker role (Aldrich and Zimmer 1986) that coordinated member-firm activities and interactions. We obtained commitment to participate in our study from the executive directors of both network administrative organizations, who then provided us with network membership directories. Total manufacturing firm members listed in each network directory were sixty and seventy-seven organizations. Unlike some networks, particularly those involving large firms, the firms in our networks had no equity ties and were linked to the broker organization loosely and voluntarily.

Preliminary interviews with the network administrators/brokers and with sample firms in both networks indicated that not all organizations listed in the membership directories were equally active in the networks. Our research questions focused on network exchanges best addressed by active participants, thus suggesting we use a sampling technique that would more likely provide a sample of active firms than random or snowball procedures (Holsti 1968; Scott 1991). Consequently, reputational samples (Burt and Minor 1983) of member companies were studied based on these firms being named by their respective network brokers as active network participants. The brokers were the appropriate key respondents to nominate a sample of network firms, given their own participation in network formation and evolution. Data were actually collected from nineteen of the twenty-two firms sampled in the first network (86 per cent) and from all twenty-three firms sampled in the second network.

The full sample of firms from the first network represented four of the five major product lines in the complete network membership directory including furniture, millwork, cabinetry and lumber remanufacturing (the arts and crafts product line was not represented in our sample). Thirteen

(60 per cent) of the twenty-two firms were small retail furniture manufacturers and the mean radius from the network broker organization for all
firms was 75 miles. Firm size ranged from one to 120 employees and from
$60,000 to $2,600,000 in gross sales. Based on firm size, product line, and
distance from the network broker organization, sample firms appeared to
be representative of the complete network. The firms in this network were
relatively homogenous regarding product line and most could be considered as potential competitors, particularly in the area of home furniture.
We adopted the naming convention of alpha-net for this network.

The sample of firms from the second network, which we called beta-net,
represented all twelve of the major product lines in the complete membership directory. Some of these product lines were similar to those of alpha-
net (e.g. millwork, furniture) but many others were different (e.g. marine
products, garden furnishings, musical instruments). The firms were located
within a mean radius of 44 miles from the network broker organization and
ranged in size from one to 125 employees and from $10,000 to
$20,000,000 in gross sales. Thus, the second network included a more
heterogeneous group of firms representing multiple product lines and
sizes. In addition, a key feature of beta-net was that firms represented
multiple points along the supplier–buyer value chain.

Data collection and analysis

In stage one of the data collection, exploratory one- to two-hour interviews
were conducted with the executive directors of the two networks' adminis-
trative/broker organizations and with CEO/managers of five member firms
from each network sample. The purpose of the open-ended interviews
was to uncover detailed information about each network and about
member-firm involvement in those networks that could be used to
formulate valid and relevant questions for the second stage survey of all
sampled firms. For instance, we asked the CEO/managers to discuss what
they believed they had learned from network involvement and how they
would characterize their involvement with member firms. Through
systematic coding and analysis of textual data (Miles and Huberman 1994)
regarding the content of interfirm exchanges, we identified response
patterns and thematic commonalities that could be readily compared across
firms and across networks (Knoke and Kuklinski 1982). Using this constant
comparison approach (Glaser and Strauss 1967), we continued our pattern
search process until few new insights occurred from the network interview
data.

In stage two of the data collection, we developed and administered a
survey to the full sample of firms in each network (including the ten stage-
one firms) based on topics and issues uncovered during the exploratory
interviews. Survey pre-testing had found that accuracy and response rates
would be impaired if respondents were required to complete time-intensive

Table 7.1 Network, firm and respondent descriptive characteristics

	Alpha-net 1989	Beta-net 1990
Year formed:		
Structure:	Network administrative organization: Part-time executive director, one part-time staff, 13-member board of directors	Network administrative organization: Full-time executive director, three full-time staff, 13-member board of directors
	Member exchanges: Monthly membership and board meetings, monthly newsletter	Member exchanges: Quarterly board meetings and newsletter, annual membership meetings
Objectives:	Joint marketing, production and development for similar-product wood manufacturers in the state	Joint marketing, production, and development for secondary wood products firms in a multi-county region of the state
Number of members listed in directory:	60 manufacturing members 9 associate members	77 manufacturing members 9 associate members
	Alpha-net sample firm/respondent characteristics	Beta-net sample firm/respondent characteristics
Mean firm size in:		
Employees:	14	26
Gross sales ($000):	550	3,300
Mean firm age (years):	15	23
Mean number of years in network at time of data collection	3.74	2.57
Respondent position	17 CEO/Founders; 2 Managers	19 CEO/Founders; 4 Managers
Mean number of years in position	11.88	11.22
Mean number of hours per month spent in network activities:	7	5

sociometric survey items on the complete network membership lists (e.g. sixty and seventy-seven manufacturing firms). Consequently, we included only the sample firms on the second-stage survey. Survey items provided descriptive organizational data as well as data on network interactions and organizational learning. Table 7.1 presents descriptive characteristics of the respondent firms.

Network participation and organizational learning

The first research question concerns whether organizational learning takes place as a result of involvement in SME networks. Our findings indicate that SMEs do achieve organizational learning through their network participation. In particular, firms achieve both internal and external learning (Day and Wensley 1988) depending upon whether they learn primarily about themselves or about other firms in their network. Table 7.2 presents a summary of both interview and survey findings regarding organizational learning within SME networks.

Internal learning through network participation

Internal learning refers to the increased knowledge, insights, or understanding that network firms gain of themselves through their network participation (Day and Wensley 1988). As Table 7.2 illustrates, exploratory interviews with network firms indicated that the ongoing exchanges among network members expanded members' understanding of their own capabilities. As an alpha-net member described, 'Spending time in other peoples' shops and looking at how they do things and how I do things really helped me learn a lot about my own strengths and weaknesses.' A beta-net respondent explained, 'It's easy to go through your career looking through your own vision. . . . If you can experience other people doing the same thing . . . it is a dose of reality and it broadens your knowledge base about yourself and others.' Thus, qualitative evidence indicated that as member firms got to know each other or watched each other's activities through their network participation, they were able to compare their own capabilities with other network firms. This comparative, or self-appraisal (Huber 1991) activity appears to allow network firms to expand awareness of their own firms' capabilities.

Since qualitative interviews suggested that network firms had expanded their understanding of their own capabilities, survey respondents were also asked to indicate whether network participation had 'clarified my understanding of my own firm's competitive capabilities' (dichotomous scale, 'yes' or 'no'). Table 7.2 illustrates that based on questionnaire responses by firms in both networks, self or internal learning did occur as a result of network involvement but that there were substantial differences across the two networks. Specifically, alpha-net respondents clarified their competitive

Table 7.2 Organizational learning within SME networks

	Alpha-net	Beta-net
Internal learning		
Interview results (representative comments):	'It's useful to compare yourself with other firms in [alpha-net] because you find out you're different in some ways that makes you feel better or makes you realize you've got lots to learn!'	'Now, through my [beta-net] contacts I know whether I am better at certain things than some guys or whether they are better than me . . . it's a learning process.'
Questionnaire results	74 per cent * 'Clarified my understanding of my own firm's competitive capabilities.'	39 per cent 'Clarified my understanding of my own firm's competitive capabilities.'
External learning		
Interview results (representative comments)	'I know more of the capabilities of the network firms [than non-network firms] . . . if you know their capabilities, you know who to deal with.'	'I've become more familiar with members [than non-members] so it's easier to communicate.'
	'With one company—a competitor—we differed so much on how we approached things but it was differences that made it possible to work so well together . . . I didn't know this until I worked with him some in [alpha-net].'	'I can know of competitors and know if their capabilities are good through network activities.'
Questionnaire results	68 per cent 'Better understand the capabilities of [alpha-net] member firms than non-member firms.'	48 per cent 'Better understand the capabilities of [beta-net] member firms than non-member firms.'
	84 per cent ** 'View competitors as potential resources to my business as a result of network membership.'	43 per cent 'View competitors as potential resources to my business as a result of network membership.'

* $p < 0.02$ comparing alpha-net and beta-net
** $p < 0.01$ comparing alpha-net and beta-net

capabilities through network participation to a much greater extent than beta-net firms: 73.7 per cent of the alpha-net sample replied positively to the survey question versus only 39.1 per cent of the beta-net sample. This difference is statistically significant at the 0.02 level using a t-test comparison of means. To summarize, while both qualitative and survey findings demonstrated that firms in both networks learned more about their own capabilities as a result of network involvement, the survey data indicated that internal learning was far more extensive among alpha-net firms than beta-net firms.

External learning through network participation

External learning refers to the increased knowledge and insights that network firms gain of other member firms, even competitors, through network participation. Table 7.2 presents qualitative evidence that network participation had, in many cases, increased members' awareness of other network firms' capabilities, thus expanding their potential resource base. For instance, an alpha-net respondent explained, 'I know more of the capabilities of the network firms [than non-network firms]. If you know their capabilities, you know who to deal with.' A beta-net member stated, 'I've become more familiar with members [than non-members] so its easier to communicate. We seem to have the same goals and a commonality of interest that I don't have with non-network firms, or don't know that I have.'

In addition to a greater awareness of members' capabilities in general, network participation also appeared to expand members' awareness of their competitors, particularly within the network. An alpha-net respondent commented, 'It is interesting how you can end up forming a relationship with someone you originally thought you'd least likely hook up with. With one company—a competitor—we differed so much on how we approached things. But it was differences that made it possible to work so well together . . . because even though we competed we also could complement each other. I worried about one thing and he worried about another.' In a second example, a beta-net member explained, 'I can know of competitors and know if their capabilities are good through network activities. Let's say I have a customer that I can't service right now . . . I ask myself, "Who could help me with this project?" And the answer is my toughest competitor, but I only know that through my involvement with him in [the network].' In sum, qualitative data indicated that network participation heightened members' awareness of other firms in their industry, and in particular, expanded members' awareness of competitors within the network.

After the qualitative interviews, the full sample of network respondents were asked questions regarding their perceptions of every other sample firm, and in particular, how perceptions of members differed from perceptions of non-members. As described above, qualitative analysis had suggested that firms might achieve external learning by increasing their understanding of member firms' capabilities over non-member firms. Consequently, we asked survey respondents to compare their network and non-network interactions using rated response scale items (i.e. a five-point scale from strongly disagree to strongly agree). In response to the question, 'I better understand the capabilities of [network] member firms than of non-member firms', 68.4 per cent of alpha-net respondents indicated they 'somewhat' or 'strongly' agreed (Table 7.2). In contrast, only 47.8 per cent of beta-net firms indicated their 'somewhat' or 'strong' agreement to the question. Thus, while both networks appeared to provide substantial external learning opportunities for members, learning was greatest in alpha-net, although the difference in these responses is not statistically significant.

Since qualitative evidence indicated that network involvement might expand members' awareness of competitors through network participation, we further explored this aspect of external learning in our questionnaire of network respondents. Specifically, survey respondents were asked to indicate whether (dichotomous, 'yes' or 'no') they 'viewed competitors as potential resources' for their businesses as a result of their network participation. Of alpha-net firms 84.2 per cent responded positively to this question, versus only 43.5 per cent of beta-net respondent firms. This difference is statistically significant at the 0.01 level using a t-test comparison of means.

Finally, we also asked survey respondents to indicate the extent (five-point scale from 'no extent' to 'great extent') to which they perceived member firms to be competitors before joining their respective networks and at the time of data collection (mean years in network=3.74 for alpha-net and 2.57 for beta-net). Obtaining an indication of respondents' competitor awareness both before and since network participation allowed us to examine how network membership affected learning about the competitive capabilities of the other firms in the network. Figures 7.1 and 7.2 graphically illustrate results for both networks. We employed an exploratory data analysis approach using UCINET (Borgatti, Everett and Freeman 1992) and KrackPlot (Krackhardt, Lundberg and O'Rourke 1993), social network analysis and graphing software, to compute network densities and changes in perceptions of competition before and after network membership. Network densities describe linkages and perceived relationships as a proportion of the total possible linkages/relationships among companies, ranging from 0 to 1 (Scott 1991).

The sociograms illustrate several things. First, while alpha-net members often viewed one another as competitors prior to network formation (thirteen of nineteen firms having thirteen competitive links), after several years of involvement in the network the total number of firms that perceived each other as competitors not only remained the same (thirteen), but the number of competitive links actually increased to twenty. In addition, while only two pairs of firms saw each other as competitors prior to network formation (indicated by a two-sided arrow), five such pairs of competitors existed after network involvement. Overall, the change in perceptions of competition among firms in alpha-net is represented by a doubling in network density from 0.04 (before) to 0.08 (after).

In contrast, competitive ties among the twenty-three sampled beta-net firms declined as a result of network involvement. Prior to network formation, twelve beta-net firms had a total of nine competitive links with one another. After being involved in the network, only nine of the twenty-three firms were seen as being linked competitively with other beta-net firms through only six competitive links. In addition, the number of dyadic pairs of firms recognizing each other as competitors went from two (pre-network) to zero (post-network). Consistent with these results, network density for beta-net dropped from 0.02 to 0.01.

To summarize, qualitative evidence suggested that SME network participation enhanced both internal and external organizational learning across the two networks. The quantitative results supported the notion that network involvement enhances organizational learning but also indicated that more alpha-net members than beta-net firms achieved both internal learning, or learning about themselves, and external learning, or learning about other members and competitors, through network involvement. Regarding external involvement, the sociograms graphically illustrate that network involvement does have an effect on what firms know about each other. What was unexpected was that for alpha-net, knowledge gained through network involvement increased the extent to which member firms saw each other as competitors, despite the fact that network success was built around cooperative relationships among members. In beta-net, enhanced knowledge from network involvement had exactly the opposite effect. We believe that these inconsistent findings regarding organizational learning across the two networks can be explained by examining key differences in network composition, but especially, by examining the role of the network broker in managing and accommodating these differences.

Network broker role

The second research question focused on how organizational learning might vary across networks depending on the role of the networks' central coordinator, or broker. Our evidence suggests that the broker's role includes two functions common to both networks that are critical to achieving SME network goals and that ultimately affect learning among network member firms. These broker functions are developing network membership and facilitating member exchanges. Broadly stated, our findings indicated that despite similarities in the general importance of these two functions across both networks, the two network brokers differed

Before Network Involvement (Density=0.04)

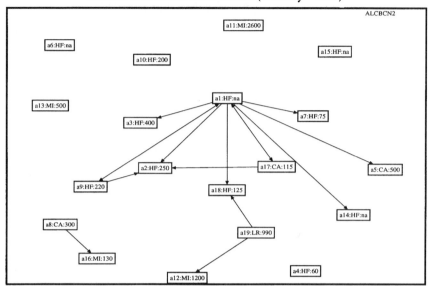

After Network Involvement (Density=0.08)

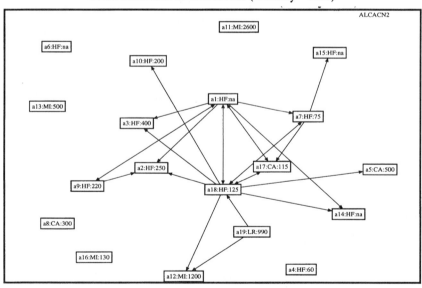

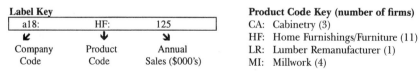

Label Key

a18:	HF:	125
Company Code	Product Code	Annual Sales ($000's)

Product Code Key (number of firms)
CA: Cabinetry (3)
HF: Home Furnishings/Furniture (11)
LR: Lumber Remanufacturer (1)
MI: Millwork (4)

Figure 7.1 Alpha-net perception of competition among sample firms

Before Network Involvement (Density=0.02)

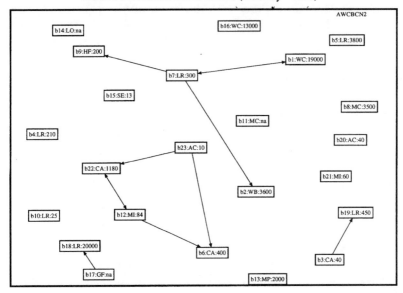

After Network Involvement (Density=0.01)

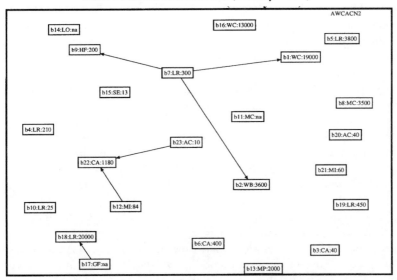

Label Key

b2 :	WB:	3600
Company Code	Product Code	Annual Sales ($000's)

Product Code Key (number of firms)

AC: Arts & Crafts (2)
CA: Cabinetry (3)
GF: Garden Furnishings (1)
HF: Home Furnishings/ Furniture (1)
LO: Logging (1)
LR: Lumber Remanufacturer (6)

MC: Musical Components (2)
MI: Millwork (4)
MP: Marine Products (1)
SE: Sports Equipment (1)
WB: Wood Broker (1)
WC: Wood Chips (2)

Figure 7.2 Beta-net perception of competition among sample firms

substantially in how they accomplished these functions. As a result, the two networks evolved quite differently, with significant consequences regarding the extent to which member firms were able to learn about themselves and other network firms.

Developing network membership

Interviews with the two networks' brokers (their executive directors) and with network members indicated that the brokers were instrumental in developing the membership of both alpha-net and beta-net. They were hired early in network formation with membership development as a key responsibility. However, qualitative data suggested that the brokers took quite different approaches to their membership development function.

One alpha-net respondent indicated that, 'while not ruling out other wood products manufacturers', the alpha-net broker focused his attention on developing network membership from the state's furniture industry, since that group comprised a wide range of 'fiercely independent' organizations with 'unique products . . . and a potential for growth'. In addition, the broker argued that focusing on membership homogeneity might strengthen the apparent benefits to potential network members: 'similar guys (firms) might see more benefits from joining the network than [when there are] a lot of different firms.' Indeed, comments from alpha-net members indicated there were potential benefits to a more homogeneous membership: 'One reason I joined is that this organization has local people in the same industry group that I'm in . . . so they know where I'm coming from.' Thus, the alpha-net broker's approach to developing network membership emphasized homogeneous, even competitor, firms within one product line (i.e. furniture). Further, the fact that most of these targeted firms did not traditionally work cooperatively within the state was of particular interest to the alpha-net broker who perceived greater organizational benefits for members from working with competitors rather than with complementary firms. Since these firms were similar in many ways, they would be able to relate to and learn from one another quite readily.

The executive director, or broker, of beta-net, also hired to develop the new network's membership, adopted a different approach to membership development. The broker described how his 'first task was membership development. I used lists of state wood manufacturers as a guide and would contact and re-contact them to join [beta-net].' In contrast to alpha-net, however, the broker's major criterion for network membership was quite broad, focusing only on 'operating as a secondary wood manufacturer' within a multi-county region of the state. Consequently, beta-net members represented twelve different product lines with no product being dominant. In contrast, alpha-net members mostly represented a single primary product line.

The beta-net broker also leveraged the credibility and existing ties of early network members for developing additional network membership. Our qualitative evidence indicated that beta-net's broker developed the network's membership by soliciting previously connected, key industry firms to join the network early in its formation. For instance, regarding the charter membership of one key member, beta-net's broker stated: 'He gave us instant credibility with the community since he is the supplier to almost all of the builders in the region.' For a second firm, the broker commented: 'From him [a second charter member] we gain his credibility and contacts as one of the larger wood manufacturers in the state.' In general, the broker emphasized that beta-net benefited from the 'community and industry credibility' that its 'membership diversity' created. In contrast to alpha-net, beta-net's broker emphasized bringing existing linkages among diverse or complementary firms into the network's membership. While there were clear advantages to building a network in this way, member-firm interaction did not need to extend much beyond those of their market-based counterparts, thus limiting incentives and opportunities to learn from one another.

Facilitating member exchanges

During interviews we asked members and network brokers to indicate how the brokers facilitated member exchanges after the network was formed. Both alpha-net and beta-net respondents described how the general meetings that took place early in the networks' evolution helped facilitate member exchanges. An alpha-net respondent stated: 'In the first year, we were getting together sometimes three or four times a month. I went to the first meetings to meet other people in my industry.' Similarly, a beta-net member described: 'In the beginning, we used to have a lot of meetings . . . at least every month. All new members would try to get together to learn about what [the network] was all about.' However, after the first year the two network brokers took different approaches to facilitating member exchanges.

Alpha-net's broker expanded the monthly membership meetings, thereby facilitating learning opportunities, moving them to different member sites around the state to accommodate different member locations. In addition, the broker mailed monthly newsletters and separate meeting agenda postcards to members to ensure that all were informed of network and other members' activities. Since alpha-net's membership included competitors, the broker had to overcome some resistance to exchange knowledge and even fear among new members. One respondent stated: 'There was a tremendous sense of paranoia and fear about the competitor . . . a lot of people were afraid to talk to other people.' The alpha-net broker purposely acted as a 'buffer' during monthly meetings between existing members and new or potential members who might be reticent to talk with other competitor members: 'At the meetings . . . I [broker] would talk to them [potential or new members] since they might feel funny talking with their competition . . . at least at first.'

The alpha-net broker's emphasis on multifirm exchanges and frequent meetings also encouraged and facilitated member learning between meetings. For instance, one member described how information on a destructive wood fungus was quickly communicated to the network membership: 'There was a fungus in some wood that occurred here and right away one member found out and began calling other members, then they called others. So we were able to tell all the members about it with our information pipeline.' In addition, alpha-net's broker argued that even though it might present more of a challenge to coordinate competitors within a network, 'it is the socialization process [among competitors] that is the single most crucial difference between networks and non-networks. I don't know exactly where this socialization process will lead us but I think it will be positive in the end.' Thus, the alpha-net broker facilitated learning through multifirm exchanges among network members, including decentralized member exchange through the 'information pipeline.'

In contrast, beta-net's broker moved to a 'more efficient' method of facilitating member exchanges after the first year. Beta-net's monthly membership meetings became annual or 'as needed' membership meetings. In addition, a newsletter was distributed quarterly to communicate network activities and a centralized 'netting circuit' replaced monthly meetings for facilitating member exchanges. The netting circuit consisted of central office staff contacting network members by phone or facsimile to inform them of specific opportunities with other members (or nonmembers). Broker knowledge of these opportunities came from outside contacts, from scanning industry publications and from members contacting the network central office. Thus, beta-net's approach emphasized dyadic, opportunity-specific member exchange of information and knowledge.

The beta-net broker described his approach to facilitating member exchanges as a 'matchmaking' strategy that attempted to connect one firm with another for mutual benefit. For instance, a beta-net member stated: 'The network lined us up with a major company we now supply products to.' Another respondent described, 'What [beta-net] is doing is eliminating the trickle down of information . . . it's much more efficient to have one central head for this information to process through.' Thus, beta-net's broker facilitated primarily dyadic member exchanges, including a more centralized exchange process (i.e. the netting circuit) than alpha-net. This approach was clearly more efficient than the more decentralized model used in alpha-net but information was channelled through and filtered by the network broker, thus limiting member-firm learning. A summary of the key findings concerning the roles and emphases of each network broker is displayed in Table 7.3.

Table 7.3 Roles and emphases of the network broker for organizational learning

	Alpha-net	Beta-net
Role of broker regarding:		
Developing Network Membership (representative comments):	'We [network broker and charter members] decided to focus on the state's furniture industry . . . a group of fiercely independent businesses . . . with unique products . . . and a potential for growth.'	'I [network broker] went out on the road to find and enlist as many of these wood companies as possible into [beta-net] . . . as far as I'm concerned, all of the state's wood manufacturers are members of [beta-net].'
	'One reason I focused on one main group [furniture] was that similar guys [firms] might see more benefits from joining the network than a lot of different ones.'	'I [network broker] tried to leverage each beta-net member . . . for instance, from [a charter member firm] we gain his credibility and contacts as one of the larger wood manufacturers in the state.'
Facilitating member exchanges (representative comments)	'We [furniture manufacturers] have . . . been really fragmented. Remember, these companies rarely talk with each other . . . so [network broker's] role was to . . . buffer the new members at the meetings . . . until they felt comfortable talking in the group.'	'We use a netting circuit to contact members about particular opportunities . . . that's when we call or fax them the information on a business opportunity as it comes in to us [network office].'
	'At the meetings . . . I [network broker] would talk to them (potential or new members) since they might feel funny talking with their competition . . . at least at first. I wanted them to carry the networking beyond the meetings . . . that's when the socialization process would start.'	'One of my most important jobs as [beta-net] executive director is to basically run a matchmaking service . . . trying to find members who can work with other members, or trying to match opportunities we hear about through the office with member companies.'
Emphasis of broker regarding:		
Developing network membership	Single product-line focus Competitor membership Few pre-network linkages	Multiple product-line focus Complementary membership Moderate pre-network linkages
Facilitating member exchanges	Decentralized processes Multifirm exchanges	Centralized processes Dyadic exchanges

Toward a theory of organizational learning through networks

March's (1991) concepts of exploratory and exploitative organizational learning provide a useful framework for distinguishing the approaches taken by the two network brokers as to their key functions, and for understanding how these different approaches affect organizational learning. An exploratory approach to organizational learning involves experimenting with new processes or frames of reference while an exploitative approach focuses on refining or extending existing processes or paradigms (Huber 1991). Thus, an exploratory approach can appear more risky at the outset and present less predictable outcomes than an exploitative approach.

Our findings suggest that alpha-net's broker emphasized less certain, more exploratory processes than beta-net's broker. The alpha-net director's interest in developing cooperative relationships among competitor firms in the furniture industry and his emphasis on group processes and multifirm communications were attempts to do things that were totally new for member firms. In contrast, beta-net's director emphasized 'more efficient' and predictable activities (i.e. exploitative processes) such as member exchanges among complementary firms or among firms with existing linkages. Indeed, the need to actively guide or manage interfirm exchanges among beta-net members was low enough that regular meetings were disbanded after the first year. Instead, when specific opportunities arose, the centralized netting circuit was employed. Thus, a more manageable and predictable process for facilitating member exchanges was used in beta-net than in alpha-net.

There are trade-offs to emphasizing predictability over uncertainty, however. Our findings suggest that organizational learning through network participation is actually increased when those interfirm linkages are among competitors rather than among buyers and suppliers or other complementary firms. In addition, the evidence indicates that network organization learning is also increased when multifirm linkages are emphasized, as in alpha-net, and when member exchanges are facilitated by decentralized processes rather than the centralized ones found in beta-net.

As in beta-net, organizations that have inherent reasons for cooperating, such as buyers and suppliers and other complementary firms, do not generally perceive themselves to be competitors. When they become members of an SME network, membership does appear to enhance knowledge and learning about the other firms in the network. However, the limited interaction among members of such heterogeneous, complementary networks means that only modest levels of organizational learning takes place, and network firms gain relatively little knowledge about their own competitiveness. In addition, if the primary mechanism for interacting with other members is when a specific opportunity arises and is presented by the network broker, then individual members have little opportunity to explore other members' capabilities and compare them with their own.

In contrast, horizontally linked firms, such as alpha-net, would have few historical exchange patterns to replicate with one another and consequently, would have more complex ties to create and coordinate once they joined the network. These ties build commitment and encourage the flow of information, thereby enhancing learning about themselves and others. As with alpha-net, small firms having the same basic product line and operating in the same geographical area are likely to see many other firms as competitors (rightfully so) prior to network involvement. After network involvement develops, an interesting learning phenomenon appears to occur. Consistent with our finding that post-network perceptions of competition can actually increase in horizontally linked networks, firms gain greater knowledge about the other firms in the network, which makes it quite clear that these firms are indeed direct competitors. At the same time, the process of network involvement builds trust among competitors so that they learn how to compete more effectively, particularly against firms outside the network. When these network firms exchange with multiple firms on a regular basis, they have an expanded opportunity to learn about the capabilities of the membership and to compare their own capabilities with other network members. Such knowledge facilitates self-learning, further enhancing the competitiveness of network members.

Conclusion

We have provided evidence that both internal and external organizational learning occurs as a result of network participation and the actions of the network broker in two key areas: developing network membership and facilitating member exchanges. Our evidence suggests that network participation provides an opportunity for SMEs to learn about their own capabilities and about their competitors in ways not available through market arrangements. Our findings also suggest that for networks of competitor firms in which the broker takes an exploratory approach to the key functions of membership development and member exchange, greater organization learning takes place than in networks where the broker takes a more incremental, exploitative approach to learning. SME network planners and organizers should not avoid developing networks of competitor firms, as long as the broker is clearly committed to exploratory learning. Although such networks are inherently more challenging to develop and maintain, our findings suggest that they have a greater potential for significant learning by network members.

Conventional wisdom is that firms learn what they can and cannot do well through interactions with customers or interactions with competitors through competitive market bidding. While these are useful ways to learn organizational capabilities, they are also difficult ways, since learning often occurs through losing an account or bid. The traditional cautions regarding network arrangements, such as organizations losing their competitive edge due to the buffering effect of network membership, do not appear to hold up in the SME networks we studied. Instead, SME members appear to go through a process of enhanced learning about themselves relative to others through cooperative activities, rather than through being 'beaten up' through competition. Network exchanges appear to provide a more advantageous context for learning about a firm's own organizational capabilities than market exchanges.

Our findings also suggest that network participation expands SMEs' awareness of other organizations in the network. Not only did network participation appear to increase network members' view of competitors as resources, but in alpha-net, members became more aware of which firms were actual competitors. Thus, previous scholars' assumptions that awareness precedes interfirm relationships (Klongan, Warren, Winkelpleck and Paulson 1976) may well depend on the context of those relationships. In an SME network context, it appears that network involvement can substantially enhance awareness of competition, while still resulting in cooperation among the firms that view themselves as competitors.

Finally, our findings suggest that when network activities and communications are primarily centralized through the network broker, as in beta-net, the learning that takes place may also be centralized. Thus, the broker, rather than the members, becomes the repository for network knowledge and opportunities. When network communications are decentralized and flow among members as well as through the broker, as in alpha-net, the learning that takes place is dispersed. Consequently, the network, comprising both members and broker, becomes the repository for knowledge and opportunities and learning is extensive. These findings are consistent with research on team communications (Rogers and Rogers 1976) and suggest that scholars and practitioners interested in documenting the outcomes of network participation, such as learning, should look more closely at the role of the network broker, particularly regarding how the broker disseminates information and opportunities.

Throughout the paper we have argued that the role of the network broker is key to understanding network learning. However, some may prefer to argue that the major difference in the two networks was the composition of participating firms. We do not deny that the relative homogeneity of alpha-net firms might have facilitated and encouraged learning, while beta-net firms might have felt that there was less to learn from firms that were different from themselves. We feel strongly, however, that it was the actions and involvement of the network broker in alpha-net that enabled significant learning to take place. Because alpha-net firms were so similar, they competed directly, minimizing the likelihood that they would ever cooperate and work with each other on their own. It was only because of the network broker, who encouraged and assisted the firms to break down their competitive instincts and build trust, that alpha-net had such strong learning.

The role of the broker in beta-net is perhaps somewhat less clear but still important. Because beta-net firms provided relatively heterogeneous, complementary services, it is reasonable to have expected high network involvement, leading to strong learning by the firms about themselves and others. That we did not find this to be the case was surprising. We saw the centralized role of beta-net's broker and his modest commitment to encouraging involvement among member firms as the prime reason for the moderate levels of learning that took place. What is not clear is how learning might be affected among firms like those in beta-net if the role of the network broker were different. Our emphasis on the importance of the broker suggests that one who strongly encouraged and facilitated interaction among complementary firms would stimulate greater organizational learning than was the case in beta-net. What we cannot tell without further research is whether learning in heterogeneous/ complementary SME networks like beta-net would have been as high as in more homogeneous/ competitive SME networks if both networks had brokers that were strong advocates of direct involvement and communication by member firms.

Because our research was limited to only two networks, it is difficult to know to what extent the findings and conclusions can be generalized to other interorganizational networks. Our use of rigorous methods of data collection, including use of both qualitative and quantitative approaches, make us confident that our results are reliable and valid. Nonetheless, we cannot be sure that significant organizational learning might not take place through other forms of interfirm involvement, including other types of network arrangements. In addition, there may be conditions present in other networks that mitigate the role of the broker regarding learning. These are clearly issues that need further investigation.

One issue that may set our study apart from others is the structure of the networks we studied. Both networks were clearly guided in their development by an autonomous broker, a role that is not always present in networks. In addition, network firms were affiliated with each other and the broker rather loosely, with no ownership or history of strong contractual ties. Many networks of business firms, especially involving larger organizations, are connected through formal contracts and/or equity ownership and there is often no independent entity, or broker, set up to manage and guide the relationship. How learning might evolve and how much firms would learn in such networks is not clear, and cannot necessarily be extrapolated from our research.

Despite these cautions, it seems clear to us that interorganizational networks for small- to medium-sized manufacturing firms can facilitate organizational learning in ways that cannot be achieved through traditional market arrangements and that the role of network broker is important for facilitating this process. Network planners and policy-makers, whether in the US, Europe, or elsewhere, need to consider not only how a broker may be useful in forming a network, but in how the broker helps to shape network composition and their impact on the extent to which learning actually takes place. It appears not to be sufficient to simply hire a broker to form a network and then assume that members will become involved with and learn from one another. While some learning does take place, as evidenced by beta-net's results, it is only when the broker takes a strong integrative role that significant learning occurs. Our findings for alpha-net indicate not only that learning takes place, but that it can occur within a context of recognized competitiveness among members that can ultimately lead to greater intranetwork cooperation and increased effectiveness in dealing with firms outside the network.

Notes

1 This research was funded by a grant from the Ewing Marion Kauffman Foundation Center for Entrepreneurial Leadership and the University of Kentucky Small Business Development Center. A version of the paper was presented at the EMOT workshop on Interfirm Networks in Modena, Italy. Travel to the workshop by the first author was funded by the European Science Foundation.
2 An analysis of the relationship between network structure and organizational outcomes using this same data set can be found in Human and Provan (1997).

Bibliography

Aldrich, H. and Zimmer, C. (1986) 'Entrepreneurship through social networks', in D. Sexton and R. Smilor (eds), *The Art and Science of Entrepreneurship*, Cambridge, MA: Ballinger, pp. 3–23.
Borgatti, S., Everett, M. and Freeman, L. (1992) *UCINET IV Version 1.0*, Columbia, SC: Analytic Technologies.
Burt, R. and Minor, M. (1983) *Applied Network Analysis: A Methodological Introduction*, Beverly Hills, CA: Sage Publications.
Cyert, R. and March, J. (1963) *A Behavioural Theory of the Firm*, Englewood Cliffs, NJ: Prentice-Hall.
Day, G. and Wensley, R. (1988) 'Assessing advantage: a framework for diagnosing competitive superiority', *Journal of Marketing*, 52: 1–20.
Eisenhardt, K. (1989) 'Building theories from case study research', *Academy of Management Review*, 14: 532–50.
Glaser, B. and Strauss, A. (1967) *The Discovery of Grounded Theory: Strategies of Qualitative Research*. London: Weidenfeld and Nicholson.
Granovetter, M. (1985) 'Economic action and social structure: the problem of embeddedness', *American Journal of Sociology*, 91: 481–510.
Hamel, G. (1991) 'Competition for competence and inter-partner learning within international strategic alliances', *Strategic Management Journal*, 12: 83–103.
Holsti, O. (1968) 'Content analysis', in G. Lindzey and E. Aronson (eds), *The Handbook of Social Psychology*, Cambridge, MA: Addison-Wesley, pp. 596–692.
Huber, G. P. (1991) 'Organizational learning: the contributing processes and the literatures.' *Organization Science*, 2: 88–115.

Human, S. E. and Provan, K. G. (1997) 'An emergent theory of structure and outcomes in small-firm strategic manufacturing networks', *Academy of Management Journal*, 40: 368–403.

Jarillo, J. (1988) 'On strategic networks', *Strategic Management Journal*, 9: 31–41.

Jick, T. (1979) 'Mixing qualitative and quantitative methods: triangulation in action', *Administrative Science Quarterly*, 24: 602–11.

Klongan, G., Warren, R., Winkelpleck, J. and Paulson, S. (1976) 'Interorganizational measurement in the social services sector: differences by hierarchical level', *Administrative Science Quarterly*, 21: 675–87.

Knoke, D. and Kuklinski, J. (1982) *Network Analysis*, Newbury Park, CA: Sage Publications.

Krackhardt, D., Lundberg, M. and O'Rourke, L. (1993) 'KrackPlot: a picture's worth a thousand words', *Connections*, 16(1/2): 37–47.

Larson, A. (1992) 'Network dyads in entrepreneurial settings: a study of the governance of exchange relationships', *Administrative Science Quarterly*, 37: 76–104.

Levitt, B. and March, J. (1988) 'Organizational learning', *Annual Review of Sociology*, 14: 319–40.

Lichtenstein, G. (1992) *A Catalogue of US Manufacturing Networks*, Gaithersburg, MD: US Department of Commerce, National Institute of Standards of Technology.

Lorenzoni, G. and Ornati, O. (1988) 'Constellations of firms and new ventures', *Journal of Business Venturing*, 3: 41–57.

Lyles, M. (1988) 'Learning among joint venture-sophisticated firms', In F. Contractor and P. Lorange (eds), *Cooperative strategies in international business*, Lexington, MA: Lexington Books, pp. 301–16.

March, J. (1991) 'Exploration and exploitation in organizational learning', *Organization Science*, 2: 71–87.

Miles, M. and Huberman, A. (1994) *An Expanded Sourcebook: Qualitative Data Analysis*, Thousand Oaks, CA: Sage Publications.

Powell, W. (1990) 'Neither market or hierarchy: Network forms of organization', in B. M. Staw and L. L. Cummings (eds) *Research in Organizational Behavior*, Greenwich, CT: JAI Press, vol. 12, pp. 295–336.

Powell, W., Koput, K. and Smith-Doerr, L. (1996) 'Interorganizational collaboration and the locus of innovation: Networks of learning in biotechnology', *Administrative Science Quarterly*, 41: 116–45.

Provan, K. (1993) 'Embeddedness, interdependence, and opportunism in organizational supplier–buyer networks', *Journal of Management*, 19: 841–56.

Rogers, E. and Rogers, R. (1976) *Communication in Organizations*, New York: Free Press.

Scott, J. (1991) *Social Network Analysis*, London: Sage Publications.

Selz, M. (1992) 'Networks help small companies think and act big', *Wall Street Journal*. 12 November, B2.

Williamson, O. (1985) *The Economic Institutions of Capitalism*, New York: Free Press.

8 Dangerous liaisons

Sharing knowledge within research and development alliances[1]

Paul B. de Laat

Introduction

Alliances between firms that involve active mutual R&D cooperation have been mushrooming since the 1980s. Such partnering is usually cast in the form of joint R&D, a research corporation or a joint venture involving mutual R&D efforts. Together, these will be designated as *R&D alliances*. In the literature, these are also referred to as 'strategic technology alliances' (Hagedoorn and Schakenraad 1992). After a rapid take-off, their growth rate seems to have stabilized at present. The actual rate is still quite high, however, and every year, hundreds of R&D alliances are being initiated.

This is a remarkable phenomenon indeed, as such alliances seem to be fraught with risks. These risks have to do with transaction-specific aspects of partnering. First, R&D alliances usually require investments into physical assets: specialized equipment, R&D buildings, production facilities and the like. Also, more often than not, investment into human assets has to be contemplated: specialists are hired for the occasion, to develop esoteric knowledge intimately connected with the goals of the alliance. Usually, such investments are, at least partly, transaction-specific: if cooperation breaks down, only part of the cost can be recuperated. Therefore, to a large extent these represent sunk cost.

Second, R&D alliances usually require the exchange of proprietary knowledge between partners, not only while cooperation is under way, but also before it actually starts. Such knowledge can be of a more formal kind, in which case transfer is easy: formulas, blueprints, designs, manuals and the like are handed over. More often, however, the more informal, tacit kind will be involved, in which case knowledge can only be transferred by people actually working together. This transfer of knowledge, either formal or informal, also represents a kind of transaction-specific investment, as knowledge, once shared, cannot be taken back from one's partner afterwards. Once a secret is shared, it is shared forever. This second kind of transaction-specific investment is much more complicated—and intriguing—than the first, as will be explained presently. Therefore I will refer to it not as sunk cost, but as *sunk knowledge*.

Both sinking cost and sinking knowledge create risks. One type of risk is common to both. If partners invest in physical or human assets that are transaction-specific, a monetary sum is put at risk. By sharing proprietary knowledge, informational value is irrevocably contributed to the alliance. Both acts, therefore, commit the investor to the alliance. At the same time, however, they generate the risk of being held up by the other, i.e. being forced to accept less favourable terms of cooperation. Without going into details, I would maintain that this kind of risk can easily be contained. Consider the total value of sunk cost and sunk knowledge for each partner; if partners to an alliance each take care to commit (more or less) equal value and keep this balance all along, they will be (more or less) equally committed to the alliance. Partners then create an equal hold on each other; blackmailing powers effectively countervail each other. For a more elaborated treatment of this proposition, see De Laat (1995).

Sinking knowledge, however, is much more complicated a phenomenon than sinking cost. Some more typical risks are associated with it. These have to do with the fact that knowledge is actually *handed over* to the other partner. Consider the situation where A shares knowledge with B. B may be tempted to apply the information in other ways than permitted by the alliance contract. This risk of *expropriation* includes first of all, that B may overstep bounds by using the knowledge in other products than agreed upon, in other markets, or both. This may involve B turning into a direct competitor. Say partners develop a common product, to be sold in different markets; B may nevertheless choose to invade A's market. Second, B may switch to direct competition, where mutual cooperation was intended. That is, A and B work together on creating, producing and selling specific products in specific markets; after some time B may choose to go it alone and challenge A in direct competition instead. Third, parties outside the alliance are possibly interested in the knowledge that has been transferred. B may then resort to selling the information for a high price, or to swapping it for other R&D secrets and the like. If such expropriation hazards materialize, for A the cooperation with B has turned sour; A wishes it had never started cooperation in the first place. The transfer of knowledge has 'boomeranged'. On top of this, of course, these risks can also be used by B to blackmail A; just the threat of expropriation may do to reap considerable benefits.

Actually, risks are even greater than sketched above. I only treated the *intended* transfer of knowledge to partners. However, one's partners may easily obtain more information than they are entitled to; this may happen by chance, or on purpose. The line between both is very thin, of course (cf. Hamel 1991). In the literature this hazard is referred to as 'leakage' or 'spillover' of information.

Note, that such backfiring hazards exist in *every* strategic alliance between firms. Some knowledge about products, processes, markets, etc., is always transferred. Partners inevitably learn from each other. However, two kinds of alliances can usefully be distinguished: *product* links, and *knowledge* links (Badaracco 1991: introduction, ch. 5). In the former, partners cooperate to get access to new products or markets. The goal of the latter, however, is to jointly create new knowledge. Such knowledge links require mutually working together on R&D problems. As can readily be seen, boomerang hazards are especially severe in knowledge links (cf. Badaracco 1991: 135–7). Such knowledge links, or R&D alliances as I have called them, are precisely the topic of this article.

These boomerang hazards are not merely figments of my imagination. Fears of this kind are actually entertained by managers involved in R&D alliances. Take, for example, a recent investigation carried out among managers of British information and communications technology firms. As major risks of partnering, 'collaborators can become competitors', and 'leakage of information' ranked very high (Littler *et al.* 1995: Table 5). Similarly, in a survey of twenty-one American R&D consortia, the inherent loss of proprietary opportunities was ranked the highest disadvantage of consortia (Souder and Nassar 1990a). In the case of the Microelectronics and Computer Technology Corporation in particular, each participant is very cautious in revealing sensitive information, for fear of helping competitors launch competing products (Werner 1993; Gibson and Rogers 1994: 369). For more details about boomerang hazards of knowledge transfer in strategic alliances in general, see Perlmutter and Heenan (1986: 142), Lei and Slocum (1992), and Yoshino and Rangan (1995: 127–30).

Hazards of knowledge transfer backfiring do not always exist fully. Knowledge may actually be 'protected' against unwanted expropriation (cf. Teece 1986). The nature of the technology counts; process innovations, for example, are more difficult to access (by reverse engineering) than product innovations. Moreover, legal instruments like copyright, patent and trademark may be effective. The more that knowledge involved in transfer is effectively protected by these mechanisms, the less boomerang hazards will be real. Also, the identity of the partner(s) counts. The more that technologies to be exchanged are complementary rather than similar, and the more that product/markets differ between partners, the less boomerang hazards have to be taken seriously.

More often than not, however, such protection is hardly sufficient, and partners to an alliance are very 'close' to each other. Then, boomerang hazards associated with knowledge transfer are very real. What should be done to contain these hazards? Some tactics suggest themselves immediately. First, partners to an alliance may use an 'avoidance' strategy. The common project that is to be undertaken is not set up as an integrated design, but is split up, as much as possible, into interconnected modules. Each module, then, is managed by different partners, at their own laboratories. This modular approach (cf. Hladik 1988; Moxon *et al.* 1988; Mangematin 1996) minimizes interaction and guarantees that knowledge transfer is minimal. Second, parties may resort to contractual arrangements. The use of knowledge confined to certain products/markets is strictly specified; also, partners are tied to clauses of confidentiality. Third, and most importantly, parties may try and create credible commitments to each other. They offer concrete guarantees that they intend to faithfully execute the agreement. By putting considerable stakes at issue, chances for loyal cooperation increase. This approach, which I have explored elsewhere (De Laat 1997), materializes first and foremost through sinking cost and sinking knowledge in mutually balanced ways, as indicated above. Moreover, setting entry fees, creating equity and taking cross-share holdings may serve the same purposes. Finally, bundling of agreements and reliance on reputation serve to stabilize alliances as well. This third approach as a whole, of course, not only tackles boomerang hazards of knowledge transfer, it also deals with opportunism in general.

Useful as these approaches may be, in this article I will explore another one. From time immemorial, people have been in need of mechanisms to ensure proper execution of agreements. Usually, parties exchanged pawns between each other, either people (*hostages*), or properties (*pledges*). Pawning in general has two features. On the one hand, the supplier comes up with a commitment to the relationship, intended to show his goodwill. On the other hand, pawns are actually handed over to one's partner, which introduces risks of expropriation and blackmail. Both formal properties of pawning may sound familiar by now: they also apply to the sharing or, for that matter, leaking of knowledge within R&D alliances. For, indeed, partners commit knowledge to the alliance, which at the same time exposes them to the risks of expropriation and blackmail. Therefore, transferring R&D knowledge—at least as far as its potential use *outside* the confines of the alliance is concerned—may be interpreted as *pawning of information*.

Of course, the analogy is not perfect (cf. De Laat 1995). Sharing secrets in R&D alliances differs in some important aspects from pawning proper. Knowledge, once shared, is duplicated; moreover, it cannot be taken back. Therefore, unlike classic pawns, informational pawns, once pledged, cannot be returned to their owner. Also, and in line with the foregoing, knowledge pawns are not meant to be temporary, they cannot be but permanent. Finally, while classic pawns are intended to support a transaction, informational pawns come about as an *unintended* by-product of knowledge transfer. Nevertheless, on account of its central feature of *ex ante* handing over of information to one's partner, knowledge transfer may be interpreted as informational pawning.

This analogy I intend to exploit as follows. I will briefly describe the age-old institution of providing hostages and/or pledges, and the problems of expropriation and blackmail these have run into. Then, I will trace the historical evolution of these institutions, precisely as a response to these problems. The analysis will mainly focus on the use of such pawns in what is known today as international relations: treaties and alliances as forged between sovereign states. I choose to do so, as it seems especially that arena, and not, for example, private law, that mostly resembles relations between firms as of today. After that analysis, I return to R&D alliances and proceed by analogy: to what extent can the more sophisticated forms of guarantee that have evolved from the more primitive forms of providing hostages and pledges be of use, after suitable modification and adaptation, in reducing boomerang hazards in R&D partnerships? Can new organizational solutions for R&D partnering be extracted from a historical analysis of guarantees of international law?

Treaty guarantees in international relations

Hostages and pledges

From ancient times onwards, hostages (Lat. *obsides*, Fr. *otages*, Ger. *Geisel*) have been used to guarantee treaty performance: one party hands over some persons to the other party as a security for the fulfilment of its undertaking. The well-being of hostages, even their lives, depended on the faithful performance of their rulers. To be effective, they had to be persons of relatively high standing and prestige, otherwise, their transfer constituted no potential harm to the party providing them. Quite often, tens and even hundreds of persons were required as hostages. Their use goes far back in time; indeed they were used by the Assyrians and Hittites, as their clay tablets testify. The Romans, in their time, also frequently resorted to the practice; in particular, they unilaterally demanded hostages from vanquished peoples. In the case of default, hostages were treated severely and often simply killed. Their use continued throughout the Middle Ages, although in time they were treated more leniently, often becoming slaves of the state. After the first millennium, hostages were often knights; and, upon default of their lord, would be imprisoned with a ransom being set for their release. Finally, in the eighteenth century, hostages ceased to be used as securities in international affairs. Of course, hostages are still a familiar phenomenon to us; as an object of exchange or as 'precautionary' measure, especially in times of war, they are still with us. That, however, concerns hostage-*taking* by force, as opposed to voluntary hostage-*posting*, which is the issue here.

Let me mention two examples. In 1524, after a military defeat, Francis I of France was in the power of Charles V of Spain. The French king was only released from prison after signing the Peace Treaty of Madrid of 14 January 1526. As a security, he had to deliver his own two sons to the Emperor in Madrid (Dumont 1726–31, IV, I: 412; also cited in Verzijl 1973: 244, and De Vattel 1758: 455). Similarly, in 1527, to cement the 'perpetual peace' between the same Francis I and Henry VIII, the English monarch sent over a whole delegation as hostage: two archbishops, eleven bishops, and twenty-eight nobles (thirteen towns were also handed over) (Phillipson 1916: 209).

As ancient a form of securing treaties is the handing over of a pledge (Lat. *pignus*, Fr. *plège*, Ger. *Pfand*). Some good is handed over to the other party to secure performance. Usually, handing over means that the pledgee actually gets it in his hands, but legal title still resides with the pledgor. If the latter actually defaults, the pledge is forfeited. Pledging between states has sometimes involved movable goods like jewels and diamonds. A famous example is Poland, which pledged its Crown Jewels to Russia in the eighteenth century (De Vattel 1758: 448; Phillimore 1855: 69). Mostly, however, immovable goods like houses, fortresses, cities and territories were pawned. In the treaty between Portugal and the Netherlands of 30 July, 1669, Cohin and Cananor in India remained part of the Dutch Republic, as security for payment by Portugal of overdue instalments of a loan (Dumont 1726–31, VII, I: 114; cited in Verzijl 1973: 295). Also, by a treaty of 1756, Corsica was pledged to France as security for the repayment of debts by Genoa (Phillipson 1916: 208; Wild 1934: 156, mistakenly refers to this as a case of hypothecation).

In the case of territory, from the nineteenth century onwards a variation has evolved: temporary military occupation. This form is less drastic than proper pawning: territory is no longer annexed, only occupied. Recent examples that come to mind involve relations between France and Germany. The Peace Treaty of Versailles, 1871, allowed Germany to keep six French *départements* under military occupation until war indemnities had been paid back by France (Phillipson 1916: 211–12). In 1919, at Versailles again, roles were reversed. France occupied the Rhineland as a guarantee for the execution of treaty stipulations by Germany, war reparation payments in particular (Wild 1934: 158–60). In international relations, most forms of pledging are now a thing of the past; only military occupation is still widely used as a means to guarantee treaties.

Such pawns, either of the human or material variety, constitute the archetype of guaranteeing engagements and treaties, by now at least 4,000 years old. Its basic logic is simple: 'Hand over to me something tangible that is valuable to you, then I will be able to trust you.' Hostages and pledges, however, run into certain basic problems that all have to do with the fact that A has actually handed over something to B. Having a hold on this, B may be tempted to exploit the situation. Historical examples include the following. Consider hostages first. Treaty performance by A notwithstanding, B may retain the hostages and blackmail A into further concessions. Also, B may try to win the hostages' allegiance and turn them against their rulers. In the case of property being pledged, the pledgee is likewise tempted. Upon contract performance, B may either simply keep the pledge, or try to extort A in exchange for its return. In the case of territories or castles being pledged, B may not only proceed to keep them, but even use them as extra resources to stage or continue a war against A.

In short, this mechanism of guaranteeing treaties may easily backfire. The heart of the problem is, of course, that someone or something is actually handed over to the party wishing to be reassured; the same problem with the same roots, it should be recalled, plagues the transfer of knowledge between R&D alliance partners. In response to this, these basic methods have, throughout history, evolved into other forms of guarantee. These developments in international guarantees will be traced below.

A word about sources and method. The first section treats so-called 'deposit with a third party'. About this subject very little has been written and, as a consequence, data had to be pieced together from various sources (mainly Verzijl 1976, and Wild 1934). The sections thereafter describe how the more primitive institutions of rendering hostages or pledges evolved into more refined forms of international guarantee. For the evolutionary scheme itself I mainly rely on Ascan Lutteroth. In his study *Der Geisel im Rechtsleben* (1922) he put forth an interesting genealogy of such developments (Lutteroth 1922: §16, §35). Although his scheme is very speculative, I cannot resist using it, but in order to provide more detail, help is sought from other authors. This is necessary, since more often than not, this German jurist is rather careless in his interpretation of treaties. The other main source is Payson Wild, whose *Sanctions and Treaty Enforcement* (1934) renders an elaborate overview of all types of guarantee ever used (not just the ones emanating from hostages and/or pledges). Also, sources listing the original documents were indispensable: Rymer's *Foedera* (1704–35), and Dumont's *Corps Universel Diplomatique du Droit des Gens* (1726–31). Finally it should be remarked, that not all forms that evolved will receive equal attention; those that I especially intend to use in the subsequent discussion of the R&D alliances of our time, will be explained more fully.

Deposit with a third party

This first section highlights not so much a new species of guarantee as a variety of it. Parties still provide hostages and/or pledges, but with one essential difference: these are not put into the hands of the other treaty partner, but forwarded to a *third party*, not involved in the treaty. Such a 'solution' doesn't seem to have been applied often, but some interesting instances have been recorded.

When in the Middle Ages kings or princes had a mutual dispute, they would often appeal to a powerful third party like the Emperor or the Pope. That party would then try to get the parties involved to agree on a settlement, either by mediation, or by arbitration. A mediator just offered his good offices to reach a solution, but had no powers to impose anything. An arbiter, on the contrary, did have the powers to pronounce a final settlement. Both roles, however, often merged into one another, if only because arbitration usually started with some attempts at reconciliation (Verzijl 1976: ch. VI).

Out of mediation, if successful, sometimes grew the role of 'trustee' for the agreement reached: hostages and/or pledges were put at the disposal of the mediator. Wild (1934: 98) mentions the treaty between Pope Urban VIII and the confederated princes of Italy (31 March 1644). Upon its conclusion, both parties entrusted hostages to Louis XIV, who had acted as mediator:

> And to ensure the observance of everything stated above, both parties will consign hostages to the King of France, to be restored to those who in good faith will have carried out everything that has been agreed upon and promised in the present treaty; and said hostages will be *officiers de guerre*, or others (. . .), in good health and of the same quality.[2]
>
> (Dumont 1726–31, VI, I: 298, XX; my translation)

Louis was only six at the time though; his mother and Cardinal Mazarin actually wielded power.

This type of deposit was found more abundantly in cases where arbitration was called for. Very often, an arbiter wanted some guarantee that parties would accept his verdict (or 'award'). Here, hostages and pledges came in handy. In 1284, for example, the Bishop of Feltre was accepted as arbiter between the De Camino and De Castelli families. The community of Treviso, i.e. the former party, handed over a fortified tower and a castle to the arbiter, while Gerardo de Castelli forwarded two of his sons as hostages (cited in Frey 1928: 178). Similarly, on 18 August 1494, a *compromissum* (agreement on arbitration) was concluded between Karel, Duke of Gelre, and the Emperor Maximilian. The Archbishop of Strasbourg became umpire (final arbiter), and to guarantee his acceptance of the future award, the duke put four cities (Tiel, Erkelens, Doesburg and Wageningen) at the archbishop's disposal (cited in Ledeboer 1986: 157).

A monetary sum could also be demanded by the arbiter to support a forthcoming treaty. For example, in 1285 King Magnus of Sweden was to arbitrate in a dispute between Norway on the one hand, and Denmark and the Hansa towns on the other. Beforehand, the king demanded payment by each party of 20,000 silver marks, to be forfeited if his award was not accepted (cited in Verzijl 1976: 210–11). Such kinds of pawn, obviously, would be futile if exchanged directly between partners.

All of the above cases involve pawns that *support* the treaty in question. The mere involvement, however, of a third party that mediates or arbitrates, allows for another interesting variety: the *object itself* that is contested between the parties, is entrusted to the third party. Consider, for example, the following case of mediation. On 25 April 1621, the Treaty of Madrid was concluded between France and Spain (the following episode is briefly alluded to, rather inaccurately, in Mérignhac 1907: 676; for more precise details of the treaty see Dumont 1726–31, V, II: 395–6). Spain agreed to render the valleys of La Valtellina (now in northern Italy) to

France, provided that some specific conditions were satisfied. As the situation was full of tension, Pope Gregorius XV proposed to mediate between the belligerents; as a result, it was agreed in August 1621, that La Valtellina was to be deposited in the hands of a Governor appointed by the Pope. This actually happened in 1623, when the Pope's brother at the head of Vatican guards occupied the valleys. One year later, though, Richelieu came to power. One of his first acts of office was to kick the Pope out of La Valtellina and occupy it. A good mediator obviously needs muscle.

Furthermore, in cases of arbitration as well, the contested objects sometimes were 'pawned' to the arbiter himself. On 30 July 1310, the Counts of Henegouwen and Vlaanderen concluded a *compromissum*. The lands that were the object of controversy were to be handed over to the arbiters immediately (cited in Ledeboer 1986: 157).

This section has considered a variation on the basic theme of providing human and/or material pawns. In it, the basic principle of providing tangible security *ex ante*, before the treaty comes into effect, is maintained. In all other forms of guarantee that later evolved from it, this principle is abandoned: only promises are forwarded, that if one party defaults, certain sanctions will come into effect. The nature of sanctions is no longer *ex ante*, but *ex post*. As remarked above, the genealogy of these guarantees, to be expounded below, is based on Lutteroth (1922).

Hypothecation, hostages ex post *and sureties*

The first development, for hostages and pledges alike, was that these were not to be provided *ab initio*, but only if and when default had taken place. For material pledges in general, this started in about the fifteenth century, when so-called hypothecation became a distinct legal possibility, particularly where immovable goods were concerned. That this variation was tried out at all simply has to do with the fact that immoveables do not run away; indeed, they are immobile. In general, though, hypothecation seems to have been applied rarely in international treaties (Phillimore 1855: 69). As far as pledges are concerned, no more fundamental changes took place after this time and in the following, therefore, they will be mentioned no more.

With regard to hostages, however, this *ex post* shift started earlier in time. From the eleventh and twelfth century onwards, in treaties between kings, princes, counts and bishops, one finds stipulations to the effect that hostages, human pawns, have to render themselves to the power of the principal only upon default by their master. Out of this 'postponed detention' grew the similar but curious practice of *Einlager*, also referred to as *obstagium tenere*. Mainly applied in matters of private law concerning monetary debts, it involved that, upon default of the debtor, his hostages (*rechte Geisel*) would ride to an inn and stay, eat and drink there at his expense. It was an effort to bring pressure to bear on the debtor; after all, his debts grew day by day.

Up to this point, subjects called upon to support a treaty played the very passive role of hostage only. As such, they bore no responsibility for the obligations of their master. Gradually, from about 1200 on, the construction of *fidejussor* appears (surety, Fr. *caution*, Ger. *Bürge*). Princes and nobles now assumed responsibility for the obligations of their lords. They became personally liable. If their master didn't perform, they were called upon to perform instead. At first, they stood surety with their body: ultimately, sureties could end up in jail. Later on, sureties became primarily liable with their property. Sometimes both types of surety were combined. A fine example is furnished by a treaty of 1103, whereby Robert, Count of Flanders, agreed to send 1,000 soldiers to Henry, King of England, if need be (Rymer 1704–35, I, I: 3; cited in Ganshof 1953: 131; cited, but wrongly interpreted, in Lutteroth 1922: 207). Twelve noble *obsides* were provided by the count. If he violated the treaty, these nobles had four months (three '*quarantaines*') to reconcile him with the king. If that failed, the nobles were either to each deliver 100 marks of silver to the king, or render themselves to him, to be imprisoned in the Tower of London. Similarly, English *obsides* were provided.

Conservatores pacis

In international relations, it is usually more complicated affairs that are at stake than simply those of a monetary nature. Therefore, the sureties just mentioned, so useful in civil matters, are only of little help to prevent or repair treaty infractions. How can a surety, for example, perform instead of his king, when the latter violates a peace treaty? For this reason, probably, the role of surety evolved further into the more active one of *conservator pacis*, *custos pacis*, or *guardien de paix*. Nobles were no longer held liable; instead, they were bound to act in such a way as to ensure that their master upheld the treaty.

According to Wild (1934: 101–3), there are two varieties. *Conservatores* of the more passive kind would merely be released from their oath to support their sovereign, to provide *auxilium et consilium*. That is, they would become impartial. As such, in the feudal world, this constituted a considerable loss of power for their sovereign. Henry, Count of Luxembourg and La Roche, swore in a treaty with Ferry, Duke of Lorraine and Marchis (14 August 1266), that 'if this covenant is not observed as it is here written, they [my subjects] shall not be obliged to aid me (. . .) with council or with any form of assistance whatsoever until the wrong shall have been repaired' (Dumont 1726–31, I, I: 224–5; cited and translated in Wild 1934: 102).[3]

In a more active vain, *custodes* upon default not only were released from their obligations, but were also bound to *shift* their allegiance to the other side. This implied that they were to take their fiefs to the other sovereign; moreover, they were to actively serve and assist the other party! An instance is furnished by the Peace Treaty of Arras between King Charles VII of

France and Count Philip of Burgundy (21 September 1435) (Dumont 1726–31, II, II: 309 ff.; cited in Verzijl 1973: 292–3). The king provided guardians of the active kind in the following terms:

> And the King will consent (. . .), that if hereafter it happens that the present treaty is violated on his part, his vassals, fiefs, and subjects, now and in the future, are no longer bound to obey and serve him, but are bound henceforth to serve said Lord of Burgundy and his successors against him, and that in said case all mentioned fiefs, vassals, subjects, and servants are absolved and released of all oaths of fidelity, (...) and of all promises and obligations to render services, to which they could have been compelled towards King Charles before (. . .).[4]
>
> (Dumont 1726–31, II, II: 314; my translation)

The Count of Burgundy, on his part, appointed guardians as well.

Third-party guarantee

As the Middle Ages drew to a close, the institution of *custos pacis* was transformed. As such, it was a cumbersome construction anyway (Lutteroth 1922: 209). On account of their position in society, vassals could hardly be expected to change sides effectively. On the other hand, vassals contemplating such a step already, got an excuse to do so. From the sixteenth century onwards, no longer did each side appoint his own *conservator pacis*; instead, a *single* third party was asked to guarantee the treaty involved *as a whole*. Such a guarantee implied that parties to a treaty authorized the guarantor to actively intervene if one or more of the treaty partners defaulted, and to use all means necessary to restore the treaty. Note, that this third-party guarantor is supposed to do exactly the same as the *conservatores pacis* treated above: actively seek to uphold treaties. The difference is, however, that by now an effort is made to seek impartial guarantors instead of partisan ones. A moot point has always been as to when the guarantor may intervene. Obviously, he should deem the treaty to have been violated. If so, is he entitled to act, or should he wait until one of the parties explicitly solicits his help?

Although some earlier intrastate treaties seem to exist, where, for example, Louis X guaranteed a treaty between a countess and some nobles (Wild 1934: 120), the first truly 'international' guarantee of the kind seems to have been instituted in 1505. To guarantee the Peace of Blois of 12 October between Ferdinand of Arragon and Louis XII of France, Henry VII of England was formally asked to act as *conservator pacis* (Dumont 1726–31, IV, I: 72–4; cited in Lutteroth 1922: 209).

Collective guarantee by more states than one also became popular from the seventeenth century onwards. The Teschen Peace Treaty between Prussia and Austria, for example, was guaranteed, in a separate treaty, by both France and Russia; both treaties were signed on 13 May 1779 (Wild 1934: 127; Verzijl 1973: 291).

Often, the role of *conservator pacis* simply evolved from mediating a treaty. After having mediated in the conclusion of the Peace Treaty of Fontainebleau between Austria and the Netherlands (8 November 1785), the French king was requested to guarantee the peace as well (Verzijl 1973: 291; Wild 1934: 120).

In this century, this role of third-party guarantor has been incorporated into the workings of the League of Nations (1920–46), and its successor, the United Nations (from 1945 onwards). In many treaties, such a role is explicitly mentioned.

Mutual guarantee

Mutual guarantee, finally, is a somewhat different form. Parties to a treaty no longer look for outside parties to act as guarantor. Instead, they guarantee its faithful execution *as between each other*. Obviously, such an arrangement only makes sense if more than two parties are involved. In actual treaties, three shades of this mutual commitment can be found (Wild 1934: 133). In its weakest form, parties merely sign a statement of mutual guarantee, without specifying what that is supposed to mean. An intermediate form of guarantee obtains when parties pledge, in addition, that upon treaty violation they will stage a conference together, where complaints are to be discussed. In its strongest form, corrective measures against the violator are mentioned explicitly.

A famous example of the latter is the Münster Treaty of 1648 between Emperor Ferdinand III and Louis XIV, King of France (Dumont 1726–31, VI, I: 450–61; cited in Wild 1934: 131). A whole series of dignitaries of the Holy Roman Empire became cosignatories: electors, margraves, counts, dukes, bishops; cities signed as well. The text of the agreement reads, that 'each and every signatory to this treaty shall be obliged to defend and protect the regulations of this peace, separately and as a whole, against anyone, of whatever religion' (Dumont 1726–31, VI, I: 459; my translation).[5] Moreover, if a party violated the agreement, and the controversy was not settled in a friendly or legal manner within three years, 'each and every signatory to this treaty shall be obliged to take counsel and join forces with the offended party, and to take up arms to redress the wrong' (Dumont 1726–31, VI, I: 459; my translation).[6]

Just as in the case of third-party guarantee, many ambiguities remain. Consider, for example, the following question. If violation by a party occurs, others are entitled and obliged to intervene. Does this apply not only collectively but also individually? That is, if one party is convinced that the mutual treaty is violated, but others do not act, is it nevertheless entitled and/or obliged to intervene?

Final remarks

With mutual guarantee, the evolution of the more 'primitive' institution of providing hostages/pledges has been exhausted. Some final remarks are in order. It should be stressed that the forms of guarantee mentioned above are by no means exclusive. Frequently, they have been used cumulatively (Schwarzenberger 1948: 89). Hostages and pledges together, pledges and sureties together, hostages and guarantor pacis together—many combinations have been used.

A nicely crafted example is the Peace Treaty of Cateau-Cambrésis between England and France, 2 April 1559 (Dumont 1726–31, V, I: 31; cited in Verzijl 1973: 293–4; see also Hume 1754–62, IV: 13–14). France was to return the fortified town of Calais to Queen Elizabeth of England, within eight years; upon failure to do so, King Henry II of France was to pay 500,000 gold crowns. In order to secure this promise, the king had to find seven or eight foreign merchants who would stand surety for this sum. Until these would be found, five noblemen were to be handed over as hostages to England immediately; these noblemen, moreover, also had to stand surety for the 500,000 crowns. So it is a chain of securities we find here. If the king defaults, the sureties are called upon to pay. If these do not materialize, the noblemen-as-sureties are requested to pay. If these do not provide the money, the noblemen-as-hostages are forfeited to the English queen. The noblemen, of course, were the most motivated group of all to perform as required; in exchange for their money, they would be set free.

It should also be remarked that this evolutionary list by no means exhausts all possible forms of treaty guarantee. According to Wild (1934), several other options exist, or have been in existence. An oath may be taken, and the Pope called upon to protect the treaty (Wild 1934: 83–95). Papal protection introduces the potential penalty of excommunication. Also, several punitive measures may be agreed upon to follow treaty violation by any one party: use of force (Wild 1934: 103–10), monetary penalties (Wild 1934: 110–15), and forfeiture of properties (Wild 1934: 115–17). Finally, treaty observance may be rewarded, monetarily or otherwise (Wild 1934: 117–18). These kinds of guarantee will not be treated here, for two reasons. First, they have not evolved out of the basic problems associated with the exchange of hostages/pledges; they have developed independently. Second, whatever the way they originated, they do not appear to be very useful. Divine or papal protection might once have been effective, nowadays they no longer seem to be so. The other measures mentioned, furthermore, do not seem to effectively strengthen good intentions, as they are just so many promises; they lack credibility. Where is the power needed to enforce them if violation takes place?

This detour into the history of diplomatic relations between sovereigns has described how the institution of pawning ran into problems of expropriation, blackmail and the like, and evolved into more sophisticated forms of guarantee. Now it is time to get back to the R&D alliances of our time. Sharing of proprietary knowledge in these alliances may in part be interpreted as the pawning of knowledge. Just as the pawning of people or property, pawning knowledge may easily backfire. If this analogy is accepted, it would seem legitimate to ask: can the forms of treaty guarantee that developed out of the primary forms of providing hostages or pledges, if properly adapted and modified, be of any use in stabilizing R&D alliances? Much can be learned from them, it would seem. To begin with, it will be argued that the idea of deposit with a third party, as treated above, may be very useful indeed.

Deposit with a third party in R&D alliances

In general, the transfer of pawns is meant to engage the provider. At the same time, however, the receiver might be tempted to abuse them; an unintended, and unfortunate consequence. Now consider a deposit with a third party as discussed above: pawns are no longer exchanged between treaty partners A and B, but deposited with a neutral party C. This is an ingenious move. Why? On the one hand, A and B still have forwarded pawns, so they are just as committed to the treaty as before. On the other hand, however, expropriation hazards have moved away from one's treaty partner to C. Provided one can be reasonably sure that C is impartial, and is not easily tempted to expropriate the pawns involved—or at least is less tempted than both A and B—the arrangement improves prospects for fruitful cooperation.

This idea, I would argue, can be usefully applied to R&D alliances. In that setting, it would require (i) the existence of something like a third party, which somehow (ii) gets a hold of the informational pawns of alliance partners involved. As to the first requirement, it would be satisfied for those alliances, where partners carry out R&D work at a *separate facility* (call it C), not in-house within the mother companies themselves. Such an arrangement is common, of course, for R&D joint ventures. Many research corporations also have their own facilities, especially in America (e.g. the Microelectronics and Computer Technology Corporation, MCC, still in existence) and in Japan (e.g. the VLSI Technology Research Corporation, concluded in 1979). Although it happens less frequently, joint R&D may also be performed in a common laboratory (e.g. the alliance between Bull, ICL and Siemens, 1984).

The second requirement is more difficult to meet. Assume, as we do throughout, that the R&D alliance is of such a kind that some R&D secrets have to be exchanged to get the alliance going. Sinking knowledge cannot be avoided. Also, of course, such transfer of knowledge continues while the common project is actually executed. How to construct an arrangement, which guarantees that C will be able to actually hold on to some, or even all, knowledge pawns entrusted to him, throughout the time that the alliance is running? How to effectively turn C into a trustee of the alliance?

My eventual proposal runs counter to current practice: I will propose exactly the *opposite* of what is usual. The easiest way, therefore, to develop my solution of 'deposit with a third party', is to start off with a description of current practice in those R&D alliances, where separate entities for co-operative R&D are created. All literature testifies to the fact that working together at a common site seriously hampers knowledge transfer back to the mother firms. A certain natural inertia is created. This is felt to be an enormous drawback. Therefore, much effort is devoted to institute policies for quick 'repatriation' of knowledge, obtained from the joint venture, back to the mother firm. These policies should go beyond simply sending back reports, articles and videotapes; more often than not, these fail to make any impact. Harrigan (1986: 150) calls such an active approach 'positive bleedthrough' of ideas.

As to joint ventures in particular, she gives the following overview of devices geared towards this goal (Harrigan 1986: ch. 7). First, the rotation of personnel between the venture and one's own research laboratories. Homecoming scientists will be able to divulge the newest findings from the joint venture. She even mentions scientists and technical personnel that rotate every month: they work at the venture for one month, then return to the mother plant for a month, and so forth. Next to this 'revolving-door' policy, it is not uncommon for research teams from a participating company to come and visit the joint venture in situ and learn about the latest developments. Such visits take place monthly. Finally, if a partner wants knowledge badly enough, he will build facilities within his wholly owned laboratories that parallel the joint venture set-up. This enables him to emulate the venture's R&D in-house, and stay up to date.

The same policies can be observed within research corporations that conduct research in-house. Peck (1986), and the thorough study by Gibson and Rogers (1994: ch. 5 in particular) give a vivid description of bleed-through policies within MCC. About twenty US firms participate in this research venture. It started off in 1982, and has its own R&D facilities at Austin, Texas. Member companies subscribe to specific technology pro-grammes. While these are carried out at Austin, three mechanisms are mainly relied upon to repatriate knowledge. First, for each programme there are quarterly meetings with member firms, in order to brief them about the progress of R&D. Second, MCC permits researchers from member companies to visit facilities, and work there for any length of time. These visits are encouraged to facilitate knowledge transfer (Evan and Olk 1990).

Third, and most important of all, an ingenious rotation policy has been instituted. The total workforce of MCC researchers who are employed to work at Austin (between 300 and 400 employees), consists mainly of independently recruited researchers from industry, universities and the like ('direct hires'; between 65 per cent and 85 per cent). The remaining personnel, however, is hired from member companies. One half of these are assigned to work at MCC on particular projects (assignees); the consortium pays for them. The other half are charged with the responsibility of regularly feeding back MCC technology to their mother laboratories (so-called shareholder liaisons, later called shareholder representatives). These representatives, paid for by the mother companies, are supposed to spend about 80 per cent of their time at Austin, doing regular science, and 20 per cent of their time back at the company, briefing their colleagues on results of the MCC programme. Every member of a specific research programme has the right to assign one such liaison representative.

MCC member companies do care about this repatriation of knowledge. Illustrative is the following episode (Harrigan 1986: 158–9; Gibson and Rogers 1994: 198, 243–4). Upon formation of MCC, member companies proposed their own candidates for its staffing. The CEO, however, was dissatisfied about their quality, and subsequently turned down 95 per cent of these scientists. Members then protested that they would have no way of repatriating knowledge back to their laboratories! There was only one way out for them: submitting better in-house candidates. As a result, the percentage of MCC personnel coming from member companies substantially increased; moreover, some of them were appointed as shareholder liaisons.

In a broader sense, effective knowledge repatriation is considered one of the key factors for the success of R&D consortia in general. After a survey of twenty-one American R&D consortia, Souder and Nassar (1990b) conclude that there is a clear correlation between effective knowledge transfer and success. Multiple transfer mechanisms were used: shareholder board meetings, technical advisory meetings, seminars, newsletters and other publications. 'Most potent' of all, however, was the use of liaison personnel.

The background of all of these practices is that partners are not just sharing technologies. They are also trying to gain as much insight as possible into the workings of the other partner. That is, they are after the other's competencies. These are basically invisible, tacit assets, embodied in people. While partnering, each is trying to outlearn the other all the time. Competition may even overtake cooperation: if the moment is opportune, no one will hesitate to break the agreement and go it alone (cf. Hamel 1991; Pucik 1991).

After this description of the usual arrangements for a joint R&D entity, I can now easily formulate my proposal for a 'trustee arrangement', in line with a deposit with a third party as practised in international relations. It takes the natural inertia of separate site arrangements as a starting point, and reinforces it; this inertia is not seen as a problem but as a blessing! At the start of cooperation, all necessary proprietary knowledge is to be transferred from the partners to the common R&D entity. From then on, basically, all repatriation of knowledge back to partners should be *suspended* until the project is entirely finished. For the time being, ideas are not supposed to bleed through. All those personnel from the mother companies who are involved should consider themselves to be on a 'secret mission'. This implies that the following rules should be respected. Personnel working for the separate entity should not rotate back regularly to their mother firms; they should be employed permanently. Revolving doors are shut so to speak. Moreover, employees coming from mother firms should be forbidden to report back, either formally or informally. All loyalties to the mother firm should be suspended for the time being. If equity is involved in the common undertaking (joint venture), it is worth considering the forwarding of stock options to C-employees, in order to effectively foster the 'new loyalty' that is required. If people are employed from outside (such as with MCC), so much the better; they have no attachment to participating partners.

This proposal, in effect, suspends the race to learn for the time being. It imposes artificial barriers, a Chinese wall, in order to pre-empt the unpleasant boomerang hazards described above. Although an author like Pucik (1991: 136) warns, in general, against setting up barriers to learning in strategic alliances, I believe that they can be useful indeed. A trade-off is thereby effectuated. Some learning speed is sacrificed; in exchange, backfiring hazards are attenuated, and cooperation therefore has more stable prospects.

It has to be taken into account, though, that this strict kind of trustee arrangement has clear implications in terms of loyalty. By letting C-employees keep the R&D results for themselves, they will not fail to identify with them, and come to consider them their 'property'. They will then try to hold on to them, and seek permission to further develop the results by themselves. The child C gets ambitions independently of his parents A and B!

Now this might be appropriate in some instances, like when parents create a joint-venture child, which they intend to let evolve into an autonomous entity in the future if he/she succeeds. Then the Chinese wall arrangement just described works well. But more usually, the common R&D undertaking is meant to be a *temporary* one, to be disbanded as soon as goals have been reached. In those cases the loyalty effect complicates back-transfer of knowledge enormously. It should be remembered, that jointly developed R&D will largely be of an informal kind; it is tacit knowledge, residing in people. If these, then, are unwilling to share, back-transfer of knowledge to mother firms is seriously jeopardized! Without trustee arrangement, we had the danger of boomerang hazards; with it, we end up with the loyalty effect. Instead of opportunistic parents who want to run away on their own, we end up with a spoilt child who wants to go on on his own! Therefore, if R&D cooperation is meant to be temporary, the strict trustee arrangement should be softened, in order to do justice to legitimate demands from mother firms that are concerned about developing in-house competencies.

One such intermediate solution, a kind of Chinese wall 'with holes', might be the following. Knowledge produced in collaboration is transferred back to participating partners' laboratories at regular intervals, say every three months (although specific technical milestones to be reached en route may determine time intervals). This back-transfer, however, never contains 'fresh' knowledge; only results up to say six months old are communicated backwards. The arrangement works as follows: at the beginning, partners transfer existing knowledge to the joint entity; after six months, this initial package is communicated back to the partners (but no more); after nine months, the new results of the first three months are relayed; after twelve months, the results obtained between months three and six are transferred back; and so on, until the project ends and all results are relayed. In general, two kinds of time interval are involved in the scheme: the deliberate delay (t_d), and the frequency of backward communication (every interval of length t_c), with $t_c \leq t_d$. Then, formally, the nth time of communication ($n \geq 1$) takes place at time $\{t_d + (n-1)t_c\}$ where all results obtained between time $(n-2)t_c$ and time $(n-1)t_c$ are released.

This mechanism ensures, on the one hand, that knowledge is regularly transferred back to partners well before the official end of the project. To some extent, the race to learn is allowed to continue. On the other hand, some newly produced knowledge is always temporarily held back from partners; this, hopefully, induces them to stay on a little longer, instead of running away. Notice the difference with the former arrangement. In the 'radical' form of trustee arrangement, informational pawns pile up, and are all held to ransom; in the softened form, only the most recent, fresh informational pawns are kept, the rest are released.

In a way, these solutions of deposit with a third party are the mirror-image of so-called 'blackboxing', as discussed by Lorange and Roos (1992: 110). They discuss the issue of how partners contributing to an alliance can protect their unique skills and know-how. One way to do so is by simply not sharing these core competencies. In their terminology: these skills are put in a black box. In our trustee arrangements something akin happens: knowledge is blackboxed, either until the end of the project, or just for a period of some months. One important difference obtains, though: partners are not holding back knowledge, but the jointly created entity instead.

In general, the need for trustee arrangements in R&D alliances all depends on how much knowledge from partners is actually put at risk. If few scientists in the alliance come from mother companies (employees are mostly 'direct hires'), and if, moreover, these transfer very little 'hot' knowledge from their home base, not many boomerang hazards are generated; as a consequence, building a Chinese wall is superfluous. The more, however, that partners send their own scientists in great numbers (assignees), and allow them to share state-of-the-art technologies with alliance partners, the more backfiring hazards become real. If so, Chinese wall solutions could impose themselves, in order to prevent repatriation of knowledge from happening too quickly.

Note, finally, that if work for the R&D alliance is carried out in the mother firms themselves ('split sites'), the trustee set-up is utterly unfeasible. No one can then really expect alliance employees, working in their home departments, to keep all the knowledge they have obtained from partner firms secret. Knowledge is bound to bleed through. Their colleagues are just too close by.

New forms of guarantee in R&D alliances

As described above, in international affairs the institution of posting hostages and/or pledges has evolved a great deal. New forms emerged: hypothecation, hostages *ex post*, sureties, *conservatores pacis*, third-party guarantee and mutual guarantee. What use can they possibly have for stabilizing R&D alliances? First some clarification is needed. In all of these subsequent forms, commitment (*ex ante*) was eliminated, to be replaced by promises (*ex post*). Moreover, these forms of guarantee didn't exclude each other. Often the basic mechanism of providing hostages/pledges continued to be used, but was strengthened by some *ex post* form of guarantee. It is in the same vein that solutions for stabilizing R&D alliances will be sought. The basic mechanism of committing knowledge remains unaltered: it will be assumed, that partners are bound to exchange proprietary knowledge and skills between them all the time. But, I ask myself, is it possible to use, *in addition* to this, any of the new forms of international guarantee, if properly transformed, to further stabilize R&D alliances?

First of all the options of hypothecation and hostages *ex post* developed. These solutions do not seem very useful in our case. One reason is that shifting pawns from *ex ante* to *ex post* reduces a tangible commitment to a mere promise; as such, much is lost. Moreover, and more importantly, it is impossible to postpone the sharing of knowledge. Secrets have to be exchanged in order to be able to start—and keep—moving together.

Thereafter, the role of standing surety was invented. Vassals were made personally responsible for the obligations of their lords. Comparing firms to states, this would translate into employees vouching for the non-opportunistic conduct of their firm. In most modern corporations there is no function, and no scope, it would seem, for such 'total' claims upon employees.

As a next step, sureties were transformed into *conservatores pacis*: vassals were no longer liable, but had to do their utmost to ensure that their lord abided by the treaty. They were bound to be 'plus royaliste que le roi'! This concept is worth giving some more consideration to. As far as R&D alliances are concerned, it can be deduced from existing literature that three elementary roles are required. First, any collaborative R&D project needs a champion who keeps the faith whatever setbacks appear along the way (Bidault and Cummings 1994). Such a champion mobilizes support for the project from all departments and personnel involved. Usually, (s)he will be a member of the team. If, say, two companies are involved, the best solution would be to have one champion accepted by both sides. But more often than not, two champions exist side by side. Then, the quality of their mutual rapport is of overarching importance. Second, every project should have a sponsor, or external champion, defending it against external attacks from higher management that might end the project (Bidault and Cummings 1994). Often, a senior manager, not directly involved, will fill this role. One sponsor for all parties in an alliance is obviously hardly possible; in practice, two sponsors are required, one on each side. Hopefully, they get along. Third, every firm in an alliance needs one or more technological gatekeepers (Hamel 1991). These route incoming requests for help from partners, in order to ensure that no company knowledge inadvertently leaks out.

These three roles are readily known. A fourth role, I would argue, can be added to them. Consider the *conservator pacis* who was to make sure that his master obeyed the treaty. Is it not perfectly feasible to transform this role, in the context of an R&D alliance, into something like a *custos collaborationis*, each participating firm appointing its own? Such a *custos* should do his utmost to ensure that members of his own company collaborate honestly and fairly with their alliance partners. If need be, they are bound to intervene actively to promote cooperation. If, for example, a firm is holding back vital information out of fear of abuse, this *custos* might try to remedy the situation. Also, complaints from other partners about expropriation of knowledge should be given a fair hearing. In a way, this new role is the opposite of the gatekeeping role; the *custos* is supposed to keep the gates open. This role obviously needs to be fulfilled by a senior manager or a board member. Possibly, the roles of champion and *custos* could be combined. And, of course, the sponsor should entirely support the role of the *custos*.

The analogy with a *conservator pacis* should, of course, not be stretched too far. If they were appointed as conservatores of the active kind, vassals would be forced to take up arms and fight their own master if need be. That means defecting to the enemy! From a *custos collaborationis* this can hardly be required. Suppose an alliance is under way between Philips and Sony, and after some time Philips starts to hold back vital knowledge, or to expropriate knowledge just obtained from Sony. Then, one cannot expect the Philips' *custos* (and champion) to take his role that literally, that he would actually go over to Sony and report the opportunistic behaviour, let alone divulge the R&D company secrets involved to the Japanese firm. Such activities, undertaken either secretly or in the open, might well cost him his job.

Active custodianship should seek a more modest form instead. A *custos* should seek to identify with the other side, and become its advocate *within* his own company. In terms of the Philips–Sony example, it would mean that the *custos* would use all his formal and informal powers within Philips to change the situation in Sony's favour; but he would stop short of actually defecting to Sony in one way or another.

As a final evolutionary step, it was no longer subjects of the states that were involved, but a separate third state that was supposed to guarantee treaty stipulations. Instead of partisan *conservatores*, one or more impartial third-party guarantors stepped in. Such a figure, I would argue, could well be used in R&D alliances. The guarantors is to oversee and monitor the collective undertaking, and to actively intervene if partners are caught cheating on each other.

What kind of actors can be asked to fulfil this role? One obvious candidate would be another company not involved in the alliance. The choice will be a hard one. On the one hand, it should have some knowledge of the matter involved, to be reasonably able to judge the situation. On the other, it shouldn't be too close to the alliance partners, for the urgent question would arise: 'Who is to control the guarantor?!' In any case, a firm with an impeccable reputation for honesty would seem a good choice. But then, if called upon, would such a company accept this task? Does it stand to gain anything?

Because of all these qualifications, one would be better advised to search for other kinds of institutions to guarantee intercompany cooperation. The list of potential candidates is long: investment banks, industry associations, governmental bodies, research institutes, universities and the like. Looking through existing literatures on R&D alliances, I came across an instance involving Italian R&D consortia where the government played precisely such a role (Tripsas *et al.* 1995). In such *Società di Ricerca*, it is mostly firms, but also research centres and universities, which take part. Upon foundation of a Società, the government, represented by IMI, a government-owned financial holding company, takes a 30 per cent share; this gives it the right of veto. Remaining shares are divided equally among participating organizations. Projects agreed upon are subsidized by IMI and managed by independent project managers appointed by the Società. These are to coordinate the efforts of participating firms. Varying from one Società to another, these projects are either executed at member's laboratories ('split sites'), or in-house at Società facilities.

What matters for our case is that a kind of third-party guarantee has been instituted with the role of *auditor*: someone who 'examines ongoing projects, and ensures firms are abiding by the intent of the original agreement' (Tripsas *et al.* 1995: 374). This role is entrusted to the acting project manager. He is allowed to visit the laboratories of participating firms in order to be able to monitor progress. Now, let me emphasize that this is extraordinary indeed. Usually, such project managers are supposed to coordinate efforts only, not to visit the actual sites where work is carried out. As a rule, those sites are out of bounds; there, functional managers reign supreme. Of course the question arises: if partners do not trust each other, can the auditor at least be trusted? From the article by Tripsas *et al.* (1995: 380) it can be concluded that project managers from the Società had indeed been able to secure such trust: 'The partners know that we will assure confidentiality on what we see during our visits to their research sites.' How they accomplished this is not explained. Would it, by any chance, simply be the basic fact that large subsidies would be put in jeopardy, if a partner refused to be 'inspected', let alone if he was caught cheating?

As a variety of third-party guarantee, mutual guarantee has also become popular between states as a means to secure treaties. Such a mutual arrangement is also a likely candidate to be applied to stabilize R&D alliances. Note, that in this respect R&D alliances have one big advantage over interstate arrangements. R&D partners may agree amongst each other to ultimately throw out a disobedient partner. States cannot avail themselves of such a clause; they are bound to live with each other.

It is usual for companies to be involved in many (R&D) alliances at the same time; also, alliances with any one partner may be multiple (cf. the networks of R&D alliances in information technologies, computers, and the like, in Hagedoorn and Schakenraad 1992). Suppose a number of companies form a new R&D alliance. Reasoning along the lines of a mutual guarantee one can imagine the following sanctions. If a partner does not cooperate loyally, the others might threaten to throw him out eventually. Moreover, they can threaten to sever the whole bundle of *other* agreements that are still in force between them and the disloyal firm. The disobedient partner not only faces the loss of one alliance, but of his position in a whole network of alliances.

Legal backing exists, at least in Europe. Since 1989, a European Economic Interest Group (EEIG) can be established. Such an EEIG resembles a cooperative. Currently it is the only supranational legal instrument to effectively regulate cooperation activities between European partners. It seems suitable for non-equity forms of cooperative R&D. The reason for mentioning this EEIG here, is that one of its clauses amounts to a strong form of mutual guarantee (article 27.2): if a member seriously fails in his obligations, or causes or threatens to cause serious disruption of the group, he may be excluded. To obtain a court order to that effect, a majority of members should agree on his exclusion.

In conclusion

We have tried, with some imagination, to apply lessons and procedures from international relations to the management of R&D alliances. It was found, in particular, that deposit with a third party might work well to mitigate boomerang hazards. If partners work together at a separate facility, that entity should continually 'hold back' at least some amount of newly developed knowledge; by doing so, partners remain attractive to each other. It has also been argued that *custodes collaborationis* might be useful. With one acting for each side, they will be able to watch over the loyalty and goodwill shown towards the other partner(s). Moreover, a case has been made for seeking a guarantee from independent parties like government, industry associations, universities and the like. Finally, mutual guarantee by partners amongst themselves has been discussed.

Some final remarks about these 'new organizational solutions' are in order. Deposit with a third party specifically mitigates against boomerang hazards of knowledge exchange. All the other forms of guarantee just mentioned do so as well. But they also do more than that: they can be used to mitigate *all other* kinds of opportunism that might occur in R&D alliances. One of the most pressing problems in R&D alliances is, for example, that partners often delegate second-rate personnel only; they cheat on expert contributions (cf. De Laat 1997). *Custodes collaborationis*, third-party guarantors, and even partners in mutual guarantee, all can be instructed to guard against that form of opportunism as well.

Furthermore, these instruments may be applied outside R&D alliances as well. *Every* kind of strategic alliance, not just R&D alliances, might profit from them. I would maintain, however, that in R&D alliances problems of opportunism are most pressing; therefore, these instruments of guarantee should preferably be tried out in that domain.

Two tasks lie ahead. In this article some new tentative insights have been developed. Further empirical research needs to be carried out in order to see if, where and how such instruments of governance are currently being used in R&D alliances. In this respect, I have a feeling that not too many instances of such use will be found. That brings me to the second task ahead. Managers should be urged to actively try out the solutions developed in this article. Are they able to create blackboxed R&D units? Can they usefully appoint *custodes collaborationis*? Are they able to work out between themselves arrangements of mutual guarantee, or can they find others—third parties—to do it for them? In the process, whenever possible, all of these solutions should also be tailored towards the specific situation of R&D. It is, after all, the unwanted proliferation of knowledge that is particularly at issue.

Notes

1 I would like to thank the participants of the EMOT workshop on 'Inter-Firm Networks: Outcomes and Policy Implications', held at Modena, 6–8 September 1996, for their useful criticisms. In particular, Anna Grandori, Stefan Klein, Bryan Mundell, Bart Nooteboom and Amalya Oliver should be mentioned here.

2 Et pour plus grande seureté de l'observation de tout ce que dessus, on consignera reciproquement des Ostages au Roy Tres-Chrestien, pour estre rendus à ceux qui de bonne foy auront executé tout ce qui a esté convenu & promis au present Traité; & lesdits Ostages seront Officiers de Guerre, ou autres (. . .), de bonne condition & égale qualité.

3   (. . .) se ces convenances n'estoyent tenuës si comme dessus est dit, ils ne devroyent aidier moy (. . .) ne de conseil, ne de aie nulle tant qu'il fut amendei.

4   Et consentira le Roi (. . .), que s'il arrivoit ci-après que de sa part fût enfraint ce présent Traité, ses Vasseaux, Feaux & Sujets présens & avenir, ne soient plus tenus de l'obéir & servir, mais soient tenus dèslors de servir mondit Seigneur de Bourgogne & ses Successeurs à l'encontre de lui & qu'audit cas tous lesdits Feaux, Vasseaux, Sujets & Serviteurs, soient absous & quittes de tous sermens de fidélité (. . .), & de toutes promesses & obligations de services en quoi ils pourroient estre tenus par avant envers le Roi Charles (. . .).

5   (. . .) teneantur omnes & singuli hujus Transactionis Consortes universas & singulas hujus Pacis Leges contra quencunque sine Religionis distinctione tueri & protegere.

6   (. . .) teneantur omnes & singuli hujus Transactionis Consortes, junctis cum Parte laesâ consiliis viribusque, Arma sumere ad repellandam Injuriam (. . .).

Bibliography

On international law

De Vattel, E. (1758) *Le Droit des Gens ou Principes de la Loi Naturelle: Appliqués à la Conduite et aux Affaires des Nations et des Souverains*, vol. 1, reproduction of books I and II of edition of 1758, Washington: Carnegie Institution, 1916.

Dumont, J. (1726–31) *Corps Universel Diplomatique du Droit des Gens: Contenant un Recueil des Traitez d'Alliance, de Paix, de Trêve (. . .) faits en Europe, depuis le Regne de l'Empereur Charlemagne jusques à présent (. . .)*, 8 vols, Amsterdam: chez P. Brunel, R. et G. Wetstein, les Janssons Waesberge, et l'Honoré et Chatelain; the Hague: chez P. Husson et Charles Levier.

Frey, S. (1928) *Das öffentlich-rechtliche Schiedsgericht in Oberitalien im XII. und XIII. Jahrhundert: Beitrag zur Geschichte völkerrechtlicher Institutionen*, Luzern: Eugen Haag.

Ganshof, F. L. (1953) *Histoire des Relations Internationales*, Tome Premier, *Le Moyen Age*, Paris: Hachette.

Hume, D. (1754–62) *The History of England from the Invasion of Julius Caesar to the Abdication of James the Second, 1688*, 6 vols, new ed., Philadelphia: Porter & Coates, s.a.

Ledeboer, L.V. (1986) *Materiaal uit gedrukte bronnen met betrekking tot publiekrechtelijke middeleeuwse arbitrages in de Nederlanden*, Leiden: Faculteit der Rechtsgeleerdheid.

Lutteroth, A. (1922) *Der Geisel im Rechtsleben: Ein Beitrag zur allgemeinen Rechtsgeschichte und dem geltenden Völkerrecht*, Breslau: Marcus Verlag.

Mérignhac, A. (1907) *Traité de Droit Public International*, Deuxième Partie, *Le Droit de la Paix*, Paris: Librairie Générale de Droit & de Jurisprudence.

Phillimore, R. (1855) *Commentaries upon International Law*, vol. II, London: Benning.

Phillipson, C. (1916) *Termination of War and Treaties of Peace*, London: Fisher Unwin.

Rymer, Th. (1704–35) *Foedera, conventiones, literae et cuiuscunque generis acta publica inter reges Angliae et alios quosvis imperatores (. . .) ab anno 1101*, 10 vols, 3rd ed., 's-Gravenhage, 1745.

Schwarzenberger, G. (1948) 'International law in early English practice', *British Year Book of International Law*, XXV: 52–90.

Verzijl, J.H.W. (1973) *International Law in Historical Perspective*, part VI, *Juridical Facts as Sources of International Rights and Obligations*, Leiden: Sijthoff.

Verzijl, J.H.W. (1976) *International Law in Historical Perspective*, part VIII, *Interstate Disputes and their Settlement*, Leiden: Sijthoff.

Wild Jr., P.S. (1934) *Sanctions and Treaty Enforcement*, Cambridge, Mass.: Harvard University Press.

On R&D alliances

Badaracco Jr., J.L. (1991) *The Knowledge Link: How Firms Compete through Strategic Alliances*, Boston, Mass.: Harvard Business School Press.

Bidault, F. and Cummings, Th. (1994) 'Innovating through alliances: expectations and limitations', *R&D Management*, 24, 1: 33–45.

Contractor, F.J. and Lorange, P. (1988) (eds) *Cooperative Strategies in International Business*, Lexington, Mass.: Lexington Books.

De Laat, P.B. (1995) 'Transaction specificity in technological alliances: from weakness to strength', paper presented at the 12th Colloquium of the European Group of Organization Studies (EGOS), Istanbul, 6–8 July.

—— (1997) 'Research and development alliances: ensuring trust by mutual commitments', in M. Ebers (ed.) *The Formation of Inter-Organizational Networks*, Oxford: Oxford University Press, 146–73.

Evan, W.M. and Olk, P. (1990) 'R&D consortia: a new organizational form', *Sloan Management Review*, Spring: 37–46.

Gibson, D.V. and Rogers, E.M. (1994) *R&D Collaboration on Trial: The Microelectronics and Computer Technology Corporation*, Boston, Mass.: Harvard Business School Press.

Hagedoorn, J. and Schakenraad, J. (1992) 'Leading companies and networks of strategic alliances in information technologies', *Research Policy*, 21: 163–90.

Hamel, G. (1991) 'Competition for competence and inter-partner learning within international strategic alliances', *Strategic Management Journal*, 12, S: 83–103.

Harrigan, K.R. (1986) *Managing for Joint Venture Success*, Lexington, Mass.: Lexington Books.

Hladik, K.J. (1988) 'R&D and international joint ventures', in F.J. Contractor and P. Lorange (eds), *Cooperative Strategies in International Business*, Lexington, Mass.: Lexington Books, 187–203.

Lei, D. and Slocum Jr., J.W. (1992) 'Global strategy, competence-building and strategic alliances', *California Management Review*, 35, 1, Fall: 81–97.

Littler, D., Leverick, F. and Bruce, M. (1995) 'Factors affecting the process of collaborative product development: a study of UK manufacturers of information and communications technology products', *Journal of Product Innovation Management*, 12: 16–32.

Lorange, P. and Roos, J. (1992) *Strategic Alliances: Formation, Implementation, and Evolution*, Cambridge, Mass./Oxford: Blackwell.

Mangematin, V. (1996) 'The simultaneous shaping of organization and technology within cooperative agreements', in R. Coombs, A. Richards, P.P. Saviotti and V. Walsh (eds) *Technological Collaboration: The Dynamics of Cooperation in Industrial Innovation*, Cheltenham: Edward Elgar, 119–41.

Moxon, R.W., Roehl, T.W. and Truitt, J.F. (1988) 'International cooperative ventures in the commercial aircraft industry: gains, sure, but what's my share?', in F.J.

Contractor and P. Lorange (eds) *Cooperative Strategies in International Business*, Lexington, Mass.: Lexington Books, 255–77.

Peck, M.J. (1986) 'Joint R&D: the case of Microelectronics and Computer Technology Corporation', *Research Policy*, 15: 219–31.

Perlmutter, H.V. and Heenan, D.A. (1986) 'Cooperate to compete globally', *Harvard Business Review*, March-April: 136–52.

Pucik, V. (1991) 'Technology transfer in strategic alliances: competitive collaboration and organizational learning', in T. Agmon and M. von Glinow (eds) *Technology Transfer in International Business*, New York: Oxford University Press, 121–38.

Souder, W.E. and Nassar, S. (1990a) 'Choosing an R&D consortium', *Research-Technology Management*, March–April, 33: 35–41.

—— (1990b) 'Managing R&D consortia for success', *Research-Technology Management*, September–October, 33: 44–50.

Teece, D.J. (1986) 'Profiting from technological innovation: implications for integration, collaboration, licensing and public policy', *Research Policy*, 15: 285–305.

Tripsas, M., Schrader, S. and Sobrero, M. (1995) 'Discouraging opportunistic behavior in collaborative R&D: a new role for government', *Research Policy*, 24: 367–89.

Werner, J. (1993) 'Towards second-generation R&D consortia', *International Journal of Technology Management*, Special Issue on Industry-University-Government Cooperation, 8, 6/7/8: 587–95.

Yoshino, M.Y. and Rangan, U.S. (1995) *Strategic Alliances: An Entrepreneurial Approach to Globalization*, Boston, Mass.: Harvard Business School Press.

Part 3
The externalities of networks

9 The costs of networked organization[1]

Peter Smith Ring

Introduction

For the managers of many firms, big and small, interorganizational collaboration is an established fact of life in the waning years of the twentieth
century. The many reasons why managers find it necessary to collaborate,
or why they deem it desirable to collaborate, have been very well
documented elsewhere (see, e.g. Beamish and Killing 1997; Ebers 1997;
Gerlach 1992; Grandori and Soda 1995; Jones, Hesterley and Borgatti
1997; Powell, Koput and Smith-Doerr 1996; Ring and Van de Ven 1994).

These same managers have found it possible, and desirable, to collaborate in ways that confound theoretical predictions. This is especially so
for theories grounded in neoclassical economics, or in the transaction cost
branch of institutional economics staked-out by Williamson (1991, 1985,
1975), and many of his followers in the management literature (Hennart
1988; Kogut 1988; Monteverde and Teece 1982; Parkhe 1993).

This chapter explores the nature of the costs that managers encounter in
the course of governing collaboration. Most managers with whom I have
had contact in the course of my research on collaboration are sensitive to
costs, and in that regard Williamson has it partially right. But, those managers who have described their collaborations to me in detail have told me
that they are sensitive to cost, but are not exclusively driven by a desire to
economize on transaction costs. Here, it appears that some economists
have it (partially) wrong. But their sin seems to be one of commission.[2] On
the other hand, the sin of the sociologists is one of omission: cost too rarely
enters into their discussion of collaborative economic exchange.

Relying primarily on the economics and management literature, the
next section of the chapter contains a basic discussion of costs associated
with economic exchange. The second section of the chapter considers the
costs of networked organization. The concluding section of the chapter is
devoted to a discussion of measurement issues, and implications for managers, public officials and scholars.

When the term governance is used, it will refer to a 'mode of organizing
transactions' (Williamson and Ouchi 1981). A transaction occurs when 'a
good or service is transferred' (Williamson 1985: 1) from use in one stage

of activity to use in another. Along a continuum defined by the (increasing) asset specificity of the good or service being transferred, markets, relational contracting and firms have been proposed by Williamson as ideal types of governance modes, and these modes of exchange (and their derivatives) tend to dominate most discussions of exchange governance (Ouchi 1980; Powell 1990; Thorelli 1988). Networked organizations, the focus of this chapter, generally employ relational contracting and its derivatives as a governance mode.

Experimentation with specific forms of relational contracting undoubtedly is accelerated by the presumed governance efficiencies of the keiretsu in Japan (see, e.g., Gerlach 1992), the chaebol in Korea (see, e.g., Steers, Shin and Ungson 1989), or the network of small, artisanal-like firms in the so-called 'Third' Italy (see, e.g., Brusco 1982; Lipparini 1995; Lorenzoni and Lipparini 1998; Piore and Sabel 1984).[3] Few of these exchange modes, however, have been subjected to methodologically rigorous longitudinal, comparative assessments of their efficiency properties. And as Scher (this volume) points out, in some cases the work does not adequately describe the complex nature of the relationships that exist between Japanese firms.

In addition, much of the conjecture about the efficiency of these kinds of relationships, at least in the management literature, focuses on transaction cost efficiencies, while generally ignoring other kinds of costs associated with these modes of exchange (e.g. production costs), or trade-offs between costs.[4] The proposition that networked organizations provide greater flexibility to managers in their pursuit of a trade-off in costs is central to the arguments made in this chapter.

Finally, in formulating the arguments made in this chapter, I also assume that the business conditions confronting a group of firms, and their managers, are uncertain, risky and turbulent. Thus, managers can be expected to look for flexible ways of structuring business deals that enable them to consider a trade-off between the kinds of cost they incur. I also make an assumption that when managers cooperate, they generally will seek high commitment relations—those in which high levels of trust exist in long-term relationships in which long-lived specific assets are invested (Helper and Levine 1992)—and both efficient and equitable outcomes over time (Ring and Van de Ven 1994).

Costs associated with economic exchange

Managers and economists (and many management scholar offspring of economists) tend to think about the concept of cost in two very different ways. For economists, a particularly important type of cost is opportunity cost: the value of what the resources employed by a firm could have produced had they been used in the production of the best alternative good (or service). Economists also deal with costs in terms such as average cost, marginal cost, fixed cost and variable cost. Reliance on concepts such as these frequently masks a need to deal more specifically with other issues related to costs, e.g. a trade-off between production costs and transaction costs, or a trade-off among production costs designed to lower learning costs or transaction costs. For managers, cost usually means the amount they have expended in producing and selling their goods and services, or the impact of production volumes on fixed and variable costs (the kinds of thinking about costs they may have learned from accountants or auditors working for their firms).

The economic well-being of firms, i.e. the ability of managers to meet their obligations to their stakeholders, depends upon the ability of these managers to minimize poor choices in the following arenas: making the wrong choice on what goods to produce (an opportunity cost issue), minimizing the costs of the resources that they will employ in producing the goods that they have chosen to produce (production, transaction and learning cost issues), minimizing the likelihood that they have chosen inappropriate technologies or inputs in producing the good (thus raising production and/or learning costs), minimizing the likelihood that they have chosen inappropriate structures for governing transactions (thus raising transaction costs). Although sometimes it is assumed that production costs are solely a function of technology and inputs, while transaction costs are solely a function of a governance structure, in this chapter it is argued that both production and transaction costs are a function of the interactions of these (and other) elements.

Finally, most managers have to take into account the issue of whether the important stakeholders of their firms will approve of the choices that they have made in combining resources and capabilities towards productive ends, or of the ways in which they have chosen to produce these goods in so far as these approaches to production have implications for social costs, or welfare costs.

Williamson (1975) certainly has done much to alter the way some economists think about cost. He has transformed Coase's (1937) arguments about transaction costs from a condition of 'much cited and little used' to one of 'much used.' Williamson characterized transaction costs as *ex ante* or *ex post*. The former include the costs of 'drafting, negotiating, and safe-guarding an agreement' (1985: 20), while the latter included 'maladaption costs . . . haggling costs . . . setup and running costs [of] . . . governance structures . . . and the bonding costs of effecting secure commitments' (1985: 21). In Figure 9.1, these costs take centre stage.

One likely consequence of this somewhat narrow approach to the issue of cost is that researchers end up ignoring the possibility that other kinds of costs also may be relevant to discussions of modes of exchange, and to governance mechanisms. As outlined in Figure 9.1, discussions of these other kinds of cost could usefully include consideration of production costs, learning costs, opportunity costs and social/welfare costs.

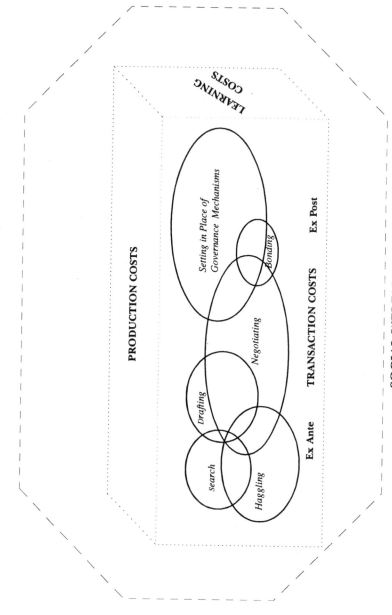

OPPORTUNITY COSTS

PRODUCTION COSTS

SOCIAL WELFARE COSTS

TRANSACTION COSTS

LEARNING COSTS

Ex Ante

Ex Post

Search

Haggling

Drafting

Negotiating

Setting in Place of Governance Mechanisms

Bonding

Figure 9.1 Costs of Exchange

The costs of networked organization

For many business firms in today's global economies, the most valuable property rights involved in exchanges between firms generally will be those that are expected to provide a basis for the generation of extra-ordinary profits, or what economists like to describe as rents (Penrose 1959, Wernerfeldt 1985). Within networked organizations these exchanges are likely to entail relationship specific, long-term investments of financial, physical, human, or social capital.[5]

It is in the nature of many of these kinds of resources or capabilities that the terms of their exchange cannot be fully specified in advance of their use in production activities. Nor is it likely that it will always be desirable that a full specification of the terms of the exchanges of these kinds of capabilities and resources should occur *ex ante*. For example, premature specification might produce both higher transaction costs and higher production costs (as a consequence of the selection of inappropriate technologies or inputs). In contrast to market transactions, in networked organizations it may not always be necessary to fully specify *ex ante* terms and conditions of an exchange such as: the choice of technologies and inputs (with attendant production cost implications); the structure of governance (a transaction cost issue); and, the sharing of information (which has production, learning, transaction, opportunity and social/ welfare cost implications).

In the discussion that follows, the initial focus is on transaction costs, then production costs. This will be followed by discussions of learning costs, opportunity costs and social/welfare costs. This is followed by a discussion of the potential for making a trade-off between these kinds of costs and a discussion of their implications for the management of networked organizations. I have chosen to avoid the use of formal propositions in an effort to enhance the reader's journey through these conjectures. The conceptual implications of the discussion should be reasonable clear to those familiar with the limitations of transaction costs economics as it is generally presented in the management literature (especially in the United States).

Transaction costs

This aspect of my discussion of the costs of networked organization assumes that one must be created (it is of course an empirical question whether networked organizations are created or can simply emerge out of embedded contexts). This assumption means that the firms will engage in searches for, and selection of, participants; discussions of the charter of the networked organization, its norms, values, governing principles; and, an undertaking of the processes that will be required to establish the governance of the networked organization. In terms that are relevant for considerations of the cost of networked organization, it is now generally accepted that *ex ante* transaction costs include those that result from searches for exchange parties in possession of resources that can not be efficiently made by a focal firm within its own boundaries.[6] In an era that demands seven sigma quality standards, and the lowest possible cost for acquired goods, the processes employed by a focal firm in its search for reliable suppliers are likely to produce costs that are non-trivial.[7] In most instances, researchers grounded in TCE would classify all of these search costs as transaction costs, and justifiably so given its static nature and focus on a comparative assessment of the efficiency properties of competing governance mechanisms in the case of a single transaction.[8]

Search costs of networked organizations can be expected to vary significantly, and are likely to be contingent on a number of factors. For example, location in so-called industrial districts may lead to lower search costs for the members of a networked organization embedded in that district (or for firms outside the district wishing to do business with firms within the district). Firms found within industrial districts may enjoy transaction cost advantages over firms that exist outside them because prospective collaborators for a networked organization form of exchange governance may already be well known to them, thus lowering search cost. This may not always be the case, however. Proximity to some firms may blind a focal firm's managers to the existence of better collaborators outside the district; firms that could help the focal firm lower learning or production costs, albeit at the expense of higher transaction (e.g. search) costs

Participation in a networked organization could lower search costs in other ways. The collective learning of the firms in a networked organization may have been acquired through individual managers who have been involved in many of the processes that are described as social integration (e.g. attending the same schools, belonging to the same social organizations, etc.) Under these conditions the transaction costs of search could be lower for individual firms in a networked organization than for their competitors outside the networked organization.

The norms that govern networked organization might also facilitate sharing of more valuable or proprietary information related to search processes among the members of a networked organization (Browning *et al.* 1995; Oliver and Libeskind 1995; Schrader 1991). Thus, participation in a networked organization may also affect the quantity and quality of search-related information, with attendant consequences for the costs of search activities for those firms.

As reflected in Figure 9.1, the haggling between parties that frequently accompanies negotiating and drafting an agreement can be an additional transaction cost of the *ex ante* variety. More haggling usually means higher transaction costs, and tends to be treated by management researchers as a sign of inefficient transacting. Attempting to safeguard a transaction may produce a different variety of costs. Safeguards may introduce third parties into the relationship; parties with different views regarding efficiency or effectiveness than those held by the parties to the exchange. When these conditions exist, uncertainty and variability in exchange relationships increases, and the costs of exchange may be adversely affected (Bromiley and Cummings 1995).

Haggling or, more generally, all other forms of negotiational costs, may also be different for firms participating in networked organizations than for those that forego this kind of governance mode. Under conditions of uncertainty, the exchange of idiosyncratic resources on a recurring basis theoretically will lead to higher negotiational costs. Members of a net-worked organization, on the other hand, may be able to rely on trust in such cases (Jones *et al.* 1997; Ring and Van de Ven 1994) to lower these negotiational costs. Developing that trust, however, may be costly (Bromiley and Cummings 1995; Ring and Van de Ven 1994).

To the degree that the passage of time may reflect the occurrence of cost, agreements on exchanges within networked organizations may occur more rapidly than in cases involving reliance on other governance modes (e.g. in the acquisition of a corporation that is publicly traded). A combination of less intensive search, more readily available information, greater awareness of the individual capabilities of the members of a networked organization, in combination can be expected to accelerate the pace of exchange processes (and can lower their costs), *ceteris paribus*.

Reliance on networked organizations as a governance mode may also lower a firm's transaction costs through substitution effects. For example, the presumed ability to rely more heavily on trust in networked organizations could eliminate the need for contracts, lawyers, or other sources of transaction costs that do not create value (Zajac and Olsen 1993; Lazerson 1988). Participation in networked organization may also lower the transaction costs of deals that take place between member and non-member firms. Collectively, the participants in a networked organizations are likely to have greater transactional exchange experience than would be the case for any single individual firm in the networked organization. Consequently, if there is a collective sharing of knowledge by members of networked organization about their individual transactional experiences with non-members, it could mediate some of the negative consequences of bounded rationality. Thus, sharing of knowledge by members of a networked organization may reduce transaction costs for individual firms in the network in those cases that involve frequent exchanges of idiosyncratic resources under conditions of high uncertainty. These conditions generally persist in high-technology industries, and this might explain the frequent occurrence of networks in these industries (e.g. Powell *et al.* 1996).

Ex post costs, generally, are even more varied than those of the *ex ante* variety. Most modern business exchange is negotiated in the present, while performance is expected to occur in the future. This generally creates greater levels of uncertainty and risk. What the parties anticipate about the future, and the future in which the administrative phases (Ring and Van de Ven 1994) of a transaction play out, frequently will turn out to be two very different worlds. Thus, the parties may find that they need to adapt their initial agreements to this new world. To the extent that they have employed collaborative practices that are more rigid, they run the risk of having generated transaction costs that are locked-in, or sunk.

Sources of *ex ante* costs will also emerge during processes of renegotiation that the parties are likely to employ in reworking their agreements. While the sources of the transaction costs may be the same (e.g. search, haggling, safeguarding), the initial conditions (Doz 1996) that led the parties to select approaches to minimizing these transaction costs, in all likelihood, will have changed. The parties may have ignored the search for the most efficient means of dealing with transaction costs *ex ante*, and incurred higher transaction costs to provide slack (Cyert and March 1963; Galbraith 1973; March and Simon 1958; Thompson 1967) in the form of access to the collective resources of a networked organization. Theoretically, this enables them to deal with ambiguity, uncertainty, or variability as it arises in the future, buffering the impact of uncertainty and variability on the production costs of the individual firms and the networked organization as a whole. Thus higher *ex ante* costs may produce lower transaction costs *ex post*. Finally, the slack that can be created by the networked organization may lead to looser coupling (Weick 1976), which in appropriate conditions (e.g. high levels of uncertainty or environmental turbulence) may lead to reduction is production and transaction costs.

Transaction costs related to safeguards also may be lower for members of networked organizations. An ability to rely more heavily on trust in governing their conduct may provide the members of the networked organization with substitutes for many of the kinds of endogenous, impersonal safeguards prescribed by Williamson as means of reducing the likelihood of opportunistic behaviour (Helper and Levine 1992; Sako 1992). A search for those safeguards (e.g. collateral, damages, third-party mediators) may lead to higher transaction costs if the parties haggle over the legal language that creates a legally binding agreement (i.e. one that has consideration and involves a meeting of the minds). These endogenous safeguards might also lead to opportunity costs such as unnecessary commitments of equity to a joint venture. The networked organization, itself, may serve as a substitute for costly exogenous safeguards (e.g. mediators, arbitrators, or the courts) in cases in which conflict does arise between parties, again leading to the possibility of lower transaction costs.

For the members of a networked organization, maladaption costs may be lower *ex post*. It is possible that less will go wrong when the parties are able to rely on trust. Aspects of their relationship that are to occur in the future do not have to be fully detailed in the present in those cases in which trust can be relied upon. If the ability to rely on trust breaks down, however, maladaption costs in such cases may be much, much higher, as the parties virtually will have to return to 'square one' in their relationship and start all over again relying on more formal (and more costly) controls. Alternatively, the relationship may be terminated bringing forth the need to consider an entirely different set of costs.

Set-up and running costs for networked organizations should be lower than those that would be associated with a series of market-based exchanges, or with a joint venture. On an ongoing basis, transactions by members of the networked organization regularly could take place within the context of established norms, SOPs, etc. *A priori*, these ought to be lower than discrete market-based exchanges. They might also be lower than exchanges taking place with a firm that suffers from a high level of bureaucracy or one in which the managers of subsidiary units enjoy relatively high degrees of decision-making autonomy.

Bonding costs, as economists know them, may decrease or vanish within networked organizations. This is not to say that bonding equivalents will be less costly. Quite the contrary, it seems quite probable that they could be very costly (Granovetter 1985; Scher, this volume). But, these kinds of binding costs are likely to have been incurred during the evolution of the networked organization and the activities that produce bonding may lead to other means for lowering transaction costs, as discussed above.

On the other hand, the costs that can arise if a relationship in a networked organization is breached certainly appear to be non-trivial. They cannot be measured just in terms of dollars or lira. Thus, breaking a bond may be much more costly in networked organizations than in other modes of exchange, especially where social capital is involved. These breaches not only may produce harm to business relationships; they may also rent the fabric of social relationships. Bonding costs may vary according to the kinds of resources that are the subject of the transaction, and the relationships that exist between the parties. All other things being equal, strangers are likely to incur higher bonding costs than those who have had prior experiences with each other (prior experience with an opportunistic party is, of course, one of the exceptions to the *ceteris paribus* condition). By their nature, however, bonding costs bind. Thus, they tend to become locked-in costs, denying the parties some degrees of freedom to deal with problems *ex post*.

The sociological research literature suggests that embeddedness could provide transaction cost advantages to firms (Grabher 1993; Granovetter 1985; Lazerson 1993). One of the problems with this literature, however, is that researchers have tended to focus on the conceptual benefits of embeddedness, and have left open the question of the empirical costs of these benefits. For example, kinship relationships (whether by blood or by marriage) are frequently cited as producing lower transaction costs (e.g. Lazerson 1988; Uzzi 1996). Kinship may lower transaction costs that flow from a search for collaborators, or a search for information. Kinship may lower the transaction costs associated with negotiating a deal (Lazerson 1988). As we shall see, however, embeddedness may also lead to costs of other types.

Embeddedness can help a firm overcome the opportunity costs (or the real learning costs) of causal ambiguity in search for collaborators who have required resources. The search costs of coping with isolating conditions (Rumelt 1984), such as unique historical conditions or social complexity (Dierickx and Cool 1989), may also be lowered when the firm in a networked organization is embedded in the social structure that surrounds the networked organization.

To conclude this discussion of transaction costs, it seems clear that *ex ante* and *ex post* costs are interdependent (Williamson, 1985: 1).[9] Williamson's (1985: 61) clear admonishment that realizing the objective of economic efficiency involves a trade-off between transaction costs and production costs is also frequently ignored, however. He observes:

> the [managerial] object is not to economize on transaction costs but to economize in both transaction and neoclassical production cost respects. [. . .] A tradeoff framework is needed to examine the production cost and transaction cost ramifications of alternative modes of organizing simultaneously.

With this 'warning' in mind, let us turn to a consideration of production costs as they relate to networked organizations.

Production costs

Production costs, as the term is employed in this chapter, include the costs of materials, labour, depreciation, inventory, the cost of capital and the like. In defining production costs it is also appropriate to include the costs of selling goods, and what Jones and Hill (1988) generally describe as bureaucratic costs (i.e. the administrative and staff costs of running a hierarchy).

It seems unlikely that managers consider the choice of governance modes primarily because of their transaction cost efficiencies. Transactions are sought because the resources that will flow to a firm from the transaction have production implications. For example, many networked organizations are being employed for purposes of collaborative R&D (Browning *et al.* 1995; Evan and Olk 1990; Powell and Brantley 1993; Saxenian 1994; Schrader 1991). Lower R&D production costs may be a result of these efforts, through efficiencies gained in consolidation of facilities, increased purchasing power, or lower administrative costs (Dyer 1996). In addition, competitors in networked organizations who are collaborating on R&D could focus on aspects of research that are within their own skill sets, developing even greater expertise leading to lower production costs in the collaborative research. Or they may find that they are able to undertake a greater number of research projects collectively than they could have done individually. This is an approach being employed by the French firm PixTech and its collaborators in the development of FED-based flat-panel display (Doz, Ring, Lenway and Murtha 1998). This approach also appears to underlie the logic of many research consortia in the US (Evan and Olk 1990; Ouchi and Kremen-Bolton 1988).

In industries in which economies of scope or scale are critical conditions for success, participants in networked organizations may be able to explore the benefits of scale economies (and lower production costs) that are derived from an ability to rely on the (temporary) excess capacity of one or more of its member firms (Uzzi 1997). Much of the research that has explored interfirm linkages in the 'Third' Italy suggests that these kinds of production cost benefits are one consequence of potentially higher transaction costs that may have been required to create and sustain these networked organizations (Lazerson 1995; Lorenzoni and Lipparini 1998; Sobrero 1997). On the other hand, our research also suggests that these kinds of production cost savings may also be obtained by more powerful firms at the expense of higher production costs (carrying excess inventory) for less powerful firms (Lazerson 1993).[10]

Co-product design and development, and other forms of innovation, by buyers and suppliers who are members of a networked organization may also lead to lower production costs (Dyer 1994; Larson 1992), under conditions in which firms along a value chain experience high degrees of resource dependency, or, where rapid changes in consumer tastes lead to the need to produce new models in shorter time frames. These kinds of activities may also reduce opportunity costs, for example, by enabling the members of a networked organization to undertake more product design efforts with a fixed amount of resources than their competitors who are relying on other modes of exchange (Bonaccorsi and Lipparini 1994). In high-volume contexts such as consumer goods industries that are globalizing, networked organization may also permit firms to employ fewer individual resources in collective distribution or service activities, further lowering their own production costs.

In networked organizations operating in embedded environments, kinship obligations may mean that lower production costs opportunities must be foregone. Further, kinship may inhibit learning and its ability to lower production (or transaction) costs in the future. In short, kinship may generate significant opportunity costs. Embedded environments that are a function of the kinds of institutional ordering described by Scher in Japan (this volume) or Soda and Usai in the Italian construction industry (this volume) can lead to higher production costs in other ways. Institutional constraints may lead to the necessity to create networks that experience higher cost structures than single firms because they forego the benefits of scale and scope economies. Or these constraints may make it harder for 'outsiders' to enter into competition in the industry, thus reducing, if not eliminating, the benefits that new resources and capabilities can provide to an industry as a whole in the form of lower production costs (realized through the diffusion of innovations brought in by outsiders).

Learning costs

March and Simon (1958) and Levitt and March (1988) argue that learning can be done by observing, or by importing. One learns by observing, by working closely with a source of knowledge. Apprentices tend to learn by observing. Learning by importing implies that a source of knowledge is more discrete and can be incorporated into an organization's knowledge base, for example, by acquiring the source(s) of knowledge. One of the potential benefits of membership in a networked organization is that both of these approaches to learning can be facilitated. Easier or quicker access to greater stocks of information may be available through participation in a networked organization, thus increasing opportunities of one or more of the firms in the networked organization to import new knowledge into its systems. In addition to codified types of knowledge (Winter 1987), participation in networked organizations is said to make sticky knowledge, tacit know-how (Teece 1987), or invisible assets (Itami 1987), more observable (i.e. accessible) to employees of its member firms (Kogut and Zander 1992; Pucik 1988). Thus, participation in a networked organization may facilitate learning because membership provides access to knowledge that would otherwise to unavailable to the employees of the firm. It might also reduce learning costs by providing access to sources of knowledge that would be very expensive to obtain through market-based transactions (e.g. acquisition of the whole to gain access to a part). People learn in different ways, and at different rates. This reality undoubtedly helps to explain the potential for differences in the profitability of competing firms within networked organizations. For example, Takahiro Fujimoto (personal communication, 1996) reports that suppliers in the Japanese automotive industry who deal with more than one manufacturer tend to be more profitable than those who have deal with only one. His studies indicate that multiple knowledge flows (which may lead to greater learning) may be partially responsible for the differences. These advantages will be extremely important in so-called knowledge-intensive industries, which may explain the frequent reliance on networked forms of organizations in biotechnology or the entertainment/telecommunications industries.

Westney (1988) argues that learning takes two forms: substantive learning and process learning. Substantive learning deals with specific types of knowledge. Process learning deals with learning how to learn. In networked organizations, both kinds of learning might be accelerated, and could be produced at lower costs.

For example, the means for discovering the existence of, or the location of industrial districts are a form of process learning. They should be considered as (process) learning costs, not transaction costs. Identifying the capabilities or resources of firms are substantive learning costs, not transaction costs. This is generalized learning that may hold future benefits for the firm.

It also seems likely that these learning costs are related to the phenomenon that economists describe as adverse selection (Balakrishnan and Koza 1993). Information asymmetries are less likely to be a function of the learning capabilities of one party than of deficiencies in process. Process learning about a partner is likely to require lots of practice in the pursuit of perfection. It seems probable that more practice can be derived from recurrent and relational contracting, than from discrete contracting (Ring and Van de Ven 1992). If that learning occurs under condition of trust, it may be less costly than process learning that would come from the same number of transactions that are viewed as being independent of each other (or that involve a variety of unrelated partners). For example, developing a relationship that is deeply personal requires lots of connected learning (Belenky *et al.* 1987; Ring 1997b). This is time consuming, and requires extensive and intensive face-to-face communication. But, connected learning can help in developing an ability to rely on trust. An ability to rely on connected ways of knowing also means that the parties very likely know a lot about what makes each other tick. Consequently, there may be fewer instances of maladaption for firms that transact within networked organizations over a sustained period of time. On the other hand, there are probably limits to the extent of process learning that is based on recurring transactions with a limited set of partners who have geared many of their processes to the ends of a networked organization.

Sustaining deep, interpersonal relationships may generate extensive process-oriented learning costs, especially in global contexts. Over time, people change. Learning that they have changed, or are changing (regardless of the sources of the change), generally requires on-going communication, generally face-to-face in nature. This kind of learning is likely to be required in all kinds of industry contexts, but will be especially important in contexts involving R&D, services and professional services. And the nature of interpersonal relationships within networked organizations is likely to vary in significant ways from the kinds of communications found in other forms of governance modes (e.g. contingent claims contracting, joint ventures). Differences in the ability to maintain deep, interpersonal relationships over time are likely to help explain variance in performance outcomes within networked organizations or in comparative assessments of different forms of collaborative governance.

Needless to say, learning requires on-going exchanges of information. In many networked organizations, information generally will be exchanged among a larger number of firms, on a more regular basis, than would be the case within a single integrated firm, or for a firm that is engaged in a series of dyadic relationships. This higher frequency of information exchange can have the effect of opening up all the firms in the networked organization to information from a greater variety of external environments; generally far more than would be available to any one of the individual firms that comprise the networked organization. Coupled with the fact that the firms in the networked organization are also likely to have complementary capabilities which give them greater levels of individual expertise, the diversity of exposure to external environments characteristic of networked organizations can mean that the information available for learning purposes is likely to be more reliable. When high levels of trust exist among members of a networked organization, it is likely that this information will be viewed as having greater validity than information provided by more remote sources (Normann 1971).

Finally, the broad range of processes that fall under the umbrella of innovation involve learning and information transfer. When information can be exchanged under conditions of trust, more valuable information tends to be exchanged (see, e.g., Oliver and Libeskind 1995). Thus, innovation costs may be lower in networked organizations, and networked organizations should be capable of producing more innovation than would occur through other forms of exchange governance, *ceteris paribus*. There are certainly indications that this is the case with networked buyer–supplier relations in the automobile industry in Japan (Helper and Sako 1995; Sako 1992; Smitka 1991) and in the United States (Dyer 1997), and in the so-called packaging valley surrounding Bologna (Bonnaccorsi and Lipparini 1994; Lipparini and Sobrero 1997). On the other hand, stable membership in a networked organization can create conditions similar to those described as 'group-think' and escalating commitment. If these conditions persist, then learning may diminish, or the costs of learning may increase (and conflict regarding the appropriateness of escalating commitments could lead to the devolution of the networked organization).

In networked organizations that are embedded, learning may be even more difficult. Knowledge may be limited simply because the members of the embedded network have been exposed to fewer sources of new, or divergent, information. Kinship ties, or other bonds that frequently hold embedded networks together, may serve as filters to the acceptance of information that diverges from accepted viewpoints. In sum, while there are indications that active participation in networked organizations may lower learning costs and facilitate innovation there is also the potential that in some contexts, such as over-embeddedness, the organizations may face higher opportunity costs.

Opportunity Costs

As was suggested earlier, the condition of embeddedness might help firms overcome the opportunity costs, as well as learning costs, created by causal ambiguity. It could also be the case that firms in networked organizations may be able to reduce opportunity costs by increasing the effective use of a fixed set of resources. The greater exposure to the environments sur-rounding networked organization should also help the firm in its effort to reduce opportunity costs by increasing their awareness of opportunities created by a dynamic environment. And the ability to react more quickly, which is said to be associated with the redundancy, slack and requisite variety attributed to networked organization, may also mean that opportunity costs are lower in this mode of exchange than would be the case in others (e.g. dyadic alliances, markets or hierarchies).

Realizing these kinds of benefits, generally, requires loose coupling within the networked organization. Enhancing an ability to minimize opportunity costs will also require regular membership changes in the overall make-up of the networked organization. Reciprocity, mutual orien-tation, mutual adaptation, or interactive learning are all activities that generally are found within networked organizations. It is in the nature of networked organizations, however, that reciprocity (or similar concepts) does not require equivalence. But they do require commitments, and the use of resources associated with making these kinds of commitments, in all likelihood, will generate opportunity costs. In addition, maintaining a networked organization over time generally means that options that might be pursued in the short term by a firm in a dyadic collaboration will have to be foregone by members of a networked organization. And the longer the networked organization maintains a stable membership, the less likely will be the case that its members will expose themselves to new environments (and the opportunities those environments can provide).

In the case of an embedded networked organization, opportunity costs may be even greater. Embedded contexts tend to produce more tightly coupled networks. Making significant changes in the design, or member-ship, of such a network is likely to be more difficult. Thus, opportunities that might be open to other forms of collaboration (consortia, multiple dyads) may have to be foregone by the members of an embedded net-worked organization. In addition, the relative stability in membership that is more characteristic of this kind of networked organization is likely to mean that fewer opportunities come to the attention of decision-makers than in other kinds of networked organizations.

Of course, these choices (as well as others discussed in this paper) reflect the varied possibilities for making a trade-off among costs that typify economic exchange, or the study of economic exchange that is not constrained by comparative assessments of the efficiency of the governance of a single transaction. These trade-offs are likely to be more pronounced in a networked organization, and may become even more diverse in nature as the size, or the complexity of its activities increase. These trade-offs are also likely to become more apparent if we assume that the products of exchange within a networked organization are influenced by the way in which the exchange is structured, or that the way an exchange is structured can be influenced by the technology or the inputs employed by members of a networked organization in designing their production activities. These kinds of choice also are likely to be more diverse in a networked organization than in a dyadic relationship simply because of the differences in the number of participants.

Social/Welfare costs

A final category of costs long recognized by economists are social or welfare costs. These may include externalities such as approaches to production by the management of a firm that lead to air or water pollution, toxic or hazardous waste, etc. They may also take the form of production designs that lead to hazards to the health and safety of the employees of the firm.

These kinds of costs can also be reflected in the distribution of rents produced by a firm. Management, acting on behalf of the owners of the firm, may be inclined to extract rents from the hourly workers in the form of lower wages. Or they may not invest in the skills of their employees, fearing that the employees will leave the firm before it has recaptured its investment in their capabilities.

Evidence provided by researchers of networked organizations indicates that these forms of governing economic exchange may produce higher or lower social costs. The member firms of the networked organization may also face higher or lower social costs. In Italy, for example, law prohibits unions from organizing certain types of firms with fifteen or fewer employees (Lazerson 1988). Researchers exploring networked organizations in Italy also report the existence of norms among employers regarding wage competition and labour poaching. In the absence of other countervailing pressures, this combination could generate higher social costs in communities in which the firms were located. And, as Soda and Usai point out in this book, networks do have their darker sides. They can facilitate collusion and corruption, with attendant social costs.

As Scher discusses in this volume, firms can use networks as a means of excluding competitors, domestic or foreign. More often than not, the potential for lowering costs (of whatever variety) through networks in such cases will not translate into lower prices for consumers. Thus, it seems likely that networked organization can lead to higher welfare costs, as well as to lower welfare costs.

Interactions between costs

Managers and economists alike have understood the potential for making a trade-off between production and transaction costs for some time. The best example, perhaps, involves industries in which scale economics are essential. There appear to be times when the production and transaction cost benefits of scale might be sacrificed in pursuit of learning. For example, tapered vertical integration is observed on occasions even in those industries in which scale economies are predicted to be a source of competitive advantage. The tapered-integrated firm does not manufacture 100 per cent of some of its components, buying the balance from suppliers. The practice may produce higher production costs (if economies of scale are lower) and higher transaction costs (if transacting in the market is costly). These costs can be traded-off against the (potentially lower) cost of learning (by doing) about the cost structure of the purchased parts, or the (potentially lower) cost of safeguarding opportunistic behaviour by managers within the firm (Dow 1987). Keeping in mind these examples of a trade-off between different types of costs within a firm, we can now turn to a more detailed discussion of the inherent potential in making a trade-off between these types of cost within a networked organization, and determine whether an understanding of the nature of these trade-offs can provide an understanding of why this form of governance mechanism, increasingly, is being employed by managers.

In conducting a search for suppliers of scarce, value-adding resources or capabilities in T_n, a focal firm learns a good deal about the general market of suppliers for this particular kind of resource. I have suggested that to the extent that this does occur, some of these costs are more properly classified as learning costs in T_{n+1}, and thereafter, particularly when the firm relies on the learning it derived from the initial search, in subsequent searches. Thus, what are initially transaction costs can become learning costs and a return on their investment is realized.

In a global economy, the successful search for resources may take the representatives of the focal firm to far-flung parts of the globe. There, they may encounter language and cultural barriers. The focal firm either will have encountered the cost of learning about the ways business deals are done in that part of the world in one of two ways: prior to arriving on the scene, or on the scene. Learning in the latter forum is likely to mean that these costs will be significantly higher, and may include the opportunity cost of losing out on a deal because of unfamiliarity with the way business is done. Again, in my view, researchers employing TCE frequently fail to distinguish between these kinds of costs, treating them all as transaction costs. This may be the case in T_n. Thereafter, however, some of these costs should be treated differently.

Haggling is another transaction cost outlined in Figure 9.1 above. In some contexts, the more the haggling the better the deal; that is, there are positive benefits to higher transaction costs—found, perhaps, in the discovery of a means of lowering production costs, building trust that leads to lower costs of governing the networked organization, or in avoiding opportunity costs. If the haggling is with external stakeholders, however, it may mean that the firms end up assuming social/welfare costs that they have avoided in the past.

As indicated above, safeguarding a transaction creates a diverse array of costs, many of which will involve a trade-off. Parties with lots of transaction experience, or with lots of experience with each other, may have a feel for what they can get away with in the form of safeguards. Learning costs, previously incurred, thus lead to lower transaction costs in the present transaction. In cases of deals with strangers from countries with poorly developed legal systems, the search for reliable third-party institutional guarantors (Commons 1924) can be costly. Hostages, in the traditional TCE sense (e.g. cheek-to-jowl plants) may be very expensive in production cost terms (e.g. foregoing the scale economies of a single plant located miles from the hostage). Thus, finding alternative governance modes (trust-based contracts relying on traditional approaches such as quanxi in China) may lead to lower production and transaction costs, but at some added expense in learning costs.

A failure to accurately predict the future (e.g. in market or factor demand) may produce increased production costs for the parties. Thus, an investment in higher transaction costs in efforts to define more accurately the respective expectations of the parties may reduce the likelihood of encountering maladaption costs *ex post*. Maladaption costs can also arise even when the parties have accurately predicted what the future holds in store for them. They may need to change terms and conditions because their objectives in the collaboration change as time progresses. The 'haggling' that occurs *ex post* may be even more intense (and possibly more costly) than that which had occurred *ex ante*, perhaps because the parties may now be attributing some fault or blame to the ways each other handled unforeseen events.

Another kind of *ex post* cost may stem from efforts to create the mechanisms required to govern the disputes that arise out of the transaction. These conflict resolution mechanisms might be relatively low-cost approaches such as third-party mediators within an industry, or more costly mechanisms such as reliance on the International Chamber of Commerce office in Stockholm. As with *ex ante* costs, some of these *ex post* costs in T_{n+1} may reflect prior learning.

The learning cost benefits of more regular exchange with a limited number of collaborators also may translate into more efficient governance over time, and may also lead to lower *ex ante* and *ex post* transaction costs with each succeeding transaction that occurs within the networked organization. Thus, it seems likely that to the extent that learning activities do occur more frequently in networked organization, than in other forms of exchange governance, the processes of learning ought to produce higher transaction costs. These higher transaction costs may be acceptable if they also translate into better outcomes, or if they translate into lower costs in other areas.

Managers and economists worry about opportunity costs. Opportunity costs will need to be considered in connection with production costs, innovation/learning costs, and transaction costs and the trade-offs that confront managers contemplating collaborations. Many managers, especially in the US, want to get right down to business when beginning a deal. They can end up ignoring opportunity costs if they fail to appreciate the benefits of really getting to know those with whom they will do the deal. These opportunity costs may show up down the road in the form of more haggling, more costly governance mechanisms, and/or in higher *ex post* production costs. Enhancing an ability to minimize opportunity costs also is likely to require regular membership changes in the overall make-up of the networked organization. Each of the examples just outlined can lead to additional transaction costs. But those additional transaction costs may be well invested if they lead to more innovations, reduced uncertainty and lower risk.

Increasingly, the management literature does focus on collaboration as a vehicle for learning (Powell and Brantley 1993). In general, however, the research on learning through alliances has not addressed the costs of learning, or the relationship between governance structure choices and possible trade-off choices among the costs of learning, producing or transacting. The long-term survival of a firm, however, may depend as much on the ability of its managers to get owners to live with the costs of innovation/learning that do not have immediate bottom line impacts, as on the ability of the managers to make appropriate trade-offs between production and transaction costs. For example, learning how to be rela-tional—process learning in Westney's terms—will generate transaction costs (with those who help the firm learn, whether the learning takes place by doing deals, or in more traditional and formal ways). But, being relational also may open up new opportunities to lower production costs (Nonoka and Takeuchi 1995; Ring and Van de Ven 1994. Sako 1992; Dyer 1996; Uzzi 1996).

In the opening paragraphs of the chapter an assertion was made that sociologists generally ignored issues of costs when dealing with interorganizational relationships. As in all generalizations, there are exceptions. One in particular provides a nice picture of the trade-offs. Lazerson (1993) makes an effort to distinguish among the various kinds of costs incurred by the firms in the Modena area, which was the subject of his study. He recognizes the costs of negotiating and administering contracts and discusses the benefits that flow from being a part of the network in reducing these kinds of costs. His work also address inventory cost issues, as well as those related to transportation. Explicit in his discussion, moreover, is the identification of the kinds of trade-offs that apparently existed between production and transaction costs in areas such as the costs of labour, quality, or the price of information. There are clear indications of transfers of production and transaction costs between members of the networks he studied (some of the dark side of the cost issues in networks), and inferences can be drawn from his discussion about benefits that are associated with carrying these costs. Hard data is lacking in Lazerson's explication of cost, however, and there is some blurring of the kinds of costs being discussed. Nonetheless, he paints a clear picture of trade-offs and the benefits that appear to flow from reliance on networked organization.

Implications and conclusions

One of the objectives with this chapter has been to demonstrate that our understanding of interfirm cooperation has produced an overly narrow view of the costs of cooperative economic exchange. Another objective was to generally demonstrate that we have very little hard data on the costs of exchange, or the trade-offs among costs that confront managers.

If the foregoing assessment of our state of knowledge about the costs of cooperation is correct, then we might wish to do something to remedy the situation. Or, we might accept the increased reliance on various forms of networked organization as a preferred mode of governance to mean that managers find the level of cost acceptable in light of the outcomes that flow from exchange governed by this mode. One potential problem with this approach is that managers may be learning; and 'the jury might still be out', as we lawyers are fond of saying. Thus, we may have to attack this issue more vigorously in our research.

Taking this as a starting point then, there appears to be a need to reach some agreement about the classification of cost. One of the problems encountered in preparing this chapter was the absence of any agreement on what costs were transaction costs, or production costs. Costs related to inventory and transportation are particularly vexing in this regard. We also need to begin to operationalize these kinds of costs in terms that make them accessible to research efforts.

My own investigations have surfaced carefully prepared budgets out-lining the transaction costs of networked organization. These included cash budgets for search, travel and lawyers; time budgets for deal-making (sometimes at the person hour level). Entertainment budgets designed to help facilitate deal-making can be found. Gaining access to contracts, and more importantly, lawyers 'work product', helps to identify sources of cost related to safeguards, bonding, etc. These kinds of archival data also make it possible, on an *ex post* basis, to identify sources of maladaption costs. More importantly, perhaps, work product provides data on trade-offs that may have been considered in terms of production costs, opportunity costs, or learning costs. These kinds of data, however, are usually very hard to come by, and in the case of networked organizations of the kinds frequently described in the literature may be irrelevant: contracts and lawyers frequently are not employed by the parties.

In such cases, we need to expand our inventory of prompts to be employed in ethnographic studies. This will require more process-oriented research, first to identify the kinds of processes that accompany the emergence, growth and dissolving over time of these modes of exchange and their firms of governance (see, e.g., Ring 1997a). From this, we can begin to define ways to explore the costs associated with these processes, and their classification. These efforts will also provide a basis for instrument construction that can be employed in large-scale survey-based research efforts.

There are a number of substantive issues related to sources of network costs that might have institutional implications (North 1990). Can the stimulation of industrial districts really be prompted by government intervention to lower transaction or production costs? Saxenian's (1994) work suggests the answer is probably no at the national level, yes at the regional level. Kanter's (1995) tales of four cities tends to confirm Saxenian's view of the advantages of working at regional levels.

Would firms make greater investments in learning costs, or improved capabilities in transacting if they could write them off for tax purposes? Should we grant investment tax credits for the setting-up costs of networked organization? Access to venture capital is an essential ingredient in networked organization designed to stimulate innovation. There may be ways that governments can help firms leverage their capital, or to manage the flow of capital on a regional basis, thus potentially lowering transaction, production, learning and/or opportunity costs. Questions such as these indicate that the costs of networked organizations can be affected not only by managers, but also by external stakeholders.

Notes

1 I would like to acknowledge the generous support of the Dipartmento di Discipline Economico-Aziendali, Universita degli Studi di Bologna, during my stay in Bologna in the summer of 1996 when this paper was initially written; Universita L. Bocconi where it was rewritten in the Spring of 1997; and the ESF-EMOT Programme for their support of my work in this area since 1993. The extremely helpful comments of participants at the EMOT Workshop, and at seminars at CNR-IRAT in Naples, and Bocconi in Milan are also gratefully acknowledged. Responsibility for errors, of course, remains with the author.
2 Lundvall's (1993) work is a carefully crafted exception to this broad characterization of the work of economists.
3 The phrase 'the Third Italy' is generally attributed to Bagnasco (1977).
4 Jones and Hill (1988) provide a seminal exception.
5 Perrone (1997) suggests that a more useful classification of these kinds of resources would include: economic capital, cultural capital, social capital and symbolic capital. His argument provides support for an assumption that exchanges within networked organizations entail a much wider variety of capabilities and resources than is possible with market-based transactions.
6 Another difficulty with Williamson's approach is the focus on intermediate goods that arises because of his frequent reliance on the efficiency of transactions within markets when compared with transactions within vertically integrated firms, and vice versa. Within-firm markets tend to be markets for intermediate goods, where the risk neutral assumption of TCE tends to hold up

well. As Radner (1992) points out, however, most transactions involve actors who are not risk neutral.

7 A discussion of these processes: negotiation, agreement, administrative, renegotiation, and the informal processes that occur in each of these formal processes—sense-making, understanding, and committing, is beyond the scope of this paper. The interested reader is directed to Doz,1996; Ring and Van de Ven 1994; Ring 1996a and 1997a for a more complete discussion of process issues.

8 A good example of the single-firm focus is the excellent empirical work of Laura Poppo (1995). She makes a significant contribution to our overall understanding of transaction costs, and to improving the operationalization of costs, but we learn little about the dynamics of the costs her managers incurred in dealing with external markets.

9 His discussion of these issues, however, points to another problem with many extant TCE-based approaches to the issue of the cost of exchange. He observes that the difficulty of quantifying these costs is mitigated by the fact that 'transaction costs are always assessed in a comparative institutional way ... accordingly it is the difference between rather than the absolute magnitude of transaction costs that matters' (Williamson 1985: 22). This may be so for economists, but for managers absolute magnitudes do matter. Thus, we need to know much more about the potential trade-off between *ex ante* and *ex post* transaction costs than is provided in the extant TCE literature. See, generally, Ring (1994) for a speculative discussion of these issues.

10 In many of these cases, excess inventory could be considered as a production cost because it is as much a result of actions by these firms to retain valued employees as it is accepting the dictates of larger, more powerful, centre-firms.

Bibliography

Bagnasco, A. (1977) *Tre Italie: La problematica territoriale dello sviluppo italiano*. Bologna: Il Mulino.

Balakrishnan, S. and Koza, M.P. (1993) 'Information asymmetry, market failure, and joint ventures: theory and evidence', *Journal of Economic Behavior and Organization*, 20: 99–117.

Beamish, P. and Killing, P. (eds) (1997) *Cooperative Strategies*: vol. 1—A North American perspective; vol. 2—A European Perspective; vol. 3—An Asian perspective, San Francisco: Jossey-Bass Publishers.

Belenky, M. F., Blythe M. C., Goldberger, N. R. and Tarule, J. M. (eds) (1986) *Women's Ways of Knowing: The Development of Self, Voice, and Mind*, New York: Basic Books.

Bonaccorsi, A. and Lipparini, A. (1994) 'Strategic partnerships in new product development: an Italian case study', *Journal of Product Innovation Management*, 11: 134–45.

Bromiley, Philip and Cummings, Larry L. (1995) 'Transactions costs in organizations with trust', in Robert J. Bies, R. J. Lewicki and Blair L. Sheppard (eds) *Research on Negotiations in Organizations* 5: 219–47, Greenwich, CT: JAI Press.

Browning, L. D., Beyer, J. M. and Shelter, J. C. (1995) 'Building cooperation in a competitive industry: SEMATECH and the semiconductor industry', *The Academy of Management Journal*, 38: 113–51.

Brusco, S. (1982) 'The Emilian model: productive decentralisation and social integration', *Cambridge Journal of Economics*, 6: 167–89.

Coase, R. H. (1937) 'The nature of the firm', *Economica*, 4, 386–405.

Cohen, M. D. and Sproull, L. S. (eds) (1996) *Organizational Learning*, Thousand Oaks, CA: Sage Publications.

Commons, J. R. (1924) *Institutional Economics*, Madison: University of Wisconsin Press.

Cyert, R. and March, J. G. (1963) *A Behavioral Theory of the Firm*, Englewood Cliffs, NJ: Prentice-Hall.

Dierickx, I. and Cool, K. (1989) 'Asset stock accumulation and sustainability of competitive advantage', *Management Science*, 35: 1504–11.

Dow, G. (1987) 'The function of authority in transaction cost economics', *Journal of Economic Behavior and Organization*, 8: 13–38.

Doz, Y. L. (1996) 'The evolution of cooperation in strategic alliances: initial conditions or learning processes?', *Strategic Management Journal*, 17: 55–83.

Doz, Y., Ring, P.S., Lenway, S. and Murtha, T. (1998) PixTech. INSEAD. Mimeo.

Dyer, J. H. (1994) 'Dedicated assets: Japan's manufacturing edge', *Harvard Business Review*, 174–8.

Dyer, J. H. (1996) 'How Chrysler created an American kieretsu', *Harvard Business Review*, 6: 42–56.

Dyer, J. H. (1997) 'Effective interfirm collaboration: how firms minimize transaction costs and maximize transaction value', *Strategic Management Journal*, 18: 535–56.

Ebers, M. (ed.) (1997) *The Formation of Inter-Organizational Networks*, Oxford: Oxford University Press.

Evan, W. M. and Olk, P. (1990) 'R&D consortia: a new organizational form', *Sloan Management review*, 31 (3), 37–46.

Galbraith, J. (1973) *Organization Design*, Reading, MA: Addison-Wesley.

Gerlach, M. L. (1992) *Alliance Capitalism: The Social Organization of Japanese Business*, Berkeley, CA: The University of California Press.

Grabher, G. (1993). *The Embedded Firm: On the Socioeconomics of Industrial Networks*. London: Routledge.

Grandori, A. and Soda, G. (1995) 'Interfirm networks: antecedents, mechanisms, and forms', *Organizational Studies*, 16: 183–214.

Granovetter, Mark (1985) 'Economic action and social structure: the problem of embeddedness', *American Journal of Sociology*, 78: 481–510.

Helper, S. R. and Sako, M. (1995) 'Supplier relations in Japan and the United States: are they converging?', *Sloan Management Review*, 36: 77–84.

Helper, S. and Levine, D. I. (1992) 'Long-term supplier relations and product-market structure', *Journal of Law, Economics and Organization*, 8, 561–82.

Hennart, Jean Francois (1988) 'A transaction costs theory of equity joint ventures', *Strategic Management Journal*, 9: 93–104.

Hill, C. W. L. (1994) 'National institutional structures, transaction cost economizing and comparative advantage', *Organization Science*, 6: 119–31.

Itami, H. 1987 *Mobilizing invisible assets*, Boston, MA: Harvard University Press.

Jones, C., Hesterley, W. S. and Borgatti, S. P. (1997) 'A general theory of network governance: exchange conditions and social mechanisms', *Academy of Management Review*, 22: 911–46.

Jones, G. R. and Hill, C. W. L. (1988) 'Transaction cost analysis of strategy-structure choice', *Strategic Management Journal*, 9: 159–72.

Kanter, R. M. (1995) *World Class*, New York: Simon and Schuster.

Kogut, Bruce (1988) 'Joint ventures: theoretical and empirical perspectives', *Strategic Management Journal*, 9: 319–32.

Kogut, B. and Zander, U. (1992) 'Knowledge of the firm: combinative capabilities and the replication of technology', *Organization Science*, 3: 383–97.

Larson, A. (1992) 'Network dyads in entrepreneurial settings: a study of the governance of exchange relationships', *Administrative Science Quarterly*, 37: 76–104.

Lazerson, M. H. (1988) 'Organizational growth of small firms: an outcome of markets and hierarchies', *American Sociological Review*, 53: 330–42.

Lazerson, M. H. (1993) 'Factory or putting-out? Knitting networks in Modena', in G. Grabher (ed.) *The Embedded Firm: On the Socioeconomics of Industrial Networks*, London: Routledge, pp. 203–26.

Lazerson, M. H. (1995) 'A new Phoenix? modern putting-out in the Modena knitwear industry', *Administrative Science Quarterly*, 40: 34–59.

Levitt, B. and March, J. G. (1988) 'Organizational learning', *Annual Review of Sociology*, 14: 319–40.

Lipparini, A. (1995). *Firm, Inter-firm Relationships, and Competitive Advantage*, Milan: Etas Libri.

Lipparini, A. and Sobrero, M. (1997) 'Coordinating multi-firm innovative processes: entrepreneur as catalyst in small-firm networks', in M. Ebers (ed.) *The Formation of Inter-Organizational Networks*, Oxford: Oxford University Press, pp. 199–219.

Lorenzoni, G. and Baden-Fuller, C. (1995) 'Creating a strategic centre to manage a web of partners', *California Management Review*, 37(3): 1–18.

Lorenzoni, G. and Lipparini, A., (1998). 'Leveraging internal and external competencies in boundary shifting strategies. A longitudinal study', University of Bologna, Faculty of Economics, Mimeo.

Lundvall, B. A. (1993) 'Explaining interfirm cooperation and innovation: limits of the transaction-cost approach', in G. Grabher, (ed.) *The Embedded Firm: On the Socioeconomics of Industrial Networks*, London: Routledge, pp. 52–64.

March, J. G. and Simon, H. A. (1958) *Organizations*, New York: John Wiley and Sons.

Monteverde, K. and Teece, D. J. (1982) 'Supplier switching costs and vertical integration in the automobile industry', *Bell Journal of Economics*, 13: 206–13.

Nonaka, I. and Takeuchi, H. (1995) *The Knowledge-Creating Company*, New York: Oxford University Press.

Normann, R. (1971) 'Organizational innovativeness: product variation and reorientation', *Administrative Science Quarterly*, 16: 203–15.

North, D. (1990) *Institutions, institutional change, and economic performance*. Cambridge, Cambridge University Press.

Oliver, A. L. and Libeskind, J. P. (1995) 'Three kinds of networking: sourcing intellectual capital in biotechnology', paper presented at the EMOT Workshop 'Industry Structure and Interorganisational Networks', Geneva, December 1–2, 1995.

Ouchi, W. G. (1980) 'Markets, bureaucracies, and clans', *Administrative Science Quarterly*, 25: 124–41.

Ouchi, W. G. and Kremen-Bolton, M. (1988) 'The logic of joint research and development', *California Management Review*, 31 (1): 9–33.

Parkhe, A. (1993) 'Strategic alliance structuring: a game theoretic and transactions cost examination of interfirm cooperation', *Academy of Management Journal*, 36: 794–829.

Penrose, E. T. (1959) *The Theory of Growth of the Firm*, London: Basil Blackwell.

Perrone, V. (1997) 'The forms of capital: exploring the complexity of strategy from a multidimensional perspective', Mimeo, University of Bocconi, Milan, Italy.

Piore, M. J. and Sabel, C. (1984). *The Second Industrial Divide*, New York: Basic Books.

Poppo, L. (1995) 'Influence activities and strategic coordination: two distinctions of internal and external markets', *Management Science*, 41: 1845–59.

Powell, W. W. (1990) 'Neither market not hierarchy: network forms of organization', in Barry M. Staw and L. L. Cummings, (eds), *Research in Organization Behavior*, Greenwich, CT: JAI Press, 12: 295–336.

Powell, W. W., and Brantley, P (1993) 'Competitive cooperation in biotechnology: learning through networks', in N. Nohria and R. Eccles (eds) *Networks and Organizations: Structure, Form, and Action*, Boston: Harvard Business School Press, pp. 366–94.

Powell, W. W., Koput, W. and Smith-Doerr, L. (1996) 'Interorganizational cooperation and the locus of innovation: networks of learning in biotechnology', *Administrative Science Quarterly*, 41: 116–45.

Pucik, V. (1988) 'Strategic alliances, organizational learning, and competitive advantage: the HRM agenda', *Human Resource Management*, 27: 77–93.

Radner, R. (1992) 'Hierarchy: the economics of managing', *Journal of Economic Issues*, 30: 1382–1415.

Ring, P. S. (1994) 'An expanded view of the cost of contracting', paper prepared for presentation at the Annual Meeting of the Academy of Management, Business Strategy and Policy Division, Distinguished Poster Session, Dallas, TX, August 10–17, 1994.

Ring, P. S. (1996a) *Networked Organization: A Resource Based Perspective*, Acta Universitatis Upsaliensie: Studia Oeronomiae Negotiorum, No. 39, Uppsala: Almquist and Wiskell International.

Ring, P. S. (1996b) 'Fragile trust and resilient trust and their roles in cooperative interorganizational relationships', *Business and Society*, 15(2): 148–75.

Ring, P. S. (1997a) 'Transacting in the state of union: A case study of exchange governed by convergent interests', *Journal of Management Studies*, 4: 1–25.

Ring, P. S. (1997b) 'Patterns of process in cooperative interorganizational relationships', in Paul Beamish and Peter Killing (eds) *Cooperative Strategies: A North American perspective*, San Francisco: Jossey-Bass Publishers, 1997, Chapter 11, pp. 286–307.

Ring, P. S., and Van de Ven, A. H. (1992) 'Structuring cooperative relationships between organizations', *Strategic Management Journal*, 13: 483–98.

Ring, P. S. and Van de Ven, A. H. (1994) 'Developmental processes in cooperative interorganizational relationships', *Academy of Management, Review* 19: 90–118.

Rumelt, R. P. (1984) 'Toward a strategic theory of the firm', in R. Lamb (ed.) *Competitive Strategic Management*, Englewood Cliffs, NJ: Prentice-Hall, pp. 556–70.

Sako, M. (1992) *Price, Quality, and Trust: Inter-firm Relations in Britain and Japan*, Cambridge: Cambridge University Press.

Saxenian, A. (1994) *Regional Advantage*, Cambridge, MA: Harvard University Press.

Schrader, S. (1991) 'Informal technology transfer between firms: cooperation through information trading', *Research Policy*, 20: 153–70.

Smitka, M. J. (1991) *Competitive Ties: Subcontracting in the Japanese Automotive Industry*, New York: Columbia University Press.

Sobrero, M. (1997) 'Structural constraints, strategic interactions and innovative processes: measuring network effects in new product development projects', paper prepared for presentation at the Annual Meeting of the Academy of Management, Boston, August 10–13, 1997.

Steers, R., Shin, Y. and Ungson, G. (1989) *The Chaebol: Korea's New Industrial Might*, New York: Harper Collins.

Teece, D. E. (1987) 'Profiting from technological innovation: implications for integration, cooperation, licensing, and public policy', in D. E. Teece (ed.) *The Competitive Challenge*, Cambridge, MA: Ballinger, pp. 185–200.

Thompson, J. C. (1967) *Organizations in Action*, New York: McGraw-Hill.

Thorelli, H. B. (1986) 'Networks: between markets and hierarchies', *Strategic Management Journal*, 7: 37–51.

Uzzi, B. (1996) 'The sources and consequences of embeddedness for the economic performance of organizations: The network effect.' *American Sociological Review*, 61: 674–98.

Uzzi, B. (1997) 'Social structure and competition in interfirm networks. The paradox of embeddedness', *Administrative Science Quarterly*, 42: 35–67.

Weick, K. (1976) 'Educational systems as loosely-coupled systems', *Administrative Science Quarterly*, 21: 1–19.

Wernerfelt, B. (1984) 'A resource based theory of the firm', *Strategic Management Journal*, 5: 171–80.

Westney, D. E. (1988) 'Domestic and foreign learning curves in managing international cooperative strategies'. In F. J. Contractor and P. Lorange (eds) *Cooperative Studies in International Business*, Lexington, MA: Lexington Books, pp. 339–46.

Williamson, O. E. (1985) *The Economic Institutions of Capitalism*, New York: The Free Press.

—— (1991) 'Comparative economic organization', *Administrative Science Quarterly*, 36, 269–96.

Wiliamson, O. E. and Ouchi, W. G. (1981) 'The markets and hierarchies program of research: origins, implications, prospects', In William Joyce and Andrew Van de Ven (eds) *Organizational Design*, New York: Wiley.

Winter, S. (1987) 'Knowledge and competence as strategic assets'. In D. E. Teece, (ed.) *The Competitive Challenge*, Cambridge, MA: Ballinger, pp. 159–84.

Zajac, E. J. and Olsen, C. P. (1993) 'From transaction cost to transaction value analysis: implications for the study of interorganizational strategies', *Journal of Management Studies*, 30: 131–45.

10 Credit rationing among small-firm networks in the London and New York garment industries[1]

Andrew Godley

Introduction

In recent years much of research into networks has emphasized the role of information linkages leading to enhanced innovation. Whether this is seen within the context of small firms in industrial districts or within larger corporations it is self-evidently a priority on the research agenda of social scientists to examine how these economic relationships are able to achieve a more efficient allocation of scarce resources than a conventional market model (Brusco 1980; Piore and Sabel 1984). This rich vein of literature has prompted a number of intriguing theoretical developments and many policy initiatives, in particular, in contributing to a renewed concern with the employment creation by the small-firm sector. However, despite the wealth of this literature, relatively little research has focused on one of the fundamental constraints on small-firm development, namely the difficulties of access to credit.

The owners and managers of small firms have for many decades complained of unfair treatment by banks. Allegedly many profitable ventures are not funded because of bankers' intransigence. This controversy has prompted much research, with, in the UK, a number of government investigations and the popularization of the idea of a small-firm sector credit-gap (Ross 1996). Recent theoretical work, however, suggests that the notion of a gap in the credit market is probably misplaced. This is because the credit market may be in equilibrium when demand and supply are not (Stiglitz and Weiss 1981; Stiglitz 1987). It is this feature of the credit market which prompts the need for credit market intermediaries to ration credit. Typically, these intermediaries are banks, but it is not inevitable that banks should be the most efficient intermediary in every situation. The purpose of this paper is to focus on how allocative efficiency may be increased when networks undertake the function of credit market intermediaries and the role of conventional banks is minimized. The particular circumstances as to when this may be an optimum solution are detailed in the next section. These are then illustrated in the following case study of the Jewish dominated garment industries of New York and London, both of which, in their formative period around the turn of the century, conformed to the model of thriving and dynamic industrial districts and where networks had developed very innovative solutions to the small-firm credit market dilemma: the soft loan society.

Networks and credit rationing

The apparent gap in the credit market is the gap between the credit demanded and supplied at a seemingly stable interest rate. But this is an interpretation of the credit market which rests on the assumption that credit is a commodity like any other, for which a market-clearing price can be found which will allow demand to equate with supply. Credit, however, is fundamentally different. In particular the price of credit—the interest rate—is not the price paid by the borrower, but the price the borrower *promises* to pay the lender. The relationship between the two is tenuous to say the least. But this element of uncertainty alone is not what gives the credit market its important characteristics. These are related to the difficulties of reducing risk by increasing the price. Again, intuitively, one would imagine that the suppliers of credit could reduce their exposure to breaches of promises by increasing the price and, thus, eliminating those who would not be able to repay the loan. The flaw in this logic is precisely that those who promise to pay more are not necessarily those who, *ex post*, will actually deliver more. Indeed, as Stiglitz and Weiss argue, 'it is not only that those offering to pay the highest interest *may* not, on average, deliver (yield) the highest expected return; but there may be systematic reasons for suspecting that those who are willing to offer to pay the highest interest rate are not among the best credit risks'. This may be because those most likely to accept high interest rates are '"risk lovers', 'opportunists' and 'crooks"' (Stiglitz and Weiss 1990: 96). There are, therefore, two important problems with the credit market. In the first instance the promise to pay a particular price is not the same as paying it. Credit markets are, therefore, characterized by incomplete contracts. Second, increasing the price in an attempt to reduce the risk may actually introduce adverse selection and incentive effects thus forcing creditworthy borrowers out of the market, and leaving bad risks behind.

This, then, explains why credit is not allocated in a market with an auctioneering process to coordinate demand and supply. It also helps to explain why specialized market intermediaries are established which ration credit. These are banks. The methods used by banks to ration credit seek to resolve the problems of asymmetric information and incomplete contracts which lie at the heart of successful coordination in the credit market. First, banks try to screen applicants by sorting them into different categories of creditworthiness. Second, they introduce some form of monitoring so as to minimize the risk of moral hazard once the loan has been granted. Third, the rough justice meted out and complained of is the sharp end of banks' methods of enforcing contracts. Of course, in the absence of perfect information, neither the screening, the monitoring, nor the enforcing functions can be performed perfectly. The cost of acquiring and processing the information required to perform these three functions even imperfectly introduces a significant cost element into the intermediation process. Moreover, this is a cost which may be higher when banks undertake the coordination process than when other groups or agents do; partly because they tend to be restricted by formal rules and procedures, and partly because borrowers have an incentive to overestimate the potential returns available on the loan. This understanding of how credit markets function points to the possibility that banks may be less efficient as intermediaries than other bodies. Banks, for example, may not be best placed to acquire the relevant information required for screening, monitoring and enforcing, and they may not be especially efficient at processing and interpreting the information that is available to them.

As in any market, the crucial function of financial intermediaries is to be able to respond to information.[2] The problem in the credit market is that important information is extremely costly to acquire and process. The theory of transactions cost attempts to explain the existence of firms as a form of organization to coordinate the transfer of economic resources. Following this theory in trying to understand the optimum form of organization in the credit market, it is possible to see that the high trans- actions costs associated with acquiring and processing relevant information in the credit market allow for the possibility of a number of different coordinating agents with very different organizational forms (Williamson 1985). In particular, the organizational forms of credit market inter- mediaries may be thought of as falling along a spectrum. This spectrum reflects the category and amount of information available to the inter- mediary and upon which its allocation decision rests. At one end will be institutions dependent upon formal quantitative data. Conventional banks may be categorized in this way; they apply a common, credit-scoring formula to all cases and so decisions are reduced to a simple quantitative equation. At the other end of the spectrum would be intermediaries who are able to use other and often informal information, usually qualitative, and perhaps even tacit. This is a category of information which ordinarily cannot be traded. Those intermediaries which are able to utilize this informal information may be more efficient than banks in those niches of the credit market where such information is valuable.

Networks then may be seen as important and possibly superior alter- natives to banks as intermediaries in those niches of the credit market where the key information is mostly non-tradeable. Certainly, both historic- ally and today, networks as organizational forms have been seen as important actors in the allocation of scarce resources to economic users.[3] The network as an organizational form is distinct from both a firm and a market, in that the actors are not linked by specific contracts to some ultimate owner of property rights, as in a firm, nor are they engaged in an auctioneering process, having to bid for resources, as in a market. Rather, networks are said to coordinate resources through cooperative strategies, with allocative decisions arrived at by consensus and through the pooling of relevant information. For the purposes of this paper, a more refined definition of networks is unimportant. The emphasis here is on the observation that any number of organizational forms may contribute to efficiency in the credit market. The appropriate question to address then, is: under what conditions will non-bank organizations (in particular, networks) be more efficient credit market intermediaries than will banks? The obvious response is to examine a number of more or less incomplete contractual relationships and assess whether banks or alternative forms of intermediary would be the more efficient coordinating mechanism. This is best seen by focusing on three important functions.

First, the function of screening applicants and sorting them into categories of creditworthiness is an area where networks may be more efficient than banks. This is because of the role of information in assessing risk. Increasingly for banks, and indeed for conventional venture capital houses, risk is assessed almost solely on the contents of the business plan, the borrower's expected rate of return and past performance. The days of individual branch managers able to use their own discretion based on non-quantifiable data are largely gone. Networks based on personal relationships may prove to have a significant competitive advantage as intermediaries because they may have access to more and better information and they may be able to interpret the information more accurately than banks. For example, an in-depth knowledge of the family background and personal integrity of a loan applicant may be seen as useful information within the orbit of a local or cultural/religious network, but not necessarily in a bank. Use of such information, however, would allow for a more efficient screening process. Networks based around industry clusters may also be better able to assess the viability of the proposed venture than banks. If there is a greater supply of relevant expertise in the network than in the bank, the former will have a considerable advantage in the screening process. However, this also implies a potential limitation to networks' efficiency premium. In particular, it would seem unlikely that they would finance entirely novel ventures in completely new areas.

The second crucial function of intermediaries in the credit market is that of monitoring borrowers. The nature of asymmetric information in the lending process means that this is a particularly difficult and expensive function for banks to perform effectively. Formal information will never be complete, however, and networks might once again have a clear advantage over banks as intermediaries in the credit markets. The exact mechanism of the monitoring function, and thus the advantage relative to the banks, will vary according to the kind of network. Industry-cluster networks will be able to monitor borrowers through the inevitable peer-monitoring in normal trading activities, for example. The most efficient form of monitoring is, however, self-monitoring, in which the borrower gives the lenders exact, honest and regular reports on the state of their investment. This sort of monitoring is much more likely in a cultural environment where moral values impose a high social cost to opportunistic behaviour.

Finally, intermediaries in the credit market must enforce their contracts, sometimes to the disadvantage of the borrower. Clearly, those inter-mediaries better at performing the first two functions of screening and monitoring loan applicants, will be better placed to bring their contracts to successful completion and thus be less dependant on efficient enforcement mechanisms for successful intermediation. However, there are also grounds for believing that networks may prove to be more efficient than banks at enforcing contract completion. This is because the normal tools of enforce-ment used by banks (forfeiting collateral and litigation) are also available for use by networks. But in certain conditions networks have access to additional tools of enforcement varying from the use of shame and exclusion in a culture/ethnic-based network to the rather severe punish-ments meted out by criminal networks such as the Mafia and Triads! It is the recent recognition of the potential advantages of the more informal methods of fulfilling these three functions which has prompted a renewed interest in the role of non-bank and informal financial intermediaries in the venture capital market (Mason and Harrison 1994).

Of course, there are, no doubt, additional costs which networks of financial intermediaries would have to bear compared to the more formal intermediaries. In particular, the opportunity costs associated with ignorance of potential advantages outside the network intermediaries. However, on balance, it might be assumed that under certain conditions network intermediaries may be more efficient than more formal ones because network intermediaries have long been able to utilize non-tradeable information in credit markets. An examination of how East European Jewish immigrant firms in the New York and London garment industries developed innovative credit market intermediaries will, hopefully, illustrate how networks are able to solve one of the fundamental constraints on small-firm growth and so enhance allocative efficiency.

Jewish soft loan societies in New York and London

The outlines of the mass migration of East European Jewry are fairly well known: between 1880 and 1914 approximately two and a half million Jews moved westwards, over three-quarters to the United States of America, some 150,000 to the United Kingdom, with smaller communities establish-ing themselves in Germany, Palestine, South Africa, Canada and Australia. They came overwhelmingly from the Russian Empire, but significant minorities also left Austria–Hungary and Romania. They settled in small regions of the poorer parts of the commercial centres in the host nations and entered the local labour markets. In both New York's Lower East Side and London's East End these new arrivals were competing overwhelmingly in just one sector, the clothing industry.

The specialization of the two Jewish immigrant economies was extreme. The clothing industry completely dominated the Jewish East End, employing around 70 per cent of the workforce. In New York's Lower East Side there was a similar bias to the garment industry with over 60 per cent employed in the clothing industry (Godley 1996a). The most common explanation for such an extreme concentration in the one industry owes little to the background of skills brought from Russia and far more to the very low start-up capital required in the clothing industry. The newly arrived immigrants in their search for new opportunities were constrained more by the almost complete absence of any asset base than a lack in the fairly basic skill levels required in most urban occupations at the time. The reason why the clothing industry rather than any other should have been characterized by such low entry costs follows from the recognition that where demand is volatile so the incentive to invest in greater amounts of fixed capital is reduced. This is because of the increased risk, when demand falls, of output falling below minimum efficient scale. This provided those manufacturers in the very seasonal clothing industry with a strong dis-incentive to increase fixed relative to variable costs. There were no great technological benefits from increasing the scale of operations when the dominant form of technology was the simple sewing machine, and so the optimum size of a clothing industry firm remained small. Thus, the barriers for new entrants remained low and it was this feature which explained its attraction to penniless Jewish immigrants. These features of the clothing industry remain to this day, especially in the very volatile womenswear sector (Waldinger 1986; Godley 1996b). Then, as now, what were normally fixed costs, typically in fixed plant and machinery, were transferred to a variable cost by purchasing sewing machines, pressing-irons and other fixtures through instalment schemes. All that was needed to start up a workshop, at least in theory, was therefore a small deposit on two sewing machines and a pressing table and the rent for a small workshop. With the typical firm so small, the organization of the industry needed to adapt. Subcontracting relations became very important as no single firm was able to complete an order on a successful design. As the industry grew so information on new designs and fabrics was pooled and quickly disseminated. Thus, a network of small firms grew very quickly, with many firms involved in single contracts, and yet no individual firm wanting to grow in size. Entry costs, therefore, remained very low.

Despite these relatively low start-up costs, the difficulty for prospective entrepreneurs from among the two Jewish immigrant communities was that even though the start-up costs might be very low, they were still beyond the scope of most immigrants' savings. The conventional response of entrepreneurs wanting to start up new businesses, but unable fully to fund the new venture from savings, is to borrow the rest. For prospective entrepreneurs needing to borrow but without any collateral to pledge as security it is invariably the case that the loan request is refused, even though the business venture may well succeed, such are the imperfections of the loans market and its intermediaries. The East European Jewish immigrants were faced with just such a credit market dilemma in turn of the century New York and London. Yet one of the striking features common to both cities' immigrant economies was the relatively efficient coordination of the credit market, despite the almost complete absence of collateral. The institutions which were developed by the two Jewish communities to resolve much of the credit gap were not banks, or any other formal lending agency. Nor were they informal networks of private lenders, but rather they were charities. These charitable lending institutions offered small, interest-free loans to entrepreneurs. They were the Jewish soft loan societies. They were able to extend credit to those who would otherwise have been denied it and so facilitated entrepreneurial entry into the immigrant trades. This section considers these two credit market inter-mediaries—the New York Hebrew Free Loan Society and the Loan Department of the London Jewish Board of Guardians—in more detail.

In New York, the Hebrew Free Loan Society was a product of immigrants meeting together and being moved by compassion to provide charitable help for fellow immigrants. Their model was the many free loan societies existing in their home countries in Eastern Europe. From very small beginnings in 1892 it became a highly successful source of venture capital in the Jewish immigrant community, styling itself the Poor Man's Bank. In London, the Loan Department of the Jewish Board of Guardians was slightly different. Its origins were in the already assimilated community of Anglo-Jewry, which had developed a distinctive philosophy of welfare. Despite these differences in philosophy, both institutions were able to maintain an astonishingly successful record as suppliers of credit to small Jewish clothing firms throughout the first half of the twentieth century (Black 1988; Godley 1996a; Lipman 1959; NYHFLS 1942; Tenenbaum 1986 and 1989).

These differences in philosophy and in the relationship with those they were trying to serve were apparent in the differences in the methods used by the two charities in allocating loans. The New York Society offered a generous screening mechanism (willing to lend unsecured small loans at a zero rate of interest to all-comers, providing they had the endorsement of other 'responsible' individuals) a sympathetic monitoring mechanism (relying on the borrower to bring weekly repayments to the office) and fairly lax enforcement—the only penalty to non-repayment was that access to further loans was denied.[4] The endorser was the key figure in the contract offered by the New York Society. He was staking his money and reputation within the community as the security for the loan. Should the borrower default it was the endorser who lost out. 'Of the borrower himself, the Society asks no questions, as to the reason for his loan, his reliability or his resources. It takes for granted that if responsible endorsers are willing to vouch for him, the risk should be taken' (NYHFLS 1942: 3). By contrast, the London Board forced the applicants to undergo a thorough investigation by the Loan Department. Evidence from the other branches of the Board's activities was taken as to their likely creditworthiness before the unsecured small loans were granted. The larger the loan the more thorough the vetting. The Board 'insisted on repayments wherever possible', and so implemented a rigorous control mechanism of monitoring and enforcing the loans, employing collectors to go to recipients and extract a weekly payment of one shilling in the pound (Lipman 1959: 121).

Both intermediaries were enormously successful in providing credit to the rapidly growing immigrant garment industries. The volume of loans increased dramatically in both communities and the majority of borrowed working capital held by Jewish firms came from these two institutions, especially in the form of initial payments for sewing machines. The impact of new and improved sewing machine technology on the clothing industry has been calculated elsewhere and estimates of productivity growth suggest that this was the period of the greatest gains in efficiency in the British and American clothing industries, and that this was mostly associated with the Jewish firms which in both cities dominated the rapidly growing womenswear sector (Godley 1995 and 1996c).

The differences in these two institutions were, in effect, marginal. As the structure of the two clothing industries changed so, it would appear, the soft loan societies were able to support the growing Jewish immigrant presence in the industry. Perhaps, the best indicator of the effectiveness of any lending agency is its default rate. This measures the proportion of the total volume of loans not repaid. The default rate is a good indicator of the effectiveness of a lending agency because it gives some sort of measure of the efficiency of the credit extended. The lower the default rate, the higher the proportion of loans successfully repaid and, by implication, the greater productivity of the capital lent. Conversely, the higher the default rate the lower the proportion repaid of total funds lent, indicating that borrowers were either unable to repay—owing to an unsuccessful investment—or unwilling—owing to dishonesty or opportunistic behaviour. It is, of course, the potential for moral hazard or other forms of opportunistic behaviour which prompts lending agencies to insist on such high levels of collateral. Where collateral is non-existent and interest rates are kept low, banks and other lending agencies often face very high default rates. Recent examples in Britain and in the Third World show that lending institutions facing these constraints have experienced default rates as high as 40 per cent.[5] The default rate for the New York Society, by contrast, was reckoned as being negligible. Almost invariably borrowers repaid. In only 2 per cent of cases was it necessary to apply to the endorsers to repay the loan. The final default rate was between one-tenth and one-half of 1 per cent of the annual volume of loans, or 'almost infinitesimal' (NYHFLS 1942: 4). The London

Board had a slightly higher default rate of 3.75 per cent in the early 1880s (which included some administration costs, though), but even this fell to a 'trifling 2.5 per cent' by 1905 (Black 1988: 94).

These very low default rates experienced by the two Jewish soft loan societies need explaining. Given the absence of complete information, much of what follows must be somewhat tentative, but the outlines of an initial explanation can be made clear. Ordinarily, a low default rate suggests a similarly low bankruptcy rate. If this was in fact the case then these Jewish immigrant entrepreneurs in London and New York would indeed have acted atypically. However, recourse to bankruptcy implies that there is some value in the firm's fixed assets for which creditors may be able to appeal. In the case of very small firms with, as has been emphasized above, very low levels of fixed capital, this was an unlikely development. These businesses could and did fail. But failure implied the inability to cover running costs and so inactivity might be temporary only. With some clothing workshops having to shut down, even temporarily during lean seasons, the repayment of any outstanding loans would have been threatened. Yet the soft loan societies were able to maintain very low levels of defaulting.

This may be thought to represent a vindication of the two charities' screening, monitoring and enforcing mechanisms. The London Board, to be sure, had a higher default rate that the New York Society, despite incorporating much more costly and rigorous procedures, but importantly the New York Society made perhaps better use of information generated by the network of Jewish garment firms. The low default rates may also reflect a willingness within the Jewish community and, in particular, within the network of Jewish garment firms, to accept mutual obligations and so to build in increasing bonds of trust within the lending process. The motivation behind the establishment of both institutions was, after all, an acknowledgement of intracommunal ties. These had a long history in the Jewish culture. The loans' zero rate of interest followed the Biblical injunction against usury, for instance. Even though the two charities had different philosophies, the much longer tradition of giving and receiving soft loans would tend to minimize the temptation to default falsely. Repeated transactions have the effect of reducing the incentive to cheat and so increase trust. The New York Society explicitly traded on intra-communal trust with its emphasis on the personal guarantee of the endorser, a feature which may partly explain the extraordinarily low default rate there. Certainly the testimonies of participants in Jewish immigrant small businesses commonly refer to the importance of easy lines of credit and how these were always available within the community. Within the Jewish immigrant communities there was a culture of trust, where lenders trusted borrowers not to default and overwhelmingly were right to do so.

It was not culture alone, however, which led to such low default rates. Development economists concerned with similar problems of extending credit to those without collateral, but in today's less developed economies, have focused on designing certain features of the loan contract in order to counter moral hazard and to increase the incentives to repay the loan. Features which appear to be important are to insist that repayments are made in regular instalments and that access to further loans is dependent upon the successful completion of any earlier loan. Both the New York Society and the London Board made regular collections, but perhaps the very low default rates experienced by these two societies can best be explained by the second feature emphasized by development economists, the restriction of future loans until outstanding ones are repaid. The possible importance of this feature of the loan contract relates to the reason why the loans were so important in the first place. The loans were important to aspiring entrepreneurs, who, with their very low capitalization, were restricted to entering those sectors with very low entry costs. Clothing was, therefore, one such industry because of its seasonality. The volatility of demand over the year contributed to the small optimum size of workshop. This very volatility of demand also led to the high probability of having to shut down the workshop. Entrepreneurs having experienced self-employment but having had to shut down may have wished to re-enter the market, and any barrier to their subsequent re-entry needed to be minimized. For that portion of the Jewish clothing entrepreneurs who depended on soft loans for their entry and re-entry into the market, the probability of needing an additional loan for subsequent re-entry would provide a powerful incentive to repay all outstanding loans.

At the heart of the problem facing small firms seeking access to credit are the costs associated with imperfect information. In many markets these transactions costs are internalized and the optimum size of firm increases. In the garment industry the nature of fashion-led demand is that the market becomes too volatile for any kind of additional investment beyond the technological imperative, and so firms remain small. In order to remain efficient compared to a single-integrated firm, these small firms need to adopt network-type relations within industrial districts. These small firms face all of the hazards of credit rationing and so represent an excellent case to study the claims of competing credit market intermediaries. Recent research of the present-day clothing industry has emphasized its ethnic bias, but the interpretation is almost solely in terms of ethnic exclusion from the general labour market. Nonetheless, this recent work has also discovered that revolving credit institutions abound within the ethnic enclaves of the various niches of the clothing industry. This example of the earlier Jewish dominated garment industries of London and New York suggest that the development of such innovative credit market inter-mediaries, like the soft loan societies, were in part responsible for the astonishing success of the Jewish clothing industries, which in turn sponsored the meteoric upward social mobility enjoyed by the second and subsequent generations of these communities in the two host nations.

The interpretation suggested here emphasizes the volatility of the industry and the importance of a high-trust culture. The volatility of demand imposed a constraint on the optimum firm size which in turn led to garment-industry networks in industrial districts. Immigrant entre-preneurs had no collateral and were denied bank finance. The response within the Jewish clothing industries was successfully to develop soft loan societies. However, their success was made possible, first, by the common recognition that individual and community interests were enmeshed. This gave the cultural context where opportunistic behaviour was minimized and trust enhanced. Second, in the volatile environment of the clothing industry every firm had a fairly high probability of needing extra working capital and not having collateral to fall back on. This gave a strong incentive to repay all past loans—non-payment of these was the principal barrier to future loans—and, additionally a strong incentive to contribute to the capital bases of the soft loan societies. They represented a very cheap and effective form of insurance. In this way the liquidity of the entire system grew, allocative efficiency increased and, consequently, total welfare enhanced.

There were additional costs, however, which this system imposed on its borrowers. As time progressed and the two garment-producing centres developed, so these costs increased. For example, the absence of bank-imposed financial self-discipline may well have been a substantial organizational opportunity cost for some of these small subcontracting firms once they had become established. The Jewish garment producers were legendary for the absence of proper internal accounting and control mechanisms (Godley 1997a; Kershen 1997). Increasingly from the 1950s and 1960s these two local industries began to contract and entrepreneurial entry began to decline (Godley 1997b). In effect these soft loan societies were coming to the end of their useful lives. Once the socio-economic context had changed, and the demand for entrepreneurial entry into the garment trades among the Jewish immigrant communities diminished, so the benefits of small soft loan societies were reduced. They operate today only as branches of communal welfare agencies.

The implications for policy-makers are not straightforward. There is, partly, a concurrence with the recent calls for an increase in the role of the informal venture capital market to facilitate start-ups; moreover, this research underlines the importance of incorporating certain essential features within loan contracts to encourage repayment and discourage opportunistic behaviour among the population of start-up entrepreneurs. However, it is emphasized here that opportunism was minimized by two factors: the peculiar characteristics of the clothing industry (and so the additional incentives to repay loans above and beyond those in the loan contracts); and the importance of a high-trust culture. For networks of small firms to be more efficient than a single integrated firm coordinating the same activities through heirarchy, a high-trust culture is essential to minimize the risk of contractual default between the different parties within the network. The problem with this conclusion is that any policy attempting to increase the trust content of a culture would appear to be fraught with difficulty and, moreover, it is not obvious that the agency best able to pursue such a goal is a national government.

Notes

1 This article has benefited from the contributions of participants at the EMOT conference at Modena. My thanks to all concerned. The usual disclaimer applies, however.
2 The information-driven view of financial intermediation is derived from Leland and Pyle (1977) and Diamond (1984).
3 For a survey see Godley and Ross (1996).
4 The details of the loan contract offered by the New York Hebrew Free Loan Society are from NYHFLS (1942) ch. 4, pp. 18–25. Also Tenenbaum (1989), pp. 215.
5 See Ross (1996), where examples are given of the Loan Guarantee Scheme of the 1980s, which experienced a default rate as high as 40 per cent, and the Development Areas Treasury Advisory Committee, with a default rate of 15 per cent. For the Third World see the World Bank's list of known lending agencies, which had an average default rate of 40 per cent, in its Lending Policy Paper on Agricultural Credit (1975).

Bibliography

Black, E. (1988) *The Social Politics of Anglo-Jewry 1880–1970*, Oxford: Oxford University Press.
Brusco, S. (1980) 'The Emilian model: productive decentralization and social integration', *Cambridge Journal of Economics*, 6.
Diamond, D. W. (1984) 'Financial intermediation and delegated monitoring', *Review of Economic Studies*, 51.
Godley, A. (1995) 'The development of the UK clothing industry, 1850–1950: output and productivity growth', *Business History*, 37.
Godley, A. (1996a) 'Jewish soft loan societies in New York and London and immigrant entrepreneurship, 1880–1914', *Business History*, 38.
Godley, A. (1996b) 'Immigrant entrepreneurs and the emergence of London's East End as an industrial district', *London Journal*, 21.
Godley A. (1996c), 'Singer in Britain: the diffusion of sewing machine technology and its impact on the clothing industry in the United Kingdom, 1860–1905', *Textile History*, 27.
Godley, A. (1997a) 'Comparative labour productivity in the American and British clothing industries, 1850–1950', *Textile History*, 28.
Godley, A. (1997b) 'The development of the clothing industry: technology and fashion', *Textile History*, 28.
Godley, A. and Ross, D. (eds) (1996) *Banks, Networks and Small Firm Finance*, London: Cass.
Kershen, A. (1997) 'Morris Cohen and the origins of the women's wholesale clothing industry in the East End', *Textile History*, 28.
Leland, H. E. and Pyle, D. H. (1977) 'Information asymmetries, financial structure and financial intermediation', *Journal of Finance*, 32.

Lipman, V. (1959) *A Century of Social Service, 1859–1959: The History of the Jewish Board of Guardians*, London: Routledge.

Mason, C. and Harrison, R. 'Informal Venture Capital in the UK', in A.Hughes and D.Storey (eds), *Finance and the Small Firm*, London: Routledge.

New York Hebrew Free Loan Society (NYHFLS) (1942), *The Poor Man's Bank: The Story of Fifty Years of Loans Without Interest*, New York: privately published.

Piore, M. J. and Sabel, C. F. (1984) *The Second Industrial Divide: Possibilities for Prosperity*, New York: Basic Books.

Ross, D. (1996) 'The unsatisfied fringe in Britain, 1930s-80s', *Business History*, 38.

Stiglitz, J. E. and Weiss A. (1981), 'Credit rationing in markets with imperfect information,' *American Economic Review*, 71.

Stiglitz, J. E. (1987) 'The causes and consequences of the dependence of quality on price', *Journal of Economic Literature*, XXV.

Stiglitz, J. E. and Weiss, A. (1990) 'Banks as social accountants and screening devices for the allocation of credit', *Greek Economic Review*, 12.

Tenenbaum, S. (1986) 'Immigrants and capital: Jewish loan societies in the United States, 1880–1940', unpublished Ph.D. thesis, Brandeis University.

Tenenbaum, S. (1989) 'Culture and context: the emergence of Hebrew free loan societies in the United States', *Social Science History*, 13.

Waldinger, R. (1986) *Through the Eye of the Needle: Immigrants and Enterprise in New York's Garment Trades*, New York: Basic Books.

Williamson, O. E. (1985) *The Economic Institutions of Capitalism: Firms, Markets, Relational Contracting*, London: Routledge.

11 The dark side of dense networks

From embeddedness to indebtedness[1]

Giuseppe Soda and Alessandro Usai

Introduction

It is often emphasized that economic life is a part of social life, to which it is bound by the norms, rules, moral obligations and other uses and customs that together make up what we call 'society'; it is therefore profoundly rooted in society, and its analysis cannot be separated from that of the (formal and tacit) values and rules governing the way in which society works.

As long ago as 1922, Max Weber highlighted the relationship between the 'cultural' artefacts of modern societies (such as religions and ideologies) and their economic behaviour. The behaviour of all economic players, including companies, is conditioned by a large number of factors, not the least of which is a 'moral' component that is expressed by conforming to a set of rules that the social system—or one of its parts—has defined as 'legitimate'. It is widely recognized that the attempt to achieve economic results is accompanied by something non-economic, such as sociability, approval or power, (Granovetter 1992: 25); economic activity is embedded in an intricate network of relationships of various kinds, content and extent.

Many authors have shown interest in the various configurations of cooperative relational structures and underlined their comparative advantages of flexibility, learning, rapidity and efficiency.[2] From a theoretical perspective, other authors have emphasized the emergence of a new form of organizational coordination—the network—as an alternative to the concepts of market and hierarchy (Powell 1990). In this new organizational form, the idea of *embeddedness* (Granovetter 1985) finds its natural home. In fact, the network concept provides a means of overcoming the dichotomous market/hierarchy view in which (as Powell said referring to Richardson 1972) 'firms are islands of planned co-ordination in a sea of market relations'. Starting from this initial stimulus, researchers started to concentrate on identifying when and how the effects of embeddedness make themselves felt.

One of the main findings has been that relationships can be seen as an asset, with economic effects. If we look at these relationships from the point of view of the individual actors, they can generally be seen as representing a type of capital inside the different competitive arenas. This has been defined as 'social capital' and, unlike financial and human capital, it is not the property of the individual players but jointly owned by the various parties involved in the relationships: 'no one player has exclusive ownership rights to social capital' (Burt 1992: 9). Social capital allows an organizational player to transform human and financial capital into profit (Granovetter 1985), and so competition and the market therefore have a 'social side'.

However, in this paper we propose to adopt the term 'relational capital' instead of 'social capital', considering that this concept should include not only the social relationships but also the formal and transactional ones. We believe that it would be more appropriate to speak of the *relational structure of competition*. Regardless of their social or transactional nature, these 'relationships' represent links between organizational players that are based on cooperation rather than competition. The set of cooperative linkages among firms represent an important form of capital that we call *relational capital*.

We also argue that traditionally the argument of embeddedness and the related concept of social capital have been usually accompanied by an implicit positive value judgement: social embeddedness is expected to lower transaction costs and to facilitate exchange. Despite this diffused attitude, some authors have hilighted the possible costs and liabilities of embeddedness (Grabher 1993; Burt 1992).

In this paper we would like to highlight some of the costs and negative effects that may be associated with a dense interorganizational network. It is clear that relational structures lead to imperfect competition, by creating entrepreneurial opportunities and advantages for certain players and not for others; we would like to describe how, under certain conditions, the web of relationships between competitors may actually create negative externalities, inefficiency and merely ephimeral advantages for the participants in the long term.

In order to explain this argument we considered the economic activities of a group of competitors—the Italian general contractors in the construction industry—and we analysed the network of relationships existing between them in the light of some basic hypotheses:

- when cooperative relationships involve a large number of competitors, it leads to a web of reciprocal obligations that represents the main entry barrier to a competitive niche;
- a large and dense network of horizontal relationships is the main determinant of the economic behaviour of the involved players, and profoundly conditions their attributes;
- the relational capital existing between companies competing in the

same niche is only profitable to the extent that the environment is munificent or places pressure on counterparts external to the niche;
- a large and dense network of horizontal relationships leads to negative externalities.

In the following pages we summarize the debate on embeddedness and we conclude trying to highlight the differences between the embeddedness concept and the relational capital concept.

Embeddedness: forms, assets and liabilities

Over the last ten years, the debate concerning the embeddedness (Granovetter 1985) of economic relationships has taken on considerable impetus. Breaking away from some of the major assumptions previously underlying economic theory, the concept of embeddedness has underlined the extent to which social (and subsequently other) relationships affect the economic relationships and behaviours of individuals and organizations.

The environment has always provided examples of long-standing economic relationships based on parallel or sometimes pre-existing social relationships. In many of these cases, the hypotheses concerning the nature of individual economic behaviour that are typical of classical, neoclassical and what Granovetter calls 'new institutional' economics (in particular, the school of transactional cost analysis) have been found to provide inadequate explanations of the observed phenomena.

In particular, the hypotheses concerning the utilitarianism or opportunism of human nature (Williamson 1975) do not seem to justify the existence or functioning of relational structures such as the frequently studied industrial districts (see Lazerson 1995; Dei Ottati 1994; Crewe 1996).

Granovetter (1985) initially used the argument of embeddedness as the foundation of a structural theory of economic behaviour. However, the first conceptual differentiation (White 1981; Burt 1982) was between structural approaches to the explanation of companies' economic behaviour and the atomistic explanations typical of the economists of the classical, neoclassical and neoinstitutional schools. The idea that many economic phenomena can be better understood by adopting a relational or structural interpretation, rather than by considering individuals or dyads of players, represents maybe the most revolutionary principle of all network theory. The social or institutional relationships of companies stop being considered frictional elements impeding perfect competition, and become the key to the interpretation of 'markets' that are actually nothing of the kind. Granovetter (1985) said that the argument of (social) embeddedness could be translated by the statement: 'the behavior and institutions to be analyzed are so constrained by ongoing social relations that to construe them as independent is a grievous misunderstanding'.

Forms of Embeddedness

Four different forms of embeddedness have been classified (Zukin and Di Maggio 1990): (1) *structural embeddedness*, which concerns the structure and quality of intercompany social ties and has been explored in studies aimed at verifying its economic effects on network-related companies and the position of these companies within the networks (Uzzi 1996); (2) *cognitive embeddedness*, which concerns the structured mental processes directing economic logic; (3) *cultural embeddedness*, which concerns the shared beliefs and values that shape economic aims; and (4) *political embeddedness*, which concerns the institutional limits on economic power and incentives. Although the last three categories refer to the concept of embeddedness in terms of a context affecting economic relationships in one way or another, the first comes closer to the structural conception of economic analysis (White 1981; Burt 1982): 'the type of network in which an organisation is embedded defines the opportunities potentially available; its position in that structure and the types of interfirm ties it maintains define access to those opportunities' (Uzzi 1996).

These beginnings led to the study of some of the economic phenomena that can typically be analysed in network terms, especially industrial districts and other types of company aggregates participating in and supported by a network of social or formal ties of various kinds.

In particular, much attention has been given to the effects of networks on the performances of companies and small industrial systems, the results of which have mostly been oriented to demonstrate that social embeddedness offers a competitive advantage to the participants in the network or to the industrial system itself.

For example, a large number of case studies of the industrial districts in Emilia Romagna (Brusco 1982; Lazerson 1988; Pyke, Beccatini and Sengenberger 1990) bear witness to the fact that, particularly for small and medium-sized companies, a network is not only capable of replacing the hierarchy in managing the relationships of economic exchange, but also manages to excel in terms of the effectiveness of the management of production activities—as in the case of the use of putting out systems (Lazerson 1993).

It has also been observed that network relations in industrial districts are sustained by factors that are typical of social embeddedness, such as esteem, solidarity, trust and non-opportunistic behaviour (Crewe 1996). All of these elements are thought to contribute towards creating the premises for the formation of a group of production enterprises that is not only highly integrated (more as a result of social rather than formal mechanisms), but also highly flexible, because each maintains a high degree of managerial autonomy and is formally responsible for its own results. In brief, it leads to a highly effective and organizationally flexible situation that has the advantages of a system without the disadvantages of a hierarchy.

If we return to the classification of embeddedness proposed by Zukin and Di Maggio, we can see that the concept of social embeddedness does not cover all of the possible forms of relation among actors in the economic environment: the literature also contains references to political embeddedness, institutional embeddedness and environmental embeddedness. Some researchers have underlined the fact that 'the environments . . . penetrate the organization, creating the lenses through which actors view the world and the very categories of structure, action and thought' (Di Maggio and Powell 1991, quoted in Halliday, Granfors and Powell 1993). Furthermore, from this point of view, a state's regulatory function is seen as playing and important role in legitimizing organizations. Other researchers have defined institutionl embeddedness as a level of connection between a population of organizations and the surrounding institutional environment, quantifying it in terms of *relational density*, or rather *the number of formal relations between the members of a population and key institutions in the environment* (Baum and Oliver 1991). It has also been claimed that a high degree of institutional embeddedness significantly increases the probability of survival and success of an organization in an environment in which institutions are capable of granting legitimacy and the access to resources.

We would add that, if what has been said above is true, the assessment of the effects of institutional embeddedness cannot be limited to identifying existing institutional ties, but must also consider the weight that these institutions have in conditioning the economic environment in question. In other words, there is a big difference between the institutional embeddedness of a company closely connected to public institutions in an economic environment in which these institutions have little effect on economic behaviour, and that of the same company in an environment in which such institutions influence economic behaviour to a large extent. Looked at in this light, the concept of institutional embeddedness makes it possible to include market regulation in the more general notion of embeddedness that we intend to adopt here. In other words, market regulation becomes one of the measures of the embeddedness (in this case *institutional*) of an economic system. The market is in fact the second theoretical dimension of our case study, which is an attempt to apply the logical dimensions of embeddedness to an entire economic system represented by the Italian construction industry.

The literature still contains only a few examples of attempts to use the concept of embeddedness at an industry and institutional level. These include the theoretical reflections of Harrison White, who sustains that every market is in reality a *social mechanism* (or network), and that every economy is an input/output network of markets. As a result, he thinks that every market should be looked at in terms of the two fundamental networks of production and exchange. Although White does not refer explicitly to social embeddedness or make a structural analysis of a specific single market, he does consider the market in network terms and defines it as a social construction (White 1993).

Furthermore, in the wake of structural thought, Granovetter has at various times pointed out that markets and industrial sectors are embedded to such an extent that their evolution does not depend upon the typical dynamics of competition, but on the relational dynamics of the players. In this sense, the current structure of the United States electricity industry (a series of large private companies, rather than one large public company or the fragmentation of electricity production among the leading national companies) is due to the fact that it was co-determined by some players who had particularly rich social relationships in key sectors of the economy (Granovetter 1992).

Cost and liabilities of embeddednes: a double-edged sword

As we have seen so far, the argument of embeddednes has often been surrounded of a 'positive flavour'.

Although economists first tended to consider embeddedness as something that was somehow 'dirtying' and only capable of muddying the crystal-clear waters of the market, the situation has been reversed over recent years—and the rediscovery of embeddedness has led to its almost unanimous acceptance as a positive factor.

The possible less desirable effects of a high degree of social embeddedness have been investigated more rarely, although it has been pointed out that it can bring with it all of the problems typical of culturally cohesive environments, such as a lack of innovation and conformist economic behaviour (Grabher 1993). However, such observations remain marginal in the strong current interest surrounding industrial districts which has even affected organizational researchers, sociologists, industrial economists and economic geographers.

Starting from the traditional concepts at the base of the embeddedness argument, in this chapter we would like to stress two different points. On the one hand we analyse a different kind of unfavourable effects, with a particular attention to the bad effects induced to the economic system. In order to do so we have to introduce the case of the construction industry in Italy. The following pages are dedicated to this issue. In addition, we try to go beyond the traditional argument of embeddednes introducing the concept of relational capital (and relational embeddedness) as a broader explanation of many economic phenomena. The relational capital can be analysed at two different levels: at the level of the single firm and at the level of the network. Each of these can help us in understanding the case study. This argument is developed in the next paragraphs.

The case of the Italian construction industry: from embeddedness to indebtedness

General description

The aim of this study is to analyse the network of relationships involving the forty-nine largest construction companies operating in Italy, concentrating on those which are in competition with each other in the 'niche' of state-financed civil works. The dynamics of this competition has been reconstructed longitudinally in order to highlight the effect of some of the profound transformations taking place in Italy between 1992 and 1996.

A preliminary analysis of the sector raises a large number of research questions concerning its particular characteristics. Why do the largest Italian companies appear to be much smaller, less diversified and less profitable than their European counterparts? Why is the level of competition between them incapable of ensuring a high level of efficiency? Why is there such widespread recourse to cooperation between formally competitive companies, and what forms does this cooperation take? What are the reasons driving these companies to cooperate with each other? What are the structural characteristics of this network of cooperation? What are the implications of this cooperation in terms of the efficiency, managerial capacity and innovativeness of the companies themselves? What are the consequences of this cooperation in terms of the efficiency of the sector as a whole and the cost of its works?

In 1980, Porter claimed that the essence of the formulation of a competitive strategy lies in relating a company to its environment (the market sector or niche in which it competes), whose structural characteristics are determined by the definition of the 'rules of the game'; he also said that the intensity of competition is rooted in the underlying economic structure of the sector itself. Using Porter's model, we first analysed the competitive arena in which Italian general contractors operate (see Table 11.1).

In particular, the intensity of competition is low because of the low level of concentration, a situation in which competitive uncertainty is known to have less effect (Pfeffer and Salancik 1978): under conditions of competitive uncertainty, interorganizational relationships (be they tacit or formalized in written agreements) make it possible to stabilize the environment and establish conditions that are more favourable for the companies.

Table 11.1 Porter's five forces model applied to the construction industry in Italy

Forces	Value
Suppliers' contractual power	LOW
Threat of new entrants	LOW
Threat of replacement products	LOW
Purchasers' contractual power	MEDIUM
Level of competition inside the sector	LOW

Competitive uncertainty and the degree of competition are factors that are generally associated with the processes of deregulation (Lang and Lockhart 1990), which give rise to what can be described as environmental 'shocks' and are capable of profoundly modifying even interorganizational company strategies (Aldrich 1979; Astley 1984; Pennings 1981). During the course of the year in which we began this study, no deregulation process was under way in the Italian construction industry: on the contrary, the dynamics of competition in the sector were embedded in a highly complex and articulated system of regulation. The Italian construction industry is much more regulated by state law than that of other countries (Soda and Usai 1995). Furthermore, the competitive niche in which we are interested here involves such a large number of companies that any increase in relational capital would be very expensive: 'the capacity of "n" organisations to communicate with each other is inversely related to the value of "n". The number of links necessary to ensure the complete interconnection of a network of 'n' organisations is $n * (n-1)/2$: if two organisations are involved, only one link is necessary; but the complete connection of ten organisations requires 45 links. Consequently, the feasibility of developing an inter-company organisation increases if there are fewer companies to coordinate' (Pfeffer and Salancik 1978: 156). Pfeffer and Salancik have also calculated that the number of intercompany links created by means of joint ventures and interlocking directorates is a function of the number of companies and the degree of competitive uncertainty measured by means of the level of concentration in the sector.

Under these conditions, we expected that the relational capital of the companies would have little weight in the acquisition and defence of competitive advantages (Pfeffer and Salancik 1978)—but, as we shall see, we were wrong.

The formal relational capital in the construction industry: the network of consortia

The cooperative relationships considered in this investigation are those represented by consortia. There is a type of coordination among Italian construction companies, the purpose of which is to ensure collaboration for the execution of one or more projects. These consortia are bureaucratic interorganizational networks, generally formalized by means of contractual agreements (Grandori and Soda 1995), and may also be associated in *joint programmes* (Oliver 1990): that is, formalized collaborative agreements relating to a well-defined project (although this is not a matter of exchange but associative relationships). As Boje and Whetten remark, we have also borne in mind the fact that joint programs are 'linkage strategies that can be used to increase the centrality of the organizations' network and the influence attributed to these organizations by other agencies in a network'

(Oliver 1990: 255). Finally, in the construction industry, these consortia are directly involved in the core business of the individual companies.[3]

Network analysis: properties and first structural findings

Our dataset consists of the structural and attributive variables relating to the individual nodes that represent the most important consortia involving the forty-nine largest Italian private, state-controlled and cooperative public works contractors. Nodes are the firms; relations are the number of consortia connecting two nodes. We constructed a 49*49 adjacency matrix in which cell Aij was set equal to 1 whenever company I and company J were bound by one cooperative relations represented, in our case, by consortia; of course, if the companies I and J were bound by ten consortia the Aij value was 10.

The logical reason for restricting the sample to largest firms was the fact that they are 'general contractors', and therefore represent a population within the universe of contractors. These firms compete in the national arena of constructions financed by the state and other public institutions. We compiled our data from a variety of construction-industry directorates; the most important was *Costruire* an annual directory in which are published the data about the Italian construction industry. Data on consortia are collected by *Costruire* directly from the firms. We checked the data with interviews of managers of the firms and we compared data with those available at the Ministry of Public Works.

Network properties

*   Transactional content: construction consortia are bureaucratic inter-company organizations that are generally association-interdependent and dedicated to joint works (Grandori and Soda 1995). They therefore do not represent a goods, service or information transaction, nor an exchange of affect, influence or power (Tichy, Tushman and Fombrum 1979; Mitchell 1969).
*   Nature of the links: all of the public construction we shall be considering here are large and the vast majority were developed by consortia. Consortia therefore represent the most important mode of awarding and executing the companies' distinctive activity of constructing, and their economic fortunes (and often their very survival) depend on the good functioning of this relationship, repeated for each work in progress. In our dataset—a matrix 49*49—each pair shows a value linkage ranging from 0 to the number of consortia in which the two firms take part. Consequently we can affirm that the final linkage resulting between two nodes also includes information about frequency and strength. The very nature of the consortia relationship means that the relational data measuring it are not 'reputational' (that is, they do

not depend in any way on the players' perceptions or judgements), but only depend on the effective existence of the consortium linkage itself. This last aspect also explains why this linkage is associative and non-directive, a factor that determines the reciprocity of the relationship and its matricial symmetry.[4]

- Structural characteristics: Figure 11.1 shows the network of relationships as these emerge from their visual examination. Although even this simple graphical analysis highlights many aspects of the breadth and diffusion of these cooperative ties, which are very frequent between these companies despite the fact that they are theoretically competing in the same niche, we shall here try to understand some of the structural properties of the network. Not only is it very large (forty-nine nodes), it is also highly interconnected. Before looking at the data in detail, it is worth understanding that this reconstruction does not derive from the collection of all of the consortia in which the forty-nine companies are involved, but from one of their sample. The first interesting aspect is that the network does not present any *isolated nodes*. Our first elaboration describes the forty-nine-firm group as a single *connected component*. Moreover, there are no *isolated sub-groups*: i.e. there are no *sub-graphs* inside which the companies collaborate, but which do not present linkages with other sub-groups. Starting from any node, it is always possible to reach any of the others. This absence of isolated nodes shows that each firm shares relational capital with another competitor. Furthermore, the absence of isolated sub-groups highlights the fact that the entire competitive niche as a whole represents a single relational environment: there are no variables (such as geographical location, for example) that are capable of determining relational sub-environments distinct from that of the niche, and the fact that the whole sector can be represented as a single relational set leads two considerations: company relational capital; network relational capital.

Company relational capital

Every company has some relational capital, which consists of its joint relationships with the others and can be measured by means of centrality indicators. Centrality can be measured in different ways; research on social network analysis suggests that each measure of centrality is associated with a different interpretation. An organization's degree of centrality is simply the number of other organizations to which the focal organization is tied. Degree is usually considered as a measure of an actor's involvement in a network (Freeman 1979). However, the level of connectivity is so high in our case that it leads to a single relational set, and so the most appropriate measure of the relational capital of the individual companies is 'betweeness centrality', which is recognized as being a measure of the power of

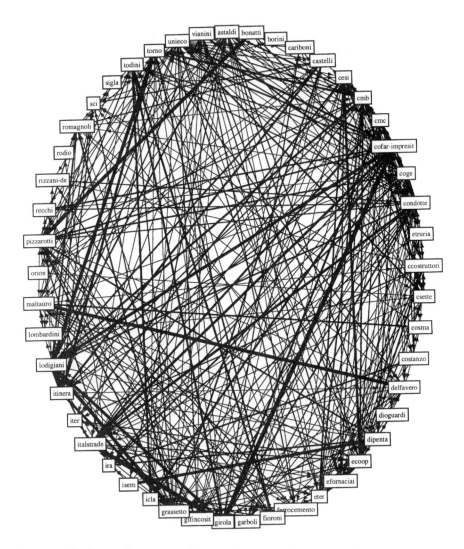

Figure 11.1 The whole network of consortia among Italian general contractors

Table 11.2 Betweeness centrality of Italian general contractors

Betweeness centrality	Dichotomized centrality	Normalized centrality
Mean	19.88	0.0176
Standard Deviation	22.40	0.0199
Centralization	—	8.24%

mediation or brokerage (Marsden 1982). The basic idea is that the power of mediation in a network having these characteristics is more important than the absolute number of cooperative ties, which represents the basis for calculating the measure of 'degree centrality'. Our observations show that the power of mediation is normally distributed among Italian general construction companies, and so there are no substantial differences in relational capital inside the network. The *normalized betweenness* of a firm is a ratio that measures the extent to which a firm in a network approaches the betweenness score of a *star* (Freeman 1979). An organization's relative betweenness can vary from a minimum of 0, when it lies on no geodesics, to maximum of 1, when the organization is, in fact, a star. The aggregate data relating to this measure is shown in Table 11.2.

The measure of betweeness centrality provides the important indication that the average power of mediation of the players is low, and this is supported by the *index of centralization*. In our case, this index measures the range of variability of the betweeness indices among the individual players, since it includes the comparison of the index of each player with the maximum value reached by the same in the group. This index reaches the maximum value of 1 (expressed as 100 per cent), which means that the reality we are looking at is close to a 'peer group network': that is, a round table at which everybody sits without the need of the mediation of someone else to ensure the circulation and exchange of information. In the network of Italian general construction companies, the index of centralization is 8.24 per cent.

Ronald Burt maintains the thesis that social capital makes it possible to transform financial and human capital into profits; we propose the more extended idea of social capital represented by relational capital. If we look at the relationship existing between a company's performance and its relational capital—measured by means of centrality measures—the correlations illustrated in Figure 11.2 emerge:

The data relating to turnover and profits have been taken from published annual reports and must therefore be considered with caution. Nevertheless, the data relating to the economic value of the portfolio of acquired orders also show the same relationship to turnover. We have found that our conception of relational capital more closely approximates betweenness centrality than either valued or dichotomized degree centrality.[5] A small difference was found in the correlation with turnover,

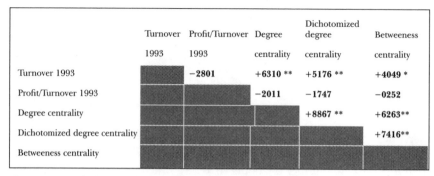

	Turnover 1993	Profit/Turnover 1993	Degree centrality	Dichotomized degree centrality	Betweeness centrality
Turnover 1993		−2801	+6310 **	+5176 **	+4049 *
Profit/Turnover 1993			−2011	−1747	−0252
Degree centrality				+8867 **	+6263**
Dichotomized degree centrality					+7416**
Betweeness centrality					

Figure 11.2 Relationship between performance and relational capital

Note: One-tailed significance: $* = 0.01$; $** = 0.001$.

even though the three measures all closely correlated with each other. The correlation between degree centrality and turnover is inevitable because a company with greater value participates in a larger number of consortia and therefore has a larger turnover. The correlation between betweeness centrality and turnover is slightly less and less statistically significant.

Network relational capital

The network of general enterprises also has its own relational capital, which is represented by the strength of its connectivity and is expressed towards the outside. We maintain that: *the greater the connectivity of the network of relationships, and the wider and more balanced the network itself (the absence of sub-groups or coalitions), the greater the amount of relational capital available to all of the companies of the network.*

As pointed out above, relational capital is never possessed by individual players but belongs to a relational set of at least minimal dimensions: that is, a dyad. The size and connectivity of the relational set of Italian general contractors, and the absence of any strong positions of dominance, lead to the creation of substantial relational capital at the level of the network—as can be presumed from its structural properties. In the first place, the diagram illustrating the interorganizational linkages among the members of the network is tightly coupled: the entire industry of general construction contractors, without any exception, can be represented as a consortia network (see Figure 11.1). We can assume that the degree of network connectivity could be considered as a *proxi* of the network relational capital. The density analysis, defined as the connection among the quantity of linkages present in the network, in comparison to the quantity of all possible linkages (Tichy, Tushman and Fombrum 1979; Wasserman and Faust 1994). The density can be expressed with different shades and it represents in our case the starting point of all our more analytic considerations.

Network density

The density of a network is the ratio of the number of ties that exist to the number of possible ties. There are two ways of measuring relational density in our type of dataset: one applies to the 'valued' matrix (with values of 0–12 being attributed to the crossings between nodes); the other to the 'dichotomized' matrix, which simply considers the absence (=0) or presence (=1) of a linkage between nodes. In our case, the 'valued' density of the Italian construction industry is 0.54, which seems to be a very high value when we bear in mind that a 49×49 matrix involves 2,401 crossings.

The 'dichotomized' density measure, which considers only the presence or absence of a linkage without any reference to its intensity value (Borgatti, Everett and Freeman 1992), is more interesting since it can be compared: the dichotomized density in our case is 0.29, which means that there are 29 linkages out of a possible 100. Given that it derives from a sample of the total number of consortia in the industry, this value is once again extremely high. In this respect, it is worth remembering that an analysis of ten kinds of cooperative agreements in the biotechnology industry (Barley, Freeman and Hybels 1991) indicated a density ranged from 0.00004 (4 for every 100,000 possible ties) for the grant network to 0.0005 (5 for every 10,000 possible ties) for equity network. It is true that this was based on a much larger sample, and it is logical to expect that network density exponentially decreases with the increase of node's number; but we should not underestimate the enormous difference observed by us, nor the fact that we have analysed just a small part of the existing consortia relationships—we put in our dataset about 35 per cent of the total consortia relationships existing among the forty-nine companies in 1993.

Network Distance

Another highly remarkable measure describing the connectivity of this network is the minimum or geodesic distance between the node pairs in the diagram. Since path length is defined as the number of nodes it includes, the geodesic distance between two nodes indicates the length of the shortest path linking them (Wasserman and Faust 1994).

In this regard, the data are intuitively even more evident. The average distance between any two nodes of the network is 1.79 (a distance of 1 means that two nodes are adjacent, whereas a distance of 2 means that there is only one intermediate node); consequently, the forty-nine nodes of the network are extremely near each other and mutually connected. The maximum distance between two nodes is 4 (it could theoretically have been as much as 48), and so the network diameter is also equal to 4.

Visually, this means that we have something that does not look like a tree, but a network with a low level of centralization and very high degree of mutual connectivity. In sociological terms, it can be said that the dispositions seem to show a large group of pairs, rather than a hierarchical structure in which eccentricity, and average and maximum distances are greater.

Finally, one last structural device underlines what we have said about distances: the high average number of geodesics, or between-node paths of minimum length (Wasserman and Faust 1994). As this is 3.67, there are almost four different paths of minimum length (with an average of 1.79) enabling any node to be reached from any other node.

Network clustering

Clustering is the analysis of the number and quality of the densest regions inside the network (Tichy, Tushman and Fombrum 1979), but we will limit ourselves here to some quantitative remarks concerning the network as a whole.

A clique is the largest complete sub-graph with a size of three nodes or more, in which each node is adjacent to all of the other nodes belonging to the sub-graph and there are no other external nodes adjacent to any of the nodes of the clique itself (Harary, Norman and Cartwright 1965). If we consider our network we find that there are about 112 cliques including five or more players.

Also when the dichotomized matrix is used with a cut-off point of more than 0 (i.e. considering only the linkages with an assigned value of more than 1—when the two firms are together in at least two consortia), the number of maximal complete sub-graphs remains very high (forty-one).

The most emblematic and somehow final factor in this first series of descriptive considerations concerning the network as a whole is the result of the n-cliques analysis. An n-clique is a maximal graph in which each pair of nodes is linked by a path whose length is equal to or less than n. A 1–clique is what we simply call a clique; a 2–clique is one in which each pair of players has to pass through at least a third in order to reach each other; and so on.

This analysis revealed the presence of four 2–cliques with thirty-eight elements each; the result of the combination of these thirty-eight elements is that only seven of the forty-nine players do not take part in these four sub-graphs.

Even more interesting is the result of the 3–clique analysis, which revealed the presence of a 3-clique with forty-seven players, thus excluding only two of the initial forty-nine constructors. We can conclude that the Italian construction industry, or rather this group of leading Italian contractors, is a 3–clique of consortia.

Effects of network relational capital

If we concentrate on the second level of the relational capital—the whole network one—we find some interesting issues.

In dense organizational networks, interests entwine and interconnect. The organizations involved in this kind of network try to use the power in order to eliminate difficulties or provide for their needs and, in attempting to achieve these goals, form external alliances and conform to the requirements of the agents with greater power (Zald 1970: 231). Zald's basic idea is that external and internal political and economic factors are inextricably bound up with each other, and organizations may use political means to alter the conditions of the external economic environment (Pfeffer and Salancik 1978). Although construction companies are constrained by their economic, social, political and legal environments, we must also remember that the same laws, social norms, values and political outcomes partially reflect action taken by the organizations themselves in order to protect their own interests of survival and growth. This power is the result of the force that the connectivity of the network has been able to exert over the other members of the organizational set (Evan 1966).

Network relational capital is founded on the institutionalized values and social norms of the sector, and affects the generation of the norms governing the organizational set and, in particular, political processes.

The Italian construction industry is highly regulated, and the importance of the economic environment diminishes as that of the political and administrative environments increases; furthermore, state and public institutions are also the 'customers' of the industry. Network relational capital was, in this case, the principal mechanism that lead to *industry self-regulation*. As Gupta and Lad (1983) pointed out, industry self-regulation is an alternative form of non-market regulation that may supplement or complement direct regulation by the government. Industry self-regulation was, in the Italian construction industry, very strong, because of the low degree of asymmetry in the distribution of power; in fact we consider that the greater the asymmetry in the distribution of power in an industry, the less the likelihood of industry self-regulation.

The existence of the process represented in Figure 11.3 was clearly described by one of the judges investigating the relationship between political power and construction companies in Italy:

'The extent of the phenomenon we are trying to fight is undoubtedly alarming. In some activities, bribery was the rule; if no bribe was requested, that was an exception. In order to circumvent legal regulations and hide wrong-doings, some contracts were split up. On the one hand, the industrialists claim that they were coerced by politicians and public officials even if there were no explicit threats; on the other hand, we have found situations in which the companies themselves were the corrupters, because they wanted to elude the regulation of the market and competition, while stipulating agreements with politicians,

(P. Davigo, in Dematté 1993)

In other words we could consider this effect as the first type of externality induced by the network on the external system.

In order to explain the strategic choices of Italian construction companies in terms of mergers and acquisitions, it must be remembered that the companies themselves are components of a larger economic and social system, and that the support of this system plays a fundamental role in determining whether or not they survive: organizational goals and activities have to be legitimized by the economic and social system as a whole. As Meyer and Rowan have pointed out (1991: 53), regardless of their specific organizational efficiency, the companies embedded in a highly elaborate institutional environment need to gain legitimacy for survival. 'Legitimation is the process whereby an organization justifies to a peer or superordinate system its right to exist [. . .]' (Maurer 1971: 361).

One contextual element is worthy of consideration: precisely because of its enormous relational capital resources, this network of cooperative relationships has exerted much greater pressure on its institutional counterparts than that of the industry's trade association. This is because the nature of the sector meant that the trade association represented a wide range of very heterogeneous interests, whereas the large construction companies identified themselves in terms of the relational capital created by means of the principal form of economic cooperation—the consortia. The pressure of relational capital was felt by the various elements involved in the organizational set: the representatives of political power, smaller companies, subcontracting mechanisms and suppliers. Naturally enough, as in a game of Chinese boxes, the mechanisms for building up relational capital at network level subsequently spread to the other niches in the sector, involving smaller companies and more circumscribed geographical areas—regions, provinces, municipalities.

Relational capital therefore has two effects:

1   at the level of individual companies, it offers greater chances of success and profits—as can be seen from our own findings;
2   at network level, the presence and power of relational capital has effects on defining the rules of the game, including those related to survival, efficiency and legitimacy (Meyer and Rowan 1991).

But we hypothesize a third effect that consists of the creation of a vicious circle which, at a macroeconomic level, is capable of producing costs and negative externalities:

1   the greater the degree of connectivity of the network of relationships,

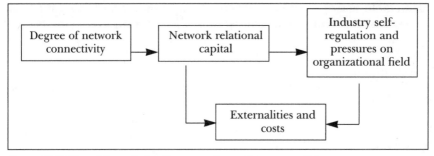

Figure 11.3 The vicious circle of costs and negative externalities

and the wider and more balanced the network itself (the absence of sub-groups or coalitions), the greater the amount of relational capital available to all of the companies of the network;

2 the greater the amount of relational capital available to the network, the greater industry self-regulation and the greater pressure it exerts on the interlocutors of the organizational set in order to reduce the sources of uncertainty and create favourable conditions for the companies belonging to the network;

3 the greater the pressure on these interlocutors, the greater the negative externalities produced by the network.

Relational capital mechanisms and effects: indebtedness and negative externalities

The network of the forty-nine leading Italian general contractors has properties and structural characteristics that are atypical for an industry theoretically governed by competitive forces. The literature contains many discussions concerning the continuum of organizational forms between companies and the market, and the characteristics of interorganizational relationship networks have always led to them being considered a distinct form (Powell 1990). One of the results of our analysis is that the pressure of competition, which should ensure the existence of industrial rivalry and the replaceability of companies on the basis of cost and/or quality functions, is not a good explanation of the recourse to cooperative agreements in the industry: these cooperative links are not based on the complementarity of technological and managerial capacities of the different companies.

The companies in a network are bound to each other by a chain of life and death, and relational capital determines a high degree of dependence between one company and the other. In addition to the absence of a market, the relational structure also shows the existence of what can be called a real *network of indebtedness* among our forty-nine general contractors (Powell 1990). The chain binding the companies summarizes their relational reciprocity and generalized risk-sharing, and this reciprocity is identifiable not so much in terms of the relationship itself, but more in terms of the structural characteristics of the network; everybody has an 'obligation' towards everybody else (either directly or through an intermediary).

Collusion is another of the many economic phenomena that can take on a different form when looked at from a network point of view. An economic situation characterized by a large (but not infinite) number of entrepreneurial opportunities should be similar to an almost perfect market. In our case, the levels of concentration show none of the signs of an oligopolistic situation, nor is it possible to trace any formal agreements designed to restrict competition. However, the presence of a significant amount of relational capital at the level of the network demonstrates that a set of producers (strongly supported by a regulatory and institutional environment which, in this case, not only represents the guarantor, but is also the principal customer of the network of producers) can construct a system of reciprocal formal and informal interdependencies and obligations that makes market mechanisms completely useless in interpreting the economic behaviour of the players. This vast system of reciprocal interconnections represents the network of indebtedness.

In our view, indebtedness is a particular form of embeddedness because it is a construct that expresses the reiteration over time of different relational patterns among a group of organizational players: it is substantially the result of the interweaving of structural, social, cultural and cognitive embeddedness (Zukin and Di Maggio 1990). The expression of these different forms of embeddedness within an interorganizational network depends on the extent to which a group of enterprises are reciprocally bound by the interconnections between their individual relational capital and the strength of the sum of their relational capital as a whole. Indebtedness therefore can be seen as a sort of intercompany law of reciprocity (Gouldner 1960). This law represents a powerful entry barrier and, in the case that the reciprocity is not respected, provides for a sanction that may even include expulsion from the network. Relational capital is a sort of 'hostage' and the mechanism of reciprocity leads to a reduction in the risk of opportunistic behaviour (Hill 1990; Williamson 1975). The economic relationships embedded in such a 'highly indebted' network respond to a logic that is different from that of the search for utility from individual transactions or relationships and, consequently, there is no reason for the existence of opportunism or even the simple 'desire to win' the competitive race because of the risk of exclusion this involves. We are therefore faced with a form of organization that is substantially different from the 'federations' whose coordination is based on forms of joint decision-making or the sharing out of total profits. The structural properties of the network of Italian general contractors seem to be much more like those of a form of integrated organization rather than a federation of companies. The 'superiority' of this form of organization may not be absolute, but it has its own specific usefulness in the environmental conditions of the sector.

Our point is that the embeddedness of economic relationships is not good or bad *per se*; but we would like to underline the fact that networks with structural properties such as those described here produce distortions that can often lead to negative externalities. In a situation where relationships of indebtedness are established between economic players in such a way that the entire market of the production of a good or service (such as the construction of public works) becomes subject to this particular form of embeddedness, then it is possible to say that cooperative relational capital 'muddies' market relationships and, although it has proved to be highly effective as a means of controlling and distributing resources for companies, its effects in terms of the public interest are not equally beneficial.

Externality has always been spoken of as one of the causes of a crisis in the market, because this way of organizing exchange is considered to be unsuitable in the case of those exchanges that have negative effects on third parties. On the other hand, it has also been said that positive externalities could be better managed within the context of reticular systems because, although these are less flexible than the market, they are much more stable. In our case, the relational network has managed competitive uncertainty by means of a profit-sharing mechanism that has had its effects on the cost of the works financed by the fiscal system. Previous studies have justified the existence of more or less tacit forms of intercompany cooperation and coordination from the point of view of the logic of profit and an overall increase in incomes on the basis that 'something is better than nothing' (Daems 1983). Furthermore, economic theory has maintained that intercompany agreements led to better results for the companies themselves and to externalities for the system.

In the following pages we would like to point out two facts that at least partially contradict this reasoning, sustaining that:

1   in the case we have examined here, the effect of indebtedness on the individual companies has been that of profoundly conditioning their competitive capacity and has thus led to the *de facto* creation of marginal companies with a lack of entrepreneurship and innovation;
2   the advantages that the companies receive from the network have proved to be limited to the period in which the network mechanisms really govern the industry and actually these advantages could only exist in highly munificent environments.

Consequences on firms and industrial structure

What effect has the network had on its member companies? Even though we cannot demonstrate this effect quantitatively, there are some elements that may help us to understand it better.

1   The high cost of public works and the widespread recourse to procedures for awarding tenders that are considered abnormal or contrary to European Community regulations.

2   The small size of the companies in comparison with their major national and international counterparts. According to the last available census, Italy has 290,000 construction companies, and the size of those involved in the field of general contracting is not only smaller than that of the other large Italian companies operating in other sectors, but also smaller than that of the leading foreign construction companies. The list of the 200 largest Italian companies includes only two construction companies, the highest placed of which is in 55th position. Furthermore, a classification of the 200 leading European constructors shows that:

   a   the first fifty include only three Italian companies (Iritecna—no. 9; Fiatimpresit—no. 34; and Cogefarimpresit—no. 48, a member of the Fiatimpresit Group and the only real civil constructor), as against fifteen French, eleven German, ten British, four Swedish, four Spanish and three Dutch companies;

   b   among the first 100 contractors, Italy's position is even weaker: in addition to those mentioned above, there is only Condotte (no. 85), which means that the Italian presence represents only 4 per cent of the leading group of European construction companies.

3   The low level of diversification. On average, the degree of diversification of the fifty largest Italian construction firms, whose size suggests that they should also be the most diversified, is 7.5 per cent of total turnover. The largest European construction companies have diversification rates that are always higher than 15 per cent and, in many cases, represent 45 per cent of the companies' business (e.g. Tarmac, George Wimpey, Dumez).

The end of the story: the crisis of indebtedness

At the beginning of 1997 the situation of the construction industry in Italy has deeply changed, in comparison with what it was in previous years. Many of the forty-nine companies considered have been acquired or they have serious financial troubles. Almost all the companies have closed their balance sheets with heavy losses and they are now indebted to the banks. The recourse to consortia in order to gain tenders has become very rare— just a few big consortia, created at the beginning of the 1990s, are still 'alive'—and the biggest companies have decided to create an independent trade association.

As a result of the profound change in the distribution of political and administrative power that has taken place in Italy since 1993, the Italian construction industry has been suffering the effects of a series of institu-

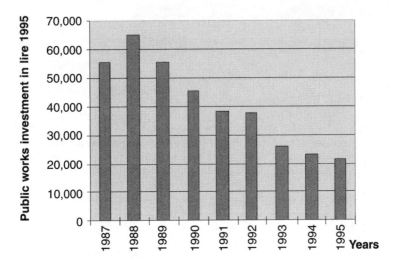

Figure 11.4 The public works market 1987–1995 (millions of lire)

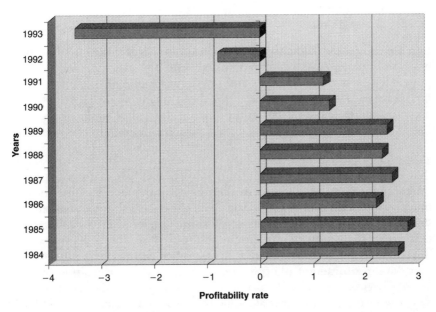

Figure 11.5 Average profitability rate of the top 100 construction companies in Italy from 1984 to 1993

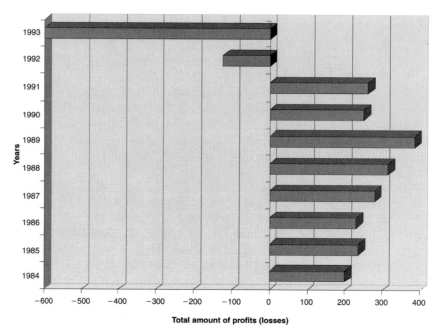

Figure 11.6 Total amount of net profits (or losses) of the top 100 construction
companies in Italy from 1984 to 1993

tional earthquakes: industry self-regulation and social norms previously
governing them have been overturned, and the clash of institutional
powers has meant that the rules and praxes that had remained unchanged
for more than thirty years have now been abandoned. This has been
accompanied by a radical fall in the demand for public works (the size of
the market) and has finally determined a radical change in the rules and
the munificence regarding the environment (see Figures 11.4, 11.5 and
11.6).

As Stigler pointed out, one of the direct consequences of the institutionalization of an economic industry is to generate a security and benefits
that the rules of competition can never assure (Stigler 1971: 3). Although it
is true that these benefits may accrue indirectly from the 'welfare state' or
directly from the industry (Stigler 1971), Peffer and Salancik have shown
that these two different interpretations of the institutionalization process
are not necessarily contradictory (Peffer and Salancik 1978: 203). In our
case, the institutional earthquake took the form of a considerable cut-back
in both the economic and 'legitimization' resources made available by the
system—and organizational survival requires both legitimacy and economic

viability. The consequence has been a paralysis of economic activity that has caused the companies serious financial problems. The companies have responded to the crisis by instituting processes of integration designed to enhance the concentration of the industry, simplifying its structure by means of mergers and acquisitions.

Conclusions

In this paper we have discussed two types of relational capital: the relational capital owned jointly by two or more companies and the relational capital owned by the network of companies as a whole. The first kind of capital is measured at a single-company level through the centrality measures—primarily betweenness centrality—whilst the second kind is measured at the whole network level by the measures of network connectiveness—density, distance, etc.

What conclusions can we draw about the final effects of these two forms of relational capital?

The first kind of relational capital—the one owned by the dyad of firms—has been a good predictor of the integration and simplification process that has occurred in the industry after the crisis already described. In this industry a high amount of relational capital between firms has pushed the companies, linked in cooperative agreements, through horizontal—mergers and acquisitions—integration processes (Soda and Usai 1996).

On the other hand, the amount of the relational capital owned by the whole network has decreased during the past few years. The conflicts among construction companies and the destructive price competition that characterise the competitive arena today, prove this situation.

The crisis of legitimacy brought new rules into play, and the first companies to succumb were those that were weak in terms of economic viability. Almost all of these firms are now suffering heavy losses. Today, many firms are virtually kept in business because they are linked to financial institutions by considerable guarantees. This is happening because the institutional crisis—which destroyed the previous relational mechanisms—has not yet created any new rules, and so uncertainty and ambiguity are leading the companies with enough financial resources, to take the easiest route in an undercapitalized industry: they are increasing their size but not their likelihood of survival.

The literature on networks has often highlighted the positive aspects of interorganizational relationships—innovation, learning and flexibility. We have underlined how, under certain conditions, a cooperative network among firms causes not only negative effects and externalities on the whole economic system, but also represents a structural source of unstable competitive advantage for the single firms in the network.

Notes

1 We are most grateful to Henry Tosi for his insightful comments and suggestions. The data and information used in this paper have been collected with the help of Tommaso Albinati and Aldo Norsa. The research programme which is the basis for this paper is jointly conducted by Giuseppe Soda and Alessandro Usai.
2 See Uzzi 1996 and Grahber 1993 for reviews.
3 The decision to privilege these consortia in constructing our dataset of interorganizational relationships was based on the results of various interviews conducted by the authors.
4 The collected data have been put in a square matrix 49*49 and have been analysed with the support of the programs UCINET IV and KrackPlot.
5 In the 'value degree centrality' we consider, for each pair, the number of consortia; in the 'dichotomized degree centrality' in each pair, relations are considered with value 1 if they exists and 0 if they do not exist.

Bibliography

Aldrich, H. (1979)*Organizations and Environment*, Englewood Cliffs, NJ: Prentice-Hall.

Astley, W. G. (1984) 'Toward an appreciation of collective strategy', *Academy of Management Review*, 9: 526–35.

Barley, S. R., Freeman, J. and Hybels, R. C. (1991) 'Strategic alliances in commercial biotechnologies', in N. Nohria and R.G. Eccles (eds), *Networks and Organizations: Structure, Form and Action*, Cambridge, Mass.: Harvard Business School Press, 1992, pp. 311–47.

Barnard, C. I. (1938) *The Functions of the Executive*, Cambridge, Mass.: Harvard University Press.

Baum, J. A. C. and Oliver, C. (1991) 'Institutional linkages and organizational mortality', *Administrative Science Quarterly*, 36: 187–218.

Borgatti, S. P., Everett, M. G. and Freeman, L. C. (1992) *UCINET IV Version 1.00*, Columbia, Analytic Technologies.

Brusco, S. (1982) 'The Emilian model: productive decentralization and social integration', *Cambridge Journal of Economics* 6(2): 167–84.

Burt, R. (1982) *Toward a Structural Theory of Action*, New York: Academic Press.

—— (1992) *Structural Holes*, Cambridge, Mass.: Harvard University Press.

Chandler, A. D. (1990) *Scale and Scope: The Dynamics of Industrial Capitalism*, Cambridge, Mass.: Harvard University Press.

Crewe, L. (1996) 'Material culture: embedded firms, organizational networks and the local economic development of a fashion quarter', *Regional Studies*,vol. 30(3): 257–72.

Daems, H. (1983) 'The determinants of hierarchical organization of industry', in Francis, Turk and Willman (eds), *Power, Efficiency and Institutions*, Heinemann, trans. into Italian 1985, as 'Dimensione di impresa e integrazione gerarchica nell'organizzazione industriale' in R.C.D. Nacamulli e A.Rugiadini (a cura di) *Organizzazione e Mercato*, Bologna Il Mulino, pp. 427–46.

Dei Ottati, G. (1991) 'The economic bases of diffuse industrialization', *International Studies of Management and Organization* 21(1): 53–75.

Dei Ottati, G. (1994) 'The industrial district transaction problems and the community market', *Cambridge Journal of Economics* 18: 529–46.

Dematté, C. (1993) 'Tempo per un nuovo inizio. Intervista al giudice Piercamillo Davigo', *Economia & Management,* Etas libri Periodici, n. 2.

Di Maggio, P. J. and POWELL, W. W. (eds) (1991) *The New Institutionalism in Organizational Analysis,* Chicago: University of Chicago Press.

Evan, W. M. (1966) 'The organization-set: toward a theory of interorganizational relations', in J. D. Thompson (ed.), *Approaches to Organizational Design,* Pittsburgh, PA: University of Pittsburgh Press, pp. 172–191.

Freeman, L .C. (1979) 'Centrality in social networks: conceptual classification', *Social Networks,* 1: 215–39.

Halliday, T. C., Granfors, M. W. and Powell, M. J. (1993) 'After mininalism: transformation of state bar associations from market dependence to state reliance, 1918 to 1950', *American Sociological Review,* 58 (August): 515–35.

Grabher, G. (ed.) (1993) *The Embedded Firm: On Socioeconomics of Industrial Networks,* London: Routledge.

Gouldner, A. W. (1960) 'The norm of reciprocity', *American Sociological Review,* 25: 161–78.

Grandori, A. (1995) *L'organizzazione delle attività economiche,* Bologna: Il Mulino.

Grandori, A. and Soda, G. (1995) 'Interfirm networks: antecedents, mechanisms and forms', *Organization Studies,* 16(2): 183–214.

Gupta, A. K and Lad, L. J. (1983) 'Industry self-regulation: an economic organizational, and political analysis', *Academy of Management Review,* 8(3): 416–25.

Granovetter, M. S. (1973) 'The strength of weak ties', *American Journal of Sociology,* 78: 1360–80.

—— (1985) 'Economic action and social structure: the problem of embeddedness', *American Journal of Sociology,* 91(3): 481–510.

—— (1992) 'Economic institution as social construction: a framework for analysis', *Acta Sociologica,* 35: 3–11.

Harary, F., Norman, R. and Cartwright, D. (1965) *Structural Models: An Introduction to the Theory of Directed Graph,* New York: Wiley.

Hill, C. W. L. (1990) 'Cooperation, opportunism, and invisible hand: implication for transaction cost theory', *Academy of Management Review,* 15(3): 500–13.

Lang, J. R. and Lockhart, D. E. (1990) 'Increased environmental uncertainty and changes in board linkage patterns', *Academy of Management Journal,* 33(1): 106–28.

Lazerson, M. (1988) 'Organizational growth of small firms: an outcome of markets and hierarchies?', *American Sociological Review* 53: 330–42.

—— (1993) 'Factory or putting out? Knitting networks in Modena', in G. Grabher (ed.), *The Embedded Firm: On Socioeconomics of Industrial Networks,* London: Routledge.

—— (1995) 'A new phoenix?: modern putting-out in the modena knitwear industry', *Administrative Science Quarterly,* 40: 34–59.

Marsden, P. V. (1982) 'Brokerage behavior in restricted exchange networks', in *Social Structure and Network Analysis,* edited by P. Marsden and N. Lin, Newbury Park: Sage Pub, pp. 201–18.

Maurer, J. G. (1971) *Readings in Organization Theory: Open-System Approaches,* New York: Random House.

Meyer, J. W. and Rowan, B. (1991) 'Institutionalized organizations: formal structure as myth and ceremony', in W. W. Powell and P. J. Di Maggio (eds), *The New Institutionalism in Organizational Analysis,* Chicago:University of Chicago Press, (first version in *The American Journal of Sociology* (1977) 83: 340–63.

Mitchell, J. C. (1969) 'The concept and use of social networks', in *Social Network in Urban Situation*, Manchester: Manchester University Press.

Oliver, C. (1990) 'Determinants of interorganizational relationships: integration and future directions', *Academy of Management Review*, 15(2): 241–65.

Pennings, J. M. (1981) 'Strategically interdependent organizations', in P. C. Nystrom and W. H. Starbuck (eds), *Handbook of Organizational Design*, vol. 1, pp. 433–55, Oxford: Oxford University Press.

Pfeffer, J. and Salancik, G. R. (1978) *The External Control of Organizations: A Resource Dependence Perspective*, New York: Harper and Row.

Porter, M. (1980) *Competitive strategies*, New York: The Free Press.

Powell, W. W. (1990) 'Neither market nor hierarchy: network forms of organization', in *Research of Organizational Behavior*, 12: 295–336.

Pyke, F., Beccatini, G. and Sengenberger, W. (eds) (1990) *Industrial Districts and Inter-Firm Cooperation in Italy*, Geneva: International Institute for Labour Studies.

Richardson, G. B. (1972) 'The organization of industry', *Economic Journal*, 82: 883–96.

—— (1994) 'The industrial district, transaction problems and the "community market"', *Cambridge Journal of Economics*, 18: 529–46.

Sapelli, S. (1990) *L'impresa come soggetto storico*, Milano: Il Saggiatore.

Soda, G. and Usai, A. (1995) Institutional embeddedness and interorganizational networks in the italian construction industry, paper presented at the EMOT Workshop 'Industry structure and interorganizational networks', 1–2 December, Geneva.

—— (1996) The strength of formal ties: intensity of ior's and horizontal integration in the italian construction industry, paper presented at the EMOT Workshop, Turin.

Stigler, G. J. (1971) 'The theory of economic regulation', *Bell Journal of Economics and Management Science*, 2: 3–21.

Swedberg, R. (1990) *Economics and Sociology*, Princeton University Press.

—— (1994) *Economia e sociologia*, Roma: Donzelli Editore.

Tichy, N., Tushman, M. and Fombrum, C. (1979) 'Social network analysis for organization', *Academy of Management Review*, 4: 507–19.

Uzzi, B. (1996) 'The sources and consequences of embeddedness for the economic performance of organizations: the network effect', *American Sociological Review*, 61 (August): 674–98.

Wasserman, S. and Faust, K. (1994) *Social Network Analysis: Methods and Applications*, Cambridge, Mass.: Cambridge University Press.

Weber, M. (1922) *Wirtschaft und Gesellschaft*, 2 vols., Tübingen: J. C. B. Mohr.

White, H. (1981) 'Where do markets come from?', *American Journal of Sociology*, 87: 517–47.

—— (1993) 'Markets, networks and control', in S. Lindenberg and H. Schreuder (eds), *Interdisciplinary Perspectives on Organization Studies*, Pergamon Press, Oxford, pp. 223–39.

Williamson, O. E. (1975) *Markets and Hierarchies: Analysis and Antitrust Implication*, New York: Free Press.

Zald, M. N. (1971) 'Political economy: a framework for comparative analysis', in M. N. Zald (ed.) *Power in Organizations*, Nashville, Tenn.: Vanderbilt University Press, pp. 221–61.

Zukin, S. and Di maggio, P. (1990) *Structures of Capital: The Social Organization of the Economy*, New York: Cambridge University Press.

12 Japanese interfirm networks
'High-trust' or relational access?

Mark J. Scher

Introduction: the vocabulary of trust

The collapse of the 'bubble economy' of the late 1980s and the ensuing asset deflation crisis threatened the very viability of the Japanese financial system and resulted in Japan's most profound economic recession since the post-war period. This in turn led to grave and unexpected economic consequences, including a major shift in interorganizational industrial networks. One serious and ongoing consequence has been the hollowing out of Japan's domestic industrial production, as primary contractors continue to expand their outsourcing of parts production overseas, abandoning their supplier networks in Japan. This trend has led to the end of such hallowed managerial practices as so-called 'lifetime employment'.

During the post-war era, Japan's economy appeared to be ever-expanding, and the existence of relational asymmetries between contractors and suppliers, for example, was subsumed under the rhetoric 'a rising tide lifts all boats' which implied that all contractors/stakeholders would be or could be considered 'winners' in spite of apparent inequities. However, following the collapse of Japan's 'bubble economy', a fundamental environmental change took place. Strategic outsourcing was extended offshore where the exploitation of economic asymmetries was far greater, leaving former domestic network producers without buyers and transforming these former comparative 'winners' into absolute losers.

Despite such major changes in Japan's economy, the reputation of Japanese interorganizational networks continues as a model of reputed economic and managerial efficiency, and network governance structures are still often said to be characterized by benevolent corporate synergism. In discussions on 'trust' in interfirm relations, the Japanese industrial group system is often held up as a leading example. According to this view, the firms in a *keiretsu* (vertically affiliated companies) are tied with bonds of trust and obligation to their members.

This chapter first briefly discusses the usages of 'trust' in Japanese business relations and whether it conforms to its Western analogues. It then examines how differences in trust are related to the differences between firms which have vertical or lateral ties and between firms as insiders or outsiders as part of a framework defined as Relational Access.

'Trust' has entered the vocabulary of organizational studies as a largely psychological concept equally applicable to intra- and interfirm relations. Trust in interfirm networks has been described as having many of the benevolent, self-protective characteristics of mutual reliance and shared confidence typically attributed to trust in the context of interpersonal relations. This is perhaps nowhere more evident than in studies on trust which cite Japanese interfirm organizational relationships as a model.

Principles of trust in organizational relationships were discussed in the social sciences as early as the late nineteenth century in Durkheim's description of the clan ([1893]1933). An institutional approach was taken by Fox (1974); and Luhmann (1979; 1988) takes a functional approach in conceptualizing trust in social relationships, again most recently in *Trust in Organizations* (Kramer and Tyler, eds, 1996); while Powell (1996) has written on trust-based forms of governance. Some cultural studies of trust, (Fukuyama 1995, for one), although overburdened with sweeping generalizations, have attracted notice in the popular media, all of which leads to the question of what is meant by trust relationships, if not 'trust' itself.

Yamagishi and Yamagishi (1994), in their comparative study of attitudes among the general population of the US and Japan, distinguish between trust and assurance. They found that the general public in Japan was significantly less 'trusting' than its American counterpart. 'Assurance', they argue, better defines Japanese attitudes, denoting an incentive structure built into a relationship to which general concepts of trust are generally irrelevant. It is therefore all the more important to define the differences in cultural attitudes and perceptions of what constitutes 'trust', since much of the current Western literature on the subject has characterized Japanese management practices as based upon trust.

The notion of assurance (as opposed to trust), as defined by Yamagishi and Yamagishi, goes to the core of much of the economic studies that view 'trust' in Japan as an implicit contractual relationship in business practices. This contractual view is perhaps no more evident than the literature on subcontracting practices. Dore (1983; 1987) and Sako (1991; 1992) have written specifically on the role of trust in Japanese subcontracting structures. These studies have largely ignored an important distinction which must be made between *keiretsu* (vertical relationships) where power relationships predominate and the collegial relationships of Japan's *kigyo shudan* (horizontal groups) which are often mistakenly referred to as *keiretsu*. It is striking that, although much of the discussion of 'trust' emanates from literature on subcontracting, issues of power in these relationships, which are never far removed, are seldom acknowledged. As will be later discussed, in neither the *keiretsu* nor *kigyo* cases do Western conceptualizations of 'trust' in business relationships apply.

This chapter begins by attempting to define what 'trust' signifies in Japanese business transactions and to question how well these definitions of trust fit Western assumptions about its nature. It should first be noted that there are separate Japanese words to describe every form of trust defined in the West as well as others without any apparent Western (or at least English) language counterpart. The range of meanings traverses the spectrum from contractual obligation, fiduciary duty, obligational trans-actions, to loyalty and those words reflecting the gamut of benevolent human feelings. These distinctions in meaning, however, are rooted in and reflect the context in which they appear.

The English word 'trust' is derived from the Old Norse *traust* meaning an obligation secured by collateral, and in Teutonic law trust was sym-bolized by a gage and pledge (token of security and forfeiture of property) and in Norman England by a bailment of actual monetary value. These transactional, essentially contractual, obligations codified in the Northern European usage of 'trust' differ from the characteristics of trust's Latin counterpart *fides*, faith, often taken as a sign of obligation expressed through allegiance or fealty.

It is not altogether surprising that similar meanings and usage of the concept of trust occur also in the hypercontextualized nature of Japanese society. A hypercontextualized society (Hall 1977) is characterized by culturally built-in schema of relationships which can and have been mistaken for trust-based relationships. In my view, the concept of trust in Japanese organizational relationships is at its core merely a metaphor of convenience used to describe practices which are not based on principles of mutual reliance or confidence but are premised on a principle I call Relational Access. In the next few pages I set forth the Relational Access framework which places trust's many attributes within the context of Japanese interfirm relations and addresses issues of 'power distance' and contextualization, parameters that are often overlooked in other models of 'trust'.

This chapter is based on extensive data drawn from multiple, in-depth interviews with the same seventy-seven Japanese bank practitioner res-pondents over a six-year period. In the course of these interviews a considerable amount of evidence was gathered which not only challenges prior assumptions of 'trust-based' perspectives, but also provides an understanding of interfirm relationships and practices.

One basic cause for the controversies over the nature of Japanese industrial groups comes from misunderstanding over terminology. Words denoting 'trust', for relationship and the varied meanings, access and *keiretsu*, among others, all have been used in ways that obscure and confuse. I discovered these inconsistencies in usage during interviews that exhaustively examined the minutiae of the daily practices of the bankers' dealings with their clients. I found major discrepancies in the commonly understood meanings of basic terminology including 'trust' and '*keiretsu*'. Such discrepancies must at least cast doubt upon the theoretical and operational positions staked out by the major participants in the current debate on the nature of trust and the so-called *keiretsu* system. The mis-characterization of the word 'trust' as an institutional concept in organizational studies literature has had a fundamental role in misleading Western views of Japanese interfirm networks and also has led to frustrating attempts to duplicate the Japanese model in other economic cultures.

Interfirm networks

The unique qualities of industrial organization in Japan have been a favourite subject of study of both economists and social scientists. In the 1970s and early 1980s game theory economists used concepts similar to trust in defining theories of self-enforcing agreements (Telser 1980). With the ascendancy of Principal-Agency Theory as the dominant paradigm in the American academy, 'trust' became an analogue for monitoring within the agency framework's design of contracts in subcontracting (Kawasaki and McMillan 1987). In the realm of the social sciences, free-floating concepts of trust have intermingled with concepts of community. Organizational sociologists and cultural anthropologists have described Japan as a 'community model' (Dore 1987); others have contrasted Japanese culture to Western culture as a 'belonging model' versus a Western 'contractual model' (Mito 1992); and within the overall context of East Asian business systems, some have viewed the Japanese model as built on high-trust communal relations of village and family and an aloof state (Whitley 1992). Noting the special character of Japanese-style capitalism, some sociologists and economists have called it 'Alliance Capitalism' (Gerlach 1992); 'Network Capitalism' (Nakatani 1990); or even 'Beyond Capitalism' (Sakakibara 1994), and more recently in the press 'crony capitalism'.

Trust relations among institutions was explored by Alan Fox (1974) who cited Japan as an example of diffuse high-trust versus low-trust relations in the US and Britain. Sako (1991; 1992) makes similar comparisons to distinguish what she terms 'arm's-length contractual relations' in Britain and 'obligational contractual relations' in Japan.

Among manufacturers and their subcontractors, it is a functional necessity that the contractor convey firm-specific details of parts design and production to the subcontractor. In Japan this 'information sharing' does not represent a matter of trust between the two so much as a matter of efficiency. In fact, this 'information sharing' favours lower transaction costs for the contractor, useful in renegotiations for price reductions, and provides the contractor's engineering and design specialists ample opportunity to monitor the supplier's operations and performance. The supplier, however, receives no extra advantage as a result of the information sharing as it is enmeshed in a captive set of group relationships that precludes the opportunity of going elsewhere.

Information sharing in service industries, such as banking, is conducted on an entirely different basis. Because financial products are generic and highly price-sensitive, one finds that the information disseminated is either minimal or often even misleading as part of a competitive bank strategy (for a full review of the role of '*dis*-information' in a critique of the agency myth of Japanese bank monitoring, see Scher 1997).

The notion of obligational relations—*giri no kankei*—has been used by Dore (1983) to define the Japanese meaning of 'trust'. The concept of *giri*, obligation, pervasive as it is in many forms of Japanese business and non-business relations, is nonetheless quite different from the concept of faith or belief in human relationships by which trust is commonly understood in Western cultures. *Giri* is often a much more mundane and measurable category of obligation in Japanese organizational culture, subject to precise calculation and repayment (Yoshino and Lifson 1986). Trust that is akin to Western notions of shared confidence and reliance is most clearly expressed in the Japanese word *shinrai*, which is applied to such human relationships as the expectations and dependency of a relationship between a mother and child. This type of dependency-based personalized trust is not normally associated with business transactions in Japan. Another word for 'trust' is the feudal term *shingi*, meaning faith, fidelity and loyalty, the Western counterpart of which is perhaps the Latin word *fides*. Both *shinrai* and *shingi* reflect trust in personal relationships, i.e. between individuals. In my interviews, respondents uniformly reported such words as 'too emotional' and not typically used to describe firm-to-firm transactions.

It was, in fact, the very absence of the occurrence of the word 'trust' in several hundred hours of interviews with bank executives over the past six years that led me to devote my most recent set of interviews (November–December 1997) to this topic. I sought to pin down what was meant by 'trust' in their own terms, under what circumstances 'trust' might be applied when describing business relationships, and what, if anything, constituted a reasonable analogue to the theoretical conceptualizations of trust as described in the literature.

I found that, if there is any word that may be used for trust in Japan in connection with business relationships, it is *shinyo*, which describes trust in terms of credibility. Sometimes used to describe interfirm relationships, i.e. between transaction partners, *shinyo* has definite business implications. The existence of *shinyo* or credibility in an interfirm relationship implies, first of all, that the relationship is longer term. It does not imply, however, the permanence needed to describe the 'high-trust fraternity' of social-class relationships described by Fox (1974). Even when *shinyo* exists in a relationship, transaction partners are closely watched, the relationship itself is reviewed every term, and it is always subject to changing conditions. *Shinyo* by its nature is easily destroyed by events, especially in times of crisis. Because *shinyo* can be undone by scandal, the threat of scandal has laid open corporate management to extortion. In the financial services industry most of the leading firms have paid hush-up money to *sokaiya* (black-mailing disrupters) to prevent embarrassing questions from being asked at annual shareholder meetings. For example, the recent collapse of Yamaichi Securities, which was abandoned by its fellow Fuyo group members, was preceded by *shinyo*-destroying scandal.

In exploring the concept of *shinyo* and other similar terms in interviews with bank and firm executives, the respondents invariably described a system that, although measured in highly reputational and highly relational terms between direct transaction partners, such as vendors and buyers, did not extend beyond the immediate partners in subcontracting group relationships. This is illustrated in my relational access continuum (see Figure 12.2). Reputation per se was, in respondents' views, based on a firm's affiliations, its size and longevity as the key determinants of overall status. Tellingly, because this system evaluates creditworthiness on the basis of that which is big, old and high priced, it does not evaluate the financial fundamentals of creditworthiness and has been a major cause of Japanese banking's bad loan crisis. Furthermore, this process of evaluating credibility, by definition, works against what is small, new and inexpensive, thus effectively keeping out newcomers and other outsiders.

The lack of codification of rules and regulations typical of high-context societies (Hall 1977) has led some social scientists to assume that, because information is most frequently transmitted on a personal level, an enhanced sense of trust exists in business relationships. However, in Japan it is well understood that interfirm relationships are not personal. Individual interactions between counterparts in transacting firms will not alter basic firm relationships so that a sense of trust on a personal level is generally irrelevant to the larger strategic issues of interfirm transactions which rely on the efficiency of long-term relationships.

Although 'trust' in some senses has been used as a metaphor to describe traditional Japanese-style business relations, *dento-teki kankei*, the relationships within these culture-bound practices are in actuality systems of long-term obligational ties and implicit contracts. The obligations implied are often inherently unequal but are nonetheless more cost effective than the sort of opportunism that dictates short-term contracts or spot-market behaviour. This system, however, has distancing mechanisms built into it that are designed to place limits on obligational ties, thus precluding the characterization of the relationship as trust-based in either psychological terms or as an article of faith.

In my view of Japan's industrial groups, principles of insider-versus-outsider, that is, 'relational access', underlie all transactions. Within Japanese interfirm and industrial group relations, core Japanese business practices are determined by sets of uncodified rules and obligations that are opaque to outsider scrutiny. The governing principle underlying these rules and obligations is relational access, a highly nuanced continuum of relationships—informal, invisible and inescapable—by which the gradations of interfirm relations from insider to outsider are determined.

The topology of interfirm networks

The principle of 'insider versus outsider' is the underpinning to the Relational Access Paradigm (Scher 1997), which is conceptualized as a three-dimensional, holistic framework encompassing the inter- and intrafirm attributes of Japanese industrial groups and their member firms. This model incorporates some of the attributes of the communal form theories of the firm and other theories, but uses as its foundation the principle of relational access. The relational access principle is described as the '*uchi-soto* (insider–outsider) continuum'. Every relationship is located along the continuum, a firm's place in the continuum determining a number of things, but chiefly its degree of access to group member firms. This insider–outsider concept of access and relationship is the glass through which Japanese industrial group relations should be viewed, and trust acquires a significance only as it is calibrated along the relational access continuum.

Hall (1977) classified Japan as a 'high-context culture',[1] indicating a high degree of shared assumptions and outlook often taken for granted by members of the society, which is maintained by extensive networks, both formal and informal, for the diffusion of uncodified information. Hofstede (1991) introduced the concept of Power Distance to examine relationships in which there were varying degrees of inequality in the concentration of authority. The Relational Access framework incorporates Hofstede's and Hall's concepts but with modifications to include two key factors. In my model, Hall's concept of high-context, low-context culture is correlated to information codification (high context/uncodified and low context/ codified), and information diffusion is correlated to Hofstede's concept of power-distance relationships. The interpretation of interfirm relations when analysed in power-distance terms makes clear significant differences between the *keiretsu*[2] characterized by feudal/asymmetrical power relations, and the *kigyo shudan* characterized by collegial/non-competitive synergistic relations. Figure 12.1 illustrates the power relationships inherent in the two differing forms, as well as the relationship between the two forms, horizontal versus vertical.

At the top of Figure 12.1 is the *zaibatsu* holding company, the apex of a pyramidal control structure. These holding companies, abolished after World War Two, were owned by the *zaibatsu* family. They held stock in the firms which today comprise the *kigyo shudan's* group member firms and their affiliated *keiretsu* firms' members. Today's *kigyo shudan* comprise a group of firms which are no longer owned by a holding company but instead are *horizontally* linked together and usually centered around the group's bank and/or trading company. For example, such former *zaibatsu* groups as Mitsui, Sumitomo, and Mitsubishi now consist of a number of related firms operating on essentially equal footing. A single member firm of such a *kigyo shudan* may in turn head a *keiretsu* of vertically affiliated

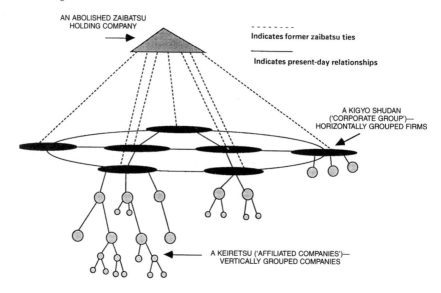

Figure 12.1 Kigyo shudan–keiretsu power relationships—a three-dimensional view

companies. The old *zaibatsu* holding company system comprised both the *kigyo shudan* and the *keiretsu* structures.

A *kigyo shudan* (horizontal corporate group) typically includes a cross-section of major industrial firms and has been frequently confused with *keiretsu*, *vertically* affiliated subordinate companies which usually reflect multi-tiered supplier and distributor relationships. The distinction between the *kigyo shudan* and *keiretsu* is important because the nature of the power relationship is not the same; in the former there is a collegial relationship among the member companies whereas in the latter there is a hierarchy between the company and its affiliated subordinates.

The *kigyo shudan* form is typified by joint projects, usually between two principal industrial members of the group which are forming a subsidiary to develop and manufacture a new product or service. Generally, the group trading company serves a supporting role in project planning, development and marketing, while among the group's financial institutions the main bank supplies financial expertise and long-term and short-term credits, and the group's trust bank may supply long-term project financing. Insurance companies, in addition to underwriting property and casualty insurance for the project, may also provide general financing, while other group companies provide project logistical support in areas such as shipping and transport, or technical expertise. However, each company's primary concern is with its own bottom line, so that depending upon the particular group, only some 20 to 30 per cent of *kigyo shudan* company contracts these days are with other group members, compared to some 80 per cent among the pre-war *zaibatsu*.

The *keiretsu* form is exemplified by such well-known Japanese sub-contracting practices as 'Just In Time' manufacturing (Fruin 1992), and black box design (Nishiguchi 1992). These practices, which shift inventory and product development costs to captive sets of subcontractors, are driven by a competitive dual-vendor pricing regime (Fruin 1992) which pits at least two suppliers for each and every component against each other. Suppliers are expected to absorb any increases in the cost of production. What may be long-term relationships within the *keiretsu* are dictated by short-term contracts that often require price reductions upon contract renewal (Sako 1992).

Some theorists have attempted to describe attributes of Japanese industrial groups to fit a market or bureaucracy profile. For example, agency economists have viewed the diffusion of information among Japanese firms in both the vertical hierarchy (*keiretsu*) and in the horizontal/collegial mode (*kigyo shudan*) as part of an agency relationship. In my view, the evidence tends to contradict such single-sided interpretation. Rather, in a high-context setting characterized by face-to-face relations, unlike either the bureaucracy or market forms, I have found that information diffusion tends to be personal, constant, wide-ranging and generally unfocused.

The Relational Access model[3] brings together some of the outstanding shared attributes of the *keiretsu*—fief form, patrimonial bureaucracy (Weber [1921]1947; Boisot 1986) and *kigyo shudan*—clan form, kinship network (Durkheim [1893]1933; Ouchi 1980). These include informal communication among firms of the group, chiefly through personal contact and membership in a culture of common values. At the same time, such attributes underscore the key distinctions between the fief form's essentially vertical mode, characterized by hierarchical relations in which control often masquerades as negotiation, and the clan form's essentially horizontal mode, which operates through collegial negotiation between related parties.

The high-context nature of Japanese society, in which communication and codification of contracts are often implicit, have misled some outside observers into the erroneous presumption that interfirm relationships are based upon trust. As can be seen in the following matrix (Figure 12.2), the upper two quadrants represent the basic dichotomy of markets versus bureaucracies typical of low-context, highly codified cultures, and the lower two quadrants represent communal forms more typical of high-context cultures such as Japan's where uncodified information and implicit contracts predominate. In this matrix the dimensions of power/control and codification/high–low context are two key factors distinguishing the forms of Japanese interfirm networks, *keiretsu* and *kigyo*. To these two factors my model adds a third, the dimension of relational access, which I will now address.

	Undiffused Information Hierarchical Power Relations	Diffused Information Horizontal Power Relations
Low context = **TRUST** Explicit contracts Codified information	**Bureaucratic combines** • Bureaucratic control of transaction costs • Information diffusion limited and under central control • Relationships impersonal and hierarchical • Submission to superordinate goals • Hierarchical coordination • No necessity to share values and beliefs • Explicit internal contracts, monitoring	**Market-based contracting** • Market/price-control mechanism • Information diffused, no control • Relationships impersonal and competitive • No superordinate goal—maximization of firm goals • Horizontal coordination through self-regulation • No necessity to share values and beliefs • Explicit market contracts, monitoring
High context = **TRUST** Implicit contracts Uncoded information	**Fiefs (patrimonial bureaucracy)** *Keiretsu* (vertical) **Asymmetrical power relationships** **Subsidiary-like Affiliations** • Information diffusion limited by lack of codification to face-to-face relationships • Relationships personal and hierarchical • Submission to superordinate goals • Hierarchical coordination • Necessity to share values and beliefs • Implict contracts may appear to outsiders as 'trust'; monitoring of subcontractor operations presumed	**Clans (kinship network)** *Kigyo shudan* (horizontal) **Collegial relationships** **Non-competitive synergistic alliances** • Information is diffused but still limited by lack of codification to face-to-face relationships • Relationships personal but non-hierarchical • Goals shared through process of negotiation • Horizontal coordination through negotiation • Necessity to share values and beliefs • Implicit relational contracts, non-monitoring; relational access presumed

= CONTROL =

Figure 12.2 Interfirm relations: trust—power/control matrix

Source: Adapted from Scher (1997), and the concepts of Boisot and Child (1988), Durkheim (1893/1933), Hall (1977), Hofstede (1991), Ouchi (1980), Weber (1921/1947), Williamson (1975).

Relational access and trust

The etymological origins of the Japanese word for relationship, *'kankei'*, is composed of two parts: *'kan'* meaning a barrier-gate and *'kei'* signifying duty to the group familial system. These two elements capture the interplay of the basic concepts contained within the meaning of 'relationship,' namely, that access is determined by the nature of the relationship. 'Access', first of all, as used in Japan, reflects a process not of opening doors but of controlling entry, determining who is allowed past the barrier-gate where passage through is determined by the specifics of the relationship. For example, in the exclusionary Japanese business practice known as *dango* (collusive rigged bidding historically rooted in the guild system) access is afforded relative to a fixed group of contractors—to the exclusion of those considered outsiders, such as domestic newcomers and foreign bidders.

In current Japanese business parlance, a relationship may be 'wet' (intimate, supportive) or 'dry' (purely transactional) or non-existent ('*kankeinai*') (no relationship and therefore no access at all). *Keiretsu torihiki*, group affiliated transactions, are mostly 'dry', in contrast to transactions based, for example, on *giri*, in which obligational indebtedness makes the relationship 'wet'. The nuanced and unstated, though understood, complexities of these relationships and the type of access each of them implies has led to the popularization among Japanese of the use of the English word 'access', which skirts around the issues of implicit barriers and control. For example, during the past several years the official Japanese language texts of Japan–US trade negotiations has employed the English 'access' written in *katakana* (Japanese phonetic alphabet) but without definition. Such lack of information and explicit definition is to be expected in an uncodified/high-context society.

It is in this context that Western scholars most often have come to mischaracterize Japanese long-term transactional relationships as dependent on 'trust'. This is not a concept or a word that is commonly used in Japan when describing *keiretsu torihiki* (group affiliated transactions). The right of 'access' provided by a *keiretsu* relationship is seen as a franchise to do business that group membership affords, hence a 'dry' relationship. The kinds of trust that are commonly referred to in business relate to credit, credit associations and the like, and trust in connection with trust companies, trust funds, trust agreements and so forth. Trust as a human value and the 'obligatedness' of a firm to behave in accordance with an individual's standard of conduct is an inappropriate expectation. This is not to say that trust does not exist in Japanese society. Trust, faith, loyalty, fidelity are marked characteristics of Japanese personal relations, but not of its intercorporate transactions.

The insider–outsider continuum

Normally the nature of transactions in the bureaucratic and the market forms are visible, with no opaque substructures to interfere with the efficient use of the market or the rational conduct of the bureaucracy. The fief (Weber's patrimonial bureaucracy) and clan forms (Durkheim's kinship network), that is, the *keiretsu* and the *kigyo shudan*, by contrast, are characterized by an opacity based on relationships and customs, the implicit rules governing access to information and commerce. Such opacity is, as discussed earlier, relative and wholly dependent on one's relationships—as an outsider trying to deal with the system or as an insider who is part of the system.

It is my view that the principle of relational access—as an *insider* or *outsider*—which ranges from 'belonging' to 'no relationship', expands the model into a holistic framework of the Japanese firm inclusive of both its inter- and intragroup relations. The relational access principle refers to the *uchi* (insider)–*soto* (outsider) continuum of graded relationships, reflecting control over access to spheres of relationships that exist within sets and subsets.

Insider–Outsider (*uchi-soto*) continuum defines where one firm stands in relationship to another firm—from the centre of group membership to the outermost sphere of the spot transactional market (no relationship). In addition, in some contexts, a firm can be an insider because it is within a larger sphere while simultaneously an outsider, depending on its relative position within the concentric spheres of relationships surrounding any Japanese firm. Table 12.1 below describes the characteristics of the insider–outsider continuum.

Table 12.1 Characteristics of the insider–outsider continuum

Insider (Uchi)	Outsider (Soto)
Access to other insiders	No relationship
Protection from outsiders	Competition
Obligations within sphere	No obligations

According to this framework, relationships follow a graded pattern based on a concentric, rather than a linear-contractual model; individuals are located in a work group, within the firm, situated in an industrial group, within a larger society (see Figure 12.3). For example, when applied to the *keiretsu* system (as illustrated in Figure 12.1), this graded system of relationships serves as an important distancing mechanism which excludes obligational relations of prime contractors from the affiliates of their subcontractors. This has had enormous implications in terms of the hollowing-out of Japanese industry in recent years as primary contractors have expanded their outsourcing of parts production overseas, abandoning their supplier networks in Japan.

This graded system of relationships, which has been conceptualized here as the insider–outsider continuum, can be applied to the four-quadrant matrix, presented earlier in Figure 12.2, to create an essentially three-

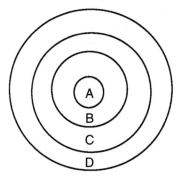

Figure 12.3 *R*-Dimension: relational access insider–outsider continuum. For example, in this illustration, Firms A and B are insiders in relationship to Firm C. Firm D is an outsider to Firms A and B. Firm C may have some kinds of relationships with Firm D because they border each other.

dimensional model. In this model, each quadrant of the matrix, representing the dichotomous forms resulting from trust, on the one hand, and control, on the other, are extended along the *uchi-soto* continuum, bringing to the fore the principle of relational access. Table 12.2 below represents the results, describing the effects of the insider-versus-outsider principle on the matrix forms.

The concept of a relational access dimension is related to the work of Grandori (1997), who has parsed the dimensions of networks into higher- and lower-degree forms of coordination modes. In actual practice, the distinctions drawn here can be seen in the differences between general trade organizations, to which there is a uniform degree of access, and the form of association typified by the *dango*, discussed earlier, in which access is limited to a fixed group of participating contractors who are part of a collusive rigged bidding system. Table 12.2 illustrates how the concept of insider-versus-outsider access works as a mechanism within the various

Table 12.2 Coordination mechanism modes

Form	Coordination mechanism	
	Stronger Insider mode	Weaker Outsider mode
Market-based contracting	franchising	market pricing
Bureaucratic combines	autocratic decision-making	democratic decision-making
Fiefs—*keiretsu* groups	obligational contracting	distance subcontracting
Clans—*kigyo* groups	joint ventures	associations

316 M. J. Scher

network forms and explains the existence of markedly different relationships within each form. By applying the principle of relational access to the *keiretsu* form, for example, we see how one form can contain the seemingly contradictory extremes of contracting loaded with obligations, on the one hand, and yet completely without obligation on the other.

Conclusion

Where a culture is built on an extensive system of informal rules and obligations, such as Japan's, some concept like trust must play a role, if only a discretionary one for the purpose of general social cohesion. The kind of trust that is evident between firms reflects a generalized expectation or reliance that decisions will be made and discretion used in service of the long-term relationship. It is my view, however, that such reliance is not chiefly grounded in a personalized form of trust or faith but rather is part of a highly contextualized set of norms by which most firms will avoid short-term opportunistic tactics to ensure long-term strategic benefits or to maintain beneficial relationships.

In fact, the durability of the concept of trust within long-term relationships, whether reflected in a firm's external transactions as a buyer or seller of goods or services or in its internal transactions as an employer with a tacit understanding of long-term employment, has been torn apart in the current crisis facing the Japanese economy, and especially within its financial institutions. The fragility of the Japanese concept of *shinyo* or credibility is starkly revealed when understood within the context of actual business practices. *Shinyo* today certainly does not qualify as a synonym for 'trust', at least not in terms of Western notions of a trusting reliance on a business relationship in times of adversity. It is important to remember that, even today, the system has not changed. Rather, the realities of that system demand a perspective unburdened by value-loaded terms, such as 'trust'.

Trust in Japanese interfirm relations has been viewed in this chapter as a metaphor for an implicit reliance among firms that each will respect certain uncodified ground rules of behaviour established by traditional practice. Because much of contracted relationships is generally implicit and therefore opaque, many Western observers have made an erroneous presumption that these interfirm relations are based on trust. This view of trust is to be distinguished from a personalized view of trust derived from human relations. Indeed, notions of trust take on a highly pragmatic character when power relations are unequal or when the relationships are with outsiders (*soto*). It is for this reason that trust in Japanese interfirm networks cannot be characterized in terms of the human feelings associated with trust; rather, it comes closest to a reliance on the traditional or long-term nature of the relationship between firms, which reflects the differences in power that affect the ability of firms to act purely self-interestedly.

Among the changes wrought by globalization was a major shift in the traditional values related to 'trust' in interfirm relations. One serious and ongoing consequence has been the hollowing-out of regional and national industrial production, where firms in a *keiretsu* move their outsourcing of parts and production from their established local and regional suppliers to cheaper overseas suppliers. The ability of organizational networks to manipulate and discard production relationships to their best advantage belies the assertion that such relationships are 'trust'-based. In sum, the metaphor of 'trust' represents a power dependency in which reliance and confidence in traditional business practices are premised on long-term relationships qualified by relational access.

Notes

1 'Culture', as used by anthropologists, is a technical term referring to a system for creating, sending, storing and processing information developed by human beings. The terms *mores, tradition, custom* and *habit* are subsumed under the umbrella of 'culture' (Hall and Hall 1990).
2 The origins of the word *keiretsu*, meaning order or succession, come out of Japan's feudal past. Its hierarchical implications can be deduced from the fact that it is used, among other things, to describe Japan's *yakuza* (crime family) structure. Its current use in describing business relationships originates in 1943 when it was first used to describe wartime munitions manufacturing subcontracting practices.
3 For a full discussion of this model, see M. J. Scher 1997.

Bibliography

Boisot, Max H. (1986) 'Markets and hierarchies in a cultural perspective', *Organization Studies*, 7: 135–8.
Dore, Ronald (1983) 'Goodwill and the spirit of market capitalism', *The British Journal of Sociology*, 34 (4): 459–82.
—— (1987) *Taking Japan Seriously*, Stanford: Stanford University Press.
Durkheim, Emile (1893) *The Division of Labor in Society*, 2nd edition (1933), trans. G. Simpson, New York: Free Press.
Fox, Alan (1974) *Beyond Contract: Work, Power and Trust Relations*, London: Faber and Faber Ltd.
Fruin, W. Mark (1992) *The Japanese Enterprise System*, New York: Oxford University Press.
Fukuyama, Francis (1995) *Trust*, New York: Free Press.
Gerlach, Michael (1992) *Alliance Capitalism: The Social Organization of Japanese Business*, Berkeley: University of California Press.
Grandori, Anna (1997) 'An organizational assessment of interfirm coordination modes', *Organization Studies*, 18: 897–925.
Hall, Edward T. (1977) *Beyond Culture*, Garden City, NY: Doubleday.
Hall, Edward T. and Hall, Mildred (1990) *Understanding Cultural Differences*, Yarmouth, ME: Intercultural Press.
Hofstede, Geert H. (1991) *Cultures and Organizations: Software of the Mind*. Maidenhead: McGraw-Hill (UK).

318 *M. J. Scher*

Kawasaki, Seiichi and McMillan, John. (1987) 'The design of contracts: evidence from Japanese subcontracting', *Journal of the Japanese and International Economies*, 1: 327–49.

Kramer, Roderick M. and Tyler, Tom R. (eds) (1996) *Trust in Organizations*. Thousand Oaks, CA: Sage Publications.

Luhmann, Niklas (1979) *Trust* and *Power*, two works, New York: John Wiley.

—— (1988) 'Familiarity, confidence, trust: problems and alternatives', in D. Gambetta (ed.) *Trust*, New York: Basil Blackwell, pp. 94–107.

Mito, Tadashi. (1992) '"Ie no ronri" to nippon shakai (2): keiyaku-gata to shozoku-gata — zangyo to tetsudai' ('"Logic of *ie*" and Japanese society (part 2): contract-model versus belonging-model—overtime work and helping-out'), *Shosai no Mado*, 3: 4–10.

Nakatani, Iwao (1990) 'Opening up fortress Japan', *Japan Echo*, 3: 8–11.

Nishiguchi, Toshihiro (1992) *Strategic Industrial Sourcing*, London: Oxford University Press.

Ouchi, William G. (1980) 'Markets, bureaucracies, and clans', *Administrative Science Quarterly*, March: 129–41.

Powell, Walter W. (1996) 'Trust-based forms of governance', in R. Kramer and T. Tyler (eds) *Trust in Organizations*, Thousand Oaks, CA: Sage Publications, pp. 51–67.

Sakakibara, Eisuke (1994) *Beyond Capitalism: The Japanese Model of Market Economics*, Lanham, MD: University Press of America/Economic Strategy Institute.

Sako, Mari (1991) 'The role of "trust" in Japanese buyer-supplier relationships', *Ricerche Economiche*, XLV, 2–3 April–September: 449–73.

—— (1992) *Prices, Quality and Trust: Inter-Firm Relations in Britain and Japan*, Cambridge, UK: Cambridge University Press.

Scher, Mark J. (1997) *Japanese Interfirm Networks and Their Main Banks*, London and New York: Macmillan Press Ltd. and St Martin's Press.

Telser, L. G. (1980) 'Theory of self-enforcing agreements', *Journal of Business*, 53:1 27–44.

Weber, Max (1921) *The Theory of Social and Economic Organization* [Wirtschaft und Gesellschaft], translated by A. M. Henderson and Talcott Parsons, edited with an introduction by T. Parsons, 1947, New York: Oxford University Press.

Whitley, Richard (1992) *Business Systems in East Asia: Firms, Markets and Societies*, London: Sage Publications.

Yamagishi, Toshio and Yamagishi, Midori (1994) 'Trust and commitment in the United States and Japan', *Motivation and Emotion*, 18:2 129–66.

Yoshino, Michael Y. and Thomas B. Lifson (1986) *The invisible link: Japan's sogo shosha and the organization of trade*, Cambridge, MA: MIT Press.

Index